WHAT'S THE POINT OF INTERNATIONAL RELATIONS?

What's the Point of International Relations casts a critical eye on what we are doing when we study and teach international relations (IR). Bringing together many of IR's leading thinkers, it presents IR as a deeply political, critical, and normative pursuit, and celebrates the discipline's growing pluralism – while also recognising that IR has not yet lived up to its potential, and has much work to do. The volume is divided into five parts:

- What is the point of IR?
- The origins of a discipline
- Policing the boundaries
- Engaging the world
- Imagining the future

Moving beyond western debate, orthodox perspectives, and uncritical histories this volume is essential reading for scholars and advanced level students concerned with the history, present, and future of international relations.

Synne L. Dyvik is Lecturer in International Relations at the University of Sussex, UK.

Jan Selby is Professor of International Relations at the University of Sussex, UK.

Rorden Wilkinson is Professor and Chair of the Department of International Relations at the University of Sussex, UK.

'We've needed this superb volume sorely for some time – a collection of fresh and invigorating essays, all responding to the editors' call for a newly 'open, political and humble' approach to our discipline. IR emerges through this fresh look not as irrelevant or hamstrung by disciplinary limitations, but as vibrant, diverse and important, and, most of all, as having a very bright future.'

– *Nicola Phillips, University of Sheffield, UK*

'Enlightening self-reflection without unhelpful narcissism or drama! These are twenty smart, thoughtful, and really productive chapters. I learned things I will use in my classes and in my own work.'

– *Robert A. Denemark, University of Delaware, USA*

'A wonderful collection of insightful essays that reveal why international relations has become one of the most exciting areas of academic work, one that has not only absorbed innovative perspectives from economics, politics, and political economy but is also becoming an influential source of ideas for these disciplines.'

– *Walden Bello, State University of New York at Binghamton, USA*

'Through a collection of consistently excellent (and valuably divergent) chapters, this timely and provocative volume calls for – and succeeds in modelling – a 'pluralist', 'dialogical', and 'political' discipline of IR. This is essential reading for anyone interested in the *purposes* of IR and how these relate to its contested past, current dynamism, and yet-uncertain future.'

– *Toni Erskine, Professor of International Politics, UNSW, Australia*

'This is an excellent collection of essays on the current state of the field – and, fortunately, much more oriented towards real-world problems than its title would suggest.'

– *Chris Brown, London School of Economics, UK*

WHAT'S THE POINT OF INTERNATIONAL RELATIONS?

Edited by Synne L. Dyvik, Jan Selby and Rorden Wilkinson

Routledge
Taylor & Francis Group
LONDON AND NEW YORK

First published 2017
by Routledge
2 Park Square, Milton Park, Abingdon, Oxon OX14 4RN

and by Routledge
711 Third Avenue, New York, NY 10017

Routledge is an imprint of the Taylor & Francis Group, an informa business

British Library Cataloguing-in-Publication Data
A catalogue record for this book is available from the British Library

Library of Congress Cataloging-in-Publication Data
A catalog record for this title has been requested

ISBN: 978-1-138-70730-6 (hbk)
ISBN: 978-1-138-70731-3 (pbk)
ISBN: 978-1-315-20146-7 (ebk)

Typeset in Bembo
by Apex CoVantage, LLC

CONTENTS

ABBREVIATIONS

AIPR	American Institute of Pacific Relations
APSA	American Political Science Association
APSR	American Political Science Review
BIS	Department for Business, Innovation, and Skills
BISA	British International Studies Association
BJP	Bharatiya Janata Party
BRICS	Brazil, Russia, India, China, South Africa
CAM	Complementary and Alternative Medicine
CDM	Clean Development Mechanism
CENISL	Center for International Studies
CIA	Central Intelligence Agency
CFR	Council on Foreign Relations
CIS	Center for International Studies
CNPS	Caucus of a New Political Science
COP21	Conference of Parties 21 (Paris Climate Conference 2015)
DfID	Department for International Development
DTT	Dichlorodiphenyltrichloroethane
ERA	Excellence in Research (Australia)
ESRC	Economic and Social Research Council (UK)
EU	European Union
FBI	Federal Bureau of Investigation
FCO	Foreign and Commonwealth Office
FIPE	Feminist International Political Economy
FLACSO	Facultad Latinoamericana de Ciencias Sociales
FPA	Foreign Policy Association
FSS	Feminist Security Studies

FTGS	Feminist Theory and Gender Studies Section of ISA
GM	Genetic Modification
HEW	Hypermasculine-Eurocentric Whiteness
IO	International Organizations
IGO	Intergovernmental Organizations
ILO	International Labour Organization
IMF	International Monetary Fund
IPCC	Intergovernmental Panel on Climate Change
IPE	International Political Economy
IPEG	International Political Economy Group at BISA
IR	International Relations
ISA	International Studies Association
ISIS	Islamic State of Iraq and the Levant
KKV	King, Keohane, and Verba
MAD	Mutually Assured Destruction
MIT	Massachusetts Institute of Technology
MM	Multiple Modernities
MoD	Ministry of Defence
NATO	North Atlantic Treaty Organization
NGO	Non-governmental Organizations
NSS	National Student Survey (UK)
PS	Political Science and Politics
RAE	Research Assessment Exercise (UK)
REF	Research Excellence Framework (UK)
RIIA	Royal Institute of International Affairs (Chatham House, UK)
RSS	Rashtriya Swayamsevak Sangh
SS	Security Studies
TRIP	Teaching, Research, and International Policy
WILPF	Women's International League for Peace and Freedom
WWI	World War I
WWII	World War II
UK	United Kingdom
UN	United Nations
UNIHP	United Nations Intellectual History Project
USA	United States of America

CONTRIBUTORS

Ken Booth, FBA, is Senior Research Associate in the Department of International Politics, Aberystwyth University, UK.

Catia C. Confortini is Associate Professor and Co-Director of the Peace and Justice Studies Program at Wellesley College, USA.

Synne L. Dyvik is Lecturer in International Relations at the University of Sussex, UK.

Patrick Thaddeus Jackson is Professor of International Studies and Associate Dean for Curriculum and Learning in the School of International Service at American University in Washington, DC, USA.

Beate Jahn is Professor of International Relations at the University of Sussex, UK.

Samuel Knafo is Senior Lecturer in International Relations at the University of Sussex, UK.

Stephanie Lawson is Professor of Politics and International Relations at Macquarie University, Australia.

L. H. M. Ling is Professor of International Affairs at The New School in New York City, USA.

Craig N. Murphy is Betty Freyhof Johnson '44 Professor of Political Science at Wellesley College, USA.

Peter Newell is Professor of International Relations at the University of Sussex, UK.

Inderjeet Parmar is Professor of International Politics at City University London, UK.

Adrienne Roberts is Lecturer in International Politics at the University of Manchester, UK.

Justin Rosenberg is Professor of International Relations at the University of Sussex, UK.

Jan Selby is Professor of International Relations at the University of Sussex, UK.

Laura Sjoberg is Associate Professor of Political Science at the University of Florida, USA.

Anna Stavrianakis is Senior Lecturer in International Relations at the University of Sussex, UK.

Jennifer Sterling-Folker is the Alan R. Bennett Honors Professor of Political Science at the University of Connecticut, USA.

Achin Vanaik is Professor of International Relations and Global Politics (Ret.) at the University of Delhi, India.

Robert Vitalis is Professor of Political Science at the University of Pennsylvania, USA.

Catherine Weaver is Associate Professor at the LBJ School of Public Affairs and the Co-Director of Innovations for Peace and Development at the University of Texas at Austin, USA.

Cynthia Weber is Professor of International Relations at the University of Sussex, UK.

Thomas G. Weiss is Presidential Professor of Political Science at The Graduate Center of The City University of New York and Director Emeritus of the Ralph Bunche Institute for International Studies, USA.

Rorden Wilkinson is Professor and Chair of the Department of International Relations at the University of Sussex, UK.

Yongjin Zhang is Professor of International Politics at the University of Bristol, UK.

ACKNOWLEDGEMENTS

This book emerges from a conference convened by the Department of International Relations at the University of Sussex in celebration of its 50th anniversary. It has been designed to cast a critical eye on what it is we think we are doing when we study and teach international relations. We took the opportunity presented by our half-century celebrations to reflect on the broader value of the discipline. In so doing we choose to eschew a more reflective, expected, and inwardly focused look back on the development of IR at Sussex, preferring instead to ask sharp questions about the purpose, value, and contribution of an academic discipline more broadly that is uncertainly defined.[1]

The conference itself was a delightfully "Sussex" affair – robust and engaged debate from start to finish. It was also provided free of charge to all attendees in the spirit of our commitment to opening up the academy – as much as we are able – as a public good. Although the event was free for all who attended, the transportation, hotel, catering, and infrastructural costs incurred were real, and a significant burden was borne. Without the generosity of the School of Global Studies and in particular its head, Andrea Cornwall, and a gift bequeathed to the IR Department that bears Norman Angell's name, we would not have been able to host the conference or to produce this book as a legacy of our quinquagenary.

Neither the conference nor the book would have been possible without the time, energy, and assistance of Kit Eves and Katy Joanna Joyce. Raphaëlle Vanden Bemen, Fernando Barrero Garrido, Luca Lo Scavo, Samuel Vavers, and Oriana Wilkinson ensured that the conference ran as smoothly as possible. Lawrence Freedman, Lene Hansen, Betsy Hartmann, John Hobson, Fabio Petito, Matthew Preston, and Teivo Teivainen – along with all of the contributors to this volume – helped make for a uniquely rich and productive discussion. Stefan Elbe, Kamran Matin, Patricia Owens, Anna Stavrianakis, and Benno Teschke chaired the panels with aplomb. And Lydia de Cruz, Nicola Parkin, Emily Ross, and the other members of the team at Routledge all helped shepherd the manuscript through production with utter professionalism. Many thanks all.

S.L.D., J.S., R.W.
Brighton, September 2016

Note

1 See Zdenek Kavan, "Memories of IR at Sussex," for an account of the development of international relations amid the South Downs. Available at: http://whatsthepointofir.com/conference-pack/

INTRODUCTION

Asking questions of, and about, IR

Synne L. Dyvik, Jan Selby and Rorden Wilkinson

What *is* the point of international relations (IR)? As a question about the purpose, value, and distinctiveness of an academic discipline the answer appears simple. Surely it is to make sense of the world around us and to generate knowledge that is beneficial to the preservation and betterment of life on this planet? Yet even the most fleeting of reflections should tell us that the answer is far from straightforward and that any attempt to work out the purpose of an academic discipline generates as many questions as it does answers.

IR as a scholarly endeavor is deeply contested, not just in terms of its purposes, subject matter, theories, and methods, but also in terms of whether it is actually a discipline or merely a field of study (see, for example, Kaplan 1961; Light and Groom 1985; Hollis and Smith 1991; Baldwin 1993; Waever 2007). However, we should not imagine that we are alone in questioning the nature of the discipline in which we operate. A cursory glance over the fence at economics, development studies, anthropology, sociology, and geography – among many others – illustrates that IR's internal disciplinary differences and doubts are far from unique (for instance, Castree, Rogers, and Sherman 2005; Seidman 2007; Lee 2009; Comaroff 2010; Cornwall and Scoones 2011; Bhambra 2014). In view of this, it would be over-ambitious of us – indeed, absurd – to try to produce a definitive statement of the point of IR, one that captures all that the discipline is and hopes to be.

"What is the point of IR?" is a question worth asking nonetheless, precisely because IR's intellectual terrain is so – and increasingly – contested. IR has become home to multiple theoretical traditions and sub-fields, and this heterogeneity arguably militates against any kind of collective endeavor, let alone cumulative knowledge building (Weiss and Wilkinson 2014). IR is often criticized as being divorced from – yet under pressure to say something meaningful about – the policy world (Walt 2005). And its comparative advantage as *the* scholarly study of the "international" faces significant challenges from other disciplines, most of which have now shed much of their erstwhile "methodological nationalism" (Martins 1974) and developed important insights and perspectives on topics which were once IR's sole preserve. These challenges are sufficiently worrisome for us – as co-authors of this introductory chapter and co-editors of this volume – to see utility in reflecting on the purpose of IR.

In so doing, we do not assume the existence of a single correct or definitive answer to the question of IR's purpose: quite the contrary. Nonetheless, we do favor a particular, if undoubtedly broad, conception of IR – both of what it is and what it should be. Five features of this "idea of IR" merit attention. We view contemporary IR as a deeply *pluralist* scholarly terrain where the diversity of theoretical, political, and methodological commitments, and of substantive interpretations, is a reason for celebration rather than for nostalgia or regret. We favor a *dialogical* model of pluralism which does not involve resorting to, and which largely abandons, the static paradigms and "*isms*" (Lake 2011) and distilled geographical perspectives (Smith 2000; Acharya and Buzan 2010) so beloved by IR textbooks. We view IR's "isms" not as incommensurable theoretical frameworks, but, at best, as starting points for conversation and, at worst, as unnecessary barriers to it. We view IR scholarship as unavoidably *political* not only in its subject matter but also in its assumptions and repercussions, having normative and critical dimensions. We favor an *open* understanding of IR's subject matter where – regardless of whether IR is conceived as a "discipline" or an "inter-discipline" or even an "un-discipline" (Sjoberg, this volume) – external boundaries and legitimate topics of enquiry are not tightly policed and where IR scholars are thus in constant dialogue not only with political scientists, but across the social sciences and beyond. Finally, we view IR, with due *humility*, not as a "master-discipline" which holds a monopoly on understanding the "international" or which, alone among the social sciences, provides the big answers to the biggest questions, but as a field that has much to learn from others, which has not yet lived up to its ambitions or potential and where much work remains to be done.

Not all of the chapters in this volume are informed by this conception of IR – indeed, there are some noteworthy and explicit departures. Nonetheless, most of this conception is shared across the volume. All of the chapters that follow emphasize and welcome IR's pluralism in one way or another. There is little reliance on "isms." All view IR as a deeply political, critical, and normative pursuit. And none of the chapters seek to demarcate what is from what is not legitimate IR enquiry. To this extent, the volume as a whole may perhaps be read not only as posing the "point of IR" question, but also as a renewed call for an open, political, and humble approach to the discipline – an ambition that is in keeping with, and reflective of, our own institution's long-standing reputation for critical and interdisciplinary scholarship and teaching.

To develop this case further and to set the scene for the volume as a whole, the remainder of this introductory chapter is organized as follows. Its first half focuses on three key questions related to "the point of IR," which flow naturally from one to another. These are:

1 What is the purpose of IR?
2 What is IR's subject matter?
3 Why bother asking about the point of IR?

For each of these questions we engage with established thinking in the field, highlight some of the key differences of perspective among our contributors, and reflect on our own views as co-authors with slightly different takes on the "point of IR." The second half of this introduction offers a guide to the remainder of the book, explaining why the volume unfolds in the way that it does and briefly summarizing each of the chapters.

Three questions

There are at least two ways in which the question "what's the point of IR?" might be read: as referring to IR's subject matter ("its point is to produce and transmit knowledge about x, y, and z"), or, alternatively, as referring to the purposes which frame and constitute it and the ends to which its subject matter is put. Here we discuss purposes first, before then turning to IR's subject matter.

What is the purpose of IR?

There was once a time – roughly between the dropping of the first atom bomb and the fall of the Berlin wall – when IR was unquestionably an American social science (Hoffmann 1977) and when the Cold War and US hegemony appeared more or less fixed – when it was still possible for many to imagine that IR was merely a science. Operating with a positivist conception of social scientific method and an insistence on the fact-value divide, and curiously blind to the unique political circumstances which were framing their work, these largely US-based scholars viewed IR's purpose as the scientific study of states and the international system. Thus a leading figure such as James Rosenau (1980, 32) could claim in all seriousness that "[a]s a focus of study, the nation-state is no different from the atom or the single cell organism," and "in terms of science-as-method" physics and foreign policy analysis were "essentially the same."

Since the 1980s, however, such views have become increasingly difficult to sustain. The end of Cold War political certainties and of the disciplinary straitjackets which were their corollary, and the ensuing rise of a plethora of alternative "reflectivist" or "post-positivist" theories and methods (Smith, Booth, and Zalewski 1996) have made it clear that, whatever else it is, IR is not *just* a science but an endeavor which has been shaped and defined in relationship with history, politics, and power. To emphasize this is not to single out IR as in any way unique: all of the modern social sciences have origins and histories which are deeply indebted to worldly developments and political projects – including, perhaps above all, the entanglements of and responses to empire. The genesis of development studies, for instance, resides in the problems of colonial administration (Kothari 2006), whereas its leading theoretical frameworks – the modernization and dependency paradigms – grew out of a strident anti-communism on the one hand (Gilman 2003) and anti-imperialist nationalism on the other, especially in Latin America (see e.g., Schuurman 1993, 3–4; Parmar 2012). Anthropology has, since its inception, had an intimate relationship with imperial encounters, interventions, and desires whether by contributing to "colonial and postcolonial essentializations of ethnic entities" (Pels 1997, 166) or by providing actionable local knowledge for counterinsurgency (González 2004). And for all its pretensions to science, even modern economics and its central concept, "the economy," arose within the context of the need to make sense of the collapse of European colonialism (Mitchell 2002, 80–119). To paraphrase Robert Cox, all "knowledge" – and not just "theory" – is ultimately "for someone and for some purpose" (Cox 1981, 128).

IR's purposes are multiple, and they have often been in tension. In the first decades of the twentieth century in the United States, as Robert Vitalis has shown, "international relations meant race relations," and "race subjection" – that is, maintaining white supremacy – was what preoccupied its first self-identified professors (2015, 1; also Vitalis this volume). During the Cold War, by contrast, this conservatism morphed in form as IR became focused on managing and, as critics subsequently argued, rationalizing the supposedly trans-historical verities of arms racing and superpower rivalry (Cox 1981; Ashley 1984; Kratochwil 1993). Tutoring the statesmen (and to a lesser extent stateswomen) of the future and providing actionable empirical evidence and insights for policy makers have also traditionally been considered key IR purposes.

At other times and in other places, however, IR's purposes have been viewed very differently. The birth of IR in the UK in 1919 was, as Ken Booth argues, self-consciously motivated by a progressivist desire to help build international peace after the catastrophe of World War I (Booth, this volume). Likewise, the explosion of "critical" approaches to IR since the end of the Cold War has been dedicated to challenging and transcending prevailing international structures, power relations, and accepted truths in a range of ways. In some accounts, for example, in Cynthia Enloe's effort to "make feminist sense of international relations," this has involved exploring places where IR had hitherto barely ventured – such as the kitchens and bedrooms of diplomatic homes and military bases – and thus recognizing that "the personal is international" and vice versa (Enloe 1990, 196). For others, for example, in Marxian or poststructuralist-inspired scholarship, it has involved work to historicize and denaturalize contemporary idioms and practices to demonstrate that change is a constant and that alternative futures are thereby possible (Cox 1981). And some critical IR research has explicitly defined itself in opposition, or as "speaking truth," to power (Wallace 1996).

What, then, is the purpose of IR? There is clearly no single answer. Different IRs are oriented toward different functions, values, and interests. Some of these may be considered progressive, others not; and it will often be a matter of debate whether, and to what extent, they should be considered progressive or not. The purposes to which IR – and indeed all disciplines – has been put have varied over time, often accommodating political projects and belief systems in racialized, gendered, and cultural ways. The traces of each of these projects should not be taken lightly, nor should it be assumed that they have been eased or expunged by today's constructions of the discipline. In many ways all disciplines retain aspects of the shape they "received" at birth, a theme we explore in Part Two of this book. More broadly, we wish to insist that, whatever else its purposes might be, IR is not just a scientific or scholarly activity, but one that also has normative and political dimensions and involves various forms of positioning in relation to power. All of the contributions to this volume adopt some such understanding of IR.

What is IR's subject matter?

This leads us to the second way "the point of IR" might be understood, relating to its subject matter. Asking how we might describe a discipline's subject matter is never the easiest of questions. Politics is variously understood as the study of government, of governance, of friendship and enmity (Schmitt 2007), and of power and its consequences – as in Lasswell's famous definition of politics as "who gets what, when, how" (1936) – all of which are quite different. Geography is variously thought of as the study of relations between humans and their physical environment and as the study of spatiality – again, quite different. And although history is undoubtedly the study of the past, this simply begs the questions "which" and "whose" past?

Yet things are arguably even less clear-cut for IR. There are two issues here: What are IR's "units" of analysis – that is, whether it should be understood as the study of relations between governments, states, or whole societies, or even any "encounter with difference across boundaries" (Jackson, this volume); and what types of relations it should study – "just" political relations, or relations of any variety? The answer of US IR during the Cold War was for the most part very narrow. Thus Kenneth Waltz (1979) famously theorized the international system as involving interactions between states alone and without any regard to these states' internal specificities (for example, constitutions or political cultures). Bruce Russet, David Singer, and Melvin Small not only assumed states to be their basic unit of analysis, but focused specifically on those they considered large enough to warrant the interest of IR scholars (1968, 933). For all of these authors, and for most scholarship of this period, IR was understood as that sub-field of political science that focused on international political (and military) relations. Moreover, for all of these authors the pursuit of a precisely defined terrain of study was in large part driven by a desire to render the study of IR "scientific," a practice that they understood as requiring variables to be clear and limited and data to be of sufficient volume and quality.

Russet, Singer, and Small, for example, "settled upon 1900" as their starting point in analyzing international relations, both because of the paucity of (quantitative) data for earlier periods and also because:

> the coding problem is markedly eased by the turn of the century [1900], by which time the unification of Germany, Italy, and Russia had been completed, almost all of the Indian subcontinent had come under the British Raj, and Africa had been largely carved up by the colonial powers. An earlier starting date would not only have necessitated a dramatically longer list, but one with a far greater likelihood of error and ambiguity.
>
> (1968, 933)

In other words, for Russet, Singer, and Small the variety and complexity of pre-1900 political systems, and the fact that they did not conform to the nation-state model universalized between 1945 and the 1960s, provided grounds for excluding everything prior to the twentieth century from our understanding of "international relations."

More recently, by contrast, far looser understandings of IR's subject matter have generally been preferred. In the view of Grieco, Ikenberry, and Mastanduno (2015, 2), "[i]nternational relations are concerned with the political, economic, social, and cultural relations between two countries or among many countries." Such formulations liberate IR from an exclusive concern with the military-political and are also less sharply state-centric – even if some ambiguity remains in the focus on "countries" (which can be read either as referring to states or to societies). Others have gone much further. Many feminist IR scholars, such as Cynthia Enloe (1990), have sought to erase the boundary between the formal and personal dimensions of international politics and to argue that the latter should be just as much part of IR's subject matter as the former. Neo-Gramscian, Foucauldian, postcolonial, and many constructivist scholars have moved away from a primary focus on inter-state (or inter-country) relations altogether to instead analyze the hegemonic ideas, the transnational class strategies, and the norms and discourses, among many other things, that circulate and are reproduced globally. Much contemporary IR examines how these ideas get translated into local arenas – effectively rejecting the discipline's erstwhile inter-state ontology in favor of one focused on global–local relations (Selby 2013). And IR has increasingly viewed itself as distinct and separate from political science – either in fact or aspiration. In the view of Justin Rosenberg (this volume), for example, IR should liberate itself entirely from "the prison of political science," and having done that should reimagine itself as the study of societal multiplicity and its consequences, whether relating to political matters or to any other dimension of human existence.

What then is IR's subject matter? Again, there is no single answer. IR's ontology – that is, the question of what constitutes the "international" and what should be included in studies of it – is not a constant, but is rather something that has evolved over time. Our concerns as IR scholars are historically contingent and have developed not only in response to particular historical events, but also evolutions in thinking and theoretical development. IR might then perhaps be described as a macro-discipline concerned with how large communities relate to one another and within which power relations are always present. It might be described as concerning itself not only with states but also with imperialism, hierarchy, war, militarism, inequality, trade, gender, race, and sexuality. IR might be described simply as a community of practice that studies these issues and more. Even we as co-editors have somewhat different views on this. Where we, and virtually all of the contributors to this volume agree, however, is in favoring an open approach that does not define IR in exclusively statist or political terms and which does not involve the tight policing of intellectual boundaries.

Why bother asking about the point of IR?

Our reasoning in wanting to reflect on "the point of IR" – its purpose and its subject matter – is that IR currently faces a series of significant challenges. These were touched upon briefly at the start of this chapter but merit revisiting. First, there is the challenge of internal heterogeneity: that IR has become home to so many contrasting theoretical traditions, styles, and substantive focuses that its coherence is in doubt. Second, there is a question of its intellectual distinctiveness and comparative advantages, both within the context of globalization and other disciplines' waning methodological nationalism. And third there are questions of practical relevance, as IR – like other fields – has been increasingly called upon to demonstrate its extra-academic worth and "impact." We consider these issues in turn.

The first of these issues we consider overblown. In a widely discussed intervention, David Lake (2011) has argued that IR has become dominated by competing "isms," which function like "sects" waging "theological debates" and have had pernicious consequences for the discipline as a whole. Elsewhere Lake has advocated "progress *within* paradigms rather than war *between* paradigms" and a continuation of what he views as a turn to "mid-level theory" (2013, 580). Others have questioned whether such disciplinary fragmentation and siloing mean that we may be witnessing "the end of IR" (Dunne, Hansen, and Wight 2013, 419). In our view, outside of the restrictive format of disciplinary textbooks, IR's "isms" do not offer discrete and mutually exclusive worldviews, but idealized tools for reflection and debate, which should be thought of less as "incommensurable paradigms" than as "intersecting sets." Thus across the Marxian tradition, some are almost constructivist in their insistence on the role of hegemonic commonsense ideas in the maintenance of international orders (Murphy 1994), others have affinities with realism in their emphasis on the enduring centrality of geopolitics (Teschke and Lacher 2007), and still others identify significant points of convergence with poststructuralist thought (Selby 2007). Equally, some poststructuralist accounts focus solely on discourse, narratives, and texts (Campbell 1992), whereas others are more materialist in their attention to embodiment, emotions, and people's experiences (Sylvester 2013; Dyvik 2017); some interpret world politics in broadly liberal internationalist terms (Dillon and Reid 2009; see Selby 2007), whereas others run close to the realist tradition in their attention to relations of power (Williams 2005). The point here is that the various schools of thought within IR have not "simply retreated to their own corners of a multifaceted boxing ring, occasionally tossing a punch in one or other direction but more often talking amongst themselves," as Lake (2013, 571) claims. In our view, IR's pluralism is less a barrier to thought and analysis than an opportunity for fertile dialogue and exchange and should, for the most part, be a cause for celebration. Indicative of this, one finds little paradigmatic positioning within the chapters that follow and scant reference to "isms," this introductory chapter aside.

By contrast, the question of IR's distinctiveness and comparative advantages we consider a major challenge. The late-twentieth-century explosion in global flows of capital, technology, people, information, and ideas – developments that are often captured under the banner of "globalization" – have been such that all social sciences now engage with the "international" to some degree, offering multi-scaled analyses of the local, regional, and national processes within the context of global ones. Moreover, some of the problems which have traditionally animated IR – war, conflict, and insecurity – are no longer exclusively or even primarily defined by inter-state logics: terrorist networks, fragile states, migration, gender and sexual violence, diseases, and climate change now all vie for policy makers' attention alongside old-style geopolitical issues, and most wars are now fought within states rather than between them. IR cannot claim anything close to a monopoly on these issues: virologists and anthropologists lead international responses to Ebola; economists and geographers dominate the study of environmental conflict; urban planners and IT specialists shape policies on infrastructure resilience and security. As an institutional corollary of this, "foreign policy" now involves a bewildering multiplicity of actors, often leaving foreign offices hollowed out and directionless, and secondary to other parts of government, international development ministries most notably (Dejevsky 2013). Combine this explosion of forms of "international relations" in practice with an open understanding of IR as a discipline and the question inevitably raises itself: What does IR have to offer that other disciplines do not?

There are various possible answers to this question, of course. IR's comparative advantage may perhaps be understood as its "strong sense of being a theory-led and theory-concerned field" (Dunne, Hansen, and Wight 2013, 420). Not dissimilarly, its role among the disciplines may be thought of as being to critique and guide others (Jahn, this volume). IR may be understood as having an "architectonic" or "directing" role in the social sciences, by virtue of focus on issues of global significance (Booth, this volume). Its distinctiveness may be defined, with reference to politics, as its especially strong focus on the international and global dimensions of governance and power. Or it may be thought of as a macro-discipline, as noted earlier. But other social sciences are hardly atheoretical or uncritical and they are hardly inattentive to the big issues or to politics and power. Moreover, the question of IR's advantages over – and more broadly its relations with – other disciplines has not exactly received much sustained scholarly attention. The *European Journal of International Relations*' widely discussed 2013 special issue on "The end of IR theory," for example, did not include any substantive analysis of other disciplines' intellectual contributions – which did not, however, prevent its editors from drawing some quite strong conclusions about IR's advantages relative to them. More thinking on this issue is undoubtedly required – starting, we would suggest, from the humble recognition that other disciplines do have a great deal to offer on classical "IR topics."

No lesser a challenge is the relationship between IR as a scholarly activity and its existing and potential non-academic audiences. IR is regularly criticized for having little to offer the policy world and more broadly for its weak social, political, and media profile (see Jahn, this volume; Sterling-Folker, this volume; Weaver, this volume). Moreover, within the UK and elsewhere, governments and funding bodies are increasingly looking for evidence of "non-academic impact," making this issue more acute. Yet, thinking through how to manage the relationship between scholarship and worldly impact is undoubtedly challenging. Here, too, we do not have a neat answer as to how IR should meet this challenge. We wish to emphasize several things nonetheless. One is that, as shown in our discussion of IR's "purposes," IR has always been a worldly discipline, shaped by and responding to global developments while simultaneously being an advocate, for good or ill, of particular political projects and agendas. If the audience for all of this has often primarily been students and fellow academics, this is no bad thing, since it is through our students that we have the greatest and richest "real world impact."

That said, IR does face particular difficulties with the impact agenda (Weaver, this volume). The rise of think tanks focused on day-to-day policy concerns and with privileged access to government is such that policy makers often see little need for academic political science or IR research (Newell and Stavrianakis, this volume). The very fact that IR's subject matter focuses on things that foreign policy makers and defense planners consider themselves experts on anyway – such as national security challenges and policy-making processes – is inevitably limiting. Moreover, IR's heavy theoretical orientation can both reduce interest in engaging with non-academic audiences and lead these audiences to doubt that the discipline has much to offer. Yet for all this, the sort of open and political approach to IR advocated here is, in our view, well suited to non-academic engagement and impact to an extent that putatively "scientific" approaches are not. As Mearsheimer and Walt (2013, 448) have recently argued, within US IR the "rise of simplistic hypothesis testing" has "increased the gulf between academia and the policy world." In other words, against what is commonly assumed, positivist IR research has rather less public and policy impact potential than more theoretically informed, critical, and political scholarship. This does not resolve the question of how IR scholars should approach the impact agenda. It does, however, suggest that there is no reason IR should shy away from to it or feel unable to respond.

How the rest of the volume unfolds

The conversation that follows is organized into five parts: what is the point of IR?; the origins of a discipline; policing the boundaries; engaging the world; and imagining the future. Although each chapter in this volume alludes to and/or discusses central aspects of all of these components, each part is designed to capture the central thrust of the concerns of our authors.

The first part tackles head on the central question of the book and offers a variety of historical, theoretical, and disciplinary reflections on the meaning, purpose, and intent of asking what the point of IR might be. Ken Booth begins by urging IR scholars and students to recognize how our very existence in the world is premised on a conception of international relations. We are all, fundamentally, "children of international relations," a recognition that not only captures our interconnectedness, but also emphasizes the importance of understanding that we are intimately interwoven with the pattern of international history. This does not, for Booth, suggest that we are determined by history or that IR as a field of study remains constant, but rather that the present is caught up in the "shock of the old." Although IR might have modest policy relevance at any given point, the discipline does have a directing role within the social sciences precisely in the way it analyzes what the "international" might be.

For Patrick Jackson, asking the question about the point of IR speaks to the discipline's anxious engagement with itself. Espousing the view that we do not need a clear answer to the question of what it "is" or what it is "for," Jackson advocates a pluralist understanding of the discipline. He argues we should give up the search for a single and coherent discipline and celebrate and work with what we have. And what we have is a common concern with the "encounter with difference across boundaries and with making whatever kind of sense we can of the dynamics of such encounters." Herein lie not only central concepts in IR, such as trade, war, and diplomacy, but also popular culture, dialogues among civilizations, and various ethical practices.

For Cynthia Weber the question posed is a seductive one in that it is so seemingly straightforward and as such can solicit seemingly straightforward answers. Taking issue with the question itself, Weber points to IR being both paranoid and hysterical about its own role, purpose, and cohesion internally as well as vis-à-vis other social science disciplines. Through the lens of psychoanalysis and queer theory she explores how paranoia and hysteria not only characterize what Weber calls "disciplinary IR," but also fester in the self-espoused "critical" camp. Through a series of truth claims about themselves and their opponents, each camp, rather than being radically different, mimics the other, thereby stabilizing disciplinary formations and disabling possibilities for critical self-reflection. This hinders deeper and important engagements with the pedagogical promise that this question seductively holds.

Beate Jahn's chapter concludes this part of the book with a staunch defense of IR. The chapter shows how the roots of IR's challenges lie less with IR itself and more with the nature of modern sciences as a whole. Through an archeological approach inspired by Michel Foucault, Jahn demonstrates how the way of "ordering things" within any modern discipline requires a kind of internal cohesion that disables an ability to see the interconnectedness between the respective and determined concerns of each discipline. This simultaneous fragmentation *between* and integration *within* disciplines leaves any modern science poorly equipped to analyze junctions and interconnections, the very elements that characterize the nature of historical and current political problems. The point of IR therefore is not to provide solutions to political problems but to show the limitations of other disciplines and to provide political actors with different interpretations of world politics.

The second part of this book looks back at the history of IR as a discipline, beginning with Craig Murphy's encouragement for us all to "dig where you stand." Murphy's excavation of early IR scholars (before we even called them "IR scholars") at Wellesley College and beyond reveals the vast array of questions and concerns that have characterized the discipline historically. Although the administration of empires and a certain "imperial anxiety" can describe the concerns of most of the discipline, there were also dissenting voices that have not been heard for political reasons found in the "racism, male chauvinism, and anti-communist hysteria that characterized elite universities in the United States and Great Britain throughout the 20th Century." Engaging with these early scholars of IR and their dissenting voices can offer the discipline an updated agenda aimed at "transforming war, the inequality of the global North and the global South, and the exploitation of working people throughout the world."

Excavating unheard voices is also the concern of Catia Confortini's chapter. Through engaging critically with the early founders and members of the Women's International League for Peace and Freedom (WILPF), Confortini uncovers their prefigurative politics and how this has had an impact upon their political agendas. In the WILPF, as in early IR, "anti-racism, anti-imperialism, and pacifism coexisted and struggled precisely with the embeddedness of racism and oppression within the organization and amongst its members." In learning from the WILPF, the task for the discipline should therefore be to develop alternative versions of ontology, methodology, and epistemology in an effort to develop a prefigurative theory "*today* with the hope and vision for a more just and peaceful *future.*"

Robert Vitalis' chapter asks what purpose IR has served and what purpose it continues to serve today. Vitalis describes the extent to which the management of race relations was a crucial concern for early-twentieth-century IR in the United States. IR at the time was "for the preservation of the white race in some accounts or for the further evolution of its genius in others, given the reality of the threat of the numerically superior but biologically inferior colored races that belted the world." The Cold War marked a shift and a forgetting of this history, moving away from the fear of a race war to the "red scare" and a focus on "American exceptionalism." Recognizing this heritage – all but erased from twenty-first-century IR syllabi – and hearing the dissenting voices within it reveal how engaging critically with these practitioner histories can help us move beyond the excuse that "back then everyone was a racist" and truly begin the hard work involved in decolonizing the academy.

Inderjeet Parmar contributes the final chapter in this part of the book on the history of the discipline of IR and its impact on the present. Connecting the dots between philanthropic funding organizations, institutions, and universities, Parmar shows how elite knowledge networks acted to consolidate US power. This history of IR means that the discipline cannot be understood on its own terms, but rather as a product of these elite forces and their knowledge networks – something that reverberates through the academy today. However, all is not lost for Parmar, as the point of IR should be to rethink this historical conception of "public IR" in new ways. This means reconsidering how we teach and research. We should be driven by engagement with non-elites outside of the mainstream organizations and settings in which IR has traditionally been more comfortable. This will then enable us to "serve our society and politics better than if we remain blinkered, uncritical, and inward looking."

The third part of the book discusses the various ways IR's boundaries have been policed and makes claims about what counts and what does not count as "proper IR." Jennifer Sterling-Folker begins with a chapter on the prominence of positivism and the role it plays in seeking policy relevance for the study of IR in the United States. Considered primarily a subfield of political science, IR's epistemological framework has largely been driven by the concerns of the US government, keenly guarded through positivist enclosures. Sterling-Folker shows how, in its desire to be relevant, American IR is "intimately connected to the American political, power project." This in turn raises some central ethical questions about the capacity of IR scholars in the United States to operate as "public intellectuals." Sterling-Folker exposes the dangers that an intellectual project of "self-reflexivity" and "speaking truth to power" holds for IR scholars professionally in the United States. Given the prominent position that positivism holds, this involves difficult political negotiations in a discipline that often seeks relevance for its own sake.

L. H. M. Ling continues the exploration of the disciplinary boundaries of IR and the dangers involved in the blind spots it engenders. Taking issue with what Ling calls "Hypermasculine-Eurocentric Whiteness" and beginning with King, Keohane, and Verba's *Designing Social Inquiry*, the chapter traces its historical roots and its impact on the discipline overall. In an effort to "undiscipline IR," Ling argues that the Buddhist tradition of *kōans* offers a way to "create cognitive and emotional space for Others." *Kōan*-izing IR's epistemology and methodology means that doubt, and self-doubt, are afforded real purchase on what we study, recognizing that "multiplicity and difference can share cognitive and emotional space with singularity and certainty."

Achin Vanaik's chapter explores Indian IR attempts to move beyond realism as the dominant theoretical paradigm. As the world faces three interlinked "horrors" – inequality, climate change, and the threat of nuclear war – the point of IR must be to tackle the economic inequality that capitalism produces, rethinking the "human–nature" relationship, while at the same time ensuring that the fight for nuclear disarmament continues. Vanaik argues that as

> India – perhaps more than any other country – best exemplifies the problems posed by this trident of issues, the task of Indian IR should be to unflinchingly

> and ruthlessly critique the policies and perspectives, nationally and internationally, that promote these dangers.

The history of India also affords lessons, given its "truly unique scale and longevity of 'unity in diversity,' its lived tolerances, its understandings of how to live with and accept inescapable differences" which can "offer lessons of global scope and application."

Laura Sjoberg's chapter concludes this part of the book by moving from thinking of IR as an "interdiscipline" to one that is much more akin to an "undiscipline." Although the term "undisciplined" might mean being a "rebel without a cause," for Sjoberg it is being a rebel *with purpose* enabling operating within an intellectual framework where exploration becomes more important than coherence. This "thinking without a net" also involves conceptualizing IR as fantasy where "an undisciplined IR would be an IR that broke the boundaries of artificial pretense with imagination – imagined possibilities, imagined worlds, imagined knowledges." For Sjoberg, an undisciplined IR can be delinquent, naughty, and stubborn, something that is likely to yield far more interesting intellectual fruit than the orthodox disciplinary boundaries that IR so heavily polices.

The fourth part of the book focuses on the increased demands made of IR scholars to have policy relevance and engage with the world of practitioners. Catherine Weaver considers the pros and cons of IR scholars remaining in their intellectual towers and rejecting engagement with public and policy audiences. Through a reflection on her own experiences, Weaver argues that "installing value (and thus incentivizing) policy engagement in IR may require constructing the means to measure policy influence in a manner commensurate to how we measure scholarly influence." What being engaged with or relevant to policy ultimately means is to be driven by "puzzles." IR scholars should "not only seek to generate knowledge" but also to "be useful to the world beyond our university walls to those who hold power," and perhaps more importantly, "to those who do not." This bridging of the gap between policy and academia does not mean the loss of the norms and rules of intellectual freedom. Rather, the end goal should be a richer and more intellectually diverse field "that empowers us, as IR scholars," not only to reflect critically "upon the politics of our time, but to attempt to change the world in which we live for the better."

This conversation about IR's role in the world is continued in Stephanie Lawson's chapter on IR theory in the Anthropocene. It takes issue with the lack of engagement with natural science in IR and how this impedes the discipline's ability to tackle what is arguably the world's greatest challenge: climate change. Taking issue with the "conservative anti-science camp," "radical anti-science camp," and "anti-science in political theory" Lawson shows the challenges IR as a discipline faces in its unwillingness to engage with the scientific basis for climate change. For Lawson, the:

> acceptance of the general idea of the social construction of reality, and of all its political implications when it comes to the exercise of power, should not

> entail rejection or dismissal of the way in which the natural or physical sciences pursue knowledge of the material world of nature.

Social constructivism and postmodernist epistemological frameworks can only get us so far, she argues, and understanding and engaging with the natural sciences has never been more important for IR. As she puts it, "if IR – and its theorization – in the contemporary world is to contribute to making it a better place, then it is indeed time for a reality check."

Thomas Weiss' contribution to the book laments the lack of attention given to international organizations (IOs) within IR and how this impairs its ability to promote positive change. Drawing on his extensive experience of working with and studying international organizations, Weiss charts the largely unknown history of the founding of United Nations (UN). From this, he offers three propositions that could enable IR to address better global problems. He argues that "if learning rather than spurning lessons is a requisite for addressing menacing trans-boundary problems, there should be not only more tolerance within the academy for policy-relevant scholarship but also more room and more rewards in regular IR departments." Weiss argues that IR must not lose sight of the grand questions that face us all and that better integrating the study of IO within IR is a crucial part of this endeavor.

The final chapter on IR's engagement with the world comes from Peter Newell and Anna Stavrianakis. Drawing on their own experiences working with policy and practice on issues relating to climate change and the arms trade, respectively, they offer an analysis of how IR scholars might engage differently. In so doing, they call into question simple distinctions between "engagement," "activism," and "scholarship as practice in its own right" and argue for a nuanced account of what the role of scholarship vis-à-vis the world of policy, practice, and activism should be. Newell and Stavrianakis also show how "understanding the nature of the relationship between academia and the world beyond the university is inherently political" and that "failure to address the politics of engagement means we run the risk of powerful academics having powerful voices with powerful people, creating a self-reproducing dynamic and diminishing the prospects of progressive change."

The final part of the book is dedicated to thinking about the future of IR in relation to itself, other disciplines, and the wider world. It begins with Justin Rosenberg's evaluation of the role of IR vis-à-vis other social sciences. Although many have argued that IR lacks a distinct intellectual and empirical endeavor, this is not the case, argues Rosenberg. His claim is that IR has a unique field of study, namely "the international," built on a recognition that "human existence is not unitary but multiple and is distributed across numerous interacting societies." This is what justifies IR as an academic discipline, he argues, but there is not yet agreement on *how* we should study the "international." For Rosenberg, one answer lies in studying the "uneven and combined development" of human societies. This concept not only captures the significance of the "international" in people's lives, but also acts as IR's "passport" out of the "prison" of political science. Only then can IR finally have real purchase in the social sciences and the humanities more broadly.

Adrienne Roberts continues this exploration into what the future may hold by analyzing the future of feminist IR. The chapter charts the often-uneasy relationship between IR and international political economy (IPE), the equally often-uneasy relationship between IR and feminism, and the developments of feminist IR in the past two decades. Rather than solely lamenting these divisions and how they might affect the impact of feminism (in all its forms) on IR as a discipline, Roberts turns the question on its head and urges IR feminist scholars of all kinds to ask themselves "what is the point of IR for feminism?" In so doing, feminists should "build bridges rather than walls, even if those bridges take us outside of the field of IR."

Samuel Knafo's chapter analyzes the lack of attention given to methodology in IR – particularly within critical approaches – and argues that the future of the discipline requires a "methodological turn." He argues that there are three main reasons for the lack of engagement with methodology in critical IR: (i) that methodology has been seen as a disciplinary device to silence critical scholarship; (ii) a sense that it puts constraints on critical thinking; and (iii) an overall privileging of ontology as a direction for scholarly enquiry. Knafo argues that many academic debates should be fought on methodological rather than ontological grounds and that the "turn to methodology is a necessary move mandated by the ethic of accountability." Moreover, "while methodological commitments can often be constraining, the point is precisely that they should force us to go in places where we would otherwise not venture."

The final chapter of the book is by Yongjin Zhang. In his contribution, Zhang uses the history of IR to imagine what IR might look like in 50 years' time. He shows how the concerns, teaching styles, theories, and ontologies of IR have shifted in the past decades and reflects on how earlier IR students and scholars could never have "envisaged either the profound and sweeping political, economic, and scientific and technological transformations of their future material world or the rapidly changing intellectual universe of IR they have helped construct." Through a reflection on central IR debates in the UK, North America, and China Zhang ponders what future IR's concerns might be. Although we may not be able to predict the future of the discipline, the history of IR shows that it is "extraordinarily resilient," able to adjust and adapt in ways that were perhaps unimaginable at its outset.

Conclusion

Our purpose in this opening chapter has not been to provide definitive answers, but rather to ask questions that encourage us to reflect on what we each believe the utility of IR is as a terrain of study. We have sought to demonstrate the ambiguities and divergent opinions on the purpose of IR and to offer some pointers about how we might make sense of this and the discipline as a whole. Inevitably what we have presented here bears the hallmarks of the eras through which we have lived and the moment in which we reside. A comparable endeavor at a different moment in time may come up with as many different views from those that we have presented here. Yet, irrespective of the instinct that some, but far from all, of us have for a small number of clear, concise statements about the point of IR, our counterparts in time would also have been as unlikely to arrive at such definitive statements. And on the balance of opinion in the pages in this volume, we should probably not try.

Where we should focus our energies, however, is working out how to communicate better with one another. We should celebrate the diversity of the discipline, encourage intellectual curiosity about the world that we live in, and reflect on how we as scholars research and teach that subject matter. We should remain open as students of the "international," not only to what this might hold but also how it changes, what it engenders, and our respective understandings thereof. We should encourage the discipline to be driven by unwavering intellectual curiosity rather than becoming consumed by policing our own borders and theoretical traditions or uncritically responding to policy needs. Our contribution to this endeavor is to use this enquiry into the purpose of IR as a small step in that direction.

Bibliography

Acharya, Amitav and Barry Buzan. Eds. 2010. *Non-Western International Relations Theory: Perspectives on and beyond Asia.* London: Routledge.

Ashley, Richard. 1984. "The Poverty of Neorealism." *International Organization* 38 (2): 225–86.

Baldwin, David A. Ed. 1993. *Neorealism and Neoliberalism: The Contemporary Debate.* New York: Columbia University Press.

Bhambra, Gurminder K. 2014. *Connected Sociologies.* London: Bloomsbury.

Campbell, David. 1992. *Writing Security: United States Foreign Policy and the Politics of Identity.* Minneapolis: Minnesota University Press.

Castree, Noel, Alisdair Rogers, and Douglas Sherman. Eds. 2005. *Questioning Geography: Essays on a Contested Discipline.* Oxford: Blackwell.

Comaroff, John. 2010. "The End of Anthropology, Again: On the Future of an In/Discipline." *American Anthropologist* 112 (4): 524–38.

Cornwall, Andrea and Ian Scoones. Eds. 2011. *Revolutionizing Development: Reflections on the Work of Robert Chambers.* London: Earthscan.

Cox, Robert. 1981. "Social Forces, States and World Orders: Beyond International Relations Theory." *Millennium* 10 (2): 126–55.

Dejevsky, Mary. 2013. "In a Globalised, Connected World, Do We Still Need the Foreign Office?" *The Guardian*, December 30. Accessed July 5, 2016. https://www.theguardian.com/commentisfree/2013/dec/30/globalised-world-foreign-office-outlived-usefulness

Dillon, Michael and Julian Reid. 2009. *The Liberal Way of War: Killing to Make Life Live.* London: Routledge.

Dunne, Tim, Lene Hansen, and Colin Wight. 2013. "The End of International Relations Theory?" *European Journal of International Relations* 19 (3): 405–25.

Dyvik, Synne L. 2017. *Gendering Counterinsurgency: Performativity, Embodiment and Experience in the Afghan 'Theatre of War.'* London: Routledge.

Enloe, Cynthia. 1990. *Bananas, Beaches and Bases: Making Feminist Sense of International Politics*. Berkeley: University of California Press.

Gilman, Nils. 2003. *Mandarins of the Future: Modernization Theory in Cold War America*. Baltimore: Johns Hopkins University Press.

González, Roberto J. Ed. 2004. *Anthropologists in the Public Sphere: Speaking Out on War, Peace and American Power*. Austin: University of Texas Press.

Grieco, Joseph, John G. Ikenberry, and Michael Mastanduno. 2015. *Introduction to International Relations: Enduring Questions & Contemporary Perspectives*. London: Palgrave.

Hollis, Martin and Steve Smith. 1991. *Explaining and Understanding International Relations*. Oxford: Clarendon Press.

Kaplan, Morton A. 1961. "Is International Relations a Discipline?" *Journal of Politics* 23 (3): 462–76.

Kothari, Uma. 2006. "From Colonialism to Development: Reflections of Former Colonial Officers." *Commonwealth and Comparative Politics* 44 (1): 118–36.

Kratochwil, Friedrich. 1993. "The Embarrassment of Changes: Neo-Realism as the Science of Realpolitik without Politics." *Review of International Studies* 19 (1): 63–80.

Lake, David A. 2011. "Why 'Isms' Are Evil: Theory, Epistemology, and Academic Sects as Impediments to Understanding and Progress." *International Studies Quarterly* 55 (2): 465–80.

———. 2013. "Theory Is Dead, Long Live Theory: The End of the Great Debates and the Rise of Eclecticism in International Relations." *European Journal of International Relations* 19 (3): 567–87.

Lasswell, Harold D. 1936. *Politics: Who Gets What, When, How*. New York: Whittlesey House.

Lee, Frederic. 2009. *A History of Heterodox Economics: Challenging the Mainstream in the Twentieth Century*. London: Routledge.

Light, Margot and A.J.R. Groom. 1985. *Contemporary International Relations: A Handbook of Current Theory*. London: Pinter.

Martins, H. 1974. "Time and Theory in Sociology." In *Approaches to Sociology*, edited by John Rex, 246–94. London: Routledge and Kegan Paul.

Mearsheimer, John J. and Stephen M. Walt. 2013. "Leaving Theory Behind: Why Simplistic Hypothesis Testing Is Bad for International Relations." *European Journal of International Relations* 19 (3): 427–57.

Mitchell, Timothy. 2002. *Rule of Experts: Egypt, Techno-Politics, Modernity*. Berkeley: University of California Press.

Murphy, Craig N. 1994. *International Organization and Industrial Change: Global Governance since 1850*. Cambridge: Polity.

Parmar, Inderjeet. 2012. *Foundations of the American Century: The Ford, Carnegie, and Rockefeller Foundations in the Rise of American Power*. New York: Columbia University Press.

Pels, Peter. 1997. "The Anthropology of Colonialism: Culture, History, and the Emergence of Western Governmentality." *Annual Review of Anthropology* 26: 163–83.

Rosenau, James. 1980. *The Scientific Study of Foreign Policy*. Dubuque, IA: Nichols Publishing Company.

Russett, Bruce M., J. David Singer, and Melvin Small. 1968. "National Political Units in the Twentieth Century: A Standardized List." *American Political Science Review* 62 (3): 932–51.

Schmitt, Carl. 2007. *The Concept of the Political*. Chicago: Chicago University Press.

Schuurman, Frans. Ed. 1993. *Beyond the Impasse: New Directions in Development Theory*. London: Zed Books.

Seidman, Steven. 2007. *Contested Knowledge: Social Theory Today*. Chichester: Wiley-Blackwell.

Selby, Jan. 2007. "Engaging Foucault: Discourse, Liberal Governance, and the Limits of Foucauldian IR." *International Relations* 21 (3): 324–45.

———. 2013. "The Myth of Liberal Peace-Building." *Conflict, Security and Development* 13 (1): 57–86.

Smith, Steve. 2000. "The Discipline of International Relations: Still an American Social Science?" *British Journal of Politics and International Relations* 2 (3): 374–402.

———, Ken Booth, and Marysia Zalewski. Eds. 1996. *International Theory: Positivism and Beyond*. Cambridge: Cambridge University Press.

Sylvester, Christine. 2013. *War as Experience: Contributions from International Relations and Feminist Analysis*. Abingdon: Routledge.

Teschke, Benno and Hannes Lacher. 2007. "The Changing 'Logics' of Capitalist Competition." *Cambridge Review of International Affairs* 20 (4): 565–80.

Vitalis, Robert. 2015. *White World Order, Black Power Politics: The Birth of American International Relations*. Ithaca: Cornell University Press.

Waever, Ole. 2007. "Still a Discipline after All These Debates?" In *International Relations Theories: Discipline and Diversity*, edited by Tim Dunne, Milja Kurki and Steve Smith, 288–308. Oxford: Oxford University Press.

Wallace, William. 1996. "Truth and Power, Monks and Technocrats: Theory and Practice in International Relations." *Review of International Studies* 22 (3): 301–22.

Walt, Stephen M. 2005. "The Relationship between Theory and Policy in International Relations." *American Review of Political Science* 8: 23–48.

Waltz, Kenneth N. 1979. *Theory of International Politics*. Reading, MA: Addison-Wesley.

Weiss, Thomas G. and Rorden Wilkinson. 2014. "Global Governance to the Rescue: Saving International Relations?" *Global Governance* 20 (1): 19–36.

Williams, Michael C. 2005. *The Realist Tradition and the Limits of International Relations*. Cambridge: Cambridge University Press.

PART ONE

What's the point of IR?

1

WHAT'S THE POINT OF IR?

The international in the invention of humanity

Ken Booth

When *IR* (uppercase and abbreviated) was born as an institutionalized academic discipline in 1919, its founders had two broad objectives: to conduct teaching and research into the manifold dimensions of international relations, and to contemplate a better future for humanity. These broad and momentous aims, for me, remain the *point* of IR nearly a century later, though obviously much has changed in the world. Critical to my argument is the profound causal significance of actually practiced *international relations* (lowercase and unabbreviated).

Born into international relations

We are children of international relations. Before any of us become students, teachers, and researchers of IR, the scaffolding of our being has been constructed by international history: this includes our chances of surviving birth, our first language, the culture into which we are socialized, the nation into which we are politicized, our economic prospects and musical tastes, and much more. The scaffolding may be rearranged, but never dismantled.

Individual identities (central to our social being) and our DNA (basic to our material being) are to a significant degree the outcomes of wars, power plays, diplomatic deals, trading arrangements, migrations, and all the structures, processes, events, attitudes, and behavior that have constituted "international history" broadly defined. Whether languages – shapers of thought as well as means of communication – have declined or flourished has been closely correlated with the exercise of political power. The worldwide prominence of English is not the result of a global urge to read Shakespeare in the original; it is a consequence of British and US geopolitical power over recent centuries. Likewise, the mix of DNA across distant populations is not simply the result of the range of Eros's arrows: we are a genetically multi-bred species because of the frequent-flyer status achieved by Eros (and barbarians) along the invasion paths, trading and migration routes, and imperial highways and seaways that have been the stuff of international relations.

It matters to us individually whether the roll of the cosmic dice placed our parents and developing selves into what international history has constituted as "Afghanistan" as opposed to the "United States," or "Russia" as opposed to "Uruguay." Specific developments play key parts. But for twists in the Second World War, I may not have been born; but for the story of the British Empire, I would surely not have a daughter-in-law from Kenya or a beloved grand daughter whose own international history means that before she can speak properly she is experiencing life through three languages. Consider your own biography and the role international history has played in what you have thought and think, done and not done, and indeed what you are able to think and do and say.

My argument is not deterministic. I am not asserting that humans are merely the ventriloquist's dummies of international history: but I do claim that what as individuals we were, are, and might become is traceable – sometimes to a profound degree – to the patterns of international history. Even how this chapter is read will in part be shaped by one's situatedness within the international.

Kenneth Waltz, IR's most influential theorist in recent decades, was not a structural determinist, but he did argue that the structure of the international system (anarchy, an uneven distribution of power, and units seeking to survive) has impressive "causal weight" (1959, 159–238; 1979, 38–101), and as such helps explain "big and important things" like war and peace (2008, 43). I accept the general thrust of this argument, but do not think Waltz pushed it *deeply* enough. Yes, system structure does help account for (but not determine) "big and important things," but its "causal weight" also shapes what I call "little and important things," like we children of the international (Booth 2014a, 4–5). In this convergence of the generally top-down concerns of structural realism since the late 1970s, and the generally bottom-up concerns of so-called alternative approaches to IR since the late 1980s, we can appreciate better the full causal power of the international on human society globally. My response to the provocation *"What's the point of IR?"* therefore begins with the causality of international relations in the manifold lifeworlds of humanity.

The shock of the old

Some of the language used earlier – wars, diplomatic deals, power plays – will no doubt attract weary criticism from those colleagues who specialize in outing what they regard as old thinking in a new world. Yet, the real shock of the old these days is not allegedly anachronistic IR-talk, but the extent to which actually practiced international relations are characterized by business as usual. Waltz rightly warned of the need to remember the persistence of the historic "texture" of international relations when tempted by images of radical change (1979, 66).

Starting in the late 1980s, the traditional concerns and approaches of mainstream (realist and liberal) IR were attacked by critics over impressed by the power of globalization and the ideas of recently discovered social theorists. Existing "IR" (obligatory scare quotes here for those critics) was challenged in two directions: its agenda was seen as increasingly out of touch, and its canon was regarded as being in urgent need of renewal (and preferably *from somewhere else* than within the established discipline). Whatever was touched in the 1990s by these Midases of Change turned into "beyond," "post," "new," or "end of."

The dazzle of change was such that sections of the discipline thought that the days of IR were numbered. James Rosenau influentially argued that world affairs were becoming "postinternational" (1990, 6). He wrote: "The very notion of 'international relations' seems obsolete in the face of an apparent trend in which more and more of the interactions that sustain world politics unfold without the direct involvement of nations or states." International relations/IR certainly had to take account of globalization: relations across borders are always affected by powerful developments in world politics, whether these are influential ideas (like religion) or substantial material changes (as with modern information technology). But Rosenau's prediction went too far. It did not follow that the globalization of world politics meant the obsolescence of IR (Booth 2014a, 94–7; Booth and Erskine 2016, 4–5).

Many of us were tempted, at some point, to exaggerate the penetration of globalization, but facts on the ground regularly demonstrate that human society globally is far from "postinternational." Indeed, the way globalization has inflamed issues at the heart of international relations – sovereignty, authority, and identity, for example – shows that globalization is stubbornly embedded in a world politics in which "the direct involvement of nations or states" remains a defining feature. Daily headlines shout this out: Putin's ambitions for Russian power! North Korea's nuclear bluster! Prioritizing "the national interest" in economic negotiations! Another failure in climate change conferences! Global levels of militarization at $1,676 billion!

Refugees provide particularly poignant evidence of the continuing grip of historic international dynamics. The refugee crisis in Europe since 2015 trumpets the shock of the old, even in a continent that seemed to be moving toward being "post-sovereign" and "post-national." Refugees are today's tragic canaries in the mine, recording the health of the international through the impact on their minds and bodies of wars, geopolitical ambitions, sovereign control, local tyranny, failed states, armies and navies, borders and border guards, passport officials, foreign ministries, nationalism, mistrust, identity politics, collective-action problems, citizenship, international organizations, sovereignty, and on and on: in other words, the historic textures of international relations. Yet within this picture is also evidence of the more humane potentialities of life under anarchy: the aspiration for better cooperation between governments, respect for individuals and meeting human rights standards, and offers of cosmopolitan hospitality. In a pre-EU world – before "everyday Europe" (McNamara 2015) – surely the crisis and humanitarian distress would have been even worse at this (still early) stage of this refugee story.

My argument about the shock of the old is not therefore that change is impossible in international relations, but rather that the present, like the past, contains a great deal of historic "texture." The international level of world politics continues to be headline-making on "big and important" things, while exercising profound influence on "small and important" things. As I have argued many times, those of us who want to build a better world will never achieve it by being unworldly about this one.

Fields, disciplines, and virgin births

Those who disparage the causal impact on human lifeworlds of states and nations and other international variables contribute to an impression of IR as an increasingly backward and marginal discipline. In contrast to the time when IR was the academic playbook of the Cold War, the view took hold in some schools of thought that the discipline of IR was on borrowed time. Unlike older, publicly prominent, and more self-confident social sciences and humanities, IR has generally been ignored by the outside world when not disparaged by hyper-globalizers. At the same time a surfeit of self-criticism and embroilment in its own theory wars has encouraged excessive introspection and the cultivation, among some, of an intellectual inferiority complex. If the academic project of IR is not to fade away – a quite irrational outcome – its proponents must be clearer about what, who, and *why* we are. For this, we need to go back to the beginning.

A *field* in academic life is an area of study relating to a particular activity, including thinking. In this regard, IR is a field focusing on a complex of relations across borders – which by definition requires input from multiple disciplines. An academic *project* is a collective intellectual endeavor in a university context. Institutionally, such a project may seek to develop a field into a discipline. A *discipline* in the traditional European sense is a distinct and systematic branch of learning, with an associated professional infrastructure. (This understanding of "discipline" is more helpful than the restrictive definition equating the word with one particular methodology.) A *subject* in a university (a particular course of study) is generally synonymous with a discipline. These distinctions – *field*, *project*, and *discipline/subject* – are logically related temporally: a project develops a field into a discipline through the establishment of departments, teaching programs, specific syllabuses, student specialisms, research projects, a professional hierarchy, subject associations, and so on.

It is often impossible to pinpoint the moment when an academic field is "invented," except in the natural sciences, where the invention may be literal. In the case of IR, we can never know when humans first started discussing the how and why of relations between distinct units (nomadic family groups and tribes, and then the first static forms of political association). What can be dated, though, are the existing written records over the millennia about the issues arising from the interactions between early civilizations, city-states, kingdoms, and empires. Over time, a field was marked out (Luard 1992 is an introductory collection) by the following, among numerous others: Mo Tzu ("Warfare Harms the State which Conducts it as Well as Mankind as a whole") in ancient China, Diogenes (the moral responsibilities of a "citizen of the world") in ancient Greece, Kautilya ("The Strategy by which Rulers should Protect their Interests") in ancient India, and Ibn Khaldun (theory of social conflict) in the Islamic world. The significance of this snapshot in relation to my overall argument is that a thoughtscape of relevant "international" concerns grew over the millennia, that it grew in different locations, and that its concerns were cross-cultural (see Bilgin 2016 on "multiple beginnings" and "connected histories").

The field was cultivated and expanded, and like much else in the century before the Great War saw a step-change in productivity, dominated by Europe. As ever, the field was written by the winners. Key writers and concerns included Clausewitz on war, Mazzini on nationalism, Marx on the proletariat, and Meinecke on *raison d'etat*. Recent disciplinary history has brought to the fore somewhat neglected nineteenth-century issues and writers – on empire, liberalism, and race relations, for example (Long and Schmidt 2005; Hobson 2012; Vitalis 2015).

Despite this picture of an ancient – if not necessarily self-conscious – field, some disciplinary historians have questioned the value of trying to explain "the history of the field" by reference to "a continuous tradition" reaching back to the ancient Greeks (Long and Schmidt 2005, 8). We can leave aside the challenge implied by the word "continuous," for history reveals an abundance of political, if not scholarly, talk about international concerns. More importantly, I want to go beyond simply claiming that an identifiable "field" of international concerns developed from ancient and multiple sites to propose that IR's agenda represents a "human universal," entirely comparable to other universals of behavior and language (see Donald E. Brown's list in Pinker 2002, 435–9). Evidence for IR's thoughtscape as a human universal is based on the engagements across time and space with issues relating to anarchy, balance of power, cosmopolitanism, domination, human nature, interdependence, law, mistrust, nationalism, peace, responsibility, uses of power, stratagems, security, sovereignty, statecraft, and much more. Recent work on "worlding" IR (for example, Tickner and Wæver 2009) does not undermine the idea of this "international" agenda as a human universal; it is a reminder instead that a productive field requires "Many Maps, Many Windows," as Mary Midgley claimed for knowledge in general (2003, 26–8, 29–35).

The discussion so far has emphasized that a thoughtscape of speculation about relations across borders stretches back millennia; that it makes no historical sense to claim that thinking about the international was "invented" in a particular place at a particular time and that a somewhat coherent field became marked out because of the universal significance of the compelling agenda of human group interaction under anarchy. Academic disciplines like IR do not miraculously emerge from nowhere. The makers of modern IR were multiple, culturally diverse, geographically disparate, and stretch back through the centuries. They provided a complex intellectual DNA, determining that at the moment of institutionalization, when IR became a disciplinary project, it was not a virgin birth.

"It ain't where you're from, it's where you're at"

If the first talk about relations between human groups is lost in time, the institutional moment is not. IR as a discipline was born in 1919, though some scholars question this "standard story" (Long and Schmidt 2005, 6), and one sometimes hears the phrase "the myth of 1919." Such revisionism suffers from critical flaws:

First: Semantic imprecision. New intellectual history is always welcome, but the most urgent need is conceptual clarity. David Long and Brian C. Schmidt (2005, 6) refer to the relationship of the Great War and "the genesis of the field *or* discipline" (emphasis added). In the previous section, I argued that "field" and "discipline" are different concepts and should be carefully separated: all academic disciplines have fields, but not all fields become academic disciplines. Imprecision on this matter is common. Robert Vitalis, for example, has described IR as "the new-field-in-formation" at the outbreak of the Great War (2005, 172) and identified Alfred Zimmern as the holder of "the first ever [Chair] created in the new field of international relations" (2005, 164). The previous section pointed to the thoughtscape of political and other relations between human groups as a truly ancient *field*. The chair to which Zimmern was appointed on 25 April 1919 was "the first ever" in a new *discipline*.

Second, self-contradiction: Long and Schmidt, as mentioned earlier, questioned the idea of "traditions of international thought" (2005, 8). Yet immediately they reversed gear and claimed that they did not wish thereby to "convey the impression that the field is devoid of any authentic traditions," nor did they want "to suggest that scholars should not study *the classic texts of international relations theory*" (emphasis added). Classic texts cannot exist in an intellectual vacuum: they are part of a field with a living history and represent the work of those writers with whom one can still have, in W. B. Gallie's felicitous phrase, a "time-transcending dialogue" (1979, 3).

Three: incomplete history. In a book seeking to add fine-grained history to IR's origins and claiming that as a profession we do not take our disciplinary history seriously enough, Long and Schmidt (2005) do not give recognition to the individual(s) who were the actual midwives at the birth of IR as a discipline in 1919, namely David Davies and his sisters Gwendoline and Margaret.

In the gap between the armistice in November 1918 and the assembling of the Peace Conference in Versailles the following January, Davies wrote to the authorities of the then University College of Wales, Aberystwyth (I am grateful to Michael Cox for a copy of this document from the university archives and much relevant intellectual inspiration). He said that "we all ardently hope it [the Peace Conference] will herald in a new world, freed from the menace of war." He recognized it would be an "immense task," requiring "energy, good will, knowledge, and enlightened public opinion in all countries." It needed "a new spirit" and "myriad agencies," and the importance of "our universities" was picked out for special mention in this task.

Davies (a Liberal MP and benefactor) wrote that it had "occurred to my sisters and myself" that the University of Wales would be willing to found a chair "in memory of the fallen students of our University." The point of this chair was "the study of those related problems of law and politics, of ethics and economics, which are raised by the project of a League of Nations, and for the encouragement of a truer understanding of civilisations other than our own." In these brief words is encapsulated *the very point* this chapter is addressing: the particular role of universities in studying the international agenda, the need for knowledge about other disciplines, the necessary search for knowledge beyond one's own culture and political horizons, engagement with real problems, and investment in the study of a better future for humanity.

This foundational inspiration can be condensed into a contemporary definition of IR with the help of a formulation I heard Charles Manning offer in the mid-1960s, when he said that he conceived IR as having "a focus but not a periphery." I express that focus as *the international level of world politics*. The idea of a "level" raises some issues, of course, but can be understood as "the transboundary interactions (including diplomacy, trade relations, war, and so on) between, *inter alia*, states, intergovernmental organisations (IGOs), powerful individual human actors, and non-state actors such as non-governmental organisations (NGOs) and multi- and transnational corporations (MNCs/TNCs)" (Booth and Erskine 2016, 296 n1). World politics, extrapolating Harold Lasswell's influential definition of politics, is "the study of *Who Gets What, When* [and] *How* globally" (Booth 1995a, 329; Booth and Erskine 2016, 5). Such a conception of the discipline has a focal point, stretch, and can be the basis for teaching and research programs.

One issue raised by critics of the so-called standard story is the significance of identity in the history of thinking about IR. I agree, and being a 1919er in this debate certainly does not mean blindness to relationships between identity and discourse or the way social practices (including academic disciplines) produce and reproduce relations of power. In a book many years ago I stressed the role of ethnocentrism in such a defining realist concern as military strategy, arguing that strategy has a logic, but also cultures (Booth 1979). In a later piece, I speculated about the character of IR in general had its origins been different. Instead of Davies and his sisters and their generation of liberal internationalist academic institution builders, I asked what IR would have become had it derived from "the life and work of the admirable black, feminist, medic she-chief of the Zulus, Dr Zungu?" (Booth 1995b, 124–6).

Such questions raise the notion of "situatedness" in theorizing, with its normative as well as empirical dimensions in the pursuit of knowledge. In this regard Robert Cox's most influential line (1981, 128) needs completing. Cox wrote that "theory is always *for* someone and *for* some purpose" (emphasis in the original): to this should be added "and is *by* someone *from* somewhere." But to recognize the significance of situatedness does not require scholars to follow the siren calls of cultural relativism or cultural appropriation. Wherever we are precisely *from*, almost every idea – good or bad – came from somewhere else in the world. Culturally speaking, humans are gloriously intermixed. What matters is not where ideas come from, but whether they travel and whether (as will be discussed later) they enhance humanity.

Bad ideas travel, as well as good, and in a field with such an ancient intellectual heritage, it is inevitable that we find skeletons in our cupboards. Workers in our field have included imperialists, racists, and extreme nationalists, among others, and most have experienced the "common sense" of patriarchy. Skeletons have been exposed by disciplinary historians, but let us not become self-righteous, for if more enlightened societies than those that now exist come about – a desperate hope – we, too, will end up as skeletons on somebody's bookshelves. Skeletons are artifacts of their time and as such need a certain understanding. Philosophers of the good life do not reject Socratic thinking because ancient Athens was a highly imperfect society by modern standards. The important thing, as Bettany Hughes writes, is the "living" Socrates, who contributes to sharpening our minds (2010, xix–xxii). Writers of the classic texts of IR also lived in imperfect societies and sometimes endorsed ideas now thought regressive, but the best of them were intellectual giants who allow us to stand on their shoulders and see further, as the old adage has it. What is more, when criticizing ethnocentric ideas in IR, as well as regressive ideas, it is well to recall that the social anthropologist I. M. Lewis called ethnocentrism "the natural condition of mankind" (1976, 13). It would therefore have been truly astonishing had ideas and practices about world politics emanating from the period of European global ascendency in the nineteenth century been other than "Eurocentric" – any more than if Imperial China had seen itself as other than the "Middle Kingdom" during its long ascendency (Booth 1979, 71).

In considering what to take from the past – the good, the bad, and the ugly – reflexivity is the key. This should help us recognize that humanity's regressive past is IR's ultimate Other, but also that it produced intellectual giants in our field with whom we can have a "time-transcending dialogue." Progress is possible: few would question that IR today is richer than 30 years ago, with greater depth, stretch, equality, and inclusiveness. The changes have been patchy, but that is another matter. Reflexivity has brought about different identities and possibilities, including ways of picking the lock of the "iron cage" of old ideas. This includes critical theory's guidance on exploring immanent potentials, which makes it rational to theorize IR in relation to a more humane humanity, structured to deepen solidarity, promote equality, universalize human rights, humanize power, and delegitimize political violence.

"Social engineers of human consciousness"

The phrase "We have words inside us" (origins explained in Booth 2007, 427) lyrically encapsulates the potential contained, often trapped, in the human species. This is particularly pertinent to how we think about the theory and practice of the international level of world politics. The character of the international in the collective consciousness will be critical to the ways human societies live together on this shrinking planet, and hence to the future of humanity.

By "humanity" here I do not simply mean our biological species, but rather the "condition or quality" attaching to humans. These might involve kindness and sympathy (being "humane") or the opposite (behaving in an all-too-human "inhuman" fashion). Actually practiced international relations are implicated in a whole range of normative outcomes, and so necessarily is IR, its academic offshoot. Scholars in this way have the role of potential "social engineers," the phrase of Philip Allott (2002, 3) in the title of this section. Theory and practice constitute a continuation of ethics by different means, and scholars become potential reality makers, whether or not an individual accepts or even recognizes such a role and whatever that individual's school of theory. The concepts of IR are open to specific cultural interpretations, as discussed earlier, but the agenda is universal in relevance and admits only a limited number of logical positions. Basic IR concepts such as the "security dilemma," for example, can be approached through "fatalist," "mitigator," and "transcender" logics only (Booth and Wheeler 2008): whichever is adopted has reality-making potentials, however minimal, through adding to the marketplace of ideas that seek to reproduce or change attitudes and behavior about how humans interact.

Two illustrations demonstrate how the quality of the international affects the quality of humanity: first, an international in which some governments target horrific and indiscriminating nuclear weapons against other societies as their "ultimate guarantors of national security" will tend to sustain a condition of humanity in which global mistrust will always poison the well of human potential; and second, an international in which war remains legitimate and militaristic values remain honored will be one in which aspirations for gender equality will always struggle. Kant encouraged us to think that if we do not get the international right, then we will not get much else right in society.

It will be apparent that I have an unashamedly positive view about the significance of the discipline of IR. At the same time, my expectations are modest about what academics can practically achieve, especially when theory/politics meet in the policy arena. The reasons for this need not be developed now, except to note that policy making and implementation and teaching and research are two very different sets of activities. What is more, ours is a passionately argumentative discipline in which theorists do not as a matter of course speak with one voice (Booth and Erskine 2016). Despite my modesty about IR's immediate policy relevance, I nevertheless think our discipline should have an "architectonic" (directing) role in the social sciences, as opposed to being somewhat marginal (Booth 2011, 337–9). The case rests on four main arguments.

First: IR focuses on issues of exceptional global significance

The international is deeply causal; we ask the biggest questions in politics in the biggest political arena; our scope is global; our time frame embraces the ancient world and the distant future; our subject matter is potentially civilization destroying; and our realities are an inconvenient truth for other disciplines.

Second: other disciplines deal with the international inadequately

There was once a case for describing IR as a "backward" discipline because of the general level of insularity in relation to relevant ideas in other disciplines. This is no longer the case, with the general rise and broadening of theoretical understanding (Booth and Erskine 2016). In contrast, one regularly sees work elsewhere dominated by statist methodology (focusing on a unit, but not in the context of its relations with others), flimsily based generalizations, and undercooked IR (Booth 2013).

Third: IR scholars are often unduly deferential to other disciplines

Our navel gazing leads us to be over-impressed by other disciplines, failing to recognize their weaknesses and unfulfilled hopes, as in the presentist tendency in writing Indian history (Khilnani 2016) and "physics envy" in economics (Ash 2016). Deference is particularly destructive, paradoxically, in IR's "enduring definition as a subfield" within "the prison of Political Science" (Rosenberg 2016 and this volume). For many of us, this means, above all, *American* political science, with its methodology obsession and superpower parochialism. To play a stronger role in academia, the IR profession needs a more self-confident self-image, transcending theory wars in the interests of engaging with the problems in and of the status quo. Greater self-confidence would surely come by spending more time with our classic texts in the original. Too often our students have their minds distorted by textbook writers and faux-radicals who flourish off the illicit earnings of a strawperson called "IR."

Four: IR has much to celebrate

If we raise our gaze above our intellectual navels, we might find time to (re)discover some excellent work in our discipline. A preliminary list for me includes general theorizing about anarchy and hierarchy; sophisticated explorations of the ethics of war and modalities of strategy; English school comparative studies of international societies; mid-range theorizing about international organizations, security regimes and communities, and global governance; historical sociology's exposing of the teleological assumptions about the rise of the nation-state; the work of "progressive realists" contemplating global reform; normative theory's examination of the idea of a just world order, including a fairer distribution of resources and sustainable relations with nature; critical perspectives on broadening and deepening the concept of security; feminist uncovering of the complexities of how power works; "World Order" thinking about global transformation and the perspective of the universal;

micro- and macro-histories of the games of nations; and much, much more. Each of these issue areas speaks to the agenda of how humans have lived, live, and might live together globally; this in turn – as argued earlier – is relevant for contemplating human flourishing at different levels, which is central to enhancing the general condition of humanity.

Champions of our discipline have a fascinating as well as a significant field in which to work, but we also have roles and responsibilities beyond the strict discipline that are vital to its flourishing (Erskine and Booth 2016). In addition to promoting IR within the social sciences, scholarship in general needs defending against threats to free speech internationally, nationally, and within universities. There is also the dark challenge to scholarly values in the expansion of the market university, with its short-termism, addiction to metrics and league tables, preference for process over outputs, valuation of managers over scholars, and the bottom line.

How, in face of such an agenda, are specialists in IR to operate as "social engineers of the human conscience"? In part, this involves the professional roles and responsibilities identified earlier; more generally, our work as "social engineers" depends on our choice of audience. In my opinion, the primary audience for IR should be society, not the state. This is not to say that individual scholars should always eschew the role of policy advisor, though those who do need to understand that they must accept the priorities of those in power. Above all, our argumentative and pluralistic discipline should practice social engineering through our students. They are the future collective conscience we can best seek to influence. Some of them will directly become engaged in relevant activities, in NGOs, the media, think tanks, and as politicians and officials; others, the majority, will become part of the bedrock of the consciousness of society as citizens, family members, voters, and civil society generally. Our students, increasingly, are global and interconnected.

Conclusion

When IR was born as an institutionalized academic project nearly a century ago, the point was to teach and research a critical level of world politics and to think about alternative futures. The global "we" in the discipline's second century will face a world historical "Great Reckoning" (Booth 2007, 395–426) in which the ideas that made humanity what it has become pose a concatenation of existential and emancipatory threats to our worldwide community of fate (Booth 2014b). In such circumstances humanity is in desperate need of improving collective decision-making in the interests of the global not the national, the many not the few, and nature not human greed.

Our disciplinary work as reality makers operating through society is necessarily long term. The American activist and writer Rebecca Solnit offers perspective. "You scatter your seeds," she wrote, "Rats might eat them, or they might rot . . . some seeds lie dormant for decades because they only germinate after fire, and sometimes the burned landscape blooms most lavishly" (2005, 93). The few of us lucky enough to have the opportunity to think and write about IR cannot ensure our seeds will ever bloom lavishly or for long, but it is in our power to try and ensure that our words are accessible as well as scholarly, are packed with an immanent critique of the present, speak in some way to and for the universal, and consider the conditions of possibility whereby actually practiced international relations might contribute, step by step, in the invention of a more humane humanity.

Bibliography

Allott, Philip. 2002. *The health of nations: Society and law beyond the state.* Cambridge: Cambridge University Press.

Ash, Timothy Garton. 2016. "When economists ignore the human factor, the rest of us pay the price", *The Guardian* (5 February).

Bilgin, Pinar. 2016. "Do IR scholars engage with the same world?" In *International relations theory today.* Edited by Ken Booth and Toni Erskine. 97–109. Cambridge: Polity.

Booth, Ken. 1979. *Strategy and ethnocentrism.* London: Croom Helm.

Booth, Ken. 1995a. "Dare not to know: International relations theory versus the future". In *International relations theory today.* Edited by Ken Booth and Steve Smith. 328–51. Cambridge: Polity.

Booth, Ken. 1995b. "Human wrongs and international relations", *International Affairs* 71 (1): 103–26.

Booth, Ken. 2007. *Theory of World Security.* Cambridge: Cambridge University Press.

Booth, Ken. 2011. "International politics: The inconvenient truth". In *Realism and world politics.* Edited by Ken Booth. 325–43. Abingdon: Routledge.

Booth, Ken. 2013. "Human development in a statist world", *International Journal of Social Economics* 40 (7): 633–47.

Booth, Ken. 2014a. *International relations: All that matters.* London: Hodder & Stoughton.

Booth, Ken. 2014b. "Global security". In *The handbook of global security policy.* Edited by Mary Kaldor and Iavor Rangelov. 11–31. Chichester: Wiley Blackwell.

Booth, Ken, and Erskine, Toni. 2016. "Introduction: The argumentative discipline". In *International relations theory today.* Edited by Ken Booth and Toni Erskine. 1–23. Cambridge: Polity.

Booth, Ken, and Wheeler, Nicholas J. 2008. *The security dilemma: Fear, cooperation and trust in world politics.* Houndmills: Palgrave Macmillan.

Cox, Robert W. 1981. "Social forces, states, and world orders: Beyond international relations", *Millennium* 10 (2): 127–55.

Erskine, Toni, and Booth, Ken. 2016. "Conclusion: Responsibility, risk, and IR theory". In *International relations theory today.* Edited by Ken Booth and Toni Erskine. 279–96. Cambridge: Polity.

Gallie, W. B. 1979. *Philosophers of peace and war: Kant, Clausewitz, Marx, Engels and Tolstoy.* Cambridge: Cambridge University Press.

Hobson, John H. 2012. *The Eurocentric conception of world politics: Western international theory, 1760–1910.* Cambridge: Cambridge University Press.

Hughes, Bettany. 2010. *The hemlock cup: Socrates, Athens and the search for the good life.* London: Jonathan Cape.

Khilnani, Sunil. 2016. *Incarnations: India in 50 lives.* London: Penguin.

Lewis, I. M. 1976. *Social anthropology in perspective.* Harmondsworth: Penguin.

Long, David, and Schmidt, Brian C., eds. 2005. *Imperialism and internationalism in the discipline of international relations.* Albany: State University of New York.

Luard, Evan, ed. 1992. *Basic texts in international relations: The evolution of ideas about international society*. Houndmills: Macmillan.

McNamara, Kathleen R. 2015. *The politics of everyday Europe: Constructing authority in the European Union*. Oxford: Oxford University Press.

Midgley, Mary. 2003. *The myths we live by*. London: Routledge.

Pinker, Steven. 2002. *The blank slate: The modern denial of human nature*. London: Penguin.

Rosenau, James R. 1990. *Turbulence in world politics*. Brighton: Harvester-Wheatsheaf.

Rosenberg, Justin. 2016. "International relations in the prison of political science", *International Relations* 30 (2): 127–53.

Solnit, Rebecca. 2005. *Hope in the dark*. Edinburgh: Canongate.

Tickner, Arlene B., and Wæver, Ole, eds. 2009. *International relations scholarship around the world*. London: Routledge.

Vitalis, Robert. 2005. "Birth of a discipline". In *Imperialism and internationalism in the discipline of international relations*. Edited by David Long and Brian C. Schmidt. 159–83. Albany: State University of New York.

Vitalis, Robert. 2015. *White world order, black power politics*. Ithaca: Cornell University Press.

Waltz, Kenneth N. 1959. *Man, the state and war*. New York: Columbia University Press.

Waltz, Kenneth N. 1979. *Theory of international politics*. New York: Random House.

Waltz, Kenneth N. 2008. "Reflections on *Theory of international politics*: A response to my critics (1986)" In *Realism and international politics*. Edited by Kenneth N. Waltz. 322–45. New York: Routledge.

2

INSECURITY REDUX

The perennial problem of "the point of IR"

Patrick Thaddeus Jackson

IR is an anxious academic endeavor. The sheer volume of ink and time expended worrying about the definition of "IR" is somewhat mind boggling, and indeed at times it seems like the chief concern of scholars who are in any sense writing "IR scholarship" is to establish whether they are, in fact, doing IR at all. Other scholarly endeavors do not seem to me to be as obsessed with the question of their own boundaries and the related issues of whether they are fields, disciplines, or something else. Although the need for academic endeavors to justify themselves as worthy knowledge-producing activities does seem to be a general feature of modern academic life, the discussions in and around IR do not seem to be able to proceed from a firm grasp of what IR *is*, which makes it somewhat difficult to spell out IR's distinctive contributions and thus to legitimate the institutional resources spent on IR programs, departments, and faculty positions.

In this chapter I do not propose to resolve the practical problem of how beleaguered IR programs make the case for their "relevance" within the contemporary neoliberal academy. Although such concerns lend some everyday urgency to the question of what IR is for (and, by implication, what IR's proper boundaries are), I want to suggest instead that we need to take a step back and think more critically about the very frame of the question. Traditionally, asking what IR is for and what IR is has called for a *singular* answer: a categorical formula that, if properly applied, could *with certainty* discriminate between IR and all manner of academic Others. The specific academic Others have not remained constant over time and space, but the quest – to be able to say with certainty what IR *is* and *is not* – has remained more or less constant over the past century of IR's existence. This intellectual insecurity is obviously related to the *organizational* insecurity of IR faculty and IR programs and to what we might call the *geopolitical* insecurity of an international realm traditionally envisioned as an arena of dangerous competition and conflict; both of those vectors of insecurity obviously color what would otherwise (but things are *never* otherwise than this, are they?) be a purely academic discussion. But for the moment I want to imagine that this *is* a purely academic discussion and to treat claims about IR's boundaries and purpose as though they were neither appeals for resources nor responses to urgent practical-political demands and see if doing so can perhaps dissolve some of IR's *intellectual* anxiety.

In my view this dis-solution comes by embracing an expansive, pluralist account of the field, which allows us to stop worrying so much about whether some topic or approach or aim is or is not IR. We do not need yet another fixed and firm definition of what IR "is" and therefore "is for." What we need instead is more useful and comprehensive definitions of the field within which a variety of theories, methodologies, and vocational orientations can fit. In effect, we need to shift the conversation from "this is/is not IR" to "why is this IR?" The open-ended question rather than the categorical statement allows for responses and dialogues, rather than procrustean efforts to fit non-traditional objects, approaches, and orientations into prefabricated definitions or efforts to storm the academic castle and throw out the rulers, only to establish new rulers in their places. And further, since the very term "IR" has all too often been used to demarcate a narrowly construed scholarly endeavor, we may need to consider abandoning it in favor of the broader term against which many foundational definitional sorties were arrayed: "international studies," an eclectic collection of theories, methodologies, and vocations united not by agreement on any of those registers, but sharing a family resemblance to one another in that they are all in some way concerned with *the encounter with difference across boundaries*. In a way I am suggesting that we return to an older way of thinking about the field, on the suspicion that if one has taken the wrong road, *regress* might be a form of *progress* (as in Lewis 2014).

Three avenues

Let me begin by identifying three avenues along which debates about IR's boundaries and purpose have traditionally unfolded. The first, a *theoretical* avenue, has involved discussions about what kinds of objects in the world count as valid things for IR scholars to study. Here we find a distinction between scholars insisting on a narrow bestiary and scholars embracing a more catholic approach. The traditional axis of debate here has involved those scholars who insist on the primacy of sovereign territorial states and inter-state political and economic relations (Waltz 1979; Keohane 1984; Wendt 1999) and those who argue that IR should also encompass the study of other kinds of actors and relations: global governance beyond formal international law (Barnett and Finnemore 2004; Avant, Finnemore, and Sell 2010), broader social forces and social structures (Wallerstein 1974; Cox 1996), flows of communication and rhetorical speech acts (Deutsch 1957; Onuf 1989), and regional and civilizational dynamics (Katzenstein 2005, 2009). A second, a *methodological* avenue, has involved debates between scholars insisting on a narrowly neopositivist account of how to do IR scholarship, emphasizing the testing of hypotheses to arrive at general laws (e.g., King, Keohane, and Verba 1994; Elman and Elman 2003), and scholars willing to countenance a broader diversity of approaches (Ackerly, Stern, and True 2006; Sil and Katzenstein 2010; Jackson 2011). A third avenue involves what we might call the *vocational orientation* of IR scholarship: questions about who the audience is for IR scholarship, what the relationship ought to be between IR scholars and the world of practical international affairs, and the like (e.g., George 1993). Across all three avenues we see the same pattern: a contrast between those who countenance only one narrow answer and those seemingly more comfortable with a diversity of orientations.

These avenues bear some probably non-accidental resemblance to the hoary old "three great debates" of introductory IR textbook lore, which are supposed to have pitted, in the first great debate, "realists" against "idealists," in the second great debate, "scientists" versus "traditionalists," and in the third great debate, "positivists" versus "post-positivists" (for a good overview see Lapid 1989; Wæver 1996). But the account of IR's history and development that uses the "great debates" framework suggests that these are discrete moments in that history, so that each debate was *resolved* in sequence and that therefore IR could move on and not have that debate again. If one takes that account on its own terms, we would now inhabit an IR defined by realism, science, and either positivism or post-positivism depending on which side one thinks "won" the third debate. Yet, a quick look around the field will immediately render this a problematic characterization, because all three of these "great debates" seem to be still going on. IR has not settled on realism, science, or positivism/post-positivism by any means, and the more one looks into the actual history of these "great debates," the clearer it becomes that they never actually took place the way that one might imagine – they are instead part of a kind of internal fairy tale that IR scholars sometimes tell themselves about where the field of IR came from and where it is going (Schmidt 1998; Vitalis 2015). The point I want to make is that these are not discrete moments in the history of IR so much as recurrent themes over the *entire* history of IR, which is why I prefer avenues to "great debates."

Also, these three avenues display a similar pattern, and that pattern *never* results in victory for the broader or pluralist end of the discussion. One reason for this, I believe, is that those arguing the narrower pole of the debate can always raise the specter of unlimited incoherence against those of a broader mind-set, implicitly or explicitly equating a catholic, pluralist attitude with the absence of standards or with a dereliction of duty. So the critics, under threat of being dismissed as irrelevant, concentrate instead on replacing the narrow end of the avenue with content more to their liking, but leave intact the notion that the avenue ought to have a narrow end in the first place. Another reason is that these three avenues are not independent of one another, but are instead hierarchically and historically arranged, so to speak: the insistence on a theoretical narrowness is reinforced by an insistence on methodological narrowness, which is in turn reinforced by an insistence on a narrow vocational orientation toward either being a policy expert or a pure academic. Thus one all too often hears that IR has to provide a framework for action rather than simply functioning as a means of understanding and explaining, and this functions as a justification for leaving aside "philosophical" questions (broader notions of theory and methodology) in order to focus on more urgently pressing matters; but almost as often, one hears that any practical recommendations are essentially tainted by their association with the extant corrupt order of things so that scholarship should be completely divorced from such mundane concerns. Either way, narrowness triumphs over breadth.

To illustrate the point, consider the reaction to Robert Cox's (1996) celebrated distinction between "problem solving" and "critical" theory. Cox proposed this distinction as a way of distinguishing between those theoretical approaches that had as their goal the maintenance and improvement of existing social arrangements and those that looked for more fundamental transformations of those arrangements. Cox clearly stated that these two forms of theory were *complementary* and that he was not calling for IR to be exclusively dominated by either; but right away certain IR scholars (e.g., Gilpin 1986) began taking the distinction as license to ignore "critical" theory on the grounds that they were interested in solving problems, whereas others took the distinction as license to completely abandon any kind of "action-guiding" recommendations in favor of general denunciations of global arrangements (as detailed in Brown 2013). So what was originally a claim on behalf of theoretical and methodological diversity – IR should contain multiple scholarly streams – was turned almost immediately into a pair of rival and exclusive claims, each of which sought to put all of IR under its ambit.

By looking at each of these three avenues in a little more detail, I hope to suggest that the narrow end of each is inadequate to any resolution of the perpetual discussion of what IR is and is for. This in turn sets up my proposal for a re-consideration of the broad end of all three avenues and of the field itself.

Scientific ontology, also known as "theory"

One of the challenges raised by the dominance of narrow construals of IR over the years is that our sense of what "theory" is or might be has been distorted, bifurcated into two mutually exclusive streams that simply increase mutual incomprehension. On one hand, we find definitions of theory that equate to well-vetted nomothetic generalizations, so that "to theorize" and "to generalize" become more or less synonymous. Thus, Andrew Moravcsik, defining a liberal theory of international politics, simply declares that "liberal theory seeks to generalize about the social conditions under which the behavior of self-interested actors converges toward cooperation or conflict" (1997, 517), but he apparently sees no need to *justify* this position. On the other hand, we find definitions of theory that place more emphasis on making sense of a situation from a particular point of view, calling attention to the operation of disciplinary and governmental power, the impact of gendered and racialized principles of order, and/or the enduring presence and persistent traces of colonialism and imperialism in global life – theory as a kind of therapeutic intervention (Blaney and Inayatullah 2009). These two streams agree on very little, because what the second calls "theory" the first calls untested conjecture, and what the first calls "theory" the second calls unreflective participation in a deeply problematic social and political order.

We cannot resolve this by choosing one of these two definitions of "theory" unless we simply want to expel the other stream's adherents from IR – which would only make sense if we were *absolutely sure* that one of these notions of "theory" was correct. Both streams can marshal compelling arguments in their favor, albeit arguments that require a prior adherence on the part of the target audience to the basic presuppositions of one or the other stream: theory-as-nomothetic-generalization scholars emphasize careful evaluation and tentative strides toward knowledge with a broader domain of applicability, which all seems too timid and too surface-level for scholars committed to a more expansive notion of theory-as-world-disclosure, and that in turn seems like speculative metaphysics or political posturing to the first group. Nor can we seamlessly put the two extremes together in some kind of two-step because doing so always privileges one or the other notion of theory: if theory-as-generalization folks put claims made by theory-as-world-disclosure scholars to the empirical test – as Price and Reus-Smit (1998) once recommended – that's a privileging of theory-as-generalization; but if theory-as-world-disclosure scholars look at empirical generalizations (such as that between democratic regime type and the absence of interstate war), they see in the generalization only the tip of the iceberg and something that has to be *theorized* before it can become a valid explanation (as in Barkawi and Laffey 1999).

In our 2013 contribution to the *European Journal of International Relations* special issue on the "end of IR theory," Daniel Nexon and I (2013) suggested that one way forward would be to adopt a definition of "theory" that sought not to choose one of these streams over the other, but instead to focus on the key family resemblances between them. In this way, both theory-as-generalization and theory-as-world-disclosure seek to provide a *scientific ontology*: a delineation of entities, processes, mechanisms, and factors that the theorist or theoretical tradition intends to use to explain some otherwise-puzzling outcome or observed state of things in the world. The most committed analyst in the theory-as-generalization stream is still producing, albeit perhaps tacitly in the course of evaluating rival explanations, a bestiary of entities and relations; and the most committed analyst in the theory-as-world-disclosure stream is still providing that bestiary with an eye toward explaining something in the world. So, at least in principle, everyone agrees that generating and refining theory is about figuring out what there is in the world and how it works, and everyone agrees that some theories accomplish these tasks better than others (although disagreements persist on which specific theories belong in which category). The point is that shifting to theory-as-scientific-ontology moves from the narrow end of the avenue toward the broad end and leaves space for *both* of these existing streams.

By way of illustration, consider Kenneth Waltz's (1979) argument that the study of international relations needed to be restricted to the study of the structure of inter-state interactions among the great powers in the international system because those interactions set the parameters for everyone and everything else. During the

Cold War, this was the bipolar rivalry between the United States and the Soviet Union. Earlier, it was the multipolar jockeying between the European imperial powers, perhaps including Japan and the United States on the periphery of the system. Understood as a scientific ontology, this is a fairly explicit attempt to produce a catalog of entities and relations. Neoliberal institutionalism (Baldwin 1993), followed by "mainstream" constructivism (Katzenstein 1996), tried to add to the bestiary, but all of these movements tended to lose sight of the main point of Waltz's original theory: to explain a "small number of big and important things," in particular, the recurrence of balances of power among the great powers. Which suggests that *other* theories might be needed to explain *other* things, and that the point of theorizing is not to "correctly" state the nature of international affairs so much as it is to produce a scientific ontology that is useful for the explanation of specific things: instead of one "international system," we would have a plethora of specifications of "the international system," each of which might be helpful for explaining a different aspect of international affairs. The move to scientific ontology thus opens up the broad end of the avenue.

Philosophical ontology, or "methodology"

The objection to such a pluralizing of explanatory intentions is generally made through an appeal to methodological issues, specifically to the supposed nature of "social science." Methodology is, in fact, a bigger barrier to dis-solving IR's perennial insecurity than theory is because under the spell of a misleadingly monolithic notion of "science" we have tended, over the decades, to insist on some unitary and foundational idea of valid knowledge as the anchor of our claims (Monteiro and Ruby 2009). It does not matter which idea of science one uses, although historically the dominant voice in these conversations in IR has belonged to neopositivism – which might help to explain why even the fiercest critics of neopositivism end up reproducing neopositivism's commitment to a *single, unified* definition that can effectively demarcate science from non-science (Taylor 1996). After all, neopositivism promises the closest thing to certainty that we can get in a post-Enlightenment era: well-vetted, as-yet-unfalsified hypothetical generalizations. Alternative methodological approaches propose well-vetted-although-unobservable causal mechanisms (critical realism), logically consistent models (analyticism), and self-aware appreciations of embedded perspectives (reflexivity) as substitutes – substitutes that are supposed to accomplish the same thing as hypothetical generalizations and hypothesis testing are supposed to accomplish for neopositivists, which is to put an end to uncertainty (as much as possible) and leave us with valid knowledge.

Yet, as I have argued in my book *The Conduct of Inquiry in International Relations* (Jackson 2011) at much greater length, none of these methodological approaches *can* fairly "win" an argument with the others because every claim made on behalf of a particular methodology against others *presumes* the superior worth of that methodology vis-à-vis the others. Each of the four methodologies I identify there has its own standards of validity, its own preferred procedures for evaluating claims, and its own sense of the epistemic status of knowledge – and these standards are logically distinct from one another. If one is not an analyticist, one does not *care* about internal logical consistency as much as one cares about other epistemic standards; if one is not a critical realist, one does not *care* about laboratory-like vetting of dispositional causal properties. And there is no reason that one *should* care, because what we have in the social sciences is a plethora of standards instead of one unequivocal one.

Moving toward the broader end of the avenue means giving up on a singular definition of methodology and accepting diversity rather than moving to shut it down. I have proposed, and continue to propose, that when we talk about methodology we are actually talking about *philosophical ontology*, which is to say, about various ways to cash out the relationship between the mind and the world. Inasmuch as these cannot be resolved,[1] what we need instead is a better *lexicon* for organizing types and styles of philosophical ontology. Just as the broad end of the theory avenue is populated by a plethora of scientific ontologies, the broad end of the methodology avenue is populated by a plethora of philosophical ontologies, all of which share a family resemblance I would characterize as a commitment to the production of *systematic, public, worldly* knowledge. But that family resemblance is the only thing holding the broad end of the avenue together.

Vocational orientation, or "bridging the gap"

Partisans of a narrowly focused IR have, however, a final trump card to play. Right from the beginning, IR was supposed to be, at least in part, about telling policy makers what to do, or perhaps telling publics what to tell policy makers what to do (Murphy 2000). The urgency of this task was thought to derive from the clear and present danger presented by international affairs. We can see this gesture clearly in the Rapporteur's Report (drawn up by C. A. W. Manning, at that time the Montague Burton Chair in International Relations at the University of London) on a 1950 international meeting of scholars to discuss the university teaching of international relations, which concludes by ascribing "the follies, in the 1930s, of the western democracies" at least in part "to the sentimentalisms, and the gullibilities, of the young" stemming from "the virtual absence in the Universities during the 1920s of provision for teaching on the contemporary layout of the diplomatic scene" (Manning 1951, 25). At about the same time, Hans Morgenthau, one of the seminal voices in the creation of international relations as a subject of study in the United States, was arguing in a paper prepared for a crucial 1954 conference on international politics sponsored by the Rockefeller Foundation (Guilhot 2008) that a good theory of international relations would be one that went beyond "rational explanation and anticipation" to provide a framework for action and thus to establish "one condition for successful action" (Morgenthau 2011, 265–266) in an era of nuclear-armed bipolar rivalry. Hence, *vocationally*, IR was supposed to be in some sense in the service of practical foreign policy and international diplomacy.

Over the course of the twentieth century, this morphed into a greater emphasis on generating in some sense valid knowledge that could be communicated to policy makers and publics. In the United States, where the entire legitimation strategy of the social sciences involved the notion that non-partisan separation from political and social life could be used to improve political and social life (Gunnell 1993), this produced a corresponding focus on specialized technical and conceptual tools for use by academics in their internal debates. The result was that the scholarly enterprise of IR and the public-policy–advising role became differentiated – not because the scholars abandoned the public and the policy makers, but because greater emphasis was placed by scholars on first figuring out what the correct thing was to say to such audiences. Taken to further institutional extremes, the differentiation of scholarly and policy worlds generated a "gap" that some subsequently tried (and keep trying) to "bridge" so that scholarly knowledge could more effectively correct and improve policy practice. Conversely, in different institutional settings, the push was for scholarship to come back to the supposedly unmediated knowledge of the subject maintained by practitioners and to remind those practitioners of the traditional lessons of worldly experience. Hedley Bull's famous comment that the analytical style practiced by the more self-consciously scientific scholars in IR "keeps them as remote from the substance of international politics as the inmates of a Victorian nunnery were from the study of sex" (1975, 26) conveys something of the spirit of the latter gesture and might be thought as a kind of reverse of the "scholarship corrects practice" position; it is, however, just as narrow as its opposite in upholding *one* vocational orientation for IR per se.

So the notion that we IR scholars have to get it right in order to tell people what to do in practical international affairs has thus never been far from the surface of the enterprise. As Manning noted, "within the circle of the social sciences the educative ideal to be served is the fostering, not of 'correct' political attitudes, but of a steadily more realistic insight into the nature of things" (1951, 22). Determining the nature of that "realistic insight" was the typical framing of calls for academic international relations to adopt one or another theoretical or methodological approach, from E. H. Carr's (1964) early advocacy through to the most recent programmatic statements of IR's scope and content, such as Amitav Acharya's call in his International Studies Association presidential address for "global IR" (Acharya 2014). It is as though our role as scholars was exhausted by our role as policy advisors, a position that presumes an essential *unity* in the relationship between scholarly knowledge and political practice. Gone, or at least driven to the margins, are the potential roles of scholarship on international affairs in the service of imagining as-yet-unseen alternative global arrangements, foregrounding issues and concerns that are not dominating policy debates, or even elucidating the basic conceptual architecture of the "world of our making" (Onuf 1989) that we find ourselves entangled in.

As an alternative, consider that perhaps the scholarly field is not just accidentally, but *essentially*, constituted by a plurality of vocational orientations and that the tensions between them unfold in a series of repeated distinctions at different levels of resolution precisely the same way that distinctions play out in any other part of the social sciences and arguably in academic life as a whole (Abbott 2001). Whereas some scholars of and scholarship on international affairs inclines toward the giving of practical policy advice either to power holders or to those outside of the formal structures of power, other scholars and scholarship do not – and this is perfectly okay. Max Weber identified "politics" and "scholarship"[2] as distinct vocations a century ago (Weber 2004), and I would suggest (and have suggested – Jackson 2010) that this distinction also recurs *within* the academy, without bringing the enterprise to a crashing halt. Indeed, it might be a healthy thing for the academic study of international affairs to be characterized by debates and discussions between those following different vocational tracks since each emphasizes things that the other does not: feasibility on the policy side, transformation on the other. The relevant space is opened more effectively by Simon Pratt's (2015) notion of "polity-relevance" than by either of the extremes of "policy-relevance" or "policy-irrelevance." And all sides of these discussions share a family resemblance in that everyone is trying to establish a discussion about the worth and status of the operative paradigms utilized by policy makers and the public, which suggests that we can neither ignore those operative paradigms nor simply presume them. These are the conversations that the broad end of the avenue affords.

Conclusion: toward international studies

The role of definitions of our enterprise is *not* to propose one or another face or wall that can be used to shut "those people" out. That would be justified only if we had a level of certainty about our definitions that, I would claim, we do not and cannot have. Instead, we should *give up* the search for a single coherent "IR" and focus instead on what we already have. Institutionally and organizationally, we have a distributed set of common conversations across journals and books and conferences (Turton 2015). Carried in those institutional networks we have debates along avenues of theory, methodology, and vocation that provide ample fodder for contentious conversations going forward.

That said, we cannot operate without intellectual definitions of the field, ways of describing to others what we do, and ways of summing up the broad shape of the enterprise for those newly entering it. Back at the field's origins, the task was to *distinguish* IR from what Morgenthau called "the tendency towards eclecticism":

> You regard as belonging to international relations everything that transcends national boundaries. Then you put everything into a bag and shake well and the only common requirement is that a thing transcend national boundaries. There is no conceptual framework.
>
> (2011, 257)

The problem is that any attempt to generate a *single* conceptual framework of the sort Morgenthau called for requires a categorical policing of the narrow end of all three of the avenues I have been discussing, and that is a recipe for unending internecine academic warfare. A "via media" (Wendt 2000) does not strike me as the way to go either, since such synthetic roads just take pieces from each of various opposed extremes and end up producing a hybrid that is either incoherent or gains its coherence from its tacit privileging of one or another of the component positions supervened on.

So what we need instead is a pithy way of summing up the core concern of scholars of international affairs, something that permits rather than shuts down debates on issues of theory, methodology, and vocation. My suggestion is that our common concern is with *the encounter with difference across boundaries* and with making whatever kind of sense we can of the dynamics of such encounters. War, trade, diplomacy, the United Nations . . . all of those fit easily, but so do concerns with popular culture, with the artistic representation of global events, with dialogues among civilizations and among communities of diverse ethical practices, and so on. Rather than a narrowing, we have an opening, such that to study international affairs and to focus on the "international" aspect of things is to foreground the way that encounter is encoded within even the most everyday objects and occasions. The result is an essentially *pedagogical* approach, such that we remember that the student of international affairs is, in Manning's (1962, 182) words, a "connoisseur-in-the-making of international relationships" regardless of how she develops her appreciation and insight.

We thus return from the narrow end of the three avenues – traditionally marked "IR" – to the broad end, for which "international studies" is probably a better name. Morgenthau is right to characterize this as a messy, incoherent place when taken *as a whole*, as though it were all *supposed* to add up to one single thing. It does not, but that is not a problem with the field; it is a problem with our expectations. And those, at least, we can change more easily than we can change the accumulated institutional legacies that so often prevent us from appreciating what we actually already have.

Notes

1 And as an aside, the irresolvability of these foundational issues is the *actual* implication of quantum mechanics for our accounts of knowledge, since there simply can be no final answer to how the mind and the world are related to one another if the very notion of mind-independent knowledge of the world is nonsensical.

2 Weber used the German word *Wissenschaft*, which is ordinarily rendered into English as "science" by those translating his lecture on the subject, but the German word has a much broader sense than "science" does in English. "Scholarship" comes closer to what Weber meant.

Bibliography

Abbott, Andrew. 2001. *Chaos of Disciplines*. Chicago: University of Chicago Press.

Acharya, Amitav. 2014. "Global International Relations (IR) and Regional Worlds." *International Studies Quarterly* 58 (4): 647–59. doi:10.1111/isqu.12171.

Ackerly, Brooke A., Maria Stern, and Jacqui True, eds. 2006. *Feminist Methodologies for International Relations*. Cambridge: Cambridge University Press.

Avant, Deborah D., Martha Finnemore, and Susan K. Sell, eds. 2010. *Who Governs the Globe?* Cambridge: Cambridge University Press.

Baldwin, David. 1993. *Neorealism and Neoliberalism.* New York: Columbia University Press.

Barkawi, Tarak, and Mark Laffey. 1999. "The Imperial Peace: Democracy, Force, and Globalization." *European Journal of International Relations* 5 (4): 403–34.

Barnett, Michael, and Martha Finnemore. 2004. *Rules for the World: International Organizations in Global Politics.* Ithaca, NY: Cornell University Press.

Blaney, David L., and Naeem Inayatullah. 2009. *Savage Economics: Wealth, Poverty and the Temporal Walls of Capitalism.* London: Routledge.

Brown, Chris. 2013. "The Poverty of Grand Theory." *European Journal of International Relations* 19 (3): 483–97. doi:10.1177/1354066113494321.

Bull, Hedley. 1975. "New Directions in the Theory of International Relations." *International Studies* 14 (2): 277–87. doi:10.1177/002088177501400204.

Carr, E. H. 1964. *The Twenty Years' Crisis, 1919–1939: An Introduction to the Study of International Relations.* New York: Harper and Row.

Cox, Robert W. 1996. "Social Forces, States, and World Orders: Beyond International Relations Theory." In *Approaches to World Order*, 85–123. Cambridge: Cambridge University Press.

Deutsch, Karl W. 1957. *Political Community and the North Atlantic Area: International Organization in the Light of Historical Experience.* Princeton: Princeton University Press.

Elman, Colin, and Miriam Fendus Elman, eds. 2003. *Progress in International Relations Theory: Appraising the Field.* Cambridge, MA: MIT Press.

George, Alexander L. 1993. *Bridging the Gap: Theory and Practice in Foreign Policy.* Washington, DC: United States Institute of Peace Press.

Gilpin, Robert. 1986. "The Richness of the Tradition of Political Realism." In *Neorealism and Its Critics*, edited by Robert O. Keohane, 301–21. New York: Columbia University Press.

Guilhot, Nicolas. 2008. "The Realist Gambit: Postwar American Political Science and the Birth of IR Theory." *International Political Sociology* 2 (4): 281–304.

Gunnell, John G. 1993. *The Descent of Political Theory: The Genealogy of an American Vocation.* Chicago: University of Chicago Press.

Jackson, Patrick Thaddeus. 2010. "What Is Theory?" In *The International Studies Encyclopedia*, edited by Robert A. Denemark. London: Blackwell Reference Online. http://www.isacompendium.com/subscriber/tocnode?id=g9781444336597_chunk_g978144433659721_ss1-5

———. 2011. *The Conduct of Inquiry in International Relations.* London: Routledge.

———, and Daniel H. Nexon. 2013. "International Theory in a Post-Paradigmatic Era: From Substantive Wagers to Scientific Ontologies." *European Journal of International Relations* 19 (3): 543–65. doi:10.1177/1354066113495482.

Katzenstein, Peter J., ed. 1996. *The Culture of National Security.* New York: Columbia University Press.

———. 2005. *A World of Regions: Asia and Europe in the American Imperium.* Ithaca, NY: Cornell University Press.

———. 2009. *Civilizations in World Politics: Plural and Pluralist Perspectives.* London: Routledge.

Keohane, Robert O. 1984. *After Hegemony: Cooperation and Discord in the World Political Economy.* Princeton: Princeton University Press.

King, Gary, Robert O. Keohane, and Sidney Verba. 1994. *Designing Social Inquiry: Scientific Inference in Qualitative Research.* Princeton: Princeton University Press.

Lapid, Yosef. 1989. "The Third Debate: On the Prospects of International Theory in a Post-Positivist Era." *International Studies Quarterly* 33 (3): 235–54.

Lewis, C. S. 2014. *The Pilgrim's Regress*. Reissue edition. Grand Rapids, MI: Wm. B. Eerdmans Publishing Co.

Manning, C. A. W. 1951. "International Relations: An Academic Discipline." In *The University Teaching of International Relations*, edited by Geoffrey L. Goodwin, 11–26. Oxford: Blackwell.

———. 1962. *The Nature of International Society*. London: John Wiley and Sons.

Monteiro, Nuno P., and Kevin G. Ruby. 2009. "IR and the False Problem of Philosophical Foundations." *International Theory* 1 (1): 15–48.

Moravcsik, Andrew. 1997. "Taking Preferences Seriously: A Liberal Theory of International Politics." *International Organization* 51 (4): 513–53.

Morgenthau, Hans J. 2011. "The Theoretical and Practical Importance of a Theory of International Relations." In *The Invention of International Relations Theory: Realism, the Rockefeller Foundation, and the 1954 Conference on Theory*, edited by Nicolas Guilhot, 263–7. New York: Columbia University Press.

Murphy, Craig N. 2000. "Critical Theory and the Democratic Impulse: Understanding a Century-Old Tradition." In *Critical Theory and World Politics*, edited by Richard Wyn Jones, 61–78. Boulder, CO: Lynne Rienner.

Onuf, Nicholas G. 1989. *World of Our Making: Rules and Rule in Social Theory and International Relations*. Columbia: University of South Carolina Press.

Pratt, Simon. 2015. "Polity Relevance and Political Science." *Said Simon*. October 14. https://saidsimon.wordpress.com/2015/10/14/polity-relevance-and-political-science/.

Price, Richard, and Christian Reus-Smit. 1998. "Dangerous Liaisons? Critical International Theory and Constructivism." *European Journal of International Relations* 4 (3): 259–94.

Schmidt, Brian C. 1998. *The Political Discourse of Anarchy: A Disciplinary History of International Relations*. Albany: State University of New York Press.

Sil, Rudra, and Peter J. Katzenstein. 2010. *Beyond Paradigms: Analytic Eclecticism in the Study of World Politics*. Houndmills: Palgrave Macmillan.

Taylor, Charles Alan. 1996. *Defining Science: A Rhetoric of Demarcation*. Madison: University of Wisconsin Press.

Turton, Helen Louise. 2015. "The Importance of Re-Affirming IR's Disciplinary Status." *International Relations* 29 (2): 244–50.

Vitalis, Robert. 2015. *White World Order, Black Power Politics: The Birth of American International Relations*. Ithaca, NY: Cornell University Press.

Wæver, Ole. 1996. "The Rise and Fall of the Inter-Paradigm Debate." In *International Theory: Positivism and Beyond*, edited by Steve Smith, Ken Booth, and Marysia Zalewski, 149–85. Cambridge: Cambridge University Press.

Wallerstein, Immanuel. 1974. *The Modern World-System: Capitalist Agriculture and the Origins of the European World-Economy in the Sixteenth Century*. New York: Academic Press.

Waltz, Kenneth N. 1979. *Theory of International Politics*. New York: McGraw-Hill.

Weber, Max. 2004. *The Vocation Lectures*. Indianapolis: Hackett Press.

Wendt, Alexander. 1999. *Social Theory of International Politics*. Cambridge: Cambridge University Press.

———. 2000. "On the Via Media: A Response to the Critics." *Review of International Studies* 26: 165–80.

3

WHAT'S THE POINT OF IR?

Or, we're so paranoid, we probably think this question is about us

Cynthia Weber

"What's the point of IR?" is a very seductive question. This is because such a seemingly simple and straightforward question makes it appear as if there are simple and straightforward answers to it. IR is awash with such answers. For example, some IR scholars find the point of IR in its distinctiveness – with its historical attention to an irreducible states system (Wight 1960) or collection of societies (Rosenberg 2006). Others find the point of IR in its refusal to claim distinctiveness, understanding it instead as another modern academic discipline (Jahn this volume) or an "un-discipline" (Sjoberg this volume) that, maybe more directly than other fields, concerns itself with "encounters with difference across [international] borders" (Jackson this volume). This leads some IR scholars to answer the question "What's the point of IR?" by celebrating some singular (Booth this volume; Rosenberg this volume) or plural (Jackson this volume; Murphy this volume) vision of the field as a way of embracing IR's pedagogical promise for academia, policy, or activism. In other words, it is by providing simple and straightforward answers to the question "What's the point of IR?" – even answers that contest and contradict one another – that IR scholars, policy makers, and activists learn about (and package what they have learned about) the academic and practical fields of IR.

It is IR's pedagogical promise that settles IR scholars and practitioners into comfortable debates about "the point of IR" and about what has been learned, can be learned, or is yet to be learned. Even pessimistic Realists, who reject Enlightenment models of learning accept some version of IR's pedagogical promise, for they embrace learning either through "real world power politics" that teaches states balance-of-power tactics (Morgenthau 1948; Waltz 1979) or through IR theories that predict the "recurrence and repetition" of such behaviors in the state system (Wight 1960). In a multiplicity of forms, then, IR seems to be confident that learning can and does take place.

These are all important interventions in the field of IR. Yet because they uncritically embrace the pedagogical promise of IR, they neglect to ask equally important questions provoked by discussions about "the point of IR." Those questions are: "Why don't we learn?" and "What gets in the way of our learning?" Posing these questions allows us to move on from celebrations of IR as a field that concerns itself with "encounters with difference across [international] borders" (Jackson this volume) to a critical analysis of the boundaries we IR scholars and practitioners put on our encounters with difference across borders that stall, inhibit, or prevent our learning.

My contention in this chapter is that IR is among the most paranoid, if not hysterical, of modern academic disciplines. For IRs of whatever sort have been formed by the paranoid question "Who is out to get us?" In practical terms, this is because IR generally understands global practices of IR to be responses to global threats. In disciplinary terms, this is because academic practices in IR are often responses to rival academic threats from beyond and especially within the discipline of IR. This leads IR scholars to ask a second question, which is "Is there enough coherence among 'us' who cohere around *a* point to make 'us' a distinct discipline at all?" This is another way of posing the hysterical question "Are 'we' a 'we'?"

In what follows, I employ the language of psychoanalysis to address this array of issues. I do so not because I am an expert or even an advocate of this sort of theory and all it implies (for a discussion of some of the merits and limitations of using psychoanalysis in IR, see Weber 1999). Rather, I do so because – in this particular case – psychoanalysis provides me with the vocabulary I need to express my concerns. For the language of psychoanalysis allows me to do three things. First, it allows me to tour IR through what psychoanalysis understands as two opposing ends of the psychological spectrum – paranoia and neurosis – and how they are related to hysteria. Second, it specifies what the key questions are with respect to paranoia, neurosis, and hysteria. The paranoid question is "Who or what is out to get us?"; the presumptively healthier neurotic question is "Have I done enough?"; the hysterical question is "Am 'I' an 'I'?" Finally, it allows me to demonstrate how, in the context of IR at least, the neurotic question returns IR scholars to the paranoid question.

My critique of paranoid readings in IR – like the title of my chapter – owes debts to queer theorist Eve Kosofsky Sedgwick's critique of paranoid readings. Sedgwick argues that paranoid readings "represent *a* way, among other ways, of seeking, finding, and organizing knowledge. Paranoia knows some things well and others poorly" (1997, 130). Yet at the same time, paranoid readings also inhibit, limit, and occlude other ways of knowing. To temper paranoia, Sedgwick developed what she called a "reparative reading," which is a "more modest and gentle way of perceiving the world, one attentive to the realness of bodies, sensations, emotions, and affects, at peace with the vertiginous contingencies of history, and at least as interested in the proximate concept of *repair* (as in reparative reading) as in revolution" (*Disgorged In Total Recall* 2012).

I do not develop a reparative reading of IR here. Instead, like Queer Theorists Robyn Wiegman and Elizabeth Wilson (2015), I use Sedgwick's critiques of paranoid readings and her critiques of binary readings more generally (and specifically of heterosexuality vs. homosexuality; Sedgwick 1985; see, in the context of IR, Sjoberg and Weber 2014; Weber 2014, 2016) to contest what Wiegman and Wilson call "the antinormativity thesis" that they claim characterizes what has become the dominant strain of contemporary Queer Studies scholarship. Wiegman and Wilson argue that this strain of Queer Studies scholarship understands and celebrates itself as a kind of paranoid Critical Theory by making antinormativity the new norm, the normative ideal, the critical position that this scholarship uncritically embraces (Wiegman and Wilson 2015).

Building on these insights, I consider what might broadly be called Disciplinary IR Theories and Critical IR Theories. Disciplinary IR Theories are ever-changing, not-necessarily unified versions of so-called "problem-solving" IR theories that uphold the dominant social and political order in the discipline and global politics. Today, they comprise Realisms, Liberalisms, and Social Constructivisms. Critical IR Theories are ever-changing, not-necessarily unified versions of so-called "alternative" IR theories that contest the dominant social and political order in the discipline and in global politics, with an eye to changing it. Today, they comprise primarily Marxisms, Poststructuralisms, and Anarchisms (Cox 1981, 128–129; Weber 2015, 29).

I suggest that if Disciplinary IR Theories understand themselves to be the hegemonic norm of something called Disciplinary IRs, then Critical IR Theories often understand themselves to be counter-hegemonic and/or anti-normative forms of Critical IRs. In so doing, Critical IRs have a tendency to establish themselves as the new norm, the normative ideal, the critical position in IR that they uncritically embrace. Both positions, I suggest, provide some insights into how IR works, yet both have their limitations. It is their limitations – how the paranoid positions of both Disciplinary IRs and Critical IRs stall, inhibit, or prevent learning in and about IR – that are the focus of this chapter.

Paranoid positions in disciplinary IRs

Paranoia enters the scene of Disciplinary IR theories and practices through four registers in which the question "What's the point of IR?" functions. These four registers are (i) rhetoric; (ii) interpellation; (iii) performativity; and (iv) locatability.

Rhetorically, the question propels (and sometimes compels) Disciplinary IR scholars to persuade others of their position by meaningfully addressing the question rationally, passionately, and ethically (even if they are not required to answer the question itself). Yet it does so by demanding that they accept how rhetoric stages reasonable, passionate, and ethical debate by demarcating specific forms of address as reasonable, ethical, and appropriately passionate. At the same time, it marks other forms of address as unreasonable, unethical, and beyond the limits of what passionate debate allows. This is the first way in which the question "What's the point of IR?" limits Disciplinary IR's engagements with some forms of IR.

Disciplinary IR types only come to address this rhetorical question because they recognize something called "IR," and they recognize themselves as somehow complicit with this "IR," possibly as "experts" or "experts-in-the-making" in relation to it. These modes of recognition – where their recognition of a particular kind of presumptively ideological "IR" is what constructs them as particular kinds of ideological agents in relation to this "IR" – is what Althusser (1971) describes as the process of interpellation. For Althusser, interpellation explains how ideological institutions and discourses rely upon social interactions to "hail" or summon individuals into these institutions and discourses. Althusser proposed the concept of interpellation to explain what he thought of as the ideological function of institutions. His argument – as it applies to how Disciplinary IR types address the question "What's the point of IR?" – is that, as they answer the call of "IR," they are constructed as ideological agents of IR. They also tend to answer this hail without wondering enough about how various ideological institutional apparatuses (from disciplines to universities to wider policy fields to formal and informal public and private "stakeholders" to whom we are held accountable) interject themselves into this scene, capture them within the laws of their specific conversational terms, and structure their discussions. Indeed, Disciplinary IR types tend to regard themselves as non-ideological agents altogether. By excluding these concerns, Disciplinary IR types again limit their engagement with "IR" and its presumed point.

Moving from an Althusserian structural analysis to a poststructuralist analysis, we can see how the question "What's the point of IR?" also has a performative function. As Judith Butler proposed the term "performativity," it refers to "that reiterative power of discourse to produce the phenomena that it regulates and constrains" (Butler 1993, 2; also Weber 1998a). Like interpellation, performativity understands agents/subjects as the products of various forms of acts (e.g., like answering the Althusserian hail to be a Disciplinary IR scholar and practitioner). Yet, in contrast to Althusser's formulation of interpellation, a performative perspective does not understand these resulting subjects to be consumed into more or less stable ideological institutional and discursive apparatuses as more or less stable subjects. Rather, a performativity perspective claims that every engagement with meaning-making – even if it is addressed by the same person to the same question, like "What's the point of IR?" – is never identical to any other engagement with meaning-making. Specifically, this has the effect of not only changing – even if slightly with each iteration of this question – what the point of IR is, but it also changes how Disciplinary IR scholars and practitioners are understood as meaningful subjects in relation to this question. In general terms, performativity in part explains how fields of theory and practice constantly change, even within what appear to be broadly stable institutional settings.

Performativity, then, explains how the question "What's the point of IR?" asks Disciplinary IR types to stabilize something called IR in order for their answers – "expert" or "naïve" as they may be – to be meaningful in relation to this field of IR that they produce through their address to it. In so doing, however, Disciplinary IR types are not necessarily asked to reflect on how "multiplicity," "difference," "temporality," "desire," and innumerable other destabilizing factors are crowded out of their conversations because their fleeting performative moments are all too often concretized into stable, enduring identities (the very things performativity calls into question). From this performative perspective, then, we see a third way in which Disciplinary IR scholars and practitioner's engagements with the question "What's the point of IR?" puts limits on "IR" and its presumed point.

These three points together constitute those Disciplinary IR types whose answers to the question "What's the point of IR?" seem to matter in Disciplinary IRs as well-behaved rhetoricians, as ideologically interpolated subjects who are in part captured by IR disciplinarily and institutionally, and as performative subjects who – often against their intentions – constantly recast what IR is and who they are as Disciplinary IR types when addressing the point of IR. So constituted, these Disciplinary IR types are finally invited to pontificate on "the point of IR" from *their* point in IR (as one or another type of scholar, practitioner, stakeholder, etc.). In other words, they are invited to locate themselves as standard bearers in relation to their authentic IR, while chastising their colleagues for their substandard answers on the basis of their inferior locational choices in relation to their authentic IR.

Collectively, these four registers of engagement about the point of IR condemn these Disciplinary IR types to exchanges like this one:

> I rightly think this because I am the right kind of Realist or Liberal or Constructivist or "fill in the blank." This means that I am within the terms of reasonable, ethical, and passionate debate that guarantees learning, through academic knowledge production and/or through meaningful action in the world.
>
> You, of course, wrongly think that because you are the wrong kind of Realist or Liberal or Constructivist or "fill in the blank" or because you are a Marxist or Poststructuralist or Anarchist or "fill in the blank" who is beyond the limits of reasonable, passionate, and ethical debate. This means that your claims to academic knowledge production and to act meaningfully in the world are at best meaningless and misguided and are at worst dangerous.

These types of exchanges are made possible because they are translations of sentences like these:

> I am the law, the real expert, the subject supposed to know, the sovereign conveyer of truth and its ethical implementation.
>
> You are the criminal, the deviant, the subject supposed to not-know-better-than-*me*, the anarchical conveyer of untruth and its unethical implementation.
>
> This makes you a threat to IR and a threat to me as the possessor of the truth of IR, as knowledge and as practice.

My suggestion here is that such positions lead Disciplinary IR scholars and practitioners to endlessly attack and maneuver around the question "What's the point of IR?" as paranoid subjects – as subjects who know someone or something is out to get them. This is because – to paraphrase Eve Sedgwick's paraphrasing of Carly Simon – "They're so paranoid, they probably think this question is about them" (Sedgwick 1997; Simon 1972). Don't they?

I think they do, in part, because this is among the things it means to be part of a discipline – and maybe especially part of a field that knows itself to be as interdisciplinary as IR knows itself to be. While my argument in this section is that Disciplinary IR types are prone to paranoia, I also think those of us who think of ourselves as Critical IR scholars – as IR scholars and practitioners who question Disciplinary IRs, who attempt to hold them to account and challenge what we see as the harmful scholarly and global practices they inform and justify in the world – may well be just as prone to paranoia. This is especially the case for Critical IR types whose embrace of radical, revolutionary, or resistive ideologies reify them into counter-hegemonic or antinormative identities.

I develop this argument in the next section, using the example of Sussex IR and its changing relationship to Critical Theory as my point of departure. I argue that paranoia enters the scene of Sussex IR through Sussex IR's embrace of the neurotic question "Am I doing enough?"

Paranoid positions in critical IRs

How Sussex IR has historically engaged with the question "What's the point of IR?" is by using it to both eschew hysteria and disavow mere paranoia. Sussex IR eschews hysteria because it knows itself to be a coherent identity, a coherent "we." This "we" that is Sussex IR also knows itself as among the world-leading intellectual centers of Critical IRs. This understanding of Sussex IR as a center for Critical IRs began to emerge in the 1980s, when some Sussex IR scholars turned toward Marxism and broadly embraced what Robert Cox called "critical theory" (1981). For some 1980s Sussex IR scholars (including me, who at the time was a Sussex MA student reading Gramsci), this meant that the point of IR was to be pointedly *against* theories and practices – from those in what later came to be known as Disciplinary IRs to those in disciplinary formations of all manner of global hegemonies – that support inequalities and injustices in their local, national, and international manifestations. Cox's understanding of "critical IRs," then, became Sussex's brand of "Critical IR."

This equation of Sussex IR with Critical IR has embedded itself since the 1980s, while expanding the range of "the critical" to include Poststructuralisms and holding on to another aspect of Sussex IR that makes it unique – its insistence that the "international" must always be analyzed in relation to the "historical" (Rosenberg 2006; Wight 1960; for critiques of these specific uses of the "historical," see Weber 1998b, 2015). Today, all Sussex IR scholars are critical and historical, but not in the same way.

Even so, in combination these broad identity markers of Sussex IR as critical and as historical are arguably what allow Sussex IR scholars to eschew hysteria. As a more or less coherent, self-assured, critically disposed identity, Sussex IR scholars seem to practice IR more as neurotic subjects than as paranoid subjects. For we endlessly ask the question, "Are we doing enough?" Sussex IR scholars do not generally pose this question in Disciplinary IR terms to ask "Am I doing enough for my discipline, for the policy world, for the Research Excellence Framework (REF)?" Rather, we each pose it in our own critical terms to ask "Am I doing enough to resist or revolt against disciplinary and institutional norms and to oppose or change the way things are in the worlds of Disciplinary IR theories, histories, and practices?"

Posing this question makes Sussex IR a uniquely critical "we" in IR terms and one that I value enormously. Yet it does mean that Sussex IR scholars as Critical IR scholars escape the rhetorical, interpolative, performative, and locational limitations that come with any engagement with the question "What's the point of IR?" This is because rhetoric, interpellation, performativity, and location still limit what IR as a discipline and as a practice can be, even when this question is engaged from a Critical IR perspective.

Rhetorically, neurotically driven Critical IR scholars, like paranoia-driven Disciplinary IR scholars, have definite (albeit different) positions on how rhetoric does and should stage reasonable, passionate, and ethical debate. And these Critical IR positions also demarcate specific forms of address as unreasonable, unethical, and beyond the limits of what passionate debate allows.

Like Disciplinary IR scholars, Critical IR scholars also answer the Althusserian hail as "experts" or "experts-in-the-making" in relation to IR theory and practice. In so doing, Critical IR scholars are not only constructed as ideological agents of IR (albeit self-consciously so), but they tend to answer this hail without wondering enough about how the Critical IR dispositions they embody are themselves part of some of the ideological institutional apparatuses of IR and how they sometimes interject themselves uncritically into this scene, capture Critical IR scholars within the laws of their specific conversational terms, and structure their critical discussions less critically than Critical IR scholars may think they do.

Like Disciplinary IR scholars, Critical IR scholars and practitioners are the performative result of their engagements with meaning-making in the field of IR, who effect changes in themselves and in IR in general with each of their unique iterative engagements with IR. These changes have expanded the field of IR over the past few decades beyond the terms imagined and often insisted upon by Disciplinary IR scholars and practitioners. Even so, Critical IR scholars and practitioners do not necessary reflect enough on which "multiplicities," "differences," "temporalities," "desires," and innumerable other destabilizing factors are crowded out of their critical conversations because their fleeting performative moments are all too often concretized into stable, enduring Critical IR identities (which performativity calls into question).

These three points together constitute Critical IR scholars whose answers to the question "What's the point of IR?" seem to matter as Critical IR rhetoricians, as ideologically interpolated subjects who are in part captured by Critical IR disciplinarily and institutionally, and as performative subjects who – often against their intentions – constantly recast what IR is and who they are as Critical IR scholars when addressing the point of IR. So constituted, these Critical IR scholars are finally invited to pontificate on "the point of IR" from *their critical* point in IR, from which they often function as standard bearers in relation to their Critical IR, while chastising their less critical colleagues for their substandard answers on the basis of their inferior locational choices in relation to their authentic Critical IR.

Collectively, these four registers of engagement about the point of IR condemn Critical IR scholars and practitioners to the same types of exchanges as their Disciplinary IR colleagues. All that is different is that the terms of these engagements – where rightness and wrongness are located – are reversed. This leads to exchanges like:

> I rightly think this because I am the right kind of Marxist or Poststructuralist or Anarchist or "fill in the blank." This means that I am within the terms of reasonable, ethical, and passionate debate that guarantee learning, through academic knowledge production and/or through meaningful action in the world.
>
> You, of course, wrongly think that because you are the wrong kind of Marxist or Poststructuralist or Anarchist or "fill in the blank" or because you are a Realist or Liberal or Constructivist or "fill in the blank" who is beyond the limits of reasonable, passionate, and ethical debate. This means that your claims to academic knowledge production and to act meaningfully in the world are at best meaningless and misguided and are at worst dangerous.

These types of exchanges are made possible by the very same understandings of the law, real expertise, sovereign knowledge, and ethical rightness, on the one hand, as opposed to criminality, deviance, lack of knowledge, and anarchical untruths and their unethical implementation as they are in relation to Disciplinary IR. What is different here is just what the right knowledge and ethical practice are, who possesses and practices them, and who the real threat to IR and to global politics.

My suggestion, then, is that even when neurosis enters the scene of IR – as it does through a neurotically driven Critical IR that finds its point in resisting, revolting against, opposing, or changing Disciplinary IRs in all their forms – this does not necessarily challenge the rhetorical, interpolative, performative, or locational terms that the question "What's the point of IR?" imposes upon all who attempt to answer it. Instead, addressing this question loops Critical IR scholars back into the very same cycles of paranoia in which their Disciplinary IR colleagues find themselves. For we Critical IR scholars also endlessly attack and maneuver around the question "What's the point of IR?" as subjects who know that someone or something is out to get us because, like our Disciplinary IR colleagues, "We're so paranoid, we probably think this question is about us" (Sedgwick 1997; Simon 1972). Don't we?

This is a shame for at least two reasons. First, it means that Critical IR scholars – like their Disciplinary IR colleagues – fail to challenge the rhetorical, interpolative, performative, and locational terms of the question "What's the point of IR?"

They often do so because they are as convinced of the pedagogical promise of their Critical IR dispositions as are Disciplinary IR scholars and practitioners. This means that Critical IR scholars are just as likely to neglect to consider how the critical terms of their "encounters with difference across [international] boundaries" also stall, inhibit, or prevent learning in and about IR. In so doing, Critical IR scholars – like their Disciplinary IR colleagues – lose opportunities for critical self-reflection about what IR was, is, and should become theoretically and practically. Instead, they all too often reaffirm their worth by staging self-affirming, enlightened, romantic interventions (see Weber 2000).

Second, it means that even though they know themselves to be working against all manner of disciplinary formations of knowledge, power, and practice, Critical IR scholars often stabilize these disciplinary formations through their opposition to them. This especially happens when Disciplinary IR and Critical IR oppose one another in a normativity vs. antinormativity dichotomy. In such a dichotomy, Disciplinary IR scholars know themselves to embody the knowledge and practice of properly normative (and presumptively good) IR, while regarding Critical IR scholars as collectively antinormative (and presumptively bad). At the same time, Critical IR scholars know themselves to be the embodiment of counter-hegemonic, antinormative knowledge and practice, as if their antinormative understanding of IR were the superior way to understand and enact IR. In other words, Critical IR scholars and practitioners embrace what Wiegman and Wilson call "the antinormativity thesis." The antinormativity thesis makes antinormativity the new norm, the normative ideal, the critical position that is uncritically embraced (Wiegman and Wilson 2015) by, in this case, the field of Critical IR.

While antinormative critiques of Disciplinary IRs offer valuable contributions to IR in general and to Critical IRs in particular, antinormative critiques can be so morally certain of their singular interpretation of history, so dogmatic in their anti-foundationalism, or so celebratory of their singular vision of "community" that they forget that "everything doesn't mean the same thing" (Wiegman 2015; quoting Sedgwick 1993, 19–20). In Sedgwick's terms, this means that these theories "can't help or can't stop or can't do anything other than prove the very same assumptions with which [they] began" (1997, 135), including proving that normativities of every variety are out to get them. This can make them no better than Disciplinary IRs that "can't help or can't stop or can't do anything other than prove the very same assumptions with which [they] began" (1997, 135), including proving that antinormativities of every variety are out to get them.

Conclusion

Disciplinary IRs and Critical IRs are led into battle against one another as normative IRs vs. antinormative IRs because they function as paranoid theories. This in part explains why they put boundaries around their encounters with differences across borders in ways that prevent learning in and about IR. So how might we proceed otherwise as IR scholars and practitioners?

Sedgwick is clear that paranoia is not something we ever escape, either as individuals or as scholars. Yet paranoia can be tempered in ways that do not give up on criticality, whether to fix problems in the prevailing social and political order or to imagine and enable alternative possibilities to achieve social and political justice. For example, IR scholars of all types might inform and perform their modes of criticality without turning criticality into a reified identity or ideology, as either Disciplinary IRs or Critical IRs. They might reject both the normativity thesis and the antinormativity thesis in favor of understanding that all of us are implicated in and never manage to escape normativities. This might help IR scholars of all types to maintain their "abiding interest[s] in contradiction and incommensurability," which can serve "as a permanent reminder . . . of the limitations of configuring any dualist account of the political as a [submissive or] transgressive ideal" (Wiegman 2015, 66).

If IR scholars were to temper their paranoid engagements with(in) IR – engagements that require them to not only know everything about IR from a Disciplinary or a Critical position but to also know who or what is out to get them – they might seek alternatives to those ways of knowing that "can't stop claiming mastery of reality as that flat, propositional object of a single verb, shivering in its threadbare near-transparency: the almost fatally thin 'to know'" (Sedgwick 2011, 212–213). They might "recognize when and where the deferral of mastery over a subject is an appropriate intellectual, ethical, and practical approach to complex political problems" (Wiegman 2012).

This, it seems to me, would make for a better way to "engage with what the field claims **most** to know" (Wiegman 2015, 50; my bold) – its point – "not by turning [our backs] on knowing, but by trying to attend to what that 'single verb' pursuit [of knowledge] is so desperate to elude" (Wiegman 2015, 55; summarizing Sedgwick 2011). In this way, IR scholars and practitioners might come to appreciate that "the work of criticism, like [the work of] politics [and ethics], requires a confrontation with convergences of every kind" (Wiegman 2015, 50), to render IRs "less destructively presumable . . . as we know [them] today" (Sedgwick 2007, 48; in Wiegman 2015, 52).

Bibliography

Althusser, Louis. 1971. "Ideology and Ideological State Apparatuses." In *Lenin and Philosophy and Other Essays*, translated by Ben Brewster. 121–176. New York: Monthly Review Press.

Booth, Ken. 2007. "The Writing on the Wall." *International Relations* 21 (3): 360–366.

Butler, Judith. 1993. *Bodies That Matter: On the Discursive Limits of "Sex"*. London: Routledge.

Cox, Robert W. 1981. "Social Forces, State and the World Order: Beyond International Theory." *Millennium* 10 (2): 126–155.

Disgorged In Total Recall. 2012. "Eve Sedgwick, Touching Feeling: Affect, Pedagogy, Performativity (2003)." Disgorged In Total Recall, June 16. Accessed 7 July 2016. http://disgorgedintotalrecall.tumblr.com/post/25250427986/eve-sedgwick-touching-feeling-affect-pedagogy

Morgenthau, Hans J. 1948. *Politics among Nations.* New York: McGraw-Hill (1993).

Rosenberg, Justin. 2006. "Why Is There No International Historical Sociology?" *European Journal of International Relations* 12 (3): 307–340.

Sedgwick, Eve Kosofsky. 1985. *Between Men: English Literature and Male Homosocial Desire.* New York: Columbia University Press.

Sedgwick, Eve Kosofsky. 1993. "Queer and Now." In *Tendencies.* 1–20. Durham: Duke University Press.

Sedgwick, Eve Kosofsky. 1997. "Paranoid Reading and Reparative Reading, or, You're So Paranoid, You Probably Think This Introduction Is about You." In *Novel Gazing: Queer Readings in Fiction*, edited by Eve Kosofsky Sedgwick. 1–37. Durham: Duke University Press.

Sedgwick, Eve Kosofsky. 2007. "Epistemology of the Closet." *Cadernos Pagu* 28: 19–54.

Sedgwick, Eve Kosofsky. 2011. *The Weather in Proust*, edited by Jonathan Goldberg and Michael Moon. Durham: Duke University Press.

Simon, Carly. 1972. "You're So Vain." Music and lyrics. BMG Rights Management US, LLC.

Sjoberg, Laura, and Cynthia Weber. Eds. 2014. "Forum on Queer International Relations." *International Studies Review* 16 (4): 596–622.

Waltz, Kenneth Neal. 1979. *Theory of International Politics.* New York: McGraw Hill.

Weber, Cynthia. 1998a. "Performative States." *Millennium: Journal of International Studies* 27 (1): 77–95.

Weber, Cynthia. 1998b. "Reading Martin Wight's 'Why Is There No International Theory?' as History." *Alternatives*: 451–469.

Weber, Cynthia. 1999. *Faking It: US Hegemony in a "Post-Phallic" Era.* Minneapolis: University of Minnesota Press.

Weber, Cynthia. 2000. "Why IR Needs Theory/Practice Debates: Or, from Enlightenment to Romanticism to Enlightened Romanticism." *Cambridge Review of International Affairs* 14 (1): 296–308.

Weber, Cynthia. 2014. "From Queer to Queer IR." *International Studies Review* 16 (4): 596–601.

Weber, Cynthia. 2015. "Why Is There No Queer International Theory?" *European Journal of International Relations* 21 (1): 27–51.

Weber, Cynthia. 2016. *Queer International Relations.* Oxford: Oxford University Press.

Wiegman, Robyn. 2012. "Eve's Triangles, or Queer Studies beside Itself." Lecture at University College Dublin Humanities Institute. Accessed 7 July 2016. http://www.ucd.ie/humanities/events/podcasts/2012/robyn-wiegman-queer-theory-anti-normativity/

Wiegman, Robyn. 2015. "Eve's Triangles, or Queer Studies beside Itself." *Differences* 26 (1): 48–73.

Wiegman, Robyn, and Elizabeth A. Wilson. 2015. "Introduction: Antinormativity's Queer Conventions." *Differences* 26 (1): 1–25.

Wight, Martin. 1960. "Why Is There No International Theory?" *International Relations* 2 (1): 35–48.

4

IN DEFENSE OF IR

Beate Jahn

What is the point of IR? For most IR scholars the answer to this question is quite straightforward: in order to prevent wars, fight poverty and inequality, spread respect for human rights, address environmental problems, and so on, we need to understand how international politics works. The point of IR, therefore, is to provide scientific analyses of the workings of international politics as the precondition for better political practice.

Alas, even a cursory glance at the current state of world affairs suggests that IR has not been very successful in its ultimate aim of improving international politics. Wars, civil conflicts, and terrorist attacks characterize world politics; the gap between the rich and the poor is increasing between and within states; economic and financial crises occur regularly; global warming is accelerating; and the human rights of women, children, migrants, prisoners, political, religious, and ethnic groups are widely and systematically violated. Hence, in the spirit of critical self-assessment, IR scholars regularly investigate where the discipline might have gone wrong and how it may improve its performance. In the first section, I will show that these analyses tend to attribute the shortcomings of IR studies to certain features of the discipline itself: the poverty of its subject matter, its internal fragmentation, and its immaturity. They also suggest that we can address these problems by following the model of, or borrowing from, other academic disciplines. In extreme cases scholars even call "for the end of IR" and its wholesale replacement with other disciplines (Burke et al. 2015).

These analyses, I argue, are partial and misleading. They fail to compare systematically the discipline of IR with other modern sciences. Hence, in the second part I locate IR within the context of the modern sciences and show that its weaknesses are rooted in the very nature of modern forms of knowledge and are common to all disciplines.[1] None of the modern sciences is in a position to offer authoritative solutions to political problems. Holding up other disciplines as the solution to IR's problems thus only perpetuates the false promise of modernity: the idea "that one can, in principle, master all things by calculation" (Weber 1948, 139). I conclude instead that taking seriously the limitations of the modern sciences leads to a different understanding of their purposes. The point of IR is not to provide solutions to practical political problems but to identify and address the blind spots of other disciplines and to furnish diverse political actors with the means for political contestation.

IR in a political context

IR scholars generally turn to the origins and history of the discipline in order to establish its purpose and assess its performance. While the timing of the origins of IR is debated and varies from country to country, there is almost unanimous agreement that the discipline developed in response to (Devetak 2012, 12) and with the aim of providing solutions for particular political problems (Schmidt 2002, 24).

In the second half of the nineteenth century, such problems included growing interdependence between states, colonial administration, imperialism and race relations, international communication, cooperation, law, and organization (Long and Schmidt 2005; Vitalis 2002); World War One (WWI) added finding "the best means of promoting peace between nations" (cited in Burchill and Linklater 2009, 6; Schmidt 1998, 155); the development of IR in the United States after World War Two (WWII) was driven to a considerable extent by the question "'What should we do?' – about the Russians, the Chinese, the bomb, the oil producers" (Hoffmann 1977, 58); and today terrorism, "failed states" and environmental challenges, to mention but a few, have joined the agenda (Burke et al. 2015).

Moreover, IR's performance in addressing these problems is systematically found wanting. The liberal focus on international law and organization in the inter-war years ended in the outbreak of WWII. The failure of these liberal policies was attributed to false ontologies – that is, to unrealistic or utopian assumptions about the nature of human beings and of international politics (overlooking the crucial role of power) (Carr 1981; Morgenthau 1993; Williams 2013, 648). WWII and especially the subsequent emergence of the Cold War also led IR scholars to criticize the methods – historical narratives – traditionally employed in IR studies. These were accused of being vulnerable to abuse by totalizing political ideologies like fascism, militarism, and communism (Biersteker 1989, 266; Bull 1966; Kaplan 1966). In the 1980s, the discipline was said to be complicit in legitimating a violent and unjust international order, largely because of its dominant epistemology – its reliance on empirical observation and rationalist assumptions that excluded other forms of knowledge and upheld existing power relations (Ashley and Walker 1990, 260, 262, 265; Lapid 1989). More recently, IR scholars failed to predict the Cold War and the latest financial crisis, and the discipline is accused of not providing the intellectual resources necessary to address the global environmental crisis (Burke et al. 2015). According to these analyses, IR did not just fail to provide solutions to these problems; it was quite regularly accused of being complicit in generating or perpetuating them.

The roots of these deficiencies, it is widely argued, lie in three main features of the discipline itself. First, IR is hampered by the "paucity" and "intellectual and moral poverty" of its subject matter. The essence of international politics is often conceived as a struggle for power and survival, as a state of war, as "the realm of recurrence and repetition" (Hoffmann 1987, 405; Waltz 1979, 69; Wight 1966, 20, 26). Unlike domestic politics, therefore, international politics is inhospitable to the pursuit of the good life, progress, and emancipation. Conversely, the argument goes, if the discipline could free itself from this heritage, if we could conceive the international sphere as, for example, an international *society*, then we would be able to mobilize the rich sociological tradition of Comte, Durkheim, Marx, and Weber (Guzzini 2013, 528) – and with it the (historically) progressive developments that characterize the domestic realm with which these authors were largely concerned. Similarly, it is argued that IR is "trapped in the thinking, knowledge, and institutions of the past;" it is "state-centric," and therefore unable to grapple with climate change which exceeds "the agency of any state, group, or the state-system itself." Addressing issues like climate change thus requires the type of knowledge we find in earth systems science that "reflects the true scale and systemic complexity of the planet" (Burke et al. 2015).

A second widely cited debilitating feature of the discipline is its internal fragmentation. IR is a "dividing discipline" (Holsti 1985), home to a wide variety of theoretical and methodological approaches, which are in turn applied to a range of issue areas. Scholars specialize, for example, in security or political economy or international institutions or norms. They approach these issues through feminist or positivist or poststructural or sociological theories. And they adopt historical or empirical or normative methods. Whereas in the past this diversity has given rise to heated exchanges, today debate is "mostly confined to within-camp issues" (Kurki 2011, 136–7; Sylvester 2013, 610, 615). This lack of debates, however, does not improve the policy relevance of IR. On the contrary, it indicates that "we do not even agree on what to discuss any more" (Waever 2007, 288), on what is, or is not, politically relevant, let alone on how best to address such issues (Holsti 1985, 5, 140).

Third, the comparatively late development of IR is sometimes interpreted as an impediment. "A discipline implies a set of skills and techniques; a body of theory and of propositions; and a subject matter" (Kaplan 1961, 464) – all of which take time to develop and refine. Here, the production of knowledge is seen as "evolutionary" or "cumulative" (Frieden and Lake 2005, 137, 145; Nau 2008, 640–1) and hence the "emerging science of international relations has a long way to go before it can be of direct use to policy makers" (Frieden and Lake 2005, 151) – unlike, for example, the discipline of economics with its sophisticated methodologies, authoritative findings, and political influence that generates "economics envy" among other academics (Hoffmann 2006, 4).

IR scholars, in sum, widely assume that the point of the discipline is to produce an accurate understanding of the dynamics of international politics that can serve as the basis for political reform. The absence of such successful reform, conversely, indicates weaknesses in IR knowledge. And these weaknesses in turn are traced back to particular features of the discipline. IR has an extremely poor conception of its own subject matter, of international relations, but it can improve its emancipatory potential by borrowing a richer conception from political theory or sociology or earth systems science. IR is internally divided and therefore unable to agree on, and address, pressing political problems. But it can improve its performance by following the example of more integrated disciplines like economics. IR is also a relatively young discipline and has not yet had sufficient time to develop, refine, and accumulate politically useful knowledge. Nonetheless, it can address this problem by patiently following the example of older academic disciplines.

In sum, the solution to IR's problems is often seen in an openness to, and borrowing from, other more mature and better integrated disciplines with a richer subject matter (Ashworth 2009, 16) – and in extreme cases in its wholesale replacement with other, more promising, or better-performing disciplines. In order to solve environmental problems, for example, we need to turn to the knowledge produced by earth systems sciences rather than that of IR (Burke et al. 2015). And yet, the claim that other disciplines are better equipped to address political problems is never substantiated: neither IR nor its theories are systematically compared with other disciplines (Bell 2009, 11). The next section thus provides a brief sketch of IR's development in the context of the modern sciences.

IR in an intellectual context

There can be no doubt that concrete political problems have played a role in the establishment and development of the discipline of IR. And yet, this political motivation is not the only relevant dimension. After all, problems of colonial administration did not arise only at the end of the nineteenth century – they were already being faced by the Spaniards in the sixteenth century (Jahn 2000; Parry 1990) and by all other colonial powers subsequently. Similarly, war had played a continuous role in European history, and the most destructive of these wars is generally taken to be the Thirty Years War and not WWI (Wilson 2010, 787). Even the attempt to systematically analyze and address the problem of war was not new, as the peace projects of thinkers like Saint Pierre, Rousseau, and Kant show (see, for example, Aiko 2006). Questions of economic development and interdependence, too, had been systematically addressed by classical authors like Adam Smith, David Ricardo, Karl Marx, Friedrich List, and others (see, for example, Heilbroner 1953). The problems the discipline of IR was supposed to address, hence, were not new, and neither was the attempt to systematically analyze them.

Instead, in contrast to earlier periods, the aim to analyze and address these problems led, at the end of the nineteenth and the beginning of the twentieth century, to the establishment of a separate field of study – the discipline of International Relations. The constitution of IR, moreover, followed the establishment of an entire wave of modern academic disciplines like history, law, economics, sociology, anthropology, and so on in the course of the nineteenth century. Hence, the discipline of IR plays a role in, and responds to, this broader context of the development of the modern sciences. Identifying its purpose thus requires reconstructing this context.

The development of the modern sciences has been analyzed by a wide variety of scholars and approaches. Historical approaches reconstruct the chronological development of the modern sciences, philosophical approaches reconstruct their internal logic, and sociological approaches reconstruct their social and political context. In contrast, I follow Michel Foucault's archeological approach. A social philosopher and historian of ideas, Foucault was interested in the relationship between knowledge and power. His genealogical method, inspired by Nietzsche and designed to uncover power and violence through an exploration of the total ideology of a particular age, has made some inroads into IR. For example, IR scholars apply Foucault's concept of biopolitics – the exercise of power through the management of human life – to international affairs. But for the exploration of the relationship between IR and other modern sciences, Foucault's early work – the archeology of knowledge – is particularly useful. It was inspired by the contradictions embedded within the modern sciences. The modern sciences, on the one hand, consist of a plurality, of a myriad of different fields, sciences, and disciplines distinguished by their particular issue areas and chronologically arising from earlier conceptions of these issues. On the other hand, the term "modern" suggests that all these different fields, sciences, and disciplines have something essential in common that sets them apart from earlier forms of knowledge. How was it possible, Foucault asked, that knowledge was simultaneously united and fragmented, the product of historical continuity and rupture?

In answer to this question, Foucault argued that we have to logically assume that knowledge consists of two different layers: its substance or content on the one hand and an underlying structure, a way of "ordering things," on the other. This deeper structural layer of knowledge he called the "episteme" and his archeology of knowledge is designed to uncover this episteme. It describes a particular way of "ordering things," a "structure of thought" that is "common to all branches of knowledge" and that "men in a particular period cannot escape" (1970, xxi; 1972, 191). The episteme, in other words, is what unites different fields of knowledge in a particular period but changes over time, thus introducing historical ruptures in the development of knowledge. It allows for the simultaneity of unity and fragmentation across space and continuity and rupture over time.

The modern episteme which underpins the modern sciences emerged at the end of the eighteenth and the beginning of the nineteenth century – a time characterized by the threat of revolution domestically and the fragmentation of empires internationally (Armitage 2013, 215, 226–30). In this context, just like the political sphere, "the epistemological field became fragmented, or rather exploded in different directions" (Foucault 1970, 220–1, 346). The modern episteme makes sense of and reproduces this fragmentation. It endows individual fragments with an internal functional coherence. Knowledge is now concerned with "the interior time of an organic structure which grows in accordance with its own necessity and develops in accordance with autochthonous laws" (Foucault 1970, 226, 265).

This way of "ordering things" in terms of their internal coherence and functionality led to the establishment of a wide range of new fields of knowledge, sciences, and disciplines. While the classical field of natural history, for example, had been concerned with establishing relations between different species and thus providing a conception of nature as a whole, the modern discipline of biology analyzes the internal functions of particular species. And while classical political economy had been concerned with the political means necessary or available to increase wealth, the modern discipline of economics analyzes the internal relations between labor, time, resources, and technology that lead to the production of wealth (Foucault 1970, 226).

Yet, by endowing individual phenomena with their own internal nature, the modern episteme severs the relations between these elements – they are not any longer part of the same space, subject to the same pressures, operating according to the same laws (Foucault 1970, 253; Ross 2008, 205). Plants, animals, human beings, nations, and cultures all have their own internal histories and develop in accordance with their own internal laws. This way of "ordering things" cannot account for the connections between different areas. Though it was clear, for example, that an animal had to feed itself in order to stay alive, grasping its links with the environment required a new field of study with its own internal laws. Hence, the modern sciences constitute

> partial totalities, totalities that turn out to be limited by fact, totalities whose frontiers can be made to move, up to a certain point, but which will never extend into the space of a definitive analysis, and will never raise themselves to the status of absolute totality.
>
> (Foucault 1970, 373)

Ironically, it is the attempt to address precisely these limitations that leads to a proliferation of new fields of study, each characterized by "poverty" and internal fragmentation.

The modern discipline of economics, for example, developed largely by shedding the "moral philosophical," "political," and "sociological" dimensions that had been part and parcel of political economy (Morgan 2008, 278) – and it left practical questions of equity unaddressed (Bannister 2008, 335–6; Morgan 2008, 297, 305; Schabas 2008, 182). The new discipline of politics, meanwhile, was concerned with government – but governments at the time did not consider the management of the economy as one of their tasks (Schabas 2008, 182). Hence, neither politics nor economics was in a position to analyze the fundamental problems created at their interface (Morgan 2008, 297, 305). This failure in turn provided the opening for the establishment of sociology – a science that posited "society" as a separate sphere between politics and economics (Bannister 2008, 329).

This dynamic of fragmentation leads not only to the constant proliferation of new fields of study, disciplines, or sciences, it also lies at the root of the relentless process of their internal "specialization" (Weber 1948, 134). Hence, for example, the division of history into national history, social history, world history, art history, the history of ideas, of agriculture, of germs, and so on (Revel 2008, 402). Further, each of these new fields of knowledge in turn engenders methodological fragmentation. Once individual phenomena have been endowed with their own internal logic, each of these logics requires appropriate methods for their analysis – leading, for example, to the fundamental divide between the natural and social sciences (Wright 2008, 117, 119). More generally, the historicist principle embedded within the modern episteme leads to the dynamic development of a huge variety of methodologies designed to study particular phenomena (Revel 2008, 403; Wright 2008, 114).

This fragmentation of the field of knowledge was seen very early on as a major obstacle – both intellectually and politically – since it led to ever smaller units of investigation and hence also diminishing returns in terms of the reach of explanations and their practical relevance (Ross 2008, 227). Yet, attempts to address this substantive and methodological fragmentation only generated new divisions, this time between theorists and specialists. While specialists carve out and investigate the internal dynamics of ever smaller pieces of the puzzle, generalists attempt to theorize the relations between these individual pieces. But the quest of theorists to reestablish connections between previously separated phenomena cannot help but generate its own form of fragmentation. Since the methodological tools available within a given field are designed to establish its internal logic, they do not lend themselves to linking that field with others. In order to establish such links, therefore, modern scientists borrow tools – concepts, metaphors, methods, theoretical approaches – from other disciplines (Foucault 1970, 357–8), leading to the fragmentation of the modern sciences along theoretical/methodological lines (Ross 2008, 235).

The emergence of IR as a separate field of study and its development follow precisely this logic. First, IR filled a space that was left unaddressed by other disciplines. Just as the newly established discipline of politics focused on the internal logic of government (Farr 2008, 309), neither economics, sociology, history, or law were conceived in such a way as to include the external relations of states (Long and Schmidt 2005). IR, in other words, owes its existence to the "poverty" of the subject matter of older modern disciplines. Indeed, early IR scholars saw themselves "as occupying a new intellectual space between established disciplines" (Vitalis 2002).

Second, even while the discipline established the international sphere as an independent issue area that functions according to its own internal rules and dynamics, the analysis of this field was right from the start undertaken through tools – concepts, theoretical approaches, methodologies – borrowed from other disciplines and fields: law, philosophy, economics, politics, diplomatic history, geography, social psychology, anthropology, eugenics, colonial administration (Burchill and Linklater 2009, 6; Devetak 2012, 5–6; Guilhot 2008, 281, 284; Vitalis 2002). Similarly, economic modeling, game theory, and hypothesis testing all originate in other disciplines (Morgan 2008, 282–3, 300). And today normative IR theory borrows from analytical philosophy, postcolonial approaches from cultural theory, international political economy is informed by economic and sociological approaches, and post-structuralism borrows from linguistic theory. Far from being "late" in picking up on new developments in the sciences, therefore, IR has always been an essentially interdisciplinary discipline (Burchill and Linklater 2009, 11; Guilhot 2008, 287–8; Vitalis 2002). What is more, when IR scholars deliberately set out to distinguish their own field from, for example, political science, they did so because the latter was adopting an extremely narrow conception of appropriate (behavioralist) methods for studying politics. It was, hence, the attempt to emancipate the discipline from the "poverty" of other sciences that contributed, ironically, to a further fragmentation of the field of knowledge and a narrow conception of IR as a separate field (Guilhot 2008, 283, 300).

Under conditions of the modern episteme, therefore, borrowing from other disciplines does not provide a solution to the ultimate limitations of modern knowledge. Attempts to broaden and enrich the subject matter of IR by borrowing from other fields simply leads to the establishment of new internalist accounts – normative, economic, aesthetic, and so on conceptions of international relations – and hence to internal fragmentation. Conversely, attempts to overcome the limitations of other disciplines by developing the internal logic of international relations leads to a narrow and impoverished conception of the subject matter and external fragmentation (Guilhot 2008, 300).

Thus, locating IR within the context of the modern sciences first shows that the characteristics generally identified with the discipline – fragmentation, poverty, immaturity – are generated by the modern episteme and thus shared by all modern sciences. Second, though there exist differences in the degree to which individual disciplines exhibit these characteristics, they do not establish a hierarchy between them because the relationship between the richness of a discipline's subject matter and its internal coherence takes the form of a trade-off – with improvements in one necessarily leading to the deterioration of the other (Ross 2008, 225, 235). In contrast to IR, economics, for example, focused on establishing a high degree of internal cohesion, but this required the systematic exclusion of issues, methods, and approaches that its core assumption of a rational economic agent could not accommodate and hence led to an increasingly narrow definition of the discipline (Bannister 2008, 335–6; Morgan 2008, 297, 300, 305). Despite this sacrifice, moreover, economics remains divided into macro- and microeconomics as well as other specializations and has been unable to overcome their separation (Morgan 2008, 278, 295).

Third, the "maturity" of a particular discipline or field of study does not enhance its capacity to address this dilemma. The dynamics of fragmentation generated by the modern episteme undermine the notion of science as a "cumulative" or "evolutionary" enterprise (Frieden and Lake 2005, 137, 145; Nau 2008, 640–1). While it certainly leads to increasingly complex and sophisticated conceptions of particular parts of the whole, as well as to new ways of dividing that whole, of creating "partial totalities" (Foucault 1970, 373), it nevertheless reproduces the core problem of the modern episteme: its inability to generate a conception of the whole. In fact, IR's "late" development does not so much signify its own limitations as those of other disciplines and the nature of modern knowledge as such.

This structural inability of the modern sciences to provide an account of the whole means that none of them is in a position to provide an authoritative account that could function as the basis for political reform. Instead, the modern sciences produce partial accounts of, and a variety of "takes" on, their respective subject matter. Moreover, this implies that such accounts are always and by definition contested. They will always leave things out, opening up the possibility, or even necessity, to frame the issue in a different way – and hence to produce a different interpretation. There is, then, no direct connection between scientific knowledge and political results. This, however, does not mean that there is no connection at all. On the contrary, the modern sciences contribute in two ways to political affairs. First, by operating in accordance with the modern episteme; that is, by providing internal accounts of particular phenomena, they rationalize and reproduce, willy-nilly, the fragmentation of modern society and politics. They are, in short, complicit in the reproduction of this system. At the same time, however, and second, they produce a multitude of analyses and interpretations that furnish a variety of political actors with the means to pursue different aims. They provide, in other words, political actors with the means for political contestation. And the outcome of these political struggles may well, on occasion, be considered "progressive."

Conclusion

The point of IR, I have tried to show, is not to provide solutions to concrete political problems. Such expectations mistake the nature of modern knowledge and its relationship to practice. They assume that modern knowledge can provide an accurate and authoritative account of the workings of (international) politics as the basis for "better" policies. In fact, however, the modern sciences provide a partial, fragmented, and contested take on the whole. The shortcomings of IR are thus common to all modern sciences.

Consequently, calls for "the end of IR" and its replacement with other disciplines or, less radically, the notion that other disciplines are better equipped to address political problems, are mistaken. The widely admired discipline of economics may well be politically influential, but it certainly has not managed to put an end to recurring economic and financial crises; similarly, as indeed the authors of the "manifesto for the end of IR" acknowledge, "by itself, earth systems science cannot tell us how to achieve social change or how to reconfigure the international" (Burke et al. 2015). In fact, such calls for "the end of IR" simply reproduce the false promise of modernity: the notion that modern scientific knowledge (in one or another form) can provide the basis for, and solution to, political problems: that we "can, in principle, master all things" (Weber 1948, 139). At best, holding out such false promises obscures and undermines the political contributions that modern sciences can and do make. At worst, it sells partial truths as total truths and thus authorizes ideologies.

The political relevance of the partiality of modern knowledge lies precisely in highlighting the limitations of all accounts, in ensuring that none can pose as *the* truth or solution to political problems, and thus in constituting politics as a field of contestation. The point of IR, therefore, is to highlight and address the limitations of other disciplines, and it is to provide political actors with different interpretations of world politics – each taking the shortcomings of others as a starting point. Viewed in this light, the fragmentation of the discipline plays a positive role, producing a multitude of different conceptions of world politics and thus diversifying and widening the political field.

IR plays a crucial role for the modern sciences and for modern politics, despite the shortcomings it shares with other disciplines as well as its particular limitations. IR, without any doubt, contributes to the reproduction of a violent and unjust international order. IR scholars thus have to identify and address the limitations of their discipline. To this end, moreover, they are right to draw on the resources of other modern sciences. These resources are not, however, useful for IR because they provide a "better" take on world politics, but rather because they provide a "different" one – just as IR, in principle, provides this service to other disciplines.

Note

1 Some of this material was first published in Jahn (2016) where I develop this argument at greater length.

Bibliography

Aiko, Yuichi. 2006. "Rousseau and Saint-Pierre's Peace Project: A Critique of 'History of International Relations Theory'." In *Classical Theory in International Relations*. Edited by Beate Jahn. 96–120. Cambridge: Cambridge University Press.

Armitage, David. 2013. *Foundations of Modern International Thought*. Cambridge: Cambridge University Press.

Ashley, Richard K. and R.B.J. Walker. 1990. "Speaking the Language of Exile: Dissident Thought in International Studies." *International Studies Quarterly* 34(3): 259–68.

Ashworth, Lucian M. 2009. "Interdisciplinarity and International Relations." *European Political Science* 8: 16–25.

Bannister, Robert C. 2008. "Sociology." In *The Cambridge History of Science*. Edited by T. M. Porter and D. Ross. 329–53. Cambridge: Cambridge University Press.

Bell, Duncan. 2009. "Writing the World: Disciplinary History and Beyond." *International Affairs* 85(1): 3–22.

Biersteker, Thomas. 1989. "Critical Reflections on Post-Positivism in International Relations." *International Studies Quarterly* 33(3): 263–7.

Bull, Hedley. 1966. "International Theory: The Case for the Classical Approach." *World Politics* 18(3): 361–77.

Burchill, Scott and Andrew Linklater. 2009. "Introduction." In *Theories of International Relations*. 4th edition. Edited by S. Burchill, A. Linklater, R. Devetak, J. Donnelly, T. Nardin, M. Paterson, C. Reus-Smit and J. True. 1–30. Basingstoke: Palgrave.

Burke, Anthony, Simon Dalby, Stefanie Fishel, Daniel Levine and Audra Mitchell. 2015. "Planet Politics: A Manifesto for the End of IR." https://worldlyir.wordpress.com Accessed 3 November 2015.

Carr, Edward H. 1981. *The Twenty Years' Crisis, 1919–1939*. London: Macmillan.

Devetak, Richard. 2012. "An Introduction to International Relations: The Origins and Changing Agendas of the Discipline." In *An Introduction to International Relations*. Edited by R. Devetak, A. Burke and J. George. 1–19. Cambridge: Cambridge University Press.

Farr, James. 2008. "Political Science." In *The Cambridge History of Science*. Edited by T. M. Porter and D. Ross. 306–28. Cambridge: Cambridge University Press.

Foucault, Michel. 1972. *The Archeology of Knowledge*. London: Tavistock.

Foucault, Michel. 1970. *The Order of Things: An Archeology of the Human Sciences*. London: Tavistock.

Frieden, Jeffrey A. and David A. Lake. 2005. "International Relations as a Social Science: Rigor and Relevance." *Annals of the American Academy of Political and Social Science* 600: 136–56.

Guilhot, Nicolas. 2008. "The Realist Gambit: Postwar American Political Science and the Birth of IR Theory." *International Political Sociology* 2: 281–304.

Guzzini, Stefano. 2013. "The Ends of International Relations Theory: Stages of Reflexivity and Modes of Theorizing." *European Journal of International Relations* 19(3): 521–41.

Heilbroner, Robert. 1953. *The Worldly Philosophers: The Lives, Times, and Ideas of the Great Economic Thinkers*. New York: Simon and Schuster.

Hoffmann, Stanley. 2006. *Chaos and Violence: What Globalization, Failed States, and Terrorism Mean for US Foreign Policy*. Lanham: Rowman and Littlefield.

Hoffmann, Stanley. 1987. *Janus and Minerva. Essays in the Theory and Practice of International Politics*. Boulder: Westview.

Hoffmann, Stanley. 1977. "An American Social Science: International Relations." *Daedalus* 106(3): 41–60.

Holsti, K. J. 1985. *The Dividing Discipline: Hegemony and Diversity in International Theory*. Boston: Allen and Unwin.

Jahn, Beate. 2016. "Theorizing the Political Relevance of International Relations Theory." *International Studies Quarterly*. doi: 1093/isq/sqw035

Jahn, Beate. 2000. *The Cultural Construction of International Relations: The Invention of the State of Nature*. Basingstoke: Palgrave.

Kaplan, Morton A. 1966. "The New Great Debate: Traditionalism vs. Science in International Relations." *World Politics* 19(1): 1–20.

Kaplan, Morton A. 1961. "Is International Relations a Discipline?" *The Journal of Politics* 23(3): 462–76.

Kurki, Milja. 2011. "The Limitations of the Critical Edge: Reflections on Critical and Philosophical IR Scholarship Today." *Millennium: Journal of International Studies* 40(1): 129–46.

Lapid, Yosef. 1989. "The Third Debate: On the Prospects of International Theory in a Post-Positivist Era." *International Studies Quarterly* 33(3): 235–54.

Long, David and Brian C. Schmidt. Eds. 2005. *Imperialism and Internationalism in the Discipline of International Relations*. Albany: State University of New York Press.

Morgan, Mary S. 2008. "Economics." In *The Cambridge History of Science*. Edited by T. M. Porter and D. Ross. 275–305. Cambridge: Cambridge University Press.

Morgenthau, Hans J. 1993. *Politics among Nations: The Struggle for Power and Peace*. New York: McGraw-Hill.

Nau, Henry R. 2008. "Scholarship and Policy-Making: Who Speaks Truth to Whom?" In *The Oxford Handbook of International Relations*. Edited by C. Reus-Smit and D. Snidal. 635–47. Oxford: Oxford University Press.

Parry, John H. 1990. *The Spanish Seaborne Empire*. Berkeley: University of California Press.

Revel, Jacques. 2008. "History and the Social Sciences." In *The Cambridge History of Science*. Edited by T. M. Porter and D. Ross. 391–404. Cambridge: Cambridge University Press.

Ross, Dorothy. 2008. "Changing Contours of the Social Science Disciplines." In *The Cambridge History of Science*. Edited by T. M. Porter and D. Ross. 205–37. Cambridge: Cambridge University Press.

Schabas, Margaret. 2008. "British Economic Theory from Locke to Marshall." In *The Cambridge History of Science*. Edited by T. M. Porter and D. Ross. 171–82. Cambridge: Cambridge University Press.

Schmidt, Brian C. 2002. "On the History and Historiography of International Relations." In *Handbook of International Relations*. Edited by W. Carlsnaes, T. Risse and B. Simmons. 3–23. London: Sage.

Schmidt, Brian C. 1998. *The Political Discourse of Anarchy. A Disciplinary History of IR*. Albany: State University of New York Press.

Sylvester, Christine. 2013. "Experiencing the End and Afterlives of International Relations/Theory." *European Journal of International Relations* 19(3): 609–26.

Vitalis, Robert. 2002. "International Studies in America." *SSRC Items and Issues* 3(3–4), 1–2, 12–16.

Waever, Ole. 2007. "Still a Discipline after All These Debates?" In *International Relations Theories: Discipline and Diversity*. Edited by Tim Dunne, Milja Kurki and Steve Smith. 288–308. Oxford: Oxford University Press.

Waltz, Kenneth W. 1979. *Theory of International Politics*. New York: McGraw-Hill.

Weber, Max. 1948. "Science as a Vocation." In *From Max Weber: Essays in Sociology*. Edited by H. H. Gerth and C. Wright Mills. 129–56. London: Routledge.

Wight, Martin. 1966. "Why Is There No International Theory?" In *Diplomatic Investigations: Essays in the Theory of International Politics*. Edited by Martin Wight and Herbert Butterfield. 17–33. London: Allen and Unwin.

Williams, Michael C. 2013. "In the Beginning: The International Relations Enlightenment and the Ends of International Relations Theory." *European Journal of International Relations* 19(3): 647–65.

Wilson, Peter H. 2010. *Europe's Tragedy: A New History of the Thirty Years War*. London: Penguin.

Wright, Johnson Kent. 2008. "History and Historicism." In *The Cambridge History of Science*. Edited by T. M. Porter and D. Ross. 113–30. Cambridge: Cambridge University Press.

PART TWO

The origins of a discipline

5

RELOCATING THE POINT OF IR IN UNDERSTANDING INDUSTRIAL-AGE GLOBAL PROBLEMS

Craig N. Murphy

IR's roots include practical studies of the four great evils of late nineteenth century imperialism: militarism, the political sabotage of the industrial working class, the immiseration of the colonized, and the associated racism that harmed citizens of color in the industrialized centers of empire. The women and men who undertook these studies inside and outside the academy treated these evils as the primary global problems of the day, problems that affect every society that no one society can solve on its own. This chapter makes the case that the growing set of global problems should remain the focus of the field.

This is not to gainsay Justin Rosenberg's argument (this volume) that the field should be the study of relations among relatively independent societies. I begin the chapter with a less sophisticated version of this ideal vision of the field and then turn to an account of the origins of the field that differs from that found in many textbooks. After returning to my thesis, the chapter ends with a brief, and I hope instructive, account of the research that led to this particular contribution that should tell us all something about how we each conceive of IR.

IR's ideal domain

At the end of John M. Hobson's *The Eurocentric Conception of World Politics*, he hopes that IR could be something more than a practice focused on the privileged few's view of the global problems of the day. By giving up our Eurocentrism, we might be able to approach the ideal that champions of mainstream IR have often claimed is the reality: the field might become a dispassionate study of the ways in which the most densely connected and largely independent human societies at any time have interacted with one another (Hobson 2012, 344). This would be a social science freed from its focus on immediate problems. Perhaps it would not be the kind of social science imagined by what Antonio Gramsci called "traditional" intellectuals – people under the delusion that their work served something other than the interests of the few – but it might the "*für ewig*" social science that Gramsci hoped to conduct in prison (Francese 2009) and that Robert W. Cox called "critical" theory (Cox 1992, 169).

Unfortunately, IR has always been caught up in contemporary politics. Perhaps that is because people within densely connected and largely self-sufficient societies are rarely deeply interested in other such places, let alone with relations among all such places. Many of us care about what we can gain from other societies. Perhaps more care about whether we should fear other societies. A few of us find those foreign places interesting, exciting, or perhaps exotic, but that is not reason enough for governments and other academic benefactors to give anyone the resources and freedom to study IR in this ideal way. That is, unless, of course, the home society has some deep reasons to fear, or hopes to gain from, other parts of the world. Finding the support needed to develop critical theory in IR is far from easy, as Cox's account of his own life makes very clear (Cox 2013). Certainly university political science departments (which, as Rosenberg [this volume] correctly laments, are the organizations in which IR is usually contained) tend to be caught up with national politics. If, in late 2015, a curious person went to the webpages of the top US IR departments (as identified by the "TRIP faculty survey," 2014) to learn about their scholarly research, the first topics she would find would be the refugee crisis in Europe, China's growing assertiveness, "The Iran Deal and What Will Follow," the power of Putin's intelligence operatives, and the connection between majoring in political science and "contemporary careers that require analytical skills."

Much of this presentism and focus on issues of interest to the US government also reflects the concerns of this generation of students. Recently, to stem a loss of majors, the political science department at Stanford radically changed its undergraduate program to focus on such global and national problems rather than on abstract subfields or research methodology (Flaherty 2015). The political science department at Duke University, for the same reason, has found its enrollments shrinking behind those of the upstart public policy program that had once been a less prestigious subfield of political science (Beyer 2015).

Even if IR must remain a present- and problem-focused academic field, it is worthwhile to keep emphasizing some of the ideals of *für ewig* critical scholars and traditional intellectuals. For example, it is important for problem solvers to be clear about the actual extent of the problem that is of interest to them. In the weeks following the November 2015 attacks on Paris (the second horrendous incident in Paris that year), very few "experts" who wrote about terrorist motivation bothered to consider databases covering the more than 60,000 attacks throughout the world since 2000. Massive attacks carried out by Islamist groups in Western Europe and the United States provided most commentators with all the information they thought they needed. Attention to the larger set of cases leads to very different conclusions about the motives, means, and opportunities that might explain the intensification of this global problem in the 21st century (Thomson-DeVeaux 2015).

Similarly, the traditional intellectual's professed concern with uncovering all the information relevant to hypothesized explanations of a particular event is of critical importance. For example, ethnographer Kristen Ghodsee (2014) has presented a powerful argument about how the global women's movement became successful, a hypothesis that contradicts mainstream liberal internationalist conclusions about cascading Western norms. The evidence for the norm cascade came from interviews with Western activists and documents in well-endowed Western archives. Ghodsee believes that the real story may be about connections between Soviet-era, Eastern European women's movements and activists in the global South. The evidence for her account comes from interviews with women in Bulgaria and southern Africa and documents in boxes shoved to the side by post-communist archivists or piled-up in overworked nongovernmental organization (NGO) offices in a few African capitals. She emphasizes the many languages that scholars need to know to uncover the whole story, as well as the willingness and courage to endure the kind of fieldwork that would be needed.

Lessons like these underlie John M. Hobson's critique of contemporary mainstream IR, and they are reflected in the work of Eric Helleiner (2015) and Robert Vitalis (2015) books that recover a more complete history of Western IR and its subfield of International Political Economy. Indeed, it would be worthwhile to uncover all of the forgotten knowledge of relations among societies that was once current in every capital around the world. However, this is work for which most of the usual sponsors are likely to find very little use when budgets become tight. The rest of this chapter aims to add to the recent work that has been done along these lines and suggest one way forward in light of those constraints.

A product of imperial anxiety

Nonetheless, it is worth thinking about where, when, and why "IR" originated. It was in the core of the European empires in the nineteenth century and largely because of concerns about administering the vast empires of the new imperialism of the industrial age.

Before there was a scholarly field of IR

Many of us first think of IR as a subject pursued in colleges and universities, organizations in which women and men are given unusual freedom in order to preserve and extend knowledge for a larger community, but these are not the only places where knowledge is preserved and extended. If we could travel back 200 years and visit the world's most populous capital cities – Beijing, London, Edo (Tokyo), Kostantiniyye (Istanbul), Paris, and Naples (Chandler 1987) – we would have been able to find four separate groups of people preserving and extending knowledge in the four fields that, when taken together, look something like IR today. To use names that would then have been used in London, these people were experts in: 1) military strategy; 2) law and diplomacy; 3) "system builders" involved with international public works (the physical systems that connected the capital to foreign lands, ports, roads, and the like (Murphy 1994, 65); and 4) political economy. Similar groups of experts could be found in other, smaller, capitals; for example, in Washington, DC, Kumasi (capital of the Asante kingdom that covered roughly the same area as modern Ghana), Cairo (nominally under Ottoman rule), Pune (soon to be conquered in the Third Anglo-Maratha War), and Rattanakosin (Bangkok).

The systems for preserving and extending knowledge about international affairs were similar in London, Paris, and Naples. However, there was diversity across the rest of the world. In the Kumasi of 1815, the lessons of statecraft were passed down orally in Akan from one office holder to the next while Muslim clerks kept diplomatic correspondence and chronicles of political events in Arabic. More significantly perhaps, the clerks kept copious records of the maintenance and traffic along the king's extensive system of roads that radiated out from the capital. Finally, many of the rites of the Odwira – the annual gathering of provincial rulers and semi-subordinate neighboring monarchs – were maintained by elaborate secret societies (Wilks 1989).

The study of international relations becomes a social science

If, in 1815, one were to have searched around the world for anything that might be considered a comprehensive textbook covering all these fields, the best might have been the second volume of the abolitionist Henry Brougham's *An Inquiry into the Colonial Policy of the European Powers* published by Longman in 1803. The book explains the "system of international relations," which is to say "the European balance of power," and the relative powers and different interests of the different European governments (Brougham 1803, 192). The book also outlines the deleterious effects of the usual system of having foreign policy dictated by a handful of men, and Brougham details the physical and political economies of the American slave system that provided Europe with so much of its wealth – the system that was, unfortunately, the various governments' most important common interest. This was, of course, a very provincial view of the combined subject matter, one that would have been of little interest in most of the world's capitals.

Forty-two years later, in 1857, Brougham would be one of the founders of the British National Association for the Promotion of Social Sciences, a reformist group that included system builders who focused on penal policy, education, public health, and poor relief at home. There were also legal scholars who worked on both law and diplomacy. In his 1880 opening address, the president of the association, Donald Mackay (who was the Scottish Lord Reay and the Dutch Baron of Ophemert and Zennewijnen) announced a new program in "International Relations," an aspect of society that had "not as yet been brought under the notice of this Association," even though it was at the intersection of the fields that had been at the center of its work since the beginning:

> Social science applied to international law embraces comparative social sciences, or the influence of existing social conditions on existing international

> relations. Our Association undertakes, therefore, to analyse the social systems of various countries; to inquire how these social systems affect their international relations, and to draw conclusions for the amendment of international law from these international relations.
>
> (Reay 1880, 11)

Lord Reay went on to give an example of the conclusions that might be reached by this new line of research. For example, he argued, the generally pacific nature of the European policies of Britain and the Netherlands stemmed from their focus on their profitable and well-governed empires, which made these governments very different from those of Germany, which had no empire, and France, whose empire was neither as beneficial nor as quiescent. Britain's imperial policy was, of course "strictly defensive," meaning the British government "will hold with an iron grip against any Power venturing to harass us, our Indian or Transatlantic route, our Indian or African frontier, or any part of our dominions" (Reay 1880, 32).

The later records of the association indicate that most of its new program in IR continued to focus on colonial administration and the threat of inter-imperial conflict. As Brian Schmidt (1998, 2) has written of the same period in the United States, these topics "represented a central dimension of the early study of international politics."

Early IR as pursued by academic critics of imperialism and racism

By 1915 things were very different than they had been a century before. For better or worse, IR had become more coherent: Europeans and North Americans controlled most of the world's capitals. Therefore the diversity of intellectual traditions influencing the four kinds of experts had declined and interests that had once been provincial could be imagined as universal. In addition, many more commentators combined two or more of the four kinds of expertise. Some even had the relative freedom provided by university positions. A few of these joined a small number of other IR scholars in writing for a larger public, that is, for more than just a handful of men who still dictated European foreign policies. The same scholars were producing courses and textbooks in "international relations" or "world politics," albeit some of the 1915 "international relations" courses were designed for all literate citizens, not just for college students. One example appeared in *The Intercollegiate Socialist*, an American journal whose first issue began with Wellesley College professor Ellen Hayes (1913, 4) praising the compassion and intellect of the 1912 "Bread and Roses" strikers in Lawrence, Massachusetts. The new IR course was for people like them, as Hayes made clear in a prefatory essay (Hayes 1915). The "Course in International Relations," designed by Jessie W. Hughan of Barnard College, included 44 readings covering international commerce, war and its causes, militarism, the peace movement, international law, proposals for a general world organization, and the policies of various socialist parties (Hughan 1915).

Only one reading (a book on militarism) by the then widely celebrated Alfred Thayer Mahan reflected the perspective that we now call "realism." The socialists overlooked most of his work because they rejected his position on a central question of the day: "the complicated problems involved in continued white supremacy over the yellow, black, and brown races." Mahan felt that maintaining such supremacy was the primary concern of IR (Shaw 1910); Hayes, Hughan, and their colleagues did not.

The syllabus included many more early liberal internationalist readings, even though the liberals' concerns were not that much different from Mahan's. Most of these studies had been sponsored by the "businessmen's peace movement" whose leading figures included textbook publisher Edwin Ginn, department store magnate Edward Filene, and Andrew Carnegie of US Steel. In 1917, W. E. B. Du Bois, a colleague of Hayes and Hughan on the board of the Intercollegiate Socialist Society, recalled the 1912 meeting of the New York Peace Society, a key organization of the businessmen's movement when Carnegie was president:

> Contempt for the weaker, lesser, blacker peoples sat enthroned. All that the society asked for was peace among the big dogs of the white world while they hunted the lesser ones. . . . Peace among the mighty and let the lesser peoples writhe. So. To many it is not war that alarms them; but the fact that those whites who should fight blacks are fighting each other.
>
> (Du Bois 1917, 447)

Of course, in 1915, some liberals' views were closer to Du Bois's, just as some socialists supported empire. In a 1902 essay discussing John A. Hobson's then recently published *Imperialism: A Study*, Max Beer (a leading German socialist essayist and historian) wrote that, in the wake of the Long Depression and the Boer uprising, "[T]he most prominent leaders of the Fabian Society turned, by way of Nietzsche, to imperialism, and saw in the suppression of universal freedom the means to a regeneration of their people." In contrast, the radical democrat "Hobson remained loyal to his democratic principles and, driven by a deep ethical conviction, sees England's remedy in the curtailment of imperialism, which he considers a sinister conspiracy of international high finance" (Beer 1902, 270).

Hobson's analysis was embraced by most of the scholars connected with *The Intercollegiate Socialist*, including Vida Scudder and Emily Balch, who were, like Hayes, Wellesley College professors.[1] The two brought Hobson to Wellesley in fall 1902 to present his conclusion in *Imperialism* to an American audience for the first time. Similarly, Jessie W. Hughan of Barnard College also acknowledged many of Hobson's conclusions in *A Study of International Government*, published eight years after the socialist syllabus (Hughan 1923).

Other scholars connected with the journal took a more radical view of imperialism, war, and the political sabotage of the industrial working class. In her essay on "Education and World Peace" that preceded Hughan's syllabus, Wellesley's Ellen Hayes wrote, "Across ocean and battlefields, I salute you, Rosa Luxemburg and you Karl Leibknecht," the authors of major studies of imperialism and militarism, respectively, who led the movement of German socialists who opposed World War I. Hayes agreed with them in their mission to assure, "no child on earth, however meanly born, is . . . held cheap and denied opportunity; nor . . . wasted in body and crushed in mind in order that others may have plentiful satisfactions" (Hayes 1915, 7). Du Bois wrote with equal passion but greater clarity about the link between the immiseration of the colonies and the position of the white working class:

> The scheme of Europe [imperialism] was no sudden invention but a way out of long, pressing difficulties. It is plain to modern white civilization that the subjection of the white working classes cannot much longer be maintained. . . . But there is a loophole. There is a chance for exploitation on an immense scale; for inordinate profit, not simply to the very rich, but to the middle class and the laborers. This chance lies in the exploitation of darker peoples. It is here that the Golden Hand still beckons; there are no labor unions or votes or questioning onlookers or inconvenient consciences. There men may be used down to the bone and shot and maimed in "punitive" expeditions when they revolt; in these dark lands "industrial development" may repeat in exaggerated form every horror of the industrial history of Europe from slavery and rape to disease and maiming with only one test of success: dividends.
>
> (Du Bois 1917, 442)

The women and men connected with *The Intercollegiate Socialist* in the United States and Hobson and his like-minded colleagues in Britain represented the best of the early IR scholars, and their concern with the interconnections among imperialism, war, the immiseration of the people of the colonies, and the conditions of the working class at home remained at the center of IR until the Cold War. Unfortunately, the Red Scare at the end of World War I pushed some of the most innovative and compassionate of these scholars out of the field. All of the Americans were subjects of government investigations at the end of World War I (Stevenson 1920) and immediately before the USA's entry into World War II (US House 1942), and the most junior of them, Balch and Hughan, were forced out of the academy. On the bright side, WWI also turned many Fabians, including Leonard and Virginia Woolf, into critics of empire, and a generation of young men and women who lived through that became critical IR scholars who would face the next Red Scare after the next war.

Robert Vitalis (2015) has helped us remember the interwar history of this part of the field. For example, an aging, race-focused Du Bois debated with a young Ralph Bunche, whose *A World View of Race* (Bunche 1936) argued that the victory of the working class was the key to the liberation of the world's people of color. When Bunche left off teaching IR at Howard for a troubled stint in the US government and then the United Nations, Eric Williams, author of the groundbreaking *Capitalism and Slavery* (Williams 1944), replaced him and continued the debate. Vitalis lets us recognize that other Pan-African leaders George Padmore, Kwame Nkrumah, and C. L. R. James were also all students or grand-students of Du Bois, and all were critical IR scholars. Similarly, W. Arthur Lewis, who as a very young man wrote his earliest and perhaps most radical work on international development under the patronage of Leonard Woolf, began as a Fabian scholar of empire, long before he became a leading economist with the UN development system and a Nobel Prize–winning economist (Murphy 2006: 119). In a comparable shift from scholarship to politics, Clemencia Lopez, a Wellesley student of Scudder, Balch, and Hayes, ended up campaigning against US occupation of her native Philippines (until it ended in 1946) and for women's equality until her death in 1963 (Prieto 2013).

Lessons for today

IR usually ignores these lineages because some of these scholars became nationalist leaders, or are remembered as intellectual fathers of Africana Studies, or, like Lewis and Bunche and fellow Nobel laureate Emily Balch, are better remembered for their contributions to global development and international peace rather than their scholarly analyses of war and empire. It would be worthwhile to be a bit more reflective about this choice. Memoirs and biographies of Balch, Lopez, Bunche, and even Lewis make it clear that their choices to move from the study of IR and imperialism into other fields were influenced by the racism, male chauvinism, and anti-communist hysteria that characterized elite universities in the United States and Great Britain throughout most of the twentieth century. These are, perhaps, the same forces that lead IR to overlook these figures, as well as less globally celebrated scholars such as Hayes, Hughan, Scudder, or Williams even though IR syllabi are still apt to include white, nationalist leaders and scholars-turned-policy makers such as Bismarck, Wilson, Kennan, or Kissinger, every one of whom shared Mahan's racist horror about the rise of non-white peoples.

No doubt, our conventional view of IR's past is partially a consequence of the fact that the scholarly enterprise first grew to its current proportions when Western anxieties about well-armed Leninist governments exceeded the original anxiety about maintaining (or reforming or overturning) imperialism and neocolonialism. Notwithstanding that, John M. Hobson (2012, 257) is certainly correct to point out that, at the end of the Cold War, the Eurocentrism of IR that was "subliminal and hidden away in the 1945–89 era" returned in all of its various concerns with maintaining, running away from, or reforming the imperialism and neocolonialism that is maintained, in large part, by the global color line.

If IR has a point – a valid justification for scholars demanding the support of our larger society for our relatively free inquiry – it comes from an updated version of the agenda of the more radical reformers and those who have sought to overthrow the system that Eurocentric IR has supported. We have a point if we are involved in a practical-critical activity aimed at transforming war, the inequality between the global North and the global South, and the exploitation of working people throughout the world. Those who investigate problems that affect everyone and that no government can solve by itself point to a larger set of issues than the ones that were the focus of radical IR a century ago. The additional global problems include climate change, degradation of the oceans and threats to biodiversity, recurrent global financial crises, pandemics, the weakening of democratic institutions by economic globalization, the nexus of the international drug and arms trades, organized crime and terrorism, the militarization of many societies, the humanitarian tragedies created by some warlords and dictators, and durable global inequalities along lines of race and gender.

Postscript: "dig where you stand"

The history of IR recounted here is meant to support and give hope to those who want to give the field a more positive purpose than the one that it often seems to have and the one that John M. Hobson has revealed. I want to end by suggesting that this history, even if it is not widely known, is real, and it may be surprisingly easy to find. Vitalis's *White World Order, Black Power Politics* revealed a great deal of it, about which I was very surprised. I read some of Du Bois's IR articles in *The Journal of Race Development*, to which Vitalis pointed, and I wondered if Du Bois wrote anything on IR in other journals, perhaps in journals more sympathetic to his point of view than the largely "liberal" *Race Development* (which – spoiler alert for those who have not read Vitalis's masterpiece – is now called *Foreign Affairs*). A quick search in Google Scholar led me to the obscure *Intercollegiate Socialist*. With a bit of trepidation, I went to WorldCat.org to find where the nearest library holding the journal would be. I expected it would be the New York Public Library, a four-hour drive away, certainly not nearby Harvard University, and certainly not what I found. It was in the Wellesley College Library. I walked over and started reading. I had known about Balch – everyone at the college knows about our only Nobel laureate whom the trustees fired for her pacifism and socialism – but I did not know she had two equally distinguished "IR" compatriots on campus or that at least one more of the Seven Sisters Colleges, Barnard, was a hotbed of *radical* IR before the textbooks tell us that the field even existed. I read some more, spending a couple of days in the Wellesley archives with the index from Vitalis's book and kept finding that the people he wrote about knew the people who were my predecessors, going all the way up to 1960 when Ralph Bunche presided over an early Wellesley public seminar on Africa where he chided Melvin Herskovits (often considered the founder of African Studies in the United States) for being overly enamored of Du Bois's racial lens on global problems, "I don't share Mr. Hershkovits' concern . . . because I think there is more real [perhaps "socialist"] internationalism in the thought and approach to be found on the African continent today than anywhere in the world" (Barnett Miller Foundation 1960, 38).

I began to think that other IR scholars might find similar histories on their own campuses. I remembered the admirable workers-oriented local history movement started by the early Swedish student of multinational corporations Sven Lindqvist (1979), "Dig where you stand." If, as Lindqvist argued, industrial workers can uncover new truths about global capitalism simply by learning how to study the documents and creating the oral histories of their own workplaces, perhaps even academic workers can do the same.

Wellesley, a critic might argue, is a special place, a college for women, a place that started with a radical mission; that is why you could find a different history of IR there. Maybe. But when most people think of "IR" together with "Wellesley," the only association is Hillary Clinton or Madeline Albright – a "special" place for IR, but certainly not radical.

Nevertheless, thinking about that question made me at least begin to think about what IR's history was at the not-so-special university in North Carolina and the college in Iowa that I had attended. I guess I already knew that at Carolina there was some connection to a more radical history of IR because the controversy over the university's publication of Williams's *Capitalism and Slavery* was still part of campus lore when I went there in the 1970s. It took a couple of Internet searches before I stumbled upon Subhinda Bose from Keotkhali, near Dacca, who began teaching "World Politics" at the University of Iowa in 1913, studied militarism and the arms trade, corresponded with Du Bois for many years, wrote "Musings on Race Prejudice" comparing the Indian and American versions – and global ramifications – of what Du Bois had discussed in the *Intercollegiate Socialist* as "The Problem of Problems," and, of course, was the first lecturer on IR at the nearby small college that I later attended (Biswas 2008).

Dig where you stand. All of us may find a different history of IR that way.

Note

1 Both were later honored for their work for peace and social justice, Balch with the 1946 Nobel Peace Prize (Nobelprize.org), Scudder with a feast day on the liturgical calendar of the Episcopal Church (Chitika 2011).

Bibliography

Barnett Miller Foundation. 1960. *Symposium on Africa*. Wellesley, MA: Wellesley College.

Beer, Max. 2012. "Party Projects in England (1902)." In *Discovering Imperialism: Social Democracy to World War I*. Edited by Richard B. Day and Daniel Gaido. 265–74. Chicago, IL: Haymarket Books.

Beyer, Adam. 2015. "PoliSci Dept. Uses New Strategies to Compete in Majors Market." *The [Duke University] Chronicle*. February 11. Accessed July 6, 2016. http://www.dukechronicle.com/article/2015/02/polisci-dept-uses-new-strategies-compete-majors-market

Biswas, Paromita. 2008. "Colonial Displacements: Nationalist Longing and Identity among Early Indian Intellectuals in the United States." PhD dissertation in History. University of California, Los Angeles.

Brougham, Henry. 1803. *An Inquiry into the Colonial Policy of the European Powers*, vol. 2. London: Longman.

Bunche, Ralph Johnson. 1936. *A World View of Race*. Washington, DC: Associates in Negro Folk Education.

Chandler, Tertius. 1987. *Four Thousand Years of Urban Growth: An Historical Census*. Lewiston: St. David's University Press.

Chitika. 2011. "Vida Dutton Scudder, American Lesbian Saint for Our Times." *Queer Saints and Martyrs (and Others)*, December 15. Accessed July 6, 2016. http://queering-the-church.blogspot.com/2011/12/vida-dutton-scudder-american-lesbian.html

Cox, Robert W. 1992. "Multilateralism and World Order." *Review of International Studies* 18 (2): 161–180.

———. 2013. *Universal Foreigner: The Individual and the World.* Singapore: World Scientific.

Du Bois, W.E.B. 1917. "Of the Culture of White Folk." *The Journal of Race Development* 7 (4): 434–447.

Flaherty, Colleen. 2015. "Rethinking Poli-Sci." *Inside Higher Ed.*, May 29. https://www.insidehighered.com/news/2015/05/29/stanford-political-science-department-overhauls-undergraduate-major

Francese, Joseph. 2009. "Thoughts on Gramsci's Need 'To Do Something 'für Ewig''." *Rethinking Marxism* 21 (1): 54–66.

Ghodsee, Kristen. 2014. "Research Note: The Historiographical Challenges of Exploring Second World – Third World Alliances in the International Women's Movement." *Global Social Policy* 14 (2): 244–264.

Hayes, Ellen. 1913. "The New Political Alignment." *The Intercollegiate Socialist* 1 (1): 3–6.

———. 1915. "Education and the World Peace." *The Intercollegiate Socialist* 3 (3): 5–7.

Helleiner, Eric. 2015. "Globalising the Classical Foundations of IPE Thought." *Contexto Internacional* 37 (3): 975–1010.

Hobson, John M. 2012. *The Eurocentric Conception of World Politics: Western International Theory, 1760–2010.* Cambridge: Cambridge University Press.

Hughan, Jessie W. 1923. *A Study of International Government.* New York: T. Y. Crowell Company.

Hughan, Jessie W., with Nicholas Kelly. 1915. "A Course in International Relations." *Intercollegiate Socialist* 3 (3).

Lindqvist, Sven. 1979. "Dig Where You Stand." *Oral History* 7 (2): 24–30.

Murphy, Craig N. 1994. *International Organization and Industrial Change: Global Governance since 1850.* Cambridge: Polity Press.

———. 2006. *The United Nations Development Programme: A Better Way?* Cambridge: Cambridge University Press.

Nobelprize.org. 1946. "Emily Greene Balch." Accessed July 6, 2016. http://www.nobelprize.org/nobel_prizes/peace/laureates/1946/balch-facts.html

———. 1950. "Ralph Bunche." Accessed July 6, 2016. http://www.nobelprize.org/nobel_prizes/peace/laureates/1950/bunche-facts.html

Prieto, Laura R. 2013. "A Delicate Subject: Clemencia López, Civilized Womanhood, and the Politics of Anti-Imperialism." *The Journal of the Gilded Age and Progressive Era* 12 (2): 199–233.

Reay, Donald Lord. 1880. "Opening Address." *Transactions of the National Association for the Promotion of the Social Sciences.* 10–36. Edinburgh Meeting.

Schmidt, Brian C. 1998. *The Political Discourse of Anarchy.* Albany: State University of New York Press.

Shaw, Albert. 1910. "Some of the Books of 1910: International and Inter-Racial Problems." *American Review of Reviews* 42 (6): 764.

Stevenson, Archibald E. Ed. 1920. *Revolutionary Radicalism: Its History, Purpose and Tactics with an Exposition and Discussion of the Steps Being Taken and Required to Curb It: Filed April 24, 1920, in the Senate of the State of New York*, 4 vols. Albany, NY: Lyon.

Thomson-DeVeaux, Amelia. 2015. "Tracking 125,000 Incidents of Global Terrorism." *FiveThirtyEight*, January 23. Accessed July 6, 2016. http://fivethirtyeight.com/features/the-paris-attacks-are-just-a-few-of-125000-entries-in-the-global-terrorism-database/

TRIP Faculty Survey in United States. "What are the Five Best PhD Programs . . .?" Accessed July 6, 2016. https://trip.wm.edu/charts/#/bargraph/37/1234

US House of Representatives, Special Committee on Un-American Activities. 1942. "Investigation of Un-American Propaganda Activities in the United States," 14+ vols. Washington, DC: US Government Printing Office.

Vitalis, Robert. 2015. *White World Order, Black Power Politics: The Birth of American International Relations*. Ithaca, NY: Cornell University Press.

Wilks, Ivor. 1989. *Asante in the Nineteenth Century: The Structure and Evolution of a Political Order*. Cambridge: Cambridge University Press.

Williams, Eric Eustace. 1944. *Capitalism and Slavery*. Chapel Hill: University of North Carolina Press.

6

PAST AS PREFIGURATIVE PRELUDE

Feminist peace activists and IR

Catia C. Confortini

The central question of this volume asks us to imagine a future for an IR theory that matters: one that has analytical and intellectual value as well as practical relevance, and one that asks itself whose interests it serves, for whom, and what purpose. In such a future, IR is unlikely to be concerned about being a discipline, at least not insofar as disciplines are in the business of disciplining. In fact, an IR that matters for the lives of people, and especially those whose lives do *not* seem to matter much to international politics, may well look like what Christine Sylvester once called "a cacophony" of voices (Sylvester 1995) when she referred to feminist IR: a mix of discordant, even unpleasantly discordant, sounds, theories, and ways to interpret the world that do not necessarily fit into a single, coherent, and neatly organized and ordered field. For one, the messiness of the world cannot be assembled in such a field. Second, coherence and unity mask, rather, exercises of power, where the so-called mainstream consistently downplays, marginalizes, or silences some of the voices in the cacophony, sometimes simply by labeling them as not IR. These imposed silences not only make IR look a lot more like a coherent field than it actually is or ought to be, but they also prevent the full exercise of our imagination. To expose the silencing is to unveil a field full of contradictions and struggles, through which the possibility of alternative worlds emerges.

For example, "revisionist" historians of international thought have brought back into light the intellectuals who were part of IR's origins but did not make it into the IR "canon" or IR textbooks (see, for example, Ashworth 2011; Ashworth 2014; Vitalis 2015). These intellectuals showed us the promise of a non-imperial IR, and the recuperation of their contributions goes hand in hand with a re-inscribing of IR's origins *both* in the justification of imperialist policies and war *and* in the study of war and imperialism as problems to be eliminated. Critical historiography reveals how, far from being the objective and value-neutral discipline that it proclaimed itself to be, IR and its self-identity were created out of specific political projects and shaped the political world "outside." The erasure of IR imperial intentions and effects was "predicated on a systematic politics of forgetting, a willful amnesia, on the question of race" (Krishna 2001, 401). In fact, this forgetting has allowed "prevalent constructions of race [to shape] visions and practices of international politics, thus helping to sustain and reproduce a deeply unjust and stratified global order" (Bell 2013, 2; see the 2001 and 2015 special issues of *Alternatives* and the 2013 special issue of the *Cambridge Review of International Affairs*).

Similarly feminists have examined gender as a primary, but largely ignored, ontological unit of IR, constitutive of the binary, hierarchical, and oppressive framing of much international thought and practice (Peterson 2008). Feminists claim that by assigning gender metaphors and meanings to theories, theorists, people, and practices, the superiority of all that is associated with men and masculinities is embedded into theory, as into all areas of life. That which is associated with women and femininity is, in parallel, devalued, subordinated, marginalized, and silenced, through the process of "feminization" (Enloe 2007). Some of the early IR feminist texts showed, for example, how IR theories were implicitly based on men's rather than women's experiences. Thus, they expressed masculinist values, while silencing those associated with femininity under the guise of objectivity (see Tickner 1988, 1992). Likewise, feminist peace research (and, more ambiguously, its feminist security studies offshoot) has looked at gender as constitutive of practices of violence (Confortini 2006; Wibben 2011; Sjoberg 2013). Feminists dig deeper into what makes violence even imaginable, thus allowing us to envision ways to transcend it, but their contributions have been all but erased from the history and self-identity of peace research (see Gleditsch et al. 2014).

Another of these silencings, and perhaps a less explored one (see Sylvester 1995; Lynch 1999; Cockburn 2007; Ashworth 2011; Confortini 2012; Eschle 2013; Frazer and Hutchings 2014; Runyan 2015 for some exceptions), is that of peace activists, and in particular of feminist peace activists. Though peace activism is inextricably linked to the emergence of peace studies and peace research (both as an autonomous field and in its incarnation as a sub-field of IR – see Kelman 1981; Thompson 1990), IR has been slow to acknowledge peace activists as contributing to the development of IR theory, again in part a reflection of IR's unacknowledged and implicit biases (Lynch 2014).

This chapter then integrates feminist peace activists into the IR cacophony to show how our field can change when their voices are no longer put on mute. Telling the story of contributions to IR from feminist peace activists is not only about building a different "common consciousness" (Vitalis 2015, 5) of IR as a field, but also about showing a practice of IR that "contributes to the transformation of global politics through its own theoretical practice" (Ackerly and True 2006, 243). Drawing from feminist peace activists' contributions is also an inoculation against IR methods of abstraction, which secure the concealment of "race, colonialism, theft, enslavement and genocide" (Gruffydd Jones 2015, 133). I adapt from social movement studies the phrase "prefigurative theory" to describe such practices, which opens the spaces of our collective (but not coherent) imagination.

After outlining the origins and value of prefigurative politics and my understanding of prefigurative theory, I describe some contributions of feminist peace activists to prefigurative IR theory along ontological, epistemological, and methodological dimensions by using examples drawn from the history of the longest-operating international women's peace organization: the Women's International League for Peace and Freedom (WILPF).

Prefigurative politics and prefigurative theory

Carl Boggs defines prefigurative politics as "the embodiment, within the ongoing practice of a movement, of those forms of social relations, decision-making, culture, and human experience that are the ultimate goal" (Boggs 1977–1978, 100). Though its origins can be undoubtedly traced to pre-Enlightenment times (see Kiersey and Vrasti 2016), the tradition of prefigurative politics goes back perhaps most famously to the anarchist and utopian experiments of the 1800s and 1900s. It finds some contemporary expressions in the African American, feminist, and student movements between the 1950s and 1970s, the Latin American *comunidades de base* in the 1980s (Epstein 1991), the Zapatista rebellious communities of Chiapas in the 1990s, and more recently the Occupy and alter-globalization movements (Kiersey and Vrasti 2016). Prefigurative politics also owes its origins to Marxist-inspired critical theory and its utopian tradition, where "the 'anticipatory consciousness' of emancipation" was seen "to be the foundation of both radical theory and radical practice" (Bronner 2000, 218).

For Wini Breines prefiguration is characterized, among other things, by "the attempt to embody personal and antihierarchical values in politics" and the experimentation with different forms of participatory democracy (Breines 1980, 421). As utopian experiments have shown, the embodiment of an imagined future is never perfect or fixed. And while these movements have often been guided by teleological visions, which themselves harbored harmful hierarchies and hidden silencings, tensions and struggles have been nestled within and across movements in messy, yet creative, cacophonies. Prefigurative politics is hard to sustain, partly because of the inevitable internal contradictions and struggles. At the same time these forms of political organizing have been ways to withstand the isolation and hostility that unpopular radical positions generated (Polletta 2002, 2). They can be seen as "a determined attempt to avoid co-optation and oligarchic transformation as well as the mantle of legitimacy accorded to those who cooperate" (Breines 1980, 427).

In this chapter, I advocate for a prefigurative IR theory which, like prefigurative politics, would reflect in our ways of doing theory *today* the hope and vision for a more just and peaceful *future*. In order to be relevant, transformative, and rebellious, IR theory *must* be prefigurative: it must remain connected with an "emancipatory outcome" (Bronner 2000, 328) and "project an egalitarian global order, . . . in which a restructuring of economic power complements an ever expanding realm of democratic action" (Bronner 2000, 303). Prefiguration in IR is all the more needed "[p]recisely because it has become impossible to rely upon teleology" or explain our commitment to emancipation with ontological or pre-political justifications (Bronner 2000, 328). Prefigurative theory opens up spaces for alternative ontologies, epistemologies, and methodologies for IR, unbound by the strictures of conventions and disciplinary power.

First, if IR theory is to be prefigurative, it needs to expand its ontological horizon, making space for alternative conceptualizations of the world, for units of analysis that go beyond the nation-state, and for ontological challenges to the primacy of violence and war. Second, the epistemological question of how we know what we know must remain suspended, as if in flux: in our theories of knowledge we need to enable the possibility of infinite knowledge sources and foundations. Finally, our methodology – or the theoretical analysis of what methods align best with our ideas about the world, the ways we acquire knowledge about it, and the ethical principles that guide our actions in and our theories about the world – should be characterized by openness to ambiguity and untidiness in order to shed some light into the complexity of the world, even of the one we intend to create. After introducing the WILPF's origins and ideology, I use examples from the organization's history to illustrate (by no means exhaustively) the possibilities of prefigurative theory through the ontological, epistemological, and methodological contributions of feminist peace activists.

The Women's International League for Peace and Freedom

Having reached its 100th birthday in 2015, the WILPF is the longest-standing international women's peace organization, with national sections on six continents and consultative status within the United Nations system. Together with a number of other NGOs, it has been instrumental in bringing about UN Security Council Resolutions on Women, Peace, and Security, and it currently plays a leading role in feminist peace advocacy internationally. Yet it is positioned in a liminal space in the international system: not easily fitting into and sometimes considered a radical challenge to the (neo)liberal and militarized international system, and yet mainstream enough to work alongside liberal international institutions.

The WILPF originated at The Hague in 1915, when 1,200 women from the suffrage and social work movements of belligerent and neutral countries met to draw proposals to end WWI (see Vellacott 1988, 1993; Rupp 1997). Though they failed in their original intent, they met again in Zürich to outline their post-war plans, in contrast with the ones that were being negotiated at the same time in Paris by victorious men. They formally established a women's peace organization, committed to the elimination of war and to broader notions of justice – including gender justice (Tripp 2006) – through the development of strong international institutions, "constructive measures of world co-operation to prevent aggression," a "new concept of 'security' not based on military power and prestige" (Bussey and Tims 1980, 177), the upholding of human rights, and an economic system based on human needs rather than profits (WILPF 1919). Among the first acts of the Zürich Congress was a resolute condemnation of the Versailles Peace Treaty, together with a cautious optimism about the nascent League of Nations. The women found that the treaty terms could not lead to a "just and lasting peace" because they exacted unfair and unnecessary burdens on the losers while sanctioning the victors' rights to the spoils of war; they denied the right to self-determination; and they imposed unilateral rather than universal disarmament, thus continuing to sanction the use of force in international relations. The women predicted that such terms would only increase animosities, poverty, and despair, which would eventually lead to another catastrophic war (WILPF 1919).

Despite global aspirations, the organization the women formed in Zürich was dominated by Euro-American members with an international secretariat based at the site of the League of Nations (Geneva). After WWII and with the establishment of the United Nations, a second international office was created in New York – today it hosts two projects of the WILPF: PeaceWomen and Reaching Critical Will. The WILPF's very origins betrayed its liminality: its founders had decades of organizing experience in feminist, socialist, labor, social work, and peace movements, but the WILPF's ideological foundations lie in the progressive era and in liberal internationalism (see Hinton 1983; Kloppenberg 1988; Lynch 1999; Confortini 2012).

In the writings of some of the WILPF's first leaders we find numerous challenges to power politics and to the racialized foundations of IR in the early twentieth century. Jane Addams, one of the organization's founders and its first international president, produced a body of work that offers a pragmatic yet radical democratic vision for national and international politics drawn from her experience and leadership in the social work and peace movements (Addams 1910, [1922] 2002; Elshtain 2002; Knight 2006, 2010; Fisher et al. 2009). Addams' friend, Emily Green Balch – the WILPF's first international secretary – was among the first to investigate the effects of the US occupation of Haiti in 1926, when she was asked by Haitian WILPF members to lead a multi-racial committee to the country. The group issued a scathing condemnation of US intervention and its paternalistic, racist practices, which they judged responsible for Haiti's appalling poverty (Balch 1927; Renda 2001; Gwynn 2010; Plastas 2011). Helena Swanwick, a British member of the WILPF, was an early pioneer in feminist IR, who analyzed and critiqued the relationship between militarism and gender roles (Ashworth 2011). Consider as well Rosa Genoni, fashion designer, feminist, socialist, and pacifist of the early 1900s, and the only Italian delegate to the International Congress of Women at The Hague in 1915. Genoni's writings rely on and reclaim the tradition, culture, and arts of working-class women in the textile industry to construct an anti-imperialist, cosmopolitan, and pacifist *Italianità* – or Italian national identity – for the newly formed Italian state, without recurring to Fascist xenophobia or imperial ambitions (see Paulicelli 2015).

Yet within the WILPF anti-racism, anti-imperialism, and pacifism coexisted and struggled precisely with the embeddedness of racism and oppression within the organization and among its members. For example, the British section of the WILPF was one of the many women's organizations that participated in the campaign against the French deployment of colonial troops in the post-WWI occupation of Germany's

Rhineland. These protests used racial stereotypes and gender tropes about dangerous black men and German women's sexual purity that were "consistent with the imperialist ideologies and racial hierarchies that formed the geopolitical view of the world in which they lived" (Kuhlman 2011, 92). They also ultimately served Germany's nationalist and re-militarizing aims. Thus paradoxically, the WILPF espoused emancipatory goals and yet was unable to free itself completely from the Zeitgeist of the moment. This example underscores how prefigurative politics may never be able to create the perfect world in any definitive way. I recapture this episode in the WILPF's history later to emphasize how, through the struggle to create a new and better world, that world is made imaginable, hence even possible. Looking at international politics through the lenses of WILPF's women's practices, we can identify a number of important theoretical contributions that offer a glimpse into the possibilities of prefigurative theory. I describe these contributions along ontological, epistemological, and methodological dimensions.

Ontology

The WILPF's ontology is dramatically different from what passes for "conventional" IR, which is too focused on the primacy of the nation-state and on an ontology of violence. "Conventional" IR's ontology prevents the enactment of prefigurative theory, as it assumes that current global organizing principles are unchanging and unchangeable. In contrast, since the organization's inception the WILPF's women have seen the world as a fluid network of transnational units. While not "assum[ing] away the importance of the global and local, or the nation-state system form" (Levitt and Khagram 2007, 4), the WILPF's founders described their organization as "international," and following WWII its officers sometimes employed the word "global" to indicate broader aspirations to transcend political boundaries (Confortini 2017). In 1946 its chairs used terms like "globalism" and "world mindedness" to mean their vision of the WILPF as "a body based on the conception of the oneness of the world" (WILPF 1946, 50). They aspired to reach out to women everywhere, finding "coworkers" in all corners of the globe (WILPF 1946, 48).

Since 1919, their constitution had proclaimed that "every nation, free or subject, and every self-governing dominion may be represented in the League" and that "any minority in a country which claims the status of a separate nationality may also form a National Section" (Balch 1938, 11). These clauses are not empty principles: though originally they likely referred to European minorities, the WILPF women discussed the implications of those words for the self-determination of the colonies at different congresses through the 1920s and 1930s (Gwynn 2010, 136). In other words, the WILPF constitution embodied an ontological vision for the world that was in contrast with dominant understandings of international politics by white US IR scholars, preoccupied with the safeguard of power politics and empire (Vitalis 2015, 11).

The WILPF also presented an alternative to IR's ontology of violence by articulating a multifaceted ontology of feminist peace through their early demands for plans to establish a system based on "principles of justice" (WILPF 1919), self-determination, democratic and transparent control of foreign policy, the creation of institutions for international cooperation, and women's equal share of "civil and political rights and responsibilities" (WILPF 1915). This ontology of peace found its way in to the academic writing produced by WILPFers like Elise Boulding, whose 2000 book *Cultures of Peace: The Hidden Side of History* is "a story of human potentials for peaceableness" (Boulding 2000, 3), or the ways in which peace cultures are enacted in day-to-day lives across the world. Boulding's work theorizes/practices a visionary ontology in contrast with an IR theory obsessed with the problem of violence even as it decries its use. This ontology is not strictly teleological or dogmatic, but rather explores the possibilities and visions already articulated (or being articulated) in the struggles of those not normally included among the ranks of so-called IR experts.

Epistemology

The previous section shows that the WILPF's structure and ways of working in the world assume an ontology of fluxes, multiple and hybrid worlds, and mutual influences (Ling 2002; Ling and Agathangelou 2009; Ling 2014), as well as an ontology of peace. Yet, what we see and understand of the world (our ontology) is accompanied by ways to decode *how* we know what we know about the world. Epistemology – or the theory/science of knowledge – helps us to understand the foundations of our knowledge about the world, how we actually acquire that knowledge (see Klotz and Lynch 2007). The WILPF's structures and ways of working reflect an understanding of epistemology as a process of knowing dependent on relationships. In the WILPF's work we see knowledge developing through "practices of engagement with others" (Confortini and Ruane 2014, 71), where "the relationship with the other is a condition for knowing in the world" (Confortini and Ruane 2014, 73). In juxtaposition to the abstract rationality of conventional IR – and, as others have noted (Cohn 1987; Ruddick 1995; Cohn 2014), of militarist thought – the WILPF's epistemology is relational and embodied, and it derives from the practice of feminist peace activism. The feminist pragmatism of Jane Addams, for example, was based on the idea that knowledge is developed through "sympathetic experience" (Elshtain 2002, xxii) with the other. Dorothy Hutchinson, the WILPF's chair in 1968, interpreted Addams' epistemological inclination this way:

> The function of WILPF has always been to study public policy, to make moral judgments based on imaginative identification with those who are victimized by inhuman public policies, and to educate ourselves and others for effective political action to change these policies.
>
> (Hutchinson 1968)

Though I have written about intelligent compassion as a methodological tool of the WILPF, this passage reflects also an epistemology of relationality, where knowledge is acquired through the exercise of moral imagination and the empathetic identification with those whom Robbie Shilliam has called "the sufferers," a term from the Anglo-Caribbean tradition that describes people who have suffered, and continue to suffer, from slavery, colonization, and their consequences (Shilliam 2013, 153).

Consider for instance the WILPF US Section's changing interpretations of the practice of "nonviolent resistance." From understanding it as an absolute refusal to perpetrate or sanction physical violence, as early as 1919 the US section of the WILPF started reading the phrase as a commitment to the eradication of the underlying causes of violence, thus tempering absolute pacifism with the need for justice in social relations. As Joyce Blackwell (2004, 6) has documented, this shift was both the result of the influence of African American women in the WILPF and a cause for increasing interest by African American women in the work of the WILPF. Likewise, the WILPF's gradual move toward unconditional support for decolonization movements (even as it decried the use of direct violence in principle) was the result of the WILPF women's attentive engagement with many of the anti-racist and anti-colonial actors of the time, particularly women (see Confortini 2011). In other words, unlike white US IR scholars of the time, the WILPF took "indigenous ideas of freedom" (Vitalis 2015, 173) seriously.

These shifts were not only political, philosophical, or normative. They were also ontological, as they reflected a rethinking of what counted as violence or freedom. And they had epistemological implications because they were the result of questioning whose knowledge counts when thinking about violence and freedom (see Ackerly and True 2006). In the next section I outline how the WILPF's methodology complemented its ontology and epistemology to make space for prefigurative politics and theory.

Methodology

I understand methodology to mean self-conscious reflections about the relationship between ontology, epistemology, and ethics (Ackerly 2000; Klotz and Lynch 2007). I have argued elsewhere that between 1945 and 1975, the WILPF's feminist critical methodology, made up of guiding criteria, deliberative inquiry, skeptical scrutiny, and intelligent compassion, "prepared the organization to be open to multiple visions of peace and alternative ways of working for it" (Confortini 2012, 120). It provided the avenue through which personal assumptions, institutional structures, and views about international politics could be transformed. For the purpose of this chapter, however, I wish to highlight that the WILPF's methodology enables the enactment of emancipatory and visionary politics and theory by compelling us to expose silences, use self-reflexivity, and "listen empathetically to others while putting our subjectivities back stage to foster the creation of hybrid subjectivities in dialogue" (Confortini and Ruane 2014, 72). These methodological practices can lead to ways of doing IR as an emancipatory project and compel us to act/theorize in prefigurative ways.

The WILPF assiduously pursued local and global interconnections, making space for conversations and learning opportunities through contacts with a wider network of people than was normally within the WILPF's geopolitical and social reach. Conscious of their own limitations and ideological biases, the WILPF women opened themselves up to "networks of interactions across national borders and between diverse peoples" (DuBois and Oliviero 2009, 1), trying to engage in collective learning and conceptualize their political practice and theory as collective (Ackerly and True 2006, 256). By searching for input from all sorts of people, including "those not conventionally credentialed" (Polletta 2002, 10), the WILPF enabled innovation and experimentation. The pursuit of solidarities was coupled with the reflexive practice of constantly reworking and rethinking the WILPF's own assumptions and policies, scouting for their exclusionary and oppressive potential. This ongoing process is evident in the WILPF's continuous debates around the question of racism.

For example, the organization as a whole was moved to distance itself somewhat from the "Rhineland Horror" campaign mentioned earlier, through the intercession of US African American member, civil rights, and suffrage activist Mary Church Terrell, who convinced Jane Addams and Emily Greene Balch of the connections between the campaign's racist ideology and the incitement of nationalist and militarist fervor (Kuhlman 2008). Eventually, the WILPF pronounced itself against ideologies of racial inferiority, as well as the deployment of French colonial troops in the Ruhr (Kuhlman 2008, 62–65).

Though the WILPF's self-assessment of its potential for racism was ongoing throughout its history, it became particularly explicit in the post-WWII era. For example, at the 1946 Congress, Gertrude Bussey of the US Section stated:

> It is hard for people who look as most of us in this group look to accept the fact that the white race is not naturally superior. We may theoretically accept this fact on the basis of both science and religion, but actually there is usually hidden in the back of our minds some vestige of prejudice which is likely to reveal itself in action.
>
> (Bussey 1946, 144)

The practice of reworking and rethinking its policies was equally explicit, as the following 1951 quote by Gertrude Baer, the WILPF's representative to the UN, illustrates:

> It seems sometimes that WILPF, too, might do a little more to help maintain flexibility in a world which is growing increasingly uniform, dull and inflexible. This very inflexibility of thought and action is a real threat to Freedom since Freedom derives from and grows and develops in differentiation. Therefore we want constant revision and re-shaping of what we are doing.
>
> (Baer 1951)

WILPF women routinely subjected their unstated assumptions about a host of issues to this ongoing reflexive process. Dorothy Hutchinson's "intelligent compassion" epistemology went hand in hand with a methodology of "empathetic cooperation" (Sylvester 1994), where WILPF women suspended their own "framework of meaning" to "accept vulnerability" and opened themselves to transformation through the encounter with the other (Wibben 2011; Confortini 2012). Attentive and empathetic listening and the search for a broad spectrum of voices through a variety of means were part of a conscious, if sometimes unstated, feminist critical methodology. This methodology was often grounded in WILPFers' own personal/political mothering and life-preserving practices and ethics of care (see Ruddick 1995; Robinson 2011), but it was also forward looking to a not-so-distant, and always provisionally articulated, emancipatory goal.

Conclusions

The WILPF has never been a part of institutional IR or at the center of global governance. Yet at times it has been considered "too mainstream" or entrenched in the postwar international system by organizations and social movements critical of this system. At the same time, it has also been considered too radical when its policies have challenged certain governments' actions (Rupp 1997, 31–33). It is an organization that navigates within the international system according to the parameters of liberalism, yet it is guided by fundamentally different ontologies, epistemologies, and methodologies. The WILPF's story is not simply one of liberal activists that leave intact the fundamentally racist, imperial, and gendered assumptions of the field, but one of activists that exposed and created cracks in the artifice and envisioned the possibilities of a different system.

Those whom the empire subjugated and even those who resisted the empire from within its margins constructed alternative theories of IR, and through them, the possibility of alternative worlds. That sometimes, or even often, those alternatives were not unequivocally anti-imperial or emancipatory, that sometimes their assumptions and actions were situated within an imperial logic, speaks of the ambivalence and difficulties of resisting and transcending that logic. But it does not invalidate the project of an IR theory that is visionary and even utopian, one whose practice embodies the world we wish to create. Because "if we concern ourselves only with what is 'pragmatic' or 'possible,' the transformative moment – the moment of prefiguration – will vanish" (Bronner 2000, interpreting Ernst Boch, 220). Normative commitment needs prefiguration even in the absence of a fixed idea or set of a priori standards for justice or emancipation because "our notion of justice needs to capture the injustices that we cannot see yet and cannot yet comprehend" (Ackerly and True 2006, 246). But we can judge theories in terms of the practical possibilities they open up (Ackerly and True 2006, 248).

The contributions of the feminist peace activists of the WILPF illustrate some of the ways in which they enacted prefigurative theory through their ontology, epistemology, and methodology. Their utopias expressed critical and feminist normative commitments, but lest one easily dismiss the pursuit of utopias as unrealistic (whatever that means), I wish to point out that there is a strategic value to utopias as well (see Polletta 2002). For one thing, imagining and explicitly enacting possible emancipatory worlds is better than the hypocritical alternative of pretending we are not already *making* possible future worlds at the expense of others with our theories. Prefigurative theory is no retreat from politics. Quite the contrary: it is a way of undermining the dominance of power politics theory when we cannot take it by storm (see Breines 1980; Polletta 2002). IR too often serves the interests of the powerful. I wish to emphasize the theoretical value of the WILPF's contributions: it is not just that prefigurative theory/politics builds spaces where the world we envision is enacted. WILPF's women also show us that *it is in thinking about how to build those spaces that we already make them.* The way we practice theory needs to be prefigurative in the sense that we need to build theory from the imagination of what we would like to see not only in our theory but also in the world.

The WILPF's women show us different ways of doing politics and IR, confronting modes of knowing and organizing that, while not completely alien or adverse to bureaucratic structures, both within their own organization as well as in the institutions of liberal-order-making (Latham 1997), seek to overturn hierarchies of power. The WILPF's story teaches IR that even critical theorists are actors within our ever-encompassing liberal order, although we do not like to think of ourselves that way. Then again, perhaps by accepting theoretical untidiness and cacophonies, acknowledging that in the end we are all liberals, we can also refuse to be "dutiful citizens" of the IR enterprise and "question the conventional categories and responsibilities of citizenship and . . . the boundaries of the political" (Polletta 2002, 230). If prefigurative theory, like prefigurative politics, can strengthen bonds of solidarity among IR scholars and develop a cooperative ethos through "communicative give and take" (Polletta 2002, 8), then by engaging in it we will be already creating the world we want, in contrast with the grinding competition and increasing marketization of academia.

Bibliography

Ackerly, Brooke A. 2000. *Political Theory and Feminist Social Criticism.* Cambridge: Cambridge University Press.

Ackerly, Brooke A. and Jacqui True. 2006. "Studying the Struggles and Wishes of the Age: Feminist Theoretical Methodology and Feminist Theoretical Methods." In *Feminist Methodologies for International Relations.* Edited by Brooke A. Ackerly, Maria Stern, and Jacqui True. 241–261. Cambridge: Cambridge University Press.

Addams, Jane. 1910. *20 Years at Hull-House.* Accessed December 8, 2015. http://digital.library.upenn.edu/women/addams/hullhouse/hullhouse.html

Addams, Jane. [1922]. 2002. *Peace and Bread in Time of War.* Urbana: University of Illinois Press.

Ashworth, Lucian M. 2011. "Feminism, War and the Prospects for Peace: Helena Swanwick (1864–1939) and the Lost Feminists of Inter-War International Relations." *International Feminist Journal of Politics* 13 (1) (March): 25–43.

Ashworth, Lucian M. 2014. *A History of International Thought: From the Origins of the Modern State to Academic International Relations.* New York: Routledge.

Baer, Gertrude. 1951. *WILPF Work at Geneva, October 1950-May 1951.* Reports 1949–1951 (Women's International League for Peace and Freedom). Swarthmore College Peace Collection. University of Colorado at Boulder, Archives.

Balch, Emily Greene. 1927. *Occupied Haiti: Being the Report of a Committee of Six Disinterested Americans Representing Organizations Exclusively American, Who, Having Personally Studied Conditions in Haiti in 1926, Favor the Restoration of the Independence of the Negro Republic.* New York: The Writers' Publishing Company.

Balch, Emily Greene. 1938. *WILPF 1915–1938: A Venture in Internationalism.* Geneva, Switzerland: Maison Internationale.

Bell, Duncan. 2013. "Race and International Relations: Introduction." *Cambridge Review of International Affairs* 26 (1): 1–4.

Blackwell, Joyce. 2004. *No Peace without Freedom: Race and the Women's International League for Peace and Freedom 1915–1975.* Carbondale: Southern Illinois University Press.

Boggs, Carl. 1977–1978. "Marxism, Prefigurative Communism, and the Problem of Workers' Control." *Radical America* 11 (6) and 12 (1) (November–February): 99–122.

Boulding, Elise. 2000. *Cultures of Peace: The Hidden Side of History.* Syracuse, NY: Syracuse University Press.

Breines, Wini. 1980. "Community and Organization: The New Left and Michels' 'Iron Law'." *Social Problems* 27 (4) (April): 419–429.

Bronner, Stephen Eric. 2000. *Ideas in Action: Political Tradition in the Twentieth Century.* New York: Rowman & Littlefield.

Bussey, Gertrude. 1946. "Political and Economic Cooperation," in *Xth International Congress of the Women's International League for Peace and Freedom at Luxembourg: August 4th–9th, 1946.* Geneva, Switzerland: WILPF, 1946. 144, microfilm reel 141.2, Swarthmore College Peace Collection. University of Colorado at Boulder, Archives.

Bussey, Gertrude and Margaret Tims. 1980. *Pioneers for Peace: Women's International League for Peace and Freedom 1915–1965.* London: WILPF British Section.

Cockburn, Cynthia. 2007. *From where we stand: war, women's activism and feminist analysis.* London and New York: Zed Books

Cohn, Carol. 1987. "Sex and Death in the Rational World of Defense Intellectuals." *Signs* 12 (4) (Summer): 687–718.

Cohn, Carol. 2014. "'Maternal Thinking' and the Concept of 'Vulnerability' in Security Paradigms, Policies, and Practices." *Journal of International Political Theory* 10 (1): 46–69.

Confortini, Catia C. 2006. "Galtung, Violence, and Gender: the case for a Peace/Studies/Feminism Alliance." *Peace & Change* 31(3) (July): 333–367

Confortini, Catia C. 2011. "Doing Feminist Peace: Feminist Critical Methodology, Decolonization and the Women's International League for Peace and Freedom (WILPF), 1945–1975." *International Feminist Journal of Politics* 13 (3): 349–370.

Confortini, Catia C. 2012. *Intelligent Compassion: Feminist Critical Methodology in the Women's International League for Peace and Freedom.* New York: Oxford University Press.

Confortini, Catia C. 2017. "The Post-War Moment: Transnational Feminist Praxis in the Women's International League for Peace and Freedom in the Aftermath of the Second World War." In *Transnational Actors in War and Peace.* Edited by Miriam Anderson and David Malet. Washington, DC: Georgetown University Press.

Confortini, Catia C. and Abigail E. Ruane. 2014. "Sara Ruddick's Maternal Thinking as Weaving Epistemology for Justpeace." *Journal of International Political Theory* 10 (1): 70–93.

DuBois, Ellen Carol and Katie Oliviero. 2009. "Circling the Globe: International Feminism Reconsidered, 1920 to 1975." *Women's Studies International Forum*, Special Issue on Circling the Globe: International Feminism Reconsidered, 1910 to 1975 32, 1.

Elshtain, Jean Bethke. 2002. *Jane Addams and the Dream of American Democracy*. New York: Basic.

Enloe, Cynthia H. 2007. *Globalization and Militarism: Feminists Make the Link*. New York: Rowman & Littlefield.

Epstein, Barbara. 1991. *Political Protest & Cultural Revolution: Non-Violent Direct Action in the 1970s and 1980s*. Berkeley: University of California Press.

Eschle, Catherine. 2013. "Gender and the Subject of (Anti)Nuclear Politics: Revisiting Women's Campaigning against the Bomb." *International Studies Quarterly* 57 (4) (December): 713–724.

Fischer, Marilyn, Carol Nackenoff and Wendy Chmielewski. Eds. 2009. *Jane Addams and the Practice of Democracy*. Champaign, IL: University of Illinois Press.

Frazer, Elizabeth and Kimberly Hutchings. 2014. "Revisiting Ruddick: Feminism, Pacifism and Non-Violence." *Journal of International Political Theory* 10 (1): 109–124.

Gleditsch, Nils Petter, Jonas Nordkvelle and Håvard Strand. 2014. "Peace Research – Just the Study of War?" *Journal of Peace Research* 51 (2): 145–158.

Gruffydd Jones, Branwen. 2015. "Le Malentendu International: Remembering International Relations with Jean-Marie Teno." *Alternatives: Global, Local, Political* 40 (2): 133–155.

Gwynn, Kristen E. 2010. *Emily Greene Balch: The Long Road to Internationalism*. Urbana: University of Illinois Press.

Hinton, James. 1983. *Labour and Socialism: A History of the British Labour Movement, 1867–1974*. Amherst: University of Massachusetts Press.

Hutchinson, Dorothy. 1968. "The Right to Be Human." Chairman's Keynote Address, 1968; Box 25, 16th International Congress Report 1966 and 17th International Congress Report 1968. WILPF Swarthmore College Peace Collection. University of Colorado at Boulder, Archives.

Kiersey, Nicholas and Wanda Vrasti. 2016. "A Convergent Genealogy? Space, Time, and the Promise of Horizontal Politics Today." *Capital & Class* 40 (1) (February): 75–94.

Kloppenberg, James T. 1988. *Uncertain Victory: Social Democracy and Progressivism in European and American Thought, 1870–1920*. New York: Oxford University Press.

Klotz, Audie and Cecelia M. Lynch. 2007. *Strategies for Research in Constructivist International Relations*. New York: Routledge.

Knight, Louise W. 2006. *Citizen: Jane Addams and the Struggle for Democracy*. Chicago: University of Chicago Press.

Knight, Louise W. 2010. *Jane Addams: Spirit in Action*. New York: W. W. Norton & Company.

Krishna, Sankaran. 2001. "Race, Amnesia, and the Education of International Relations." *Alternatives: Global, Local, Political* 26 (4): 401–424.

Kuhlman, Erika. 2008. *Reconstructing Patriarchy after the Great War: Women, Gender, and Postwar Reconciliation between Nations*. New York: Palgrave Macmillan.

Kuhlman, Erika. 2011. "The Rhineland Horror Campaign and the Aftermath of War." In *Aftermaths of War: Women's Movements and Female Activists, 1918–1923*. Edited by Ingrid Sharp and Matthew Stibbe. 89–113. Leiden and Boston: Brill.

Latham, Robert. 1997. *The Liberal Moment*. New York: Columbia University Press.

Levitt, Peggy and Sanjeev Khagram. 2007. "Constructing Transnational Studies." In *The Transnational Studies Reader: Intersections and Innovations*. Edited by Sanjeev Khagram and Peggy Levitt. 1–23. New York: Routledge.

Lynch, Cecelia. 1999. *Beyond Appeasement: Interpreting Interwar Peace Movements in World Politics.* Ithaca, NY: Cornell University Press.

Lynch, Cecelia. 2014. *Interpreting International Politics.* New York: Routledge.

Paulicelli, Eugenia. 2015. *Rosa Genoni. La Moda è una cosa seria: Milano Expo 1906 e la Grande Guerra.* Milano: Deleyva Editore.

Peterson, V. Spike. 2008. "Shifting Ground(s), Remapping Strategies and Triad Analytics Revisited: 2008." In *Globalization: Theory and Practice*, 3rd Edition. Edited by Eleonore Kofman and Gillian Youngs. 101–114. London: Continuum.

Plastas, Melinda. 2011. *A Band of Noble Women: Racial Politics in the Women's Peace Movement.* Syracuse, NY: Syracuse University Press.

Polletta, Francesca. 2002. *Freedom Is an Endless Meeting: Democracy in American Social Movements.* Chicago: University of Chicago Press.

Renda, Mary A. 2001. *Taking Haiti: Military Occupation and the Culture of U.S. Imperialism, 1915–1940.* Chapel Hill: University of North Carolina Press.

Robinson, Fiona. 2011. *The Ethics of Care: A Feminist Approach to Human Security.* Philadelphia, PA: Temple University Press.

Rowbotham, Sheila, Lynne Segal and Hilary Wainwright. 2013. *Beyond the Fragments: Feminism and the Making of Socialism.* London: Merlin Press.

Ruddick, Sara. 1995. *Maternal Thinking: Toward a Politics of Peace*, 2nd edition. Boston, MA: Beacon Press.

Runyan, Anne Sisson. 2015. "Going Greenham/Going Gaga on Peace and Security." *Critical Studies on Security* 3 (2): 216–219. http://dx.doi.org/10.1080/21624887.2015.1047158:1-4.

Rupp, Leila J. 1997. *Worlds of Women: The Making of an International Women's Movement.* Princeton, NJ: Princeton University Press.

Sjoberg, Laura. 2013. *Gendering Global Conflict: Toward a Feminist Theory of War.* New York: Columbia University Press.

Sylvester, Christine. 1994. "Empathetic Cooperation: A Feminist Method for IR." *Millennium: Journal of International Studies* 23 (2): 315–334.

Sylvester, Christine. 1995. "Riding the Hyphens of Feminism, Peace, and Place in Four-(Or More) Part Cacophony." *Women's Studies Quarterly* 23 (3–4) (Fall): 136–146.

Tickner, J. Ann. 1988. "Hans Morgenthau's Principles of Political Realism: A Feminist Reformulation." *Millennium* 17 (3): 429–440.

Tickner, J. Ann. 1992. *Gender in International Relations.* New York: Columbia University Press.

Tripp, Aili Mari. 2006. "The Evolution of Transnational Feminisms." In *Global Feminism: Transnational Women's Activism, Organizing, and Human Rights.* Edited by Myra Marx Ferree and Aili Mari Tripp. 51–75. New York: New York University Press.

Vellacott, Jo. 1988. "Women, Peace and Internationalism, 1914–1920: Finding New Words and Creating New Methods." In *Peace Movements and Political Cultures.* Edited by Charles Chatfield and Peter Van den Dungen. 106–124. Knoxville: University of Tennessee Press.

Vellacott, Jo. 1993. "A Place for Pacifism and Transnationalism in Feminist Theory: The Early Work of the Women's International League for Peace and Freedom." *Women's History Review* 2 (1) (March): 23–56.

Vitalis, Robert. 2015. *White World Order, Black Power Politics: The Birth of American International Relations.* New York: Cornell University Press.

Wibben, Annick. 2011. *Feminist Security Studies: A Narrative Approach.* New York: Routledge.

WILPF. 1915. *Resolutions.* http://www.wilpfinternational.org/resolutions-from-wilpfs-triennial-congresses/

WILPF. 1919. *Resolutions*. http://www.wilpfinternational.org/resolutions-from-wilpfs-triennial-congresses/

WILPF. 1946. *Xth International Congress of the Women's International League for Peace and Freedom*. Luxembourg: Women's International League for Peace and Freedom, August 4. WILPF Swarthmore College Peace Collection. University of Colorado at Boulder, Archives.

7

BEYOND PRACTITIONER HISTORIES OF INTERNATIONAL RELATIONS

Or, the stories that professors like to tell (about) themselves

Robert Vitalis

This chapter addresses the question: who and what is international relations for? Its vantage is the early and largely unknown institutional history of the segregated academy and discipline in the United States, concentrating on the period between 1900 and 1940 and based primarily on unpublished papers of individuals and institutions. It then turns, more speculatively, to the next few, seemingly better known, decades, when a new Cold War cohort began the process of forgetting the same institutional history and substituting a set of myths about the past. It concludes by considering some implications for two kinds of related histories: of the discipline in the United Kingdom and elsewhere and of the until-now-unknown history of the discipline's pioneering women. It also suggests why such histories might matter to those overwhelmingly white men and smaller number of white women who identify as professors of international relations today.

What comprises the discipline for these purposes? It includes the scholars and impresarios at departments under various names at Clark, Columbia, Harvard, and Princeton universities; the universities of Chicago, Pennsylvania, and Wisconsin; and the historically black Howard University, among others. It takes in the main journals in which the professors and others published in those decades, starting with the *Annals of the American Academy of Political and Social Science*, *Political Science Quarterly*, the *Journal of Race Development* (which became the *Journal of International Relations* and, subsequently, *Foreign Affairs*), the *American Political Science Review*, the *American Journal of Sociology*, *Pacific Affairs*, and the *Journal of Negro Education*. Beyond these academic departments that were the main institutions that promoted research, teaching, and the dissemination of ideas during IR's formative years in the United States we also need to count the Council on Foreign Relations, the Foreign Policy Association (FPA), the then far more important Institute of Pacific Relations, the Williamstown Institute of Politics, the early international relations committees of the Social Science Research Council, and the Yale Institute of International Studies.

Finally, there are the tomes, textbooks, radio broadcasts, and scholarly and popular articles on the subject that circulated in the period.

The published and unpublished records of individuals and organizations make the answer incontrovertible: in those decades, IR was for the preservation of the white race in some accounts or for the further evolution of its genius in others, given the reality of the threat of the numerically superior but biologically inferior colored races that belted the world. Conflict avoidance would require the marshaling and synthesizing of insights from various disciplines. As the works of pioneering and today mostly unknown scholars George Hubbard Blakeslee, Raymond Leslie Buell, William Burgess, Archibald Cary Coolidge, Edward Mead Earle, Ellsworth Huntington, Parker Moon, Paul Reinsch, Leo Rowe, William Franklin Willoughby, and Quincy Wright, among others, make clear, IR theory took the ordering principle of hierarchy as its starting point. That is, different logics and processes were at work and, thus, different rules applied across the biological boundary dividing white peoples from the inferior races found in Indian Territory, New Mexico, the Philippines, the Caribbean, Africa, and Oceania. So US professors viewed the "Negro problem" in the American South and the phenomenon of miscegenation as falling within the new interdisciplinary field.

The "new" imperialism of the late nineteenth century, sometimes referred to as the process of "race subjection," and in particular the McKinley administration's conquests in the Caribbean and Asia, had multiplied the country's "race problems" and increased the likelihood of conflict across what W. E. B. Du Bois in 1898 called "the color line." A century or more later we tend to view Du Bois as a visionary who was pointing theory in a direction that has yet to gain much traction. Grappling with the color line idea would thus seem long overdue. In fact, back then the argument hardly represented the dissident edge of American social scientific thought. Rather it is the premise from which the contending perspectives on the best means to preserve or advance Caucasian hegemony began. It is Du Bois's heretical prescription for freedom now (or sooner) rather than later or never that distinguishes him and the black thinkers that he influenced from the preferences of the discipline's great white fathers.

Charles E. Merriam, the first political scientist hired at the University of Chicago and one of the giants of the early twentieth-century social sciences, discussed these epoch-making developments in his 1924 state-of-the-field essay, "Recent Tendencies in Political Thought." Deepening industrialism had given rise to the penetration of the "backward states of the world," which he also describes as "the invasion of the tropical by the temperate zone." The resulting multiplication of race problems constituted "storm centers of political theory and practice." The "harsh jangle of imperialism" was one important effect of these contacts. A second consequence was the revival of the doctrine of self-determination, which "found abundant expression in political-racial propaganda and in military theory" in Europe and Japan and in the "movements for political autonomy" in India, South Africa, Egypt, and Ireland (Merriam 1924, 1–4). The next year, Columbia's Parker Moon came out with his *Syllabus on International Relations* (1925), organized conceptually around the three themes or units – nationalism and war, imperialism, and militarism and armaments – and followed up with his most famous work, *Imperialism and World Politics* (1926).

To men like Moon, Merriam, and George Hubbard Blakeslee, the co-founder of the first IR journal, the *Journal of Race Development*, a leading scholar of US–East Asian relations, and one of the organizers in 1925 of the Institute for Pacific Relations, the (barely) established social science disciplines appeared inadequate to the task of managing the myriad challenges of what Harvard's Raymond Leslie Buell called "complex interdependence" (1925, 5), from race mixing to armed revolt against the "White Man's Rule" (57). What the increasing contacts across the world's imagined biological borders demanded, and the new interdisciplinary science promised, was a revised view of and upgraded techniques for colonial administration and the management of race subjection. The theory and practice of "race development" focused on control over and enhancement of the labor power of the semi-civilized races through tutelage or uplift. Race development held out the prospect of a more peaceful and prosperous white hegemony while reducing the threat of race war that preoccupied self-identified white elites in the United States and elsewhere in the 1890s, 1920s, and 1950s.

Although unknown now, Buell was the most prolific IR scholar and public intellectual of the 1920s and 1930s, the author of the main textbook in use in the 1920s – *International Relations* (1925), organized virtually identically to Moon's syllabus – and the first political scientist to do field work in Africa, decades earlier than today's intellectual historians believe to be the case (Gilman 2003, 118). It resulted in his monumental two-volume study, *The Native Problem in Africa* (1928). Buell had also resigned his Harvard position in 1927 to devote himself full time to public policy advocacy. He took over from Columbia's leading new historian of imperialism in the Near East, Edward Mead Earle, as research director and ultimately head of the Foreign Policy Association (FPA), a nation-wide membership organization and progressive counterpart to the Council on Foreign Relations.

The records of Buell and of the FPA document his prodigious efforts at and objectives in publicizing the resurgence of ideas about militant racial supremacy and the forward march of economic imperialism after the war, the failures of the League of Nations Mandate System, the exploitative labor regime in place in the Firestone plantations in Liberia, the disastrous new restrictions on Asian migration to the United States, the dangers of settler colonialism in Kenya, and the continuing abuses in US-occupied Haiti. He also tried but failed to set up an Institute of Interracial Problems at Princeton as part of its planned School of International Affairs. The Depression years put many such plans on hold. For example, the Social Science Research Council closed down its IR committee for lack of funds and then scrambled to respond to the outbreak of WWII. As for Buell, he gradually shifted his political allegiance after Roosevelt's New Deal to the internationalist (Willkie) wing of the Republican Party and joined media mogul Henry R. Luce's organization (*Time*, *Life*, *Fortune*). One fact, he believed, distinguished him from the many converts among the professors to the side of US interventionism and "power politics" in the late 1930s and early 1940s, men such as ex-socialist Reinhold Niebuhr; Nicholas John Spykman, the sociologist and sharp critic of capitalist imperialism in Asia (Spykman 1926) who, as head of Yale's new Institute for International Studies, reinvented himself as a geostrategist; Ed Earle, by then at the School of Advanced Study in Princeton, New Jersey, another "disenchanted Wilsonian" who would bring John Halford Mackinder's classic study of geopolitics *Democratic Ideals and Reality* (1919) back into print (Vitalis 2012); or the young William T. R. ("Bill") Fox, who went on to coin the term "superpower." Buell remained an outspoken critic of imperialism as a main source of insecurity and war, until his tragic, early death in 1944.

The origin myths IR scholars in the United States began to tell after 1945 – which are repeated semester after semester today – render invisible the men, institutions, and arguments summarized here. Earle, through his war-time, Carnegie Corporation–funded seminar on military affairs at the School of Advanced Study (Ekbladh 2011/12), and Fox, an early champion of E. H. Carr's *Twenty Years Crisis*, together with his colleagues at the Yale Institute of International Studies, did much to advance the fiction of the so-called great debate between liberalism and realism (Schmidt 1988) and to reboot IR for the new "American century." They did so with the objective of "clarifying the task of statesmen, diplomatists and military planners charged with assuring the survival and future position in the world of the particular state they are serving" (Fox 1985, 18–19). It was a dramatic realignment, as Fox described it toward the end of his career in the 1980s, although the new self-identified national security experts encountered some stumbling blocks. When Institute of International Studies member A. Whitney Griswold took over as president of Yale, he demanded more scholarship through engagement with the established social sciences – since, he said, neither political science nor international relations was a real discipline – and an end to the "mimeographed reports" and "short books" of the kind usually associated with think tanks and government agencies (Vitalis 2015, 119). Seven leading IR faculty left for Princeton, bringing the journal *World Politics* with them, forming the core of a new Rockefeller Foundation-funded Center for International Studies (CIS). Fox moved to Columbia to direct the new Institute for War and Peace Studies. At MIT, Max Milliken kick-started a second policy-oriented Center for International Studies (CENIS) the same year, with the Central Intelligence Agency's (CIA's) support (Kuklick 2006, 84–85).

Were one so disposed, it might be possible to explain the postwar American discipline's turn from the study of imperialism and its consequences, its waning obsession with race war, and the quiet trade of its social Darwinist and Neo-Lamarkian commitments (Hobson 2012) in exchange for the timeless traditions of Thucydides, Machiavelli, and so forth entirely in terms of developments "internal" to it. So, one might point to the outsized influence on the discipline of émigré thinkers such as Hans Morgenthau, Robert Strausz-Hupé, and others trained in the legal tradition of colony-less Weimar Germany rather than the Jim Crow United States (Guilhot 2014). The problem, however, is that multiple disciplines and subfields in the Cold War American academy all moved in the same direction at the same time. A new-found faith in "American exceptionalism" took hold. Sociology and history forgot and forgave US imperialism and racism, too, even in the absence of an influx of émigrés (Vitalis 2007, 7; Go 2013). And the small but highly motivated "militant right" in postwar American IR theory (together with various sociologists, anthropologists, and eugenicists) that made the case anew for worldwide white supremacy also counted émigrés among its ranks.

What "context" might therefore help to account for the seeming repudiation of a discipline's long entanglement with racism and empire? One could point to the dramatic transformation of the US position, from rising regional imperial power in the Caribbean and the Pacific to global hegemon. The struggle with the Soviet Union and the advent of the nuclear era posed challenges to which "primitive" versions of complex interdependence and race development theory had no answers. Still, there are problems. Decolonization was arguably the single most significant transformation of the last century. Anti-imperialist movements proliferated across the globe. More UN General Assembly resolutions focused on racism than any other issue in the 1950s and 1960s (Lauren 1996, 4). Yet it is impossible to name a single American IR scholar after 1945 known primarily for work on these issues. One cannot help but consider the possibility that ideology triumphed over the theorists' new-found commitment to render the world as it "really" is in an era when US officials worked overtime to deflect and depoliticize these very challenges. At home, during the second "Red Scare" in the 1950s, their methods included government harassment, Federal Bureau of Investigation (FBI) surveillance, the threat of job loss, and even prison time, which affected, among others, the leading African American critics of global white supremacy (Von Eschen 1997).

The histories that historians, sociologists, and literary theorists began to teach about their disciplines after WWII all also resembled the first practitioner histories of IR in a key respect. The early black writers and thinkers who contested the racist foundations of knowledge were scrubbed from the record as cleanly as were traces of the repudiated beliefs themselves. I recall the contributions of the "Howard [University] School" of IR theory (see Vitalis 2015), comprising Chicago- and Harvard-trained specialists in the 1920s, 1930s, and 1940s who explained racial science as the ideological prop for slavery and related forms of colonial subjugation (Bunche 1936, Williams 1944, Locke 1992 [1915/16]), while pioneering such fields as arms control (Tate 1942), the workings of the League of Nations Mandate System (Logan 1928, 1942), US-Haitian relations (Logan 1941), and the course of imperialism in the Pacific (Tate 1965), the latter at a time when the subject allegedly held no value for the study of IR.

If even W. E. B. Du Bois – the giant of the twentieth century, whose once controversial analysis of the colonial roots of WWI predated Lenin's *Imperialism* – disappeared from the reading lists, then his heirs did not stand a chance. Consider the reputational curve of Du Bois's two explosive essay collections, *Souls of Black Folk* (1903) and *Darkwater* (1920), the former now routinely considered one of the greatest books of the twentieth century and the latter drawn in part on work first published in the *Journal of Race Development*. The books were read, referenced, and treated as essential sources for international relations when they first appeared, but for decades after WWII the only citations to them appeared almost exclusively in *Phylon* and the *Journal of Negro Education*, the two main outlets for African Americans in the segregated university system. No wonder that Harold Isaacs, a journalist and one-time comrade of Leon Trotsky who, improbably, was named a professor of political science at MIT's Center for International Studies, once inquired if he could take Du Bois's books for his own library since none had been borrowed for decades. Their subsequent canonization as essential works of history, criticism, and diasporic theory (Henderson n.d.) and the restoration of his place in the history of twentieth-century political thought more generally are the outcome of the black power movement's rise on American campuses (Biondi 2012) and thus the partial breakdown of the all-white departments.

Africana studies and faculty of color in the United States have driven the creation of new research fields and reoriented existing ones, from the sociology of the Black Atlantic and the political science of race and immigration to literary studies of the Harlem Renaissance and the historiography of the US Civil War. For example, today Du Bois's *Black Reconstruction in America* (1935) appears on virtually any syllabus on the subject, although it went unreferenced in sociologist Barrington Moore's *Social Origins of Dictatorship and Democracy* (1966). Practitioners' understandings of the effects of racism on the part of their own disciplines have changed less or more slowly (Steinmetz 2013, Morris 2015), even in fields where black scholars have come to occupy leading positions. The discipline of IR in the United States remained largely insulated from the black studies revolution, a subject that deserves more study. In certain respects, it thus looks nearly the same today as it did in 1970.

Conclusion

Needless to say, there is much more to learn about the past. For one thing, the postwar discipline in the United Kingdom turned toward rather than away from the study of race and decolonization, although this topic has not received the attention it deserves. The *Times* editor and one-time member of Milner's Round Table, H. V. Hodson (1950), addressed Chatham House arguing that race relations likely posed an even greater threat to civilization than the struggle with communism. Leaving aside his unabashed defense of white supremacy, Hodson called for the creation of a new institute on race, and two years later the Royal Institute of International Affairs (RIIA) appointed Sir Malcolm Hailey, the career Indian hand, as head of a new board of studies on race relations. The Rockefeller Foundation funded its burgeoning research program until 1958 when its director, the novelist, Philip Mason, split from the RIIA to found an independent Institute of Race Relations (Sivanathan 2008). It appears that the early twentieth-century anxieties about white survival in the United States and other settler colonies (Lake and Reynolds 2008, Cotton 2009), which drove the creation of the American discipline, had reached London. Why? As Tolentino describes the break represented by decolonization: the colonial question in Europe was fast becoming the immigration question (2013).

Another subject about which we know next to nothing is the experience of the first women to gain PhDs in the subject and their subsequent teaching and research careers. The first waves of feminist and now gender and IR theorists that have reanimated critique and opened up new areas of inquiry fit the pattern discussed in this chapter. It has proceeded to date without looking back at the practitioner histories themselves with their silence and evasion about women such as Merzi Tate or Vera Micheles Dean, who succeeded Buell at the FPA and then went on to teach at Rochester and New York Universities in the late 1950s. We have yet to wrestle adequately with the "rise of feminism," despite Merriam's identification of it back in 1924 as the third epoch-making process – together with racism and imperialism – with which political theory would have to contend.

Practitioner histories help to sustain the illusions on which the daily practices of disciplines such as international relations depend: the steady advance of knowledge, the autonomy of scientists, the free play of ideas, and the rest. Arguably nothing exposes the extent of those illusions more than that moment when, in the words of William Langer, "international relations meant race relations" (1977, 81) in a country that to early IR theorists resembled South Africa. The constitutive force of racism appears at once unimaginable, since no practitioner history to date acknowledges it, let alone considers its effects, and simultaneously not worth discussing, since, to anticipate the response, "back then everyone was racist." That said, the hope is that an unvarnished account of its role in the founding of the US profession will matter to those critical IR theorists today studying racism and global hierarchy and those seeking to "decolonize the academy."

Bibliography

Biondi, Martha. 2012. *The Black Revolution on Campus*. Berkeley: University of California Press.

Buell, Raymond. 1925. *International Relations*. New York: Henry Holt.

———. 1928. *The Native Problem in Africa*. Two volumes. New York: Macmillan.

Bunche, Ralph. 1936. *A World View of Race*. Washington, DC: The Associates in Negro Folk Education.

Cotton, James. 2009. "Imperialism and Internationalism in Early Australian International Relations: The Contribution of W. Harrison Moore." *Australian Journal of Political Science* 44: 639–657.

DuBois, W.E.B. 1903. *Souls of Black Folk: Essays and Sketches*. Chicago: A. C. McClurg.

———. 1920. *Darkwater: Voices from within the Well*. New York: Harcourt, Brace, and Howe.

———. 1935. *Black Reconstruction: An Essay toward a History of the Part Which Black Folk Played in the Attempt to Reconstruct Democracy in America*. New York: Harcourt, Brace.

Ekbladh, David. 2011/12. "Present at the Creation: Edward Mead Earle and the Depression-Era Origins of Security Studies." *International Security* 36: 107–141.

Fox, William. 1985. "Geopolitics and International Relations." In *On Geopolitics: Classical and Nuclear*, edited by Ciro Zoppo and Charles Zorgbibe, 15–44. Dordrecht: Martinus Nijhoff.

Gilman, Nils. 2003. *Mandarins of the Future: Modernization Theory in Cold War America*. Baltimore: Johns Hopkins University Press.

Go, Julian. 2013. "Sociology's Imperial Unconscious: The Emergence of American Sociology in the Context of Empire." In *Sociology and Empire: The Imperial Entanglements of a Discipline*, edited by George Steinmetz, 83–105. Durham: Duke University Press.

Guilhot, Nicolas. 2014. "Imperial Realism: Post-War IR Theory and Decolonisation." *International History Review* 36: 698–720.

Henderson, Errol. n.d. "Black Culture and Revolution in the United States: The Black Power Era."

Hobson, John. 2012. *The Eurocentric Conception of World Politics: Western International Theory, 1760–2010.* Cambridge: Cambridge University Press.

Hodson, Henry. 1950. "Race Relations in the Commonwealth." *International Affairs* 26: 305–315.

Kuklick, Bruce. 2006. *Blind Oracles: Intellectuals and War from Kennan to Kissinger.* Princeton: Princeton University Press.

Lake, Marilyn and Henry Reynolds. 2008. *Drawing the Global Color Line: White Men's Countries and the International Challenge of Racial Equality.* Cambridge: Cambridge University Press.

Langer, William. 1977. *In and Out of the Ivory Tower: The Autobiography of William L. Langer.* New York: Neale Watsun Academic Publications.

Lauren, Paul. 1996 [1988]. *Power and Prejudice: The Politics and Diplomacy of Discrimination.* 2nd edition. Boulder: Westview.

Locke, Alain. 1992 [1915/16]. *Race Contacts and International Relations.* Edited and with an introduction by Jeffrey Stewart. Washington, DC: Howard University Press.

Logan, Rayford. 1928. "The Operation of the Mandate System in Africa." *Journal of Negro History* 13: 423–477.

———. 1941. *The Diplomatic Relations of the United States with Haiti, 1776–1891.* Chapel Hill: University of North Carolina Press.

———. 1942. *The Operation of the Mandate System in Africa, 1919–1927.* Washington, DC: Foundation Publishers.

Merriam, Charles. 1924. "Recent Tendencies in Political Thought." In *History of Political Theories: Recent Times*, edited by Charles Merriam and Harry Elmer Barnes, 1–45. New York: Macmillan.

Moon, Parker. 1925. *Syllabus on International Relation.* New York: Macmillan.

———. 1926. *Imperialism and World Politics.* New York: Macmillan.

Morris, Aldon. 2015. *The Scholar Denied: W. E. B. DuBois and the Birth of Modern Sociology.* Berkeley: University of California.

Schmidt, Brian. 1988. *The Political Discourse of Anarchy: A Disciplinary History of International Relations.* New York: State University of New York Press.

Sivanathan, Ambalavaner. 2008. "Race and Resistance: The IRR Story." *Race and Class* 50: 1–30.

Spykman, Nicholas. 1926. "The Social Background of Asiatic Nationalism." *American Journal of Sociology* 32: 396–411.

Steinmetz, George, ed. 2013. *Sociology and Empire: The Imperial Entanglements of a Discipline.* Durham: Duke University Press.

Tate, Merze. 1942. *The Disarmament Illusion: The Movement for a Limitation of Armaments to 1907.* New York: Macmillan.

———. 1965. *The United States and the Hawaiian Kingdom.* New Haven: Yale University Press.

Tolentino, Cynthia. 2013. "From Unincorporated Territory to Commonwealth: Connecting Decolonization and U.S. Empire." *Mémoire(s), identité(s), marginalité(s) dans le monde occidental contemporain* 10. Accessed April 26, 2016. http://mimmoc.revues.org/1392

Vitalis, Robert. 2007. *America's Kingdom: Mythmaking on the Saudi Oil Frontier*. Palo Alto: Stanford University Press.

———. 2012. Review of David Ekbladh, "Present at the Creation," *H-Diplo*, 15 June 2012. http://www.h-net.org/~diplo/ISSF/PDF/ISSF-AR14.pdf.

———. 2015. *White World Order, Black Power Politics: The Birth of American International Relations*. Ithaca: Cornell University Press.

Von Eschen, Penny. 1997. *Race against Empire: Black Americans and Anticolonialism, 1937–1957*. Ithaca: Cornell University Press.

Williams, Eric. 1944. *Capitalism and Slavery*. Chapel Hill: University of North Carolina Press.

8

HOW ELITE NETWORKS SHAPE THE CONTOURS OF THE DISCIPLINE AND WHAT WE MIGHT DO ABOUT IT

Inderjeet Parmar

> "What is this thing called International Relations in the 'English-speaking countries' other than the 'study' about how to 'run the world from positions of strength'? . . . There was no 'science of international relations' . . . The subject so-called was an ideology of control masking as a proper academic discipline."
>
> (Carr quoted in Vitalis 2015, 1)

International Relations (IR), area studies, and the other major social sciences are products of Anglo-American early twentieth-century hegemonic elite knowledge networks aimed at securing elite and imperial-state interests in a world rocked by war, revolution and change, particularly after WWI. The main contours of IR are hardly the product of a liberal-pluralistic free market of ideas nor even of inward-looking disciplinary developments, but of elite attempts to construct a "scientific" discipline capable of comprehending and managing a changing world to protect western (imperial) interests. This represented an attempt at ruling-class intellectual and political hegemony against the forces of radical change brought about by capitalist industrialization, urbanization and mass immigration, especially in the United States. Thus, I argue that IR's principal aim has been, and largely remains, to develop ideas that legitimize or protect the status quo or manage crises facing ruling elites to maintain intact, or through superficial reforms, an unjust national/global imperial order, with Anglo-American power at its core (Hobson 2013; Parmar 2012; Vitalis 2015). International Relations was born as "race relations" – to manage the *racial* balance of power at a time of growing anti-colonial resistance – so W. E. B. DuBois (1903) was hardly alone when he famously noted this. Yet, so stunning has the silence on the race question been in the self-understandings of Anglo-American scholars of their discipline that Du Bois is left standing alone and outside of the considerations of most IR scholars (Furedi 1998; Vitalis 2015). The fundamental aim of IR and the other social sciences has been to put knowledge to work and "relate knowledge to action," as the Rockefeller Foundation put it (Parmar 2002, 244).

Yet, the development of IR, area studies and development studies, among others, has hardly been uninterrupted. There are disruptions and ruptures in a world of unequal powers and peoples, and the voices of the unheard sometimes echo in the corridors of power, usually as threats and warnings. Crises provide potential for change both within the disciplines as well as to develop the more critical role scholars might play in broadening the range of issues and questions – choices – for public debate. As ever, when the dominant forces that control funding – and decide what the problems are that require research, with what methods and perspectives – see threats, they divert resources to head off opposition through reform, the net result of which is the prevention of fundamental change. In this process, I argue, the elite knowledge network, frequently funded by pioneering American foundations such as the Ford, Rockefeller, Carnegie and other corporate "philanthropies," plays a decisive role. I argue that the elite knowledge network – defined as flows of people, ideas and funding around a complex of knowledge, political, corporate, governmental and other institutions – is the principal power technology that develops and maintains elite hegemony along the lines Antonio Gramsci referred to in his writings – the means by which the ruling class maintains its grip on the hearts and minds of the masses, albeit through an apparently "free" press, supposedly apolitical schools, political parties, elections and so on (Hoare and Nowell-Smith 1971). This represents nothing less than the construction of "empires of the mind," drawing the boundaries of thinkable thought and directing into relatively safe channels any currents of dissent or rebellion. Some might be tempted to call this "soft power," but there is nothing very soft about it – it is lethal in its consequences when practiced in an unjust, class-ridden, racial-imperial order.

There is a relatively small proportion of IR scholars who are completely integrated into the mentalities and institutions of the status quo, who frequent foreign and defense ministries, congressional or parliamentary committees, establishment think tanks and media outlets, who provide advice based on shared worldviews (Anderson 2013b). Most of us are, however, most of the time, in a state of contained political irrelevance, particularly in the sense of having little impact in public debates or even bringing to light latent public concerns. This is regardless of how critical our teaching and research is or might be. As part of the elite knowledge network – at least of its outer circles – there is a small proportion of IR and other scholars who manage to engage in the public sphere without being part of the status quo; it is this group that needs to increase in political significance. The question is how to do it. The chapter ends with a few suggestions of what might be done, limited though it must necessarily be given the structural forces that shape our discipline, as well as the limits allowed by the confines of this book. Under pressure though it is, the university is an intellectually contested space, occupied by students from broader swathes of society than ever before, that is still an oasis of relatively free debate and argument in which empires of the mind may be challenged by critical scholars with unorthodox views and rigorous empirical research. We need to work out ways to maximize this potential.

Knowledge, power and networks

The power of intellectuals, ideas and especially of elite knowledge networks is best appreciated in and through a Gramscian perspective, the focal point of which is "hegemony." "Hegemony" here is understood as a set of processes by which a group, class or state – through a combination of persuasion and coercion – is able to attain "buy in" from other groups, classes or states for its own objectives, values and interests. In order to establish hegemony, the hegemonic power or group normally, culturally, intellectually, financially, or militarily penetrates the target group or society/ state, thereby providing significant impetus in socializing elements in the target group. While there is a bargain struck between hegemonic forces and target groups, it is normally characterized by inequality of rewards (Parmar 2012).

The Gramscian view notes the existence of important protective layers of pro-status quo ideology and institutions that actively struggle to shape consciousness. It is the role of "organic intellectuals" to develop and disseminate dominant ideas, to make "commonsense" of what are, in reality, ideas that principally support the ruling class. Politics and the state are sites of struggle between rival ideas and regimes. Through bargaining and building, enduring coalitions that cut across class and ethno-racial cleavages are formed by the dominant concepts that underlies a particular set of political and economic arrangements: a regime. As political regimes – or hegemonic projects and alliances – are made up of cross-class coalitions, they require public opinion mobilizations to convince the masses – or at least a critical proportion of them – that they have a stake in current arrangements. In short, the coalition, or historic bloc, is generated and sustained by the "consent of the governed" under the hegemonic leadership of politicians and intellectuals of the capitalist class. Because consent is so vital to political arrangements, it is engineered by elites through numerous channels that involve the state and organizations such as elite universities, influential think tanks like the Council on Foreign Relations and the major foundations (Arnove 1980; Berman 1983; Hoare and Nowell-Smith 1971).

A significant role is played in the development of knowledge by institutions that concentrate funds and (attempt to) build hegemonic knowledge networks. Knowledge flows are unequal: some are excluded from knowledge flows, while others are included on certain terms; some kinds of knowledge are privileged, while others are marginalized; some intellectuals are central, others peripheral. Knowledge flows, however, are not just unequal: they also re-orient "mentalities" or "mind-sets" particularly by shifting scholars' reference points from their locale to a broader logic. Philanthropic foundations which, as Dwight MacDonald famously noted, are pots of money surrounded by people who want some, are among the strategic leading players in the intellectual field: they have great influence in determining – through targeted and large-scale grant making – who defines what is legitimate and illegitimate knowledge. Their power to establish new disciplines – such as international relations – as well as their theoretical, methodological and empirical preoccupations, are always devices for promoting symbolic domination.

Knowledge networks are, at least in part, aimed at the incorporation and employment of intellectuals, thereby consolidating their attachment to existing political arrangements and processes of change. Intellectual unemployment or under-incorporation within elite cultural and political institutions has long been associated with political radicalism, while integration tends to lead to greater levels of political moderation (Brym 1980). Funding bodies create strong networks precisely to recruit and mobilize the most promising academic intellectuals for a whole range of large-scale projects, including assisting the development of the American state in domestic and foreign affairs. The intellectuals so mobilized are provided with career-building opportunities, well-funded programs and opportunities for policy influence and tend therefore to produce research of a utilitarian, technocratic character that is methodologically compatible with the positivistic orientations of foundation leaders. This is not to suggest that foundations directly "interfere" with researchers or research results, let alone pressure researchers. It is only to suggest that given the conditions of near-perpetual financial crisis within academic institutions, large-scale funding programs prove very attractive to researchers and influence selection of research topics, research questions and methodologies. It is plainly possible that researchers could always draw conclusions radically at odds with funders' implicit or explicit intentions, thereby challenging hegemonic thinking. Yet, past research may have serious consequences for future funding, encouraging a culture of self-censorship (Laski 1930; McGoey 2015).

IR as a product of a state–private network

IR as a discipline emerged from a number of sources, including reactions to world war, anti-colonial revolt and socialist revolution, and from a number of institutional sources, such as Anglo-American peace planners at Paris in 1919, Chatham House and the Council on Foreign Relations (CFR) and the major American foundations – Carnegie, Rockefeller and Ford. Locked in close relationships with state elites, funded by J. P. Morgan bankers like Thomas W. Lamont and corporate foundations, IR emerged from international law in the United States and history in the United Kingdom and gradually found a home in various university chairs and departments. IR operated in and around the League of Nations system and reacted against the collapse of the Wilsonian liberal dream. Management of the global color line and of domestic public opinion were significant preoccupations of the founders of Chatham House and the CFR (Parmar 2000).

Alongside IR, there also proliferated area studies, strategic studies, development studies – each in its own way developing ways to know and act on the world, becoming separate-but-related university disciplines, with their own professional societies, academic journals and annual conferences. Such networks operated to nurture people and ideas, develop orthodoxies and marginalize rival approaches – manufacturing empires of the mind.

The post-1918 period witnessed a massive effort at national network building by foundations in the United States. Rockefeller and Carnegie funded liberal internationalist/anti-isolationist think tanks, university research institutes and publicity organizations: CFR (1921), Foreign Policy Association (FPA, 1918), League of Nations Association (1923) and numerous World Affairs Councils. The foundations built an historic bloc behind the hegemonic project of liberal internationalist globalism (and anti-isolationism) that consisted of corporations, organized labor, intellectuals/students and racial minorities, for example. Such groupings, with their varied interests, were leashed to the globalist vision that included an open trading system, full employment, "anti-fascism" abroad and "anti-racism" at home (although in very limited ways) and world peace underwritten by American power.

Concretely to promote liberal internationalism, Carnegie philanthropies supported numerous universities in establishing IR courses in the 1920s and 1930s, as well as local library "international corners" and radio broadcasts across the country. The crowning achievements of this "movement" were the Yale Institute of International Studies and the programs established at Princeton under the leadership of Edward Meade Earle: together, Yale and Princeton led the way in establishing IR as an academic discipline and, even more significantly, in establishing Realism – the centrality and *inevitability of power politics and the necessity of American global interventionism* – as the discipline's dominant postwar paradigm. The Yale Institute trained hundreds of undergraduates and graduate students for state service or academia, launching its journal, *World Politics*, in 1948. Well-known IR alumni include Bernard C. Cohen and Lucian Pye. Other alumni went on to join important US foreign policy–related institutions such as the CFR, FPA, Foreign Service and State Department.

Additionally, the early stirrings of the massive postwar area studies phenomenon were the work of the big foundations from as early as the 1930s, in the case of Soviet Studies, as was their postwar development and maturity. Asian, African and Latin American Studies thrived as those regions became objects of American attention because of their strategic location, raw materials, market potential or place in Cold War competition. For example, a Carnegie Corporation internal report by Columbia University historian, Nathaniel Peffer, concluded that the Rockefeller-Carnegie-funded American Institute of Pacific Relations (AIPR) was responsible for increasing consciousness of the Far East in the United States and inspiring teaching of Pacific area studies and establishing Far Eastern studies departments in schools, colleges and universities (Parmar 2012).

Located at prestigious universities such as Harvard, Columbia and Chicago, area studies programs featured funded chairs, departments, professional associations, conferences, doctoral students and research fellowships. Relatively small investments had powerful "multiplier" effects as the symbolic power of the Ivy League encouraged other universities to invest in their own programs. The foundations' efforts in this area were assisted by regular advice and encouragement by an enlarged postwar State Department that yearned for trained graduate students for public service and a more internationally conscious American public. The State Department more closely oriented the teaching of IR at Yale, for example, to the department's concerns. In 1944 a committee investigated "what the educational process can do to produce good decision-makers in the field of international relations," mainly to improve the caliber of graduate students entering government service and to provide in-service training to practicing diplomats (Parmar 2015, 70).

In addition, the strongly pro-interventionist foundations actively funded the mid- to late-1930s campaigns to "educate" various elements of elite opinion, particularly pacifist and isolationist students at leading universities, and regional notables in isolationist parts of the United States. The League of Nations Association, for example, which was heavily funded by the Rockefeller Foundation, sponsored college-based Model League of Nations Assemblies and ran national competitions for school children to "to train an elite to think, feel and act internationally" (Parmar 2015, 67).

The American foundations' international network building was as strategic as their national enterprises. Rockefeller officials noted when selecting London-based colleges (such as the London School of Economics) for investment that London's worldwide imperial network offered opportunities to influence the questions and methods of research across the British Empire.

It is unsurprising, therefore, that the foundations funded the long-term cooperative efforts of the American CFR with its British counterpart, the Royal Institute of International Affairs (RIIA, also known as Chatham House). Founded as two branches of one Institute of International Affairs, the CFR and Chatham House became national organizations in the early 1920s. Nevertheless, their cooperation remained "special": they were champions of Anglo-American cooperation and, indeed, alliance, as the best way of combating "aggressors" and securing world peace and prosperity. They established joint conferences and study groups from the 1920s right into the Cold War, informal and semi-formal diplomacy that shadowed their official counterparts in their respective governments – for example, on naval matters, trade, war debts and postwar issues in the Pacific region, among others. While they did not "resolve" problems, they created spaces within which policy-oriented elites were able frankly to air their grievances and indicate how much political room for maneuver their respective governments enjoyed. They also reinforced habits of Anglo-American dialogue. During the Second World War – the high point of the CFR-RIIA's cooperation – the two groups' leaders, which included numerous leading scholars like Arnold Toynbee, Charles Kingsley Webster, Isaiah Bowman, James Shotwell, Quincy Wright and Alvin Hansen, together with their respective governments, planned the postwar international institutional architecture that became known as the Bretton Woods system: the International Monetary Fund (IMF), the International Bank for Reconstruction and Development (IBRD, and later, albeit somewhat differently, the World Bank) and the United Nations. In regard to the latter, the role of the CFR as an organization, and of Isaiah Bowman, is well documented. It is clear that, for Bowman and the CFR, the UN was for the maintenance of national security, and international organization would be the route to avoiding "conventional forms of imperialism." American power would be exercised through an American-led "international" system (Parmar 2004).

Finally, the foundation-supported area studies programs provided an additional avenue for "thickening" American elite networks with other countries and strategic world regions. John Ikenberry, referring to the building of the British Empire in India, states that "[a] necessary condition for the emergence of both informal and formal empire is the explicit, physical penetration of peripheral society by metropolitan agents. Whether officials, soldiers, traders, financiers, or missionaries [to these add professors, research fellows and doctoral students] these agents serve as the medium through which socialization occurs" (quoted in Parmar 2012, para 57). Postwar US-based area studies programs provide an excellent example of such "socialization."

Building on American domestic area studies networks – with their attendant professional societies, journals and conferences – foundations funded network construction in target regions and countries. That is, foundations encouraged field-based studies by American scholars in Africa, Asia and Latin America, as well as building prestigious "centers of excellence" and expertise in those regions. Doctoral and post-doctoral fellowships were established, beginning a flow of scholars and students around US elite university-based networks, with the usual multiplier effects. Whole careers were built by the tremendous levels of funding from the Ford Foundation through its Foreign Areas Fellowship Program, for example. These networks helped to create and sustain bonds of scholarly cooperation between elite American universities' area studies (and other) programs, the US Department of State and strategic overseas regions.

It was through such network flows – of money, scholars and ideas – that modernization theory was established as the paradigm for the economic development of "backward" countries during the 1950s to 1970s. Strongly driven by Cold War competition, as well as the historic American desire for global hegemony, modernizers favored market-oriented, non-nationalist and non-communist roads to economic development in the Third World. An excellent example of such thinking, and its underlying political assumptions, is represented in a confidential 1954 memorandum to CIA director Allen Dulles from Max Millikan and Walt Rostow. In it, they argue that the American economy can continue to grow only if the world economy grows. Specifically, the "underdeveloped" regions needed "the mobilization of capital; the development of 'know-how,'" among other things. For the latter, Millikan and Rostow recommended "international collaborations between universities, management associations, medical societies, and trade unions for education, research, and training." All this could be achieved only through a system of international organizations, including the UN and the International Labor Organization (ILO). Although denying any intention of interfering in other countries' internal affairs, Millikan and Rostow added that the United States must develop "an [international] environment in which societies which directly or indirectly menace ours will not evolve" (Parmar 2012, para 59).

Collaborations between Ford-funded American economists and Indonesian economists in the 1950s and 1960s, for example, had profound effects on that nation's political and economic development, especially after the overthrow of the leftist-nationalist, Sukarno, in 1966. This involved direct and violent involvement of the Ford-funded and US-trained economists, the "Beautiful Berkeley Boys," and many of their students, in the destabilization and removal of Sukarno, not to mention the bloodbath that occurred against members of the Communist Party of Indonesia. Similar outcomes may also be noted with regard to Rockefeller- and Ford-funded social scientists – the so-called Chicago Boys – in Chile before and after the military coup by General Pinochet in 1973 (Parmar 2015). The ideological, ideational and institutional collaborations at the heart of these networks integrated Third World elites, or at least important sections of them, into American (and western) networks, promoting non-national, cosmopolitan logics among them, as well as the promise of well-funded research programs and prestigious careers.

Perry Anderson's articles (2013a and b) in the *New Left Review* – "Imperium" and "Consilium" – indicate the institutional complex of professional public policy schools that have developed over decades to nurture the ideas and train the practitioners of American power. They firmly locate IR and its various schools in a state-private network that performs the principal functions of elite networks – socialization, training, cohesion, consensus building and development of concepts to protect and promote American power. British IR has its own origins and trajectories but may also be located in similar pathways – with Chatham House and its American foundation backers as a significant force (Parmar 1992, 2004, 2012).

Overall, such organic intellectuals' work functions largely to elaborate a consensus for the "harmonization" of divergent social and economic forces and the perpetuation of unequal systems of national and global power. By constructing knowledge networks, the most powerful states, in which the richest funders are based, develop a system of flows of people, ideas and money suited to the maintenance of the existing global hierarchy of power. Global South intellectuals are incorporated into network spaces constructed, funded and heavily influenced – if not led and populated – by scholars, foundation, corporate and state elites from the metropolitan core. The former are, to an extent, transformed into cosmopolitans or transnational forces, responding, to an increasing degree, to extra-national, global logics (Tickner 2013). Crudely, such "extraction" of intellectuals approximates the extraction of resources, the global flows of wealth from the less developed to developed nations. Foundations have helped to develop spaces which "house" global elites, within which elites circulate and communicate with each other, developing ideas, programs and, most of all, symbolic capital, enduring empires of the mind.

Foundations build networks for their own sake because they produce results by virtue of merely being constructed (that is, because of a range of "internal" functions they perform), and second because networks achieve ends other than those publicly stated (their "external" functions). Foundation networks foster and create frames of thought that cohere to the network; they generously finance spaces for the production and legitimization of particular types of knowledge; networks build careers and reputations; they fund key scholars, policy makers, universities, journals, professional societies and associations, connecting scholars from the "core" metropolitan centers with those in the "periphery"; networks provide sources of employment for intellectuals within a system of "safe" ideas, strengthening some ideas, combating others and, merely through generating and disseminating ideas and empirical research, preventing, or at least making a lot less likely, "other thoughts"; networks identify and develop pro-US elite cadres that, in the Cold War, backed (and benefitted from) capitalist modernization strategies and which, today, back and benefit from neoliberal globalization strategies.

Can IR be more critical and relevant?

IR, then, is hardly to be understood in its own terms only, but rather as the product of larger historical and elite forces and of elite knowledge networks. It has become a major university discipline attracting large numbers of students at all levels. Recruitment has benefitted from world-historical developments and crises – the end of the Cold War, 9/11, wars of aggression in Iraq and Afghanistan, the rise of Islamic State, global power shifts and the like. Yet, beyond some problem-solving, policy-oriented work that is neither critical nor oriented toward structural change and some engagement with civil society actors, IR scholars do not in any large numbers appear to play a role in broader political life and public debate. Why is this the case, and how might we think about changing this state of affairs?

There are numerous structural impediments to greater levels of public engagement, as well as deeply ingrained scholars' self-concepts. The changing character of the British university in the twenty-first century – abolition of the block grant, fees, competition within the state sector and between it and a politically encouraged for-profit private sector – promotes an environment that values particular kinds of knowledge, including that which produces employable graduates and usable knowledge. This accentuates but does not fundamentally alter the direction of travel since the inception of IR.

The Research Assessment Exercise/Research Excellence Framework (RAE/REF) systems have had major effects on academics' priorities and time with its focus on research rankings, appointments to that end, marketing, research programs and topics and approaches congenial to "top" journals. The university as a public good, a space for critical thought and discussion, is placed under greater stress because of market forces, regulatory regimes and political pressure.

Structurally, departments' and universities' promotion processes probably play a role in narrowing scholars' conceptions of their role. Although the REF "impact agenda" demands increasing attention, promotion committees value publications in "high-impact" journals and university presses, which clearly affects the ways in which scholars work and think, socializing them in a language that is far from comprehensible beyond a narrow sub-field, let alone to a broader public. The pressure to conform varies but is significant and increased by various external research quality regimes.

Workloads have increased as market pressures have risen and student numbers have grown and in response to the National Student Survey (NSS) regime. The greater pressure to produce employable graduates with marketable competences itself leads to greater emphasis on providing useful knowledge at the expense of critical thought. This dovetails with increasing opportunities, and pressure, for external consultancy fees, which increases scholars' engagement but also tends to skew scholars' agendas away from general and theoretical problems to more practical matters. The sources of prestige also shift away from one's own scholarly peers toward political and governmental decision makers, threatening to convert the scholar into an adjunct of the civil service or political machine. Powerful funding agency priorities, shifting with governmental priorities, influence research agendas and seem to value policy-oriented useful research and economic growth more than critical work that does not share policy makers' assumptions.

Levels of administrative support vary but remain insufficient to permit greater time for scholars to engage in research, teaching and public engagement. Administrators, under pressure to re-engineer the university and to report on progress toward meeting external criteria of quality, impose change and patterns of uniformity often clashing with the *laissez faire* approaches of academics, hindering academic work and increasing workloads.

Added to this are widespread self-concepts of what it is to be a scholar, some of which militate against public engagement: that they are producers of knowledge for its own sake and are too theoretical or esoteric to be relevant beyond the field.

Possible ways forward?

We should begin closer to home and develop greater engagement across the university to broader cross-sections of students and faculty, especially as increasing numbers and proportions of 18- to 21-year-olds attend university. In addition, we must develop different conceptions of our students as learners and diffusers, increasing their opportunities for engagement in the public sphere via various media and other forms at an early stage. The training of doctoral candidates might include writing for and speaking to broader audiences, by going out into schools or other organized communities. An intellectual shift away from "employability" toward student placements at a range of "political" organizations – including campaigning organizations – allows students to "test" their knowledge against specific real-world forces. Universities should develop outward-facing centers for public debate and the understanding of global issues, reducing the gap between local communities and universities; more closely embed the academic community into their locale; and become a resource for the local community, including schools, local campaign organizations, community activists and councils.

In short, there is scope to develop a conception of a "public IR" driven by research and engagement with concerns of non-elites outside mainstream organizations and settings, breaking the centrality of the core and its myths of self-constitution (Lawson 2008). This could exploit the opportunity offered by the REF "impact" agenda to broaden engagement from policy elites to broader publics. This requires a commitment from university leaders to provide administrative support and periods of leave for scholars to engage.

Just as a century ago, we have global rivalries in ideas and projects, and we must step out of our paradigms and our structurally and self-imposed "empires of the mind" – or what Eric Herring (2006) refers to as "disciplined minds" – to be a lot more critical and see the world from a variety of angles and not just the traditions in which we are steeped. There is a whole world out there we are barely glimpsing, let alone studying and taking seriously, and questions that we too frequently do not even know to ask. That may allow us to serve our society and politics better than if we remain blinkered, uncritical and inward looking.

Bibliography

Anderson, Perry. 2013a. "Imperium," *New Left Review* 83.

Anderson, Perry. 2013b. "Consilium," *New Left Review* 83.

Arnove, Robert F. 1980. *Philanthropy and Cultural Imperialism*. Boston: G. K. Hall.

Berman, Edward H. 1983. *The Ideology of Philanthropy: The Influence of the Carnegie, Ford and Rockefeller Foundations on American Foreign Policy*. Albany: SUNY Press.

Brym, Robert. 1980. *Intellectuals and Politics*. London: George Unwin.

Carr, E. H. 1939/2001. *The Twenty Years' Crisis: An Introduction to the Study of International Relations*. Basingstoke: Palgrave, 2001.

DuBois, W. E. B. 1903. *The Souls of Black Folk*. Chicago: A. C. McClurg.

Furedi, Frank. 1998. *The Silent War: Imperialism and the Changing Perception of Race*. London: Pluto Press.

Herring, Eric. 2006. "Remaking the mainstream: The case for activist IR scholarship," *Millennium: Journal of International Studies* 35 (1): 105–118.

Hoare, Quintin and G. Nowell-Smith. 1971. *Selections from the Prison Notebooks of Antonio Gramsci*. London: Lawrence and Wishart.

Hobson, John. 2013. *The Eurocentric Conception of World Politics*. Cambridge: Cambridge University Press.

Laski, Harold. 1930. *The Dangers of Obedience and Other Essays*. London: Harper and Brothers.

McGoey, Lynsey. 2015. *No Such Thing as a Free Gift: The Gates Foundation and the Price of Philanthropy*. London: Verso.

Parmar, Inderjeet. 1992. "Chatham house and the Anglo-American alliance," *Diplomacy and Statecraft* 3 (1): 23–47.

Parmar, Inderjeet. 2000. "Engineering consent: The Carnegie Endowment for International Peace and the mobilization of American public opinion, 1939–1945," *Review of International Studies* 26 (1): 35–48.

Parmar, Inderjeet. 2002. "American foundations and the development of international knowledge networks," *Global Networks* 2 (1): 13–30.

Parmar, Inderjeet. 2004. *Think Tanks and Power in Foreign Policy: A Comparative Study of the Role and Influence of the Council on Foreign Relations and the Royal Institute of International Affairs, 1939–1945*. Basingstoke: Palgrave.

Parmar, Inderjeet. 2012. "Foundation networks and American hegemony," *European Journal of American Studies* 7 (1) (Spring).

Parmar, Inderjeet. 2015. *Foundations of the American Century: The Ford, Carnegie, and Rockefeller Foundations in the Rise of American Power*. New York: Columbia University Press.

Tickner, Arlene B. 2013. "Core, periphery and (neo) imperialist international relations," *European Journal of International Relations* 19 (3): 627–646.

Vitalis, Robert. 2015. *White World Order, Black Power Politics: The Birth of American International Relations*. Ithaca: Cornell University Press.

PART THREE
Policing the boundaries

9

BE CAREFUL WHAT YOU WISH FOR

Positivism and the desire for relevance in the American study of IR

Jennifer Sterling-Folker

For many American IR scholars, the point of studying IR is to serve as public intellectuals who can provide coherent ideas, information, and advice about global affairs to citizens, policy makers, activists, journalists, and other interested parties. Here the "modifier American has to be taken seriously," as Katznelson and Milner (2002, 3–4) observe, because in the American academic setting the study of IR is typically housed within political science departments as one of several subfields. As a result, American IR shares with American political science what Katznelson and Milner observe are "the marks of its origin" (see also Rosenberg this volume). These include not only a deep commitment to American liberalism and the modern state (see also Oren 2003; Smith 2002), but also the epistemological conversations and debates that have characterized political science's disciplinary history.[1] And because IR shares political science's sense of purpose in that context, the "core question shaping the future of the discipline," according to Flinders and John (2013, 222; emphasis added), is not "'should political science be relevant?' but 'how can political science be *more* relevant?'"

This disciplinary desire for relevance and engagement is often treated as so obvious and natural that it hardly needs justification. Büger and Gadinger (2007) point out there are different interpretations of what it means to be relevant and, from a critical theoretical perspective, American IR scholars already heavily influence the world in some very negative ways. Yet the more popular and, as Flinders and John (2013, 225) note, "fairly broad and widespread perception" in America is instead "that the discipline has become socially irrelevant and politically disconnected." There is practically a cottage industry of texts decrying our irrelevance and elaborating ways to become better public intellectuals (for example, Ericksson and Sundelius 2005; Flinders and John 2013; Jentleson and Ratner 2011; Lepgold and Nincic 2001; Walt 2005). In them, we are exhorted to be more attentive to the substantive and practical needs of policy makers and to couch our interactions in consumer-friendly ways. Yet this begs a fundamental question: what we are doing instead that is making us so inattentive and incomprehensible?

To most disciplinary observers, the blame goes to positivism as the preferred epistemology of the American political science discipline and, by extension, its IR subfield. American IR graduate students are heavily schooled in this epistemological position, which assumes there is an objective social world that can be observed and measured utilizing procedures and techniques drawn largely from the natural sciences (Ricci 1984; Smith 1997). Because it is often the *only* epistemological perspective taught, it is common for most American political science graduate students and scholars to know nothing of other epistemological choices. In this way, positivism, or behavioralism as it was often called in the American context, is naturalized as the common sense of the discipline. Yet from a public intellectual perspective, positivism has proven problematic because it puts a premium on methodology over results and envisions incremental knowledge production. What positivism produces, then, is often relatively obvious or uninteresting and difficult to understand in the absence of similar methodological training. This has generated successive waves of American disciplinary discontent and soul searching among proponents and critics alike, who believe that it is our adherence to positivism that prevents us from being more socially relevant and politically influential.

This chapter examines the relationship between positivism and public intellectualism in the American disciplinary context and asks to what extent is positivism the problem in this relationship? I am not a huge fan of positivism, but the successive waves of disciplinary discontent revolving around it are so intimately entwined with the desire for relevance that I suspect more is at play here than epistemological preferences. Relevance, like beauty, is in the eye of the beholder, which suggests that *for what* or *to whom* American political scientists and IR scholars wish to be relevant is just as important for understanding their discontent with positivism as its own attributes. Examining this desire for relevance reveals substantive end-goals intimately connected to the American political power project. It therefore raises important ethical questions about our relationship to the American national context, our role as public intellectuals in reifying American power, and the impact our reification has on global affairs. This chapter considers these issues and concludes with a discussion of the dangers posed by our desire to be useful to a particular, relatively powerful, national context. In doing so, it suggests that while the desire for relevance is in keeping with that context, it is also an ethically questionable position.

Positivism and its discontents

Writing in 1996, just four years before a disgruntled letter to the *American Political Science Review* (APSR) editor would culminate in the Political Science Perestroika movement of the early 2000s, the editors of a state-of-the-art handbook claimed there was "striking evidence of the professional maturation" of the discipline (Goodin and Klingemann 1996, 3). This assessment was premised on the "increasingly shared overarching intellectual agenda" and "methodological tool-kit" within the American discipline which the editors argued promoted synthesis and sub-disciplinary exchange (Goodin and Klingemann 1996, 3–4). What was shared, Goodin and Klingemann assumed, was a vision of science involving "systematic inquiry building toward an ever more highly-differentiated set of ordered propositions about the empirical world" (Waldo 1975; cited in Goodin and Klingemann 1996, 9). This, Almond (1996, 82) claimed in the same volume, should be the "privileged" vision of American disciplinary history, "measured by the increase of knowledge based on evidence and inference," and hence "progressive" by nature.

Reflected in Goodin, Klingemann, and Almond's claims about the American political science discipline is the deep yet implicit commitment to behavioralism, itself an application of Popperian-positivist tenets about how to proceed with scientific inquiry. Empirical observation and data collection could be subjected to hypothesis building and methodologically rigorous testing that could be replicated and, if incorrectly conducted, potentially falsifiable. Underlying this epistemological preference for what is observable, testable, and falsifiable is a normative assumption that "adherence to the scientific method must lead eventually to cumulative and useful knowledge" (Ricci 1984, 142). As one of the early leading behavioralists David Easton (1969, 1054) put this in 1969, "the history of the natural sciences shows us how slowly basic research moves," and so the "seemingly remote, often minute details . . . are the building blocks of the edifice in which more reliable understanding occurs." Cumulative knowledge is gained only through the adherence to a positivist methodological toolkit, a point that Easton repeatedly endorsed even as he was criticizing behavioralism for its lack of relevance and ethical concerns.

It is no small matter, then, that positivism is the coherence at the heart of such an optimist vision of the discipline. Without it, there can be no accumulated knowledge and no relevance beyond the walls of the academy for the American political scientist and IR scholar. As such, positivism is treated by its adherents as the gold standard by which all other approaches may be assessed. Not surprisingly, we see its practitioners repeatedly claiming that we can "include the work of opposing schools, insofar as it meets these standards" (Almond 1996, 82) or that "unless a theory makes some sort of causal statement, it cannot be deemed to explain anything" (Sanders 2010, 40). Steve Smith (2002, 72) provides a number of other examples of this sort of disciplinary gatekeeping in American IR, noting that alternative approaches are often "dismissed as intellectually weak, as illegitimate" in what is essentially "the homeland of the mainstream of the (IR) discipline" (See also Levine and Barder 2014). This has ramifications for knowledge production beyond the American shores, as Arlene Tickner (2013) demonstrates, since it reinforces the preference for positivism on a global scale and core–periphery relations in the process.

Of course as the very term suggests, this sort of gatekeeping is precisely what academic *disciplines* do. Disciplines police their boundaries by claiming exclusive knowledge of a subject and developing professional networks and procedures to vet the credentials of potential members. As Büger and Gadinger (2007, 103) observe, "practices of disciplinarity require practices of exclusion," because "by drawing and maintaining boundaries, professional identities and roles are preserved." Boundary setting and maintenance involve high stakes not just for any given individual (whose career and livelihood depend on meeting these professional standards) but the disciplinary collective as a whole, which can expect societal support and prestige in return for the knowledge it produces.

Adherents to positivism often try to soften this disciplining image. Goodin and Klingemann (1996, 5) acknowledge, for example, that "the community of scholars which collectively constitutes a discipline does exercise a strict supervisory function," but they urge us to think of it instead as a "useful self-binding mechanism." That is, "subjecting oneself to the discipline of a discipline . . . is conducive to more and indisputably better work." The added advantage, they go on to say, is that "the simple sharing of 'nuts and bolts' – the building blocks of science – goes a long way toward consolidating a shared sense of the discipline" (Goodin and Klingemann 1996, 14). But given that "better" is defined here as a version of positivism, we begin to see why calls for analytical coherence should be viewed with considerable antipathy. Coherence is too often evoked as a desirable analytical and disciplinary goal masking specific epistemological commitments. It is, as Anne Norton (2004, 78) has observed, "the all-too-imperial desire for a rule, a single standard that can measure all, a maxim that applies in every case." And the specific intent of coherence in this context is to restrain analytical alternatives for the sake of disciplinary unity.

It is another matter, however, as to whether such obvious (and arguably inept) attempts at gatekeeping add up to a hegemonic epistemological perspective so powerful that opponents and their careers are silenced in the process. A great many anecdotal stories about epistemological discrimination of this sort in hiring and tenure decisions circulate in the discipline. A number of studies have documented the extent to which positivism remains the intellectual bedrock for some of the better-known and hence more highly ranked American political science journals (Bennett, Barth, and Rutherford 2003; Pion-Berlin and Cleary 2005; Yanow 2003; Yanow and Schwartz-Shea 2010). And concern over epistemological bias was one of the concerns driving the early 2000s Perestroika movement in the discipline.

The Perestroika movement began when a widely circulated letter from an anonymous "Mr. Perestroika" was sent to the editors of *Political Science and Politics* (PS) and to APSR, the latter being the premier journal of the American Political Science Association (APSA). The published letter in October 2000 included a list of 10 complaints about the *APSR*, the association, and the profession at large, including their lack of relevance and methodological, ethnic, and gender diversity. Letters and short essays in its support flooded into *PS* and the *APSR* in subsequent months and represented, as one letter signed by over 200 political scientists put it, an "extraordinary outpouring of frustration with the current state of the American Political Science Review, the *APSA*, and the profession generally" (An Open Letter 2000).

At first glance, then, while we can assume positivism's epistemological dominance over the American study of IR, the Perestroika movement itself belies the notion that critics are necessarily silenced in or driven out of the discipline. The original *APSR* correspondence garnered support from quite a few well-placed and influential scholars, and numerous articles and an edited volume about the movement were subsequently published (Bennett 2002; Caterino 2010; Luke and McGovern 2010; Monroe 2005; Rigger 2009; Yanow and Schwartz-Shea 2010). In fact, when Perestroika is placed within an historical context, it appears that epistemological dissension of one sort or another has been a feature of the discipline all along (Dryzek 2005; Ricci 1984). "Perestroika did not write on a blank slate," as Susanne Rudolph (2005, 14) observes, because "challenges to a prevailing behaviorist hegemony had already been raised in the late 1960s by the Caucus of a New Political Science (CNPS)." While the CNPS had been motivated primarily by resistance to America's Vietnam War and its persistent racism and sexism, Rudolph (2005, 14) notes, it also had "a recessive epistemological dimension," because it, too, had "felt that political science had become indifferent to the great social issues of the day" and "was increasingly fixated on technique and methodological precision."

In fact, there have been at least five revolutionary movements in the discipline's history according to John Dryzek (2006), who points out that only two of these movements – statism and behavioralism – succeeded in resetting the discipline's epistemological and methodological agenda. In both cases, analytical opposition appeared afterward and, in the case of behavioralism, has produced successive waves of visible dissatisfaction within the discipline's professional association and its journals. Such dissatisfaction is a collection of disparate complaints ranging from concerns over methodological preferences, hiring and tenure practices, editorial procedures, and professional association requirements, to the desire for greater public and political relevance. What seems to unite such concerns into an opposition movement at any given moment in time is typically a "shared condition of marginalization" (Luke and McGovern 2010, 730) combined with an acute "lack of enthusiasm for the monopoly claims of the scientific trope" (Rudolph 2005, 16).

There are divisions on the scientific side to be sure, with little common ground between behavioral empiricism and political scientists who favor rational choice formal modeling, for example. Critics often lump these together, yet rational choice has little to do with empirical data collection and relies instead on economic models that assume actor preferences in order to analyze strategic interaction in a highly abstract and often mathematical fashion. Yet the lack of epistemological unity within the opposition may give some form of scientism, and hence positivism, an advantage. As Rudolph (2005, 15) notes of the scientists, "when methodological disputation breaks out, advocates of these tendencies can unite" since they appear to "have common opponents." This united front means that the epistemological opposition, even when motivated, numerous, and working in concert, must wage an uphill battle for change. And, according to Dryzek (2006, 487), "no reform movement has ever succeeded if it opposed the actual practice of the discipline in a way that met with explicit resistance from practitioners." Given that positivism is what much of American political science practices, the discipline seems particularly difficult to reform as a result. As Luke and McGovern (2010, 731) observed in their retrospective of the Perestroika movement that appeared 10 years later, the "stubborn facts about the discipline's progress endure. Like the earlier CNPS, the

Perestroika movement's disaffection with the practices of political science has not led to a grander vision of what political science in the United States should be."

Yet this also suggests, counter-intuitively, that ongoing collective dissatisfaction with disciplinary epistemological practices may be the disciplinary norm, not the anomaly. Quite a number of disciplinary histories have suggested that collective dissatisfaction with American political science's preference for positivism "has been constitutive of the discipline from the beginning, not a feature that arrived with behavioralism or rational choice theory" (Dryzek 2005, 515). While disciplinary historians disagree over the exact combination of elements that reproduce this dissatisfaction on a regular basis, common to all their accounts is an analytical conflict between scientific inquiry and the discipline's subject matter (Crawford 2000; Levine and Barder 2014; Ricci 1984; Seidelman and Harpham 1985; Smith 1997, 2002). As Ricci (1984, 70) puts it, "there may be something special about the end purpose of political science which turns out to be incompatible with its means." Similarly, Smith (1997, 253) argues that this incompatibility has "contributed to periodic debunkings of the prevailing forms of political science, followed by quests for a 'new science of politics' that can fulfill both desires better." Yet because each quest fails to address the fundamental incompatibility between ends and means, the discipline reenacts collective dissatisfaction with each successive generation of political scientists. The result, as Smith (1997) puts it, is a discipline "still blowing in the wind."

The obvious answer for most dissatisfied observers of the discipline is to give up the means, that is, the commitment to scientific inquiry. This seems like the correct answer given the enormous ontological and epistemological issues that arise when the social is studied as if it were scientifically objective. Yet it is also an impractical and unlikely solution given the American political, economic, and social milieu's preference for scientific inquiry and data; the ongoing professional inducements for satisfying that preference; and existing vested interests in scientific inquiry among the discipline's practitioners. As Lowi (1992, 3) puts it, "[the American] government has become intensely committed to science," and it

> is an inherent part of the new, bureaucratized state, in at least two dimensions: First, it involves a commitment to building science as an institution, that is, a commitment to government for science; and second, it involves a commitment to government by science – that is to say, it involves scientific decision making.

Smith (2005, 526) also notes the historical professional incentives for embracing a form of scientism involving statistical analysis and mathematics. Tickner's (2013, 642) analysis of global knowledge production underscores just how entrenched positivism is, leading her to observe that stepping outside it "is not so simple."

This answer also avoids the question of what exactly science is supposed to be incompatible with and why. The presumption in much of the disciplinary historical literature is that the ends, however defined, are appropriate and that the burden of proof lies squarely with scientific inquiry generally and positivism specifically. Yet to what extent might our ends, and the ways in which we define our scholarly purpose in relationship to them, be as responsible for our collective dissatisfaction as is scientific inquiry itself? An alternative approach to the disciplinary ends–means incompatibility, then, is to consider our subject matter and our purpose as scholars in relationship to that subject matter.

Relevance and its discontents

It is probably no surprise that American political scientists and IR scholars have tended to be concerned with subjects that are central to the American political experience. Ricci (1984) and Smith (1997) both identify democracy as the central concern of the discipline. More specifically it is the "*devotion* to democratic politics" (Ricci 1984, 24, emphasis added) and the desire "to *serve* American democracy" (Smith 1997, 253, emphasis added) that has driven disciplinary scholarship. In other words, our purpose has been not just to study democracy as impassive or indifferent observers, but to transmit knowledge of how to maintain and improve it in our teaching and scholarship. The ends–means incompatibility with positivism comes about because "a science of human political behavior thus can seem to debunk the self-understandings of democratic participants and the meaningfulness of their conscious choices" (Smith 1997, 257). Or, as Ricci (1984, 24) puts it, scientific "studies do not always shed positive light on the very object of their inquiries." This produces Ricci's disciplinary "tragedy," since the more we commit to positivism as a means to understanding our subject matter, the further we move from our ends of supporting and improving it.[2]

An alternative perspective on the discipline's foundational subject matter is offered by Katznelson and Milner (2002), who argue that democracy was a linked but subordinate concern to liberalism and its relationship to the modern state.[3] "About liberalism," they observe, "the founders of political science were rarely ambivalent," but "about democracy, they were more so" (Katznelson and Milner 2002, 10). Similarly, Theodore Lowi (1992, 2) places the relationship between the discipline and the modern American state at the center of his disciplinary overview, arguing that "the early APSA was a kind of *counter*intelligentsia formed in defense of a state that did not yet exist" and, as a result, political science has "no concept of an alternative regime in the United States." Lowi (1992, 1) goes on to assert that American political science and, by implication, its study of IR, "is a product of the state," which means the relationship between scholarship and subject matter was never, nor could it have been, impassive or indifferent. American political science was instead "a quest to understand and secure liberal regimes against competitors, such as monarchies and illiberal empires," while simultaneously being shaped by "the desire to control and contain the state by civil society" (Katznelson and Milner 2002, 8, 10).

Seen in this context, it becomes less clear that the failures of American political science and IR are because of positivism per se. Rather the central problem for positivism may be the desire among American political scientists and IR scholars to be *relevant* to the things that they study. It is a desire that appears to precede epistemological training in the discipline since it is voiced by both proponents and opponents of positivism alike. David Easton's "Credo of Behavioralism" (1965, 7), which promoted positivism as a favored means of knowledge production, was followed four years later by his "Credo of Relevance" (1969, 1052), a call to overcome behaviorialism's "ideology of empirical conservatism" and "reach out to the real needs of mankind in a time of crisis." This was the special responsibility of the intellectual, he argued, who had "the obligation to implement his knowledge" and "protect the humane values of civilization." Yet what constituted "humane values," "civilization," or even "mankind" was clearly informed by Easton's own national context. Thus his desire for relevance and to fulfill the "special responsibility" of the public intellectual was universalizing in scope but narrow in content.

At no point, however, did Easton entertain the possibility of abandoning positivism as he understood it. To do so would have meant sacrifice of "those criteria which have proved most successful in developing reliable understanding" and which "help to protect the professional scientist from the pressures of society for quick answers" (1969, 1054). Rather, what Easton had in mind was a positivism that kept "alive and active the legitimate long-range interests of all science" even as it embraced values and sought political engagement (1969, 1056; see also Satori 2004). Most positivists propose this kind of balancing act between their epistemology and public engagement, arguing as Flinders and John (2013, 224) do, that, "the trick then for the profession is to find a way to encourage greater technical sophistication . . . but at the same time to ensure that political scientists are encouraged to communicate the findings from this research to the wider world."

The idea that the public intellectual has an ethical responsibility for solving contemporary problems is a primary motivation for positivism's most outspoken critics as well. After having criticized Easton heavily for his scientific pretensions, Ricci's (1984, 304) summation of what is wrong with the discipline – "political studies suffer from overemphasizing science while paying insufficient attention to the realm of morals" – comes strikingly close to Easton's final assessment. In another example, Gregory Kasza (2001, 597) argued in a letter defending the Perestroika movement that one reason "to stop the hard-science project is that its scholarship is increasingly irrelevant to the normative and practical problems of real politics." In its place he argued for an "ecumenical science" that would "unite scholars of diverse methods and approaches around the study of substantive political problems" (Kasza 2001, 598). In the same *PS* issue, another Perestroika supporter lamented that the "scholarly mindset" for statistical analysis "has marginalized the field" so that "policy makers, journalists, and informed citizens have no interest in what most of our modern political scientists have to say about politics" (Brunori 2001, 598–9).

Yet the problem with this collective desire for relevance and social problem-solving is how closely it aligns with and is reflective of the values, judgments, and interests of the democratic, liberal American state. These are political projects in their own right, they are intimately linked to American power and its projection, and their promotion has practical and ethical implications for the rest of the globe. For all its reliance on science and technocracy, the American democratic, liberal state has also thrived (particularly since the mid-twentieth century) on a belief in its own self-importance in determining outcomes for everyone else. Most American IR scholars and political scientists therefore treat democracy, liberalism, and the American state as naturally and obviously desirable end goals or, at the very least, value neutral. The call for relevance to these political projects reflects, as Norton (2004, 68) has observed, a belief "that the vocation of the political scientist is to act in the world for the improvement of the world" and to "move with the good will, the generous heart, the parochial judge consistent with the American historical, political and cultural imagination." Not surprisingly, then, many of the most basic theoretical propositions in the study of American political science and IR (whether realist, liberal, or constructivist) rest on the assumption that what is good for America is good for the rest of the world. They reflect what George Lawson (2008, 26) has referred to as "the cult of the public intellectual," who "fail to engage formatively with the world beyond and outside the West," and so offer a "stilted picture of the world concerned with what 'we' can do either to or for 'them.'"

To make matters worse, there is on the part of American IR scholars almost no attempt to "avoid false universalizations of a specific culture and to analyze the symbolic gains generated by a specific group's own interest in universalism" (Bigo 2011, 233). Of course, one of the reasons the American discipline embraced positivism was to avoid this basic sociology-of-knowledge problem. Positivism's objectification of facts and its rejection of normative concerns were seen as a means to overcome personal and contextual biases (Eagleton-Pierce 2016, 809; Easton 1969, 1057). That solution, however, was a contextual bias in itself. It fitted with the needs of the American state, as both Lowi (1992) and Oren (2003) have argued, which rewarded the scientific, technocratic knowledge produced by the discipline's subscription to positivism, thereby reinforcing it. The hegemony that positivism enjoys is, as it turns out, "to a large extent a product of its compatibility with bureaucratic thoughtways, rather than the result of successful discourse within political science" (Lowi 1992, 3). This casts doubts on the claim that positivism makes communication with policy makers more difficult, since an innate scientific commitment is shared by the American academy and its state. It also helps explain how positivism can be simultaneously hegemonic and a source of continual discontent within large swaths of the discipline.

Yet positivism's critics hardly escape the problem by merely eschewing the methods the American state favors. Their disagreement with it often boils down to whether it makes us as useful as possible to our own social milieu and the political projects it promotes at home and abroad. Debate over epistemology becomes the routine practice of the discipline, thereby masking our collective servitude to be relevant to democracy, liberalism, and the American state. It is this purpose that serves as our common sense, binding us into an academic, professional collective. But because there is almost no practice of reflexivity in American political science, there is almost no recognition that academics "are especially fragile regarding the field of power of the national state from which they have received their education" (Bigo 2011, 230). Instead, American political scientists and IR scholars enthusiastically embrace their role as promoters of democracy, liberalism, and the state and, as Levine and Barder (2014, 865) observe, rarely question what "policymakers wish to steer us toward" or "the moral quality of their goals and the cultural contextual value systems from which those moral considerations spring." Small wonder, then, that Norton (2004, 69), among others, has "come to distrust the scholar activist."

Conclusions

What emerges from this disciplinary historical analysis is less a picture of positivist dominance and more an ongoing disciplinary debate over how best to serve and promote democracy, liberalism, and the state, all of which are largely defined by the specific American national and historical context.[4] If, as Jeffrey Isaac (2015, 273) has put it succinctly, our "*raison d'être* [is] to develop publicly relevant and meaningful knowledge about the world or politics," then positivism may be objectionable because its demands for logic, evidence, causality, and slowly accumulated knowledge clash with a missionary zeal for improving the world right now and according to a particular democratic-liberal vision. Hence the analytical means adopted by most of the profession clashes with the public ends to which the profession aspires. Positivism is not a particularly good epistemological vehicle for achieving the kind of relevance craved by most American political scientists and IR scholars, and yet they seem to be stuck with it.

The unlikely option, then, is that we abandon positivism, because some form of scientism and publically available (i.e., published) results is preferred by the American milieu and the university setting in which academics operate. As Büger and Gadinger (2007, 104) observe,

> [U]nder the conditions of a democratic system, scientists need to justify their existence and the resources they are granted before a wider audience. With presence in the public sphere a group of scientists can easily acquire more resources, but with a lack of such presence they are more likely to lose resources.

Small wonder, then, that positivism has become an embedded disciplinary practice. Alternatively most scholars who recognize the dangers of Lawson's "cult of the public intellectual" (2008) argue that we need to encourage the practice of disciplinary self-reflexivity. "What needs to be objectified," observes Eagleton-Pierce (2016, 816), "are the social conditions that have formed the theorist" and "how the academy is situated in relation to other structures of power in domestic societies and cross-nationally" (see also Berling and Bueger 2013). Self-reflexivity would encourage us to play what Zambernardi (2016, 5) has argued is the "ironic" role "of ensuring that rival explanations can be heard for each problem," rather than the "heroic" role "of providing scientifically derived knowledge by which foreign policy may be guided."

This is a worthy goal, and yet our own scholarly relationship to the larger democratic–liberal–state matrix still remains highly problematic. Given that transmitting ideas about self-reflexivity involves participating in standard disciplinary activity, how can we avoid reproducing the disciplinary common sense and its desires? That is, how can we speak except through the very disciplinary practices that inculcate this common sense? In recognizing the inherent danger of participating in the project of relevancy, Smith (1997, 276) cautioned us that we should "define an intellectual agenda that does not simply maintain and extend the political understandings favored by the powerful." Both Norton (2004) and Smith (1997) recommended instead that we "speak truth to power," as did Morgenthau and many others before them. According to Smith (1997, 276), "we academic political scientists are best equipped institutionally to challenge prevailing wisdom and explore what may prove to be truths about politics that are neglected or unpopular because they go against the grain."

Of course, the terms "speaking" and "truth" deserve critical analysis and self-reflexivity as well. After all, whose truth? On what grounds do we claim a truth position outside the disciplinary common sense? In what ways is this purpose an abdication of responsibility or even an embrace of fatalism? After all, why speak at all? In the context of this chapter, however, the unfortunate conclusion about positivism and relevance must be that, given the historical relationship between the discipline and its social milieu, "speaking truth to power" is the surest path to irrelevancy. The exercise of critical self-reflexivity seems to demand self-imposed professional marginalization in the American context. One senses this in Smith's (1997, 278) own characterization of scholars as "intellectual gadflies" who court "unpopularity by offering suggestions that markets are not likely to reward and that people in power are not likely to approve." The notion that public intellectualism is a political project in its own right with serious ethical implications, and so we should stop promoting it as our purpose, is certainly one of those unpopular suggestions.

Notes

1 Thus when Goodin and Klingemann (1996, 38) took stock of the discipline's shared methodological toolkit through a bibliometric profile of its "integrators," they naturally included IR (although they were also forced to admit that it was one of several subfields exhibiting "a lot of independent development," 25).

2 Ricci (1984, 297) is even more specific about our role and this conflict later: "no matter how important the moral framework of life may be, political science, as practiced scientifically, can pay very little attention to distinctions as basic as those between good and evil. Yet talking to citizens about how to attain the former and avoid the latter has long been a primary mission of those who care deeply about the foundations of social order."

3 They distinguish between liberalism as "the doctrine fashioned in early modern Europe to guide relations between states and their citizens," and democracy, involving concerns over "membership" and "the institutions that would represent the majority and constrain the executive" (2002, 4, 6).

4 While I have focused on the specifics of the American case, the desire for academic relevance and to what or whom would be a concern in any national context, even as the specifics would vary. If some part of the desire for relevance is a response to the demands of liberal democracies, then their current ubiquity would even promote it.

Bibliography

Almond, Gabriel. 1996. "Political Science: The History of the Discipline," in *A New Handbook of Political Science*. Edited by Robert E. Goodin and Hans-Dieter Klingemann. 50–96. Oxford: Oxford University Press.

"An Open Letter to the APSA Leadership and Members." 2000. *PS: Political Science and Politics*. 33 (4) (December): 735–737.

Bennett, Andrew, Aharon Barth, and Kenneth R. Rutherford. 2003. "Do We Preach What We Practice? A Survey of Methods in Political Science Journals and Curricula," *PS: Political Science and Politics*. 36 (July): 381–386.

Bennett, Stephen Earl. 2002. "'Perestroika' Lost: Why the Latest 'Reform' Movement in Political Science Should Fail," *PS: Political Science and Politics*. 35 (2): 177–179.

Berling, Trine Villumsen and Christian Bueger. 2013. "Practical Reflexivity and Political Science: Strategies for Relating Scholarship and Political Practice," *PS: Political Science and Politics*. 46 (1): 115–119.

Bigo, Didier. 2011. "Pierre Bourdieu and International Relations: Power of Practices, Practices of Power," *International Political Sociology*. 5: 225–258.

Brunori, David. 2001. "Opening More Doors," *PS: Political Science and Politics*. 34 (3): 598–599.

Büger, C. and F. Gadinger. 2007. "Reassembling and Dissecting: International Relations Practice from a Science Studies Perspective," *International Studies Perspectives*. 8 (1): 90–110.

Caterino, Brian. 2010. "Perestroika's Last Stand," *PS: Political Science & Politics*. 43 (4) (October): 753–754.

Crawford, Robert M. 2000. *Idealism and Realism in International Relations*. London: Routledge.

Dryzek, John S. 2005. "A Pox on Perestroika, a Hex on Hegemony: Toward a Critical Political Science," in *Perestroika: The Raucous Rebellion in Political Science*. Edited by Kristen Renwick Monroe. 509–525. New Haven: Yale University Press.

Dryzek, John S. 2006. "Revolutions without Enemies: Key Transformations in Political Science," *American Political Science Review*. 4 (November): 487–492.

Eagleton-Pierce, Matthew. 2016. "Advancing a Reflexive International Relations," *Millennium: Journal of International Studies*. 39 (3): 805–823.

Easton, David. 1965. *A Framework for Political Analysis*. Englewood Cliffs, NJ: Prentice-Hall.

Easton, David. 1969. "The New Revolution in Political Science," *American Political Science Review*. 63 (4) (December): 1051–1061.

Ericksson, Johan and Bengt Sundelius. 2005. "Molding Minds That Form Policy: How to Make Research Useful," *International Studies Perspectives*. 6: 51–71.

Flinders, Matthew and Peter John. 2013. "The Future of Political Science," *Political Studies Review*. 11: 222–227.

Goodin, Robert E. and Hans-Dieter Klingemann. 1996. "Political Science: The Discipline," in *A New Handbook of Political Science*. Edited by Robert E. Goodin and Hans-Dieter Klingemann. 3–26. Oxford: Oxford University Press.

Isaac, Jeffrey C. 2015. "For a More Public Political Science," *Perspectives on Politics*. 13 (2) (June): 269–282.

Jentleson, Bruce W. and Ely Ratner. 2011. "Bridging the Beltway – Ivory Tower Gap," *International Studies Review*. 13 (1): 6–11.

Kasza, Gregory. 2001. "Perestroika: For an Ecumenical Science of Politics," *PS: Political Science and Politics*. 34 (3): 597–599.

Katznelson, Ira and Helen V. Milner. 2002. "American Political Science: The Discipline's State and the State of the Discipline," in *Political Science: The State of the Discipline III*. Edited by Ira Katznelson and Helen V. Milner. 1–26. New York: Norton.

Lawson, George. 2008. "For a Public International Relations," *International Political Sociology*. 2 (1): 17–37.

Lepgold, Joseph and Miroslave Nincic. 2001. *Beyond the Ivory Tower: International Relations Theory and the Issue of Policy Relevance*. New York, NY: Columbia University Press.

Levine, Daniel J. and Alexander D. Barder. 2014. "The Closing of the American Mind: 'American School' International Relations and the State of Grand Theory," *European Journal of International Relations*. 20 (4): 863–888.

Lowi, Theodore J. 1992. "The State in Political Science: How We Became What We Study," *American Political Science Review*. 86 (March): 1–7.

Luke, Timothy W. and Patrick J. McGovern. 2010. "The Rebels' Yell: Mr. Perestroika and the Causes of This Rebellion in Context," *PS: Political Science and Politics*. 43 (4): 729–731.

Monroe, Kristen Renwick. 2005. Ed. *Perestroika: The Raucous Rebellion in Political Science*. New Haven: Yale University Press.

Norton, Anne. 2004. "Political Science as a Vocation," in *Problems and Methods in the Study of Politics*. Edited by Ian Shapiro, Rogers M. Smith, and Tarek E. Masoud. 67–83. Cambridge: Cambridge University Press.

Oren, Ido. 2003. *Our Enemies and US: America's Rivalries and the Making of Political Science*. Ithaca, NY: Cornell University Press.

Pion-Berlin, David and Dan Cleary. 2005. "Methodological Bias in the APSR," in *Perestroika: The Raucous Rebellion in Political Science*. Edited by Kristen Renwick Monroe. 304–323. New Haven: Yale University Press.

Ricci, David M. 1984. *Tragedy of Political Science: Politics, Scholarship, and Democracy*. New Haven: Yale University Press.

Rigger, Shelley. 2009. "The Perestroika Movement in American Political Science and Its Lessons for Chinese Political Studies," *Journal of Chinese Political Science*. 14: 369–382.

Rudolph, Susanne. 2005. "Perestroika and Its Other," in *Perestroika: The Raucous Rebellion in Political Science*. Edited by Kristen Renwick Monroe. 12–21. New Haven: Yale University Press.

Sanders, David. 2010. "Behavioral Analysis," in *Theory and Methods in Political Science*, 3rd ed. Edited by David Marsh and Gerry Stoker. 23–42. London: Palgrave Macmillan.

Satori, Giovanni. 2004. "Where Is Political Science Going?," Special Symposium in *PS: Political Science and Politics*. 37 (October): 785–787.

Seidelman, Raymond and Edward J. Harpham. 1985. *Disenchanted Realists: Political Science and the American Crisis*. Albany, NY: SUNY Press.

Smith, Rogers. 1997. "Still Blowing in the Wind: The American Quest for a Democratic, Scientific Political Science," *Daedalus*. 126 (Winter): 253–287.

Smith, Rogers. 2005. "Of Means and Meaning: The Challenges of Doing Good Political Science," in *Perestroika: The Raucous Rebellion in Political Science*. Edited by Kristen Renwick Monroe. 525–534. New Haven: Yale University Press.

Smith, Steve. 2002. "The United States and the Discipline of International Relations: 'Hegemonic Country, Hegemonic Discipline'," *International Studies Review*. 4 (2): 67–85.

Tickner, Arlene B. 2013. "Core, Periphery and (Neo)imperialist International Relations," *European Journal of International Relations*. 19 (3): 627–646.

Walt, Stephen. 2005. "The Relationship between Theory and Policy in International Relations," *Annual Review of Political Science*. 8: 23–48.

Yanow, Dvora. 2003. "Practicing Discipline," *PS-WASHINGTON-*. 36 (3): 397–400.

Yanow, Dvora and Peregrine Schwartz-Shea. 2010. "Perestroika Ten Years after: Reflections on Methodological Diversity," *PS: Political Science & Politics*. 43 (4): 741–745.

Zambernardi, Lorenzo. 2016. "Politics Is Too Important to Be Left to Political Scientists: A Critique of the Theory – Policy Nexus in International Relations," *European Journal of International Relations*. 22 (1): 3–23.

10

DON'T FLATTER YOURSELF

World politics as we know it is changing and so must disciplinary IR

L.H.M. Ling

Given its epistemic history, it is patently clear to me that Disciplinary IR has always been – and continues to serve as – a source of colonial management disguised as knowledge production (Hagmann and Biersteker 2012; Hobson 2012; Ling 2014c; Vitalis 2015). For this reason, I prefer to call Disciplinary IR by what it is: Hypermasculine-Eurocentric Whiteness (HEW). *Hypermasculinity* refers to an ideology that denigrates anything smacking of the feminine: e.g., welfare, intellection, compassion (Nandy 1988). Imperial England used it to colonize India and other parts of the world. *Eurocentrism* regards all things European – people, customs, languages, institutions, philosophies, even fashions and lifestyles – as definitive of "civilization" (Gong 1984; Anghie 2005; Aydin 2007; Bowden 2009; Suzuki 2009). And *Whiteness* constructs a racialized order of privilege and entitlement derived from all of the above (Baldwin 1984; Biss 2015). (Please note: because HEW is based on *ideology*, not biology, it is possible for non-white, non-males to uphold and perpetuate it just as many white males do not.)

HEW has intensified in world politics since 2001. Ever since al Qaeda's attacks on New York and Washington on 9/11, followed by shootings and bombings across the globe but especially in Paris in November 2015, elites in the West have felt justified to return to colonial supremacy in both rhetoric and strategy. On ISIS, for example, US Senator and 2016 presidential candidate Marco Rubio has declared: "In this is a clash of civilizations, either we win, or they win" (Rubio 2015). Others, like French philosopher and public intellectual Bernard-Henri Lévy, predict a third world war in the making: "Today there is again the world war of [sic] which Europe after America is the target" (Rose 2015). Yet the mastermind behind 9/11, Osama bin Laden, had rationalized the attacks as *retribution*: "What the United States tastes today is a very small thing compared to what we have tasted for tens of years. Our nation has been tasting this humiliation and contempt for more than 80 years" (BBC 2001). In other words, they attack us because we had attacked *them* – and over long periods of time.

The discipline itself rationalizes this kind of endless violence. It infiltrates not only what we teach but also how we relate to one another. Let me explain. At a workshop I attended in fall 2015, the discussion turned to IR in Asia. One distinguished professor asserted: "the 'high temple of Westphalianism' is in South Korea and Japan, as much as Thailand and Cambodia. In fact, post-Westphalian thought may be more prevalent in Europe." He concluded with a smile: "So we return to Europe." In other words, despite their access to thousands of years of history, politics, and culture, Asians cannot think in any terms other than those given to them by the West – indeed, they worship blindly at the feet of the Westphalian God; meanwhile, the West remains ever dynamic even in self-critique. So "we return to Europe" – not the diverse, multi-cultural continent of today but yesterday's preserve of colonial-patriarchal whiteness – as the center of all action and thought. Another professor emeritus proclaimed that "the unification of China is actually very Westphalian." Even though China unified in the third century BCE and the Westphalian Treaty was signed in 1648, *20 centuries later*, this professor emeritus would never consider Westphalia in any way "Chinese." For him, Westphalia applies to all, at all times and in all places, going forwards *and* back.

One could dismiss these comments as idiosyncratic but the ideology they express is not. As this chapter shows, these views reflect the very training that Disciplinary IR perpetrates, especially because of its *religious* roots in the Protestant Ethic. One key propagator was John Locke. Preaching frugality as a virtue, he accounted for how and why Proper Protestant Patriarchs could/should educate social "inferiors" like women and children, servants and slaves, not to mention the colonized Other (Dienstag 1996). Kipling called this sense of duty the "white man's burden."

I have long encountered this ideology. It has dogged my study of IR from undergraduate days to the present, in published papers and reviewers' comments, and through conversations with colleagues and friends alike. Encountering it again at this workshop, I suddenly found myself short of breath (Chinese medicine refers to this life-giving force as *qi*). I could not speak even as I wanted to shout: "*Don't flatter yourself.* The world has changed and so must you!" Instead, a profound sense of anger and sadness welled inside. And for a fleeting moment, as I sat in that room with these smug high priests of Disciplinary IR, I suddenly understood ISIS and why so many have joined it. I, too, wanted to bomb the hell out of this world politics. *Let's kill the bastards!* But the moment passed, for I knew that was exactly what HEW wanted. After all, there is no greater justification for the Self than when Others mirror it.

My question thus becomes: "How can we *emancipate* IR?" It needs emancipation not just intellectually and politically but also spiritually. Despite our best efforts to resist and reform, critique and interrogate, Disciplinary IR still mires us in violence. For a way out and *non*-violently, I draw on the ancient Buddhist practice of *kōans*. These seek to "loosen" ways of thinking and feeling that shackle us to established icons, rituals, thoughts, or traditions – even reason itself – so that an enlightenment of the spirit may unfold. *Kōans* typically come in the form of an absurdity, paradox, or *non-sequitur.* A self-knowing laugh, Zen Buddhists believe, enables one to open the heart-mind-soul to understanding and compassion. For this reason, any method that does so qualifies as a *kōan*. Recent attempts on social media to poke fun at ISIS provide one example. That these make people laugh, thereby leaving them less terrified or angry or simply paralyzed, demonstrate a *kōanic* method at work. It counters terrorism by dissolving it.

The chapter begins with a standard manual of training in Disciplinary IR: *Designing Social Inquiry* by King, Keohane, and Verba or KKV (1994). Though dated, KKV still represents the core concepts and methods, norms and principles of Disciplinary IR. Through criteria like *parsimony*, *rigor*, and *autonomy*, KKV extends to social science the Protestant Ethic, long established by a secular parson like Locke. I conclude with the implications of *kōanizing* IR.

Hypermasculine-Eurocentric Whiteness: Disciplinary IR in action

KKV stresses parsimony, rigor, and autonomy as essential criteria for an "objective," "valid" social science. The manual advises the aspiring IR scholar accordingly:

1 **Parsimony**. KKV emphasizes parsimony as the defining criterion of good social science. In "*explaining as much as possible with as little as possible*" (King, Keohane, and Verba 1994, 28, original emphases), the properly trained IR scholar achieves order and control: "If we can accurately explain what at first appears to be a complicated effect with a single causal variable or a few variables, the *leverage* we have over a problem is very high" (King, Keohane, and Verba 1994, 29, original emphasis). Such parsimony requires rigor, both analytical and personal.
2 **Rigor.** Nature, KKV cautions, could drown us in its "blooming, buzzing" randomness. For this reason, we need rigorous methods. These help to uncover an internal logic ("rules") to the particulars we observe, thereby enabling generalization. Causality emerges when behavior or patterns conform to rules, and inference gains validity when it is able to capture causality through "valid procedures" (King, Keohane, and Verba 1994, 34). Rigor ensures autonomy in the pursuit of science.
3 **Autonomy**. Most of all, a scientific life requires a lonely, detached sovereignty. Even when standing on the shoulders of giants, the KKV scholar, like his cousin in natural science, remains an autonomous, solitary figure. (I use the male pronoun deliberately here. After all, who can afford the illusion of "independence" and "autonomy"? Certainly not those who must care for others, especially if they are very young and/or very old.) Skepticism trumps all in KKV. No personal experiences, memories, hopes, and/or aspirations matter. "When told A causes B," KKV instructs, "someone who 'thinks like a social scientist' asks whether that connection is a true causal one" (King, Keohane, and Verba 1994, 30).

Put differently, only results matter. "[N]o one cares what we think – the scholarly community only cares what we can demonstrate" (King, Keohane, and Verba 1994, 15).

Science as a community judges what is "good" research (i.e., "valid inferences") through conventions set down by precedents (i.e., "well-established procedures of inquiry") (King, Keohane, and Verba 1994, 6). Indeed, the individual cannot theorize about the subject under study or why we study what we do or question its fundaments. In KKV-world, neither rules nor patterns in social life have anything to do with the agents of that social life. KKV allows for interpretation only when it narrates the "causal effects" of the "real world." And such approximation is possible only when certainty is established despite the constant reality of uncertainty. "Without a reasonable estimate of uncertainty," KKV instructs, "a description of the real world or an inference about a causal effect in the real world is uninterpretable" (King, Keohane, and Verba 1994, 9).

KKV underscores that only one answer or type of understanding can prevail. If Explanations B, C, or D emerge, then each must show how it adds "extra value" (what Lakatos [1970] called a "progressive research program") to the original Explanation A to obtain validation. The analyst can only replace Explanation A with a better, more comprehensive alternative rather than ask: How do Explanations A, B, C, and D *interact* and what insights can we gain therein? With singularity and certainty, the KKV analyst gains not just knowledge but also social power. Strategies for action thus reflect the expert's predictions based on formulaic abstractions, rather than any understanding drawn from local contexts or sources. These attributes of "valid social science" reflect a legacy of the Protestant Ethic, as defined by one of its leading proponents: John Locke.

Locke's paradox

Many have wondered about Locke's paradox. How could someone who believed in individual liberty also condone slavery? Locke's commitment to parsimony, rigor, and autonomy, I submit, accounts for this contradiction and his ability to bridge it. I derive this understanding from Dienstag's (1996) exemplary article on Locke, "Serving God and Mammon." Dienstag himself does not use these categories but they fit substantively:

1 **Parsimony as Virtue in Labor and Frugality**. For Locke, labor serves as a source of salvation for all, even slaves. Such freedom would grant more than physical liberty; it would bring about a moral and intellectual emancipation as well. "Slavery, for [Locke]," writes Dienstag (1996, 503), "is something that can appear in thought as well as in action." Such emancipation, in turn, requires parsimony in action and thought: that is, frugality as a virtue. Savings are for re-investment, not immediate consumption or enjoyment (Locke would disapprove strongly, I suspect, of contemporary capitalism with its neoliberal glee for instant gratification). Extravagance squanders the fruits of one's labor and, by extension, one's virtue. To follow the dictates of frugality, one must instill a sense of rigor – and that comes only from education.

2 **Rigor through Discipline and Education**. Lockean education "chastens." One must suffer in body and soul to learn: "Rather than book learning, it is the conditioning of the body and the spirit that most concern Locke. His concern is manifested in a chastening education meant to impose a severe discipline upon children from the earliest possible age . . . The target of this training is not just the body but the mind as well. Through severity Locke aims to foster good morals" (Dienstag 1996, 502). Above all else, Protestant education prevents surrender to sin. Locke explicitly admitted as much: "Whoever will list himself under the banner of Christ, must, in the first place, and above all things, make war upon his own lusts and vices" (Locke quoted in Dienstag 1996, 502).

3 **Manly Autonomy**. Freedom arrives when the mind rules the body, enabling a manly autonomy: "The self-denial that was enforced on the child by his teacher is, for the adult, enforced on his body by his mind . . . And this notion of liberty means that the mind should not be subject, as far as possible, to the influence of physical pleasure and pain. It is this conception of freedom which allows Locke to equate such threats to liberty as the physical temptation to pleasure and the threat of injury at the hands of an absolute government: Both threaten to make concerns of the body overwhelm the freedom of thought . . . The Protestant Ethic allows Locke to be equally hostile to authoritarian government and physical pleasure. One does not seek freedom from absolute government in order to pursue one's wants but to fulfill one's duties" (Dienstag 1996, 503).

From this brief exposition, we see how KKV smuggles in Locke's Protestant Ethic to discipline IR. Its lofty claim of a "valid social science" actually covers for something quite different. As demonstrated by Locke himself, the *real* purpose of parsimony, rigor, and autonomy is to emancipate both body and soul from sin and temptation. The "concerns of the body" cannot – must not – "overwhelm the freedom of thought." Otherwise, women and other sources of unmanliness could gain the upper hand. Chaos would ensue. To prevent such an aberration, Disciplinary IR must follow Locke's Proper Protestant Patriarch: it must "educate" and "discipline" all Others, especially if deemed "savage" (Sampson 2002). Given that Locke considered members of his own family – i.e., women and children – as part of the "inferior" Other, then all those who fall outside of his Self identity, including males who may be white but Catholic, must abide by Hypermasculine-Eurocentric Whiteness. And if not, woe to the "deviant," the "indigene," the "colonized," the "slave"!

It should be clear by now: Disciplinary IR cannot deal with Others. As taught by KKV via John Locke, Disciplinary IR cannot meet the Other on its own terms – even when structures and actors change (Shiraishi 2012). Given that absolute control over both body and mind are not possible – at least, not all the time – HEW must concentrate all its efforts and resources on maintaining the Self. Such unrelenting Self-absorption *necessarily* interprets any kind of departure from singularity and certainty – i.e., multiplicity and difference – as confusion (Prozorov 2014) or threat (Inayatullah and Blaney 2003). Consequently, HEW seeks always to reduce or contain or, best of all, erase the Other, both externally *and* internally (Shaw 2008). Such insecurity and pathos in the Self, now transplanted to the State, can only enrage Others and lead to predictable outcomes. Violence thus bedevils both Self and Other.

We need to undiscipline IR. *Kōans* can help.

Undisciplining IR: *kōanic* relief

Buddhist *kōans* originated in Tang China as "public records" (*gong an*). These presented a case on trial through argumentation and speech, reasoning and judgment. Later, this practice became known in Japan as *kōan* and subsequently entered the West under this term. Reflecting its origin in Daoist and Hindu dialectics, augmented by traditional Chinese literary games like competition, on-the-spot spontaneity, turning the tables, and mind-to-mind transmission (Hori 2003), a *kōan* aims to startle one from complacency in thought or worship. Usually, this takes the form of *non-sequiturs*, puzzles, or funny stories. "*Kōans* exhaust the logical activity of the mind so that the mind will break out of its conventional view of the nature of reality" (Grenard 2008, 153).

A well-known *kōan* tradition comes from the Japanese Zen master, Dōgen (1200–1253). He often rewrote original *kōans* with commentaries to reverse conventional understandings so as "to support several different didactic and metaphysical positions concerning the doctrines, rituals, and practices of Zen monastic life" (Heine 2004, 5). One example involves an old woman and a monk. A monk encounters an old woman selling rice cakes by the side of a road. He asks for one but she poses a question. On the condition that he is able to answer it, she will give him a rice cake. She then asks a deep, almost mystical question regarding the Buddhist concept of the "ungraspable mind." The monk is struck speechless and the old woman leaves without selling him a rice cake.

Heine (2004, 9) writes:

> Dōgen's commentary tries to reverse the conventional understanding by criticizing the woman as well as [the monk]. Dōgen points out that while [the monk] thought that he was "checking out" the old woman, it turned out that she had checked him out and found him wanting. [Dōgen] challenges [the monk] for not asking in response to her query, "If I cannot answer your question, what would you say?" But Dōgen also suggests that she should have said, "Venerable priest, if you cannot answer my question, try asking me a question to see if I can answer you."

Dōgen's commentary, Heine suggests, encourages both the monk and the old woman to begin a dialogue by asking questions. In this way, they may begin to engage with each other, rather than stay in their respective, socially assigned identities as "venerable monk" and "old woman who sells rice cakes." The monk could enact Buddhist humility by ceding religious authority to the old woman. And the old woman could enact her dignity as a person who is worthy of asking and answering a question to a venerable monk.

Kōans need not stem from Buddhism, per se, or even Asian culture. Similar kinds of subversion enjoy a long-standing tradition in the West as well (note Aristophanes' comic-caustic plays in ancient Greece as well as contemporary programs like *The Daily Show with Jon Stewart*). Indeed, any method that shakes us from standard thinking, stimulates self-reflection, and provokes detachment from icons qualifies as a *kōan*.

Making fun of ISIS

Recent attempts at ridiculing ISIS provide a kind of *kōanic* relief from terrorism (Gunter 2015). "These people are not a true representation of Islam and so by mocking them, it is a way to show that we are against them," explains the producer of a satirical show in Lebanon (McLaughlin 2015). Through songs, skits, plays, and posters, dissidents expose the hypocrisy and ad-hockery of ISIS: e.g., the drunkard who's in charge of banning alcohol, militants who propagandize a medieval way of life on their cellphones while riding in cabs, soldiers who "play air guitar with rifles and juggle with human skulls" (McLaughlin 2015). The Internet has also Photoshopped yellow rubber ducks onto the heads of ISIS militants. One poster shows a duckified ISIS militant with the headline, "Interview with Abu Muquack." The interview proceeds accordingly: "Quack quack quack quack . . . Quack!"

In laughing at ISIS, we open up cognitive and emotional space from terror. From this basis, we can engage with the Other on its own terms, possibly finding commonalities previously not detected. In interviews with twenty-somethings in Paris, London, and Barcelona, "as well as with captured ISIS fighters in Iraq and Jabhat an-Nusra (al-Qaeda) fighters from Syria," two researchers have found that Western arrogance, contempt, and ignorance account for why Muslim youths from the West want to join ISIS to fight the West (Atran and Hamid 2015):

> They [Western society] teach us to work hard to buy a nice car and nice clothes but that isn't happiness. I was a third-class human because I wasn't integrated into a corrupted system. But I didn't want to be a street gangster. So, I and my friends simply decided to go around and invite people to join Islam. The other Muslim groups in the city just talk. They think a true Muslim state will just rain from heaven on them without fighting and striving hard on the path of Allah.
>
> (24-year-old male recruit to Jabhat an-Nusra in Syria)

Indeed, ISIS wants the Other to remain alienated:

> ISIS has managed to insert itself, with no small amount of cunning, and with acute sensitivity to feelings of humiliation, into two of the most intractable conflicts of our time: the relationship of European societies to their internal,

> Muslim 'others' and the sectarian power struggles that have engulfed the lands of Iraq and Syria since 2003.
>
> (Shatz 2015, 14)

Kōanizing IR

We need to *kōanize* IR. Elsewhere, I detail what this process entails (Ling 2016a). Here, I comment only on how *kōans* can help loosen the Protestant grip on IR by creating cognitive and emotional space for Others. I draw on the four basic components of a *kōanic* method: (1) questioning assumptions, (2) investigating possibilities for action, (3) breaking through words and letters, and (4) cutting attachment to one's own awakening.

In questioning assumptions, *kōans* open the possibility of dialogue between constructed opposites. As underscored by his commentary on the old woman and the monk, Dōgen suggests questions based on mutual respect as the best way to proceed. In this way, singularity and certainty can meet their nemeses, multiplicity and difference, on equal terms. Clashes may occur but, over time, something else wholly unexpected happens: enlightenment. Instead of the Protestant version of enlightenment, defined as the conquest of one realm (mind) over another (body), *kōans* simply awaken us to the possibility of compassion (Hori 2003). It arises from what may seem a counter-intuitive realization: that is, when we extend compassion to the Self, instead of imposing strictures and taboos, we extend compassion to the Other as well. From this basis, possibilities for innovative action emerge. We no longer "educate" Others, as preached by Locke; instead, we embark on a journey of *self*-discovery. It breaks through "words and letters," leading to a trans-subjective fusion. We begin to realize "you are in me just as I am in you" (Ling 2014a).

The Buddhist monk and teacher, Thich Nhat Hanh (1987), calls it "interbeing." More than simply imagining the Other, interbeing requires actual engagement. Thich Nhat Hanh elaborates:

> What are we to be in touch with? The answer is reality, the reality of the world and the reality of the [true] mind . . . Getting in touch with true mind is like digging deep in the soil and reaching a hidden source that fills our well with fresh water. When we discover our true mind, we are filled with understanding and compassion, which nourishes us and those around us as well.
>
> (Nhat Hanh 1998, 3)

Still, we need to "cut attachment to one's own enlightenment." *Kōans* prevent reproducing another binary, now perhaps framed as Buddhist awakening versus Protestant freedom, by recognizing the necessity of duality *within* non-duality. Otherwise, another duality would prevail. Even as we seek integration across opposites, *kōans* remind us, each element retains its own specificity. This reflects Buddhism's grounding in *Advaita* monism (Shahi and Ascione 2015) as much as *Daoist* dialectics (Ling 2014a). I review the latter here briefly.

Yin/yang dialectics

The *Daodejing* (*Classic of the Way*, Ames and Hall 2003) posits two polar opposites that are also ontologically equal. *Yin*, the black sphere, represents the "female" principle; *yang*, the white sphere, comprises the "male" principle. Each opposes the other (black versus white), but each also exists within the other (black-within-white, white-within-black). An inherent simultaneity follows: conflicts and contradictions (*yin* versus *yang*) operate in tandem with complicities and connections (*yin*-within-*yang*, *yang*-within-*yin*). In this way, the *dao* accounts for continuity *and* change, connections *and* conflicts, masculinity *and* femininity, duality *and* non-duality. For this reason, the *Daodejing* teaches balance or harmony between *yin* and *yang* to realize the totality of the Way.

Kōans draw on *yin/yang* dialectics to integrate opposites. One method comes from what Zen Buddhism calls the five-rank protocol (Loori 2009). The first two ranks – "the relative within the absolute" and "the absolute within the relative" – caution, in effect, that appearances can be deceiving. Things may seem different on the surface (e.g., *yin* vs. *yang*) but they share a common essence underneath (e.g., *yin*-within-*yang*, *yang*-within-*yin*). Even so, the common essence in different things does not negate each entity's unique qualities (e.g., *yin* still conveys all things "feminine;" *yang*, all that is "masculine"). From these two ranks, the third one – "coming from within the absolute" – becomes possible. Here, we begin to see and treat the two parts, relative (*yin*) and absolute (*yang*), as one. Compassion arises and enlightenment begins. A fourth rank – "arriving at mutual integration" – urges action based on this insight. "At this stage, the absolute and relative are integrated, but they're still two things" (Loori 2009, xxvii). For this reason, we need a fifth rank – "unity attained" – to affirm "[t]here is no more duality. [The entity] is one thing – neither absolute nor relative, up nor down, profane nor holy, good nor bad, male nor female" (Loori 2009, xxvii).

With *yin/yang* dialectics, we have Disciplinary IR *and kōanic* IR *along with* their integration. Parsimony, rigor, and autonomy do not disappear; neither do their polar opposites in excess, flexibility, and relationality. Both contribute to the totality of world politics. *Each also exists within the other.* In recognizing that parsimony-rigor-autonomy operates within excess-flexibility-relationality, like Islamic science (Zaid 2003) – as much as the reverse – like neoliberal capitalism (Chang 2007, 2010), one can no longer set up a global hierarchy of asymmetrical norms. Indeed, any supposed conquest or triumph imposed by one realm (e.g., Protestant-Self-Mind) over another (ISIS-Other-Body) simply redounds back to haunt the source. In short, targeting the Other also hurts the Self. Accordingly, a war-like, hegemonic ultimatum becomes impossible. A *kōanic* method dismantles chest-beating claims like "either we win or they win." Under *kōanic* IR, we all lose and win together.

Conclusion

Kōans rouse those who are asleep, not just intellectually and politically, but also emotionally and spiritually. Here, awakening means realizing our essential but dynamic non-duality (compassion) in a dualistic (passionate) world. For this reason, a *kōan* raises doubt – especially self-doubt. Doing so simultaneously brackets the familiar and highlights the unfamiliar. Distinctions between Self and Other, Subject and Object, fall aside, no longer occupying the center of our concerns, yet they remain distinctively present at the same time.

Kōanizing IR enables what Feyerabend (1999) called a "richness of being." Multiplicity and difference can share cognitive and emotional space with singularity and certainty. It is the tension between them that stimulates creativity and learning, like the parodies of ISIS that we so desperately need in today's world politics. "Digging deep in the soil" of our souls to reach that "hidden source [of nourishing] fresh water" enables an openness to the absurd, the nonsensical, and the hermeneutic. It helps to shift the deadly consequences of the self-righteous and self-referential, like those high priests of Disciplinary IR I encountered at the workshop in the fall of 2015. With cognitive levity, the study and practice of world politics can attain some semblance of reason, reality, and sustainable knowledge (Särmä 2014). By the latter, I mean a recognition of the ontological parity of all: even an old woman who sells rice cakes by the side of a road could equal or surpass a venerable master monk in her knowledge of Buddhist doctrine. From this basis, real engagement can take place between Self and Other. We may paddle closer, then, to a *kōanic* shore: "awakened wisdom and selfless compassion" (Hori 2003, 6).

Bibliography

Ames, Roger T. and David L. Hall. 2003. Trans. *Dao De Jing: A Philosophical Translation.* New York: Ballantine Books.

Anghie, Anthony. 2005. *Imperialism, Sovereignty, and the Making of International Law.* Cambridge: Cambridge University Press.

Anonymous. 2015. "The Mystery of ISIS." *New York Review of Books*, 13 August. Accessed November 29,2015. http://www.nybooks.com/articles/archives/2015/aug/13/mystery-isis/

Atran, Scott and Nafees Hamid. 2015. "Paris: The War ISIS Wants." *New York Review of Books Daily*, 16 November. Accessed December 1, 2015. http://www.nybooks.com/blogs/nyrblog/2015/nov/16/paris-attacks-isis-strategy-chaos/

Aydin, Cemil. 2007. *The Politics of Anti-Westernism in Asia: Visions of World Order in Pan-Islamic and Pan-Asian Thought.* New York: Columbia University Press.

Baldwin, James. 1984. "On Being White. . . And Other Lies." Accessed December 31, 2015. http://www.cwsworkshop.org/pdfs/CARC/Family_Herstories/2_On_Being_White.PDF

BBC. 2001. "Bin Laden's Warning: Full Text." *BBC*, 7 October. Accessed July 7, 2016. http://news.bbc.co.uk/2/hi/south_asia/1585636.stm

Biss, Eula. 2015. "Debt: Reckoning with What Is Owed – and What Can Never Be Paid." *New York Times Magazine*, 6 December: 50–51, 83.

Bowden, Brett. 2009. *The Empire of Civilization: The Evolution of an Imperial Idea.* Chicago: The University of Chicago Press.

Chang, Ha-Joon. 2007. *Kicking Away the Ladder: Development Strategy in Historical Perspective.* London: Anthem Press.

Chang, Ha-Joon. 2010. *23 Things They Don't Tell You about Capitalism.* New York: Bloomsbury Press.

Dienstag, Joshua Foa. 1996. "Serving God and Mammon: The Lockean Sympathy in Early American Political Thought." *American Political Science Review* 90 (3) September: 497–511.

Gong, Gerrit W. 1984. *The Standard of "Civilization" in International Society*. Oxford: Clarendon Press.

Grenard, Jerry L. 2008. "The Phenomenology of Koan Meditation in Zen Buddhism." *Journal of Phenomenological Psychology* 39: 151–188.

Gunter, Joel. 2015. "ISIS Mocked with Rubber Ducks as Internet Fights Terror with Humour." *The Guardian*, 28 November. Accessed December 1, 2015. http://www.theguardian.com/world/2015/nov/28/isis-fighters-rubber-ducks-reddit-4chan

Hagmann, Jonas and Thomas J. Biersteker. 2012. "Beyond the Published Discipline: Towards a Critical Pedagogy of International Studies." *European Journal of International Relations* 20 (2): 291–315.

Heine, Steven. 2004. "Kōans in the Dōgen Tradition: How and Why Dōgen Does What He Does with Kōans." *Philosophy East & West* 54 (1) January: 1–19.

Hobson, John M. 2012. *The Eurocentric Conception of World Politics: Western International Relations Theory, 1760–2010*. Cambridge: Cambridge University Press.

Hori, Victor Sōgen. 2003. *Zen Sand: The Book of Capping Phrases for Kōan Practice*. Honolulu: University of Hawai'i Press.

Inayatullah, Naeem and David Blaney. 2003. *International Relations and the Problem of Difference*. London: Taylor & Francis.

Lakatos, Imre. 1970. "Falsification and the Methodology of Scientific Research Programmes." In *Criticism and the Growth of Knowledge*. Edited by Imre Lakatos and Alan Musgrove. 170–196. Cambridge: Cambridge University Press.

Ling, L. H. M. 2014a. *The Dao of World Politics: Towards a Post-Westphalian, Worldist International Relations*. London: Routledge.

Ling, L. H. M. 2014b. "Decolonizing the International: Towards Multiple Emotional Worlds." *International Theory* 6 (3) November: 579–583.

Ling, L. H. M. 2014c. "Hobson's Eurocentric World Politics: The Journey Begins." *Millennium: Journal of International Studies* 42 (2): 456–463.

Ling, L. H. M. 2016a. "*Kōanizing* IR: Flipping the Logic of Epistemic Violence." Keynote address for a symposium on "Beyond 'West' and 'Rest': A Critical Inquiry into the Dichotomized Ontology of International Relations." Ryukoku University, Kyoto, 27 February 2016.

Ling, L. H. M. 2016b. "What's in a Name? A Critical Interrogation of the *Chinese* School of *IR*." In *Constructing a Chinese School(s) of IR: Ongoing Debates and Critical Assessment*. Edited by Richard Little, Yongjin Zhang, and Simon Chang. 17–35. London: Routledge.

Loori, John Daido. 2009. *The True Dharma Eye: Zen Master Dōgen's Three Hundred Kōans*, translated by Kazuaki Tanahashi and John Daido Loori. Boston: Shambhala.

McLaughlin, Jenna. 2015. "The Case for Making Fun of ISIS." *Mother Jones*, 6 March. Accessed November 29, 2015. http://www.motherjones.com/politics/2015/03/snl-dakota-johnson-isis-middle-east-satirical-cartoons

Nandy, Ashis. 1988. *The Intimate Enemy: The Psychology of Colonialism*. New Delhi: Oxford University Press.

Nhat Hanh, Thich. 1998. *Interbeing: Fourteen Guidelines for Engaged Buddhism*. Berkeley: Parallax Books.

Prozorov, Sergei. 2014. *Ontology and World Politics*. London: Routledge.

Rose, Charlie. 2015. "Paris Terror Attacks." November 16, 2015. Accessed July 7, 2016. https://charlierose.com/videos/22388

Rubio, Marco. 2015. "This Is a Clash of Civilizations: Either They Win or We Win." *YouTube*, 14 November. Accessed July 7, 2016. https://www.youtube.com/watch?v=q8qa2ZRaOmc

Sampson, A. B. 2002. "Tropical Anarchy: Waltz, Wendt, and the Way We Imagine International Politics." *Alternatives: Global, Local, Political* 27 (4): 429–457.

Särmä, Saara. 2014. *Junk Feminism and Nuclear Wannabes: Collaging Parodies of Iran and North Korea*. PhD Dissertation, School of Management, University of Tampere, 5 September.

Shahi, Deepshikha and Gennaro Ascione. 2015. "Rethinking the Absence of Post-Western International Relations Theory in India: 'Advaitic Monism' as an Alternative Epistemological Resource." *European Journal of International Relations* 22 (2): 313–334.

Shatz, Adam. 2015. "Magical Thinking about ISIS." *London Review of Books* 37 (23), 3 December: 11–14.

Shaw, Karena. 2008. *Indigeneity and Political Theory: Sovereignty and the Limits of the Political*. New York: Routledge.

Shiraishi, Takeshi. 2012. "The Rise of China and Its Implications for East Asia." In *Sinicization and the Rise of China: Civilizational Processes beyond East and West*. Edited by Peter J. Katzenstein. 120–150. London: Routledge.

Suzuki, Shogo. 2009. *Civilization and Empire: China and Japan's Encounter with European International Society*. New York: Routledge.

Vitalis, Robert. 2015. *White World Order, Black Power Politics: The Birth of American International Relations*. Ithaca: Cornell University Press.

Zaid, Ahmad. 2003. *The Epistemology of Ibn Khaldun*. London: Routledge Curzon.

11

INDIAN IR

Older and newer orientations

Achin Vanaik

Since the turn of the new millennium, developments in IR and elsewhere have had an important and expanding resonance in Indian IR as well. This has generated newer directions in the discourse in India that need to be explored for their possible consequences for future policy, practice and activism even though the dominant current continues to understand IR as being about state foreign policy behavior and advocacy. Despite a considerable time lag compared to even China, there is now growing awareness of a multiplicity of approaches going beyond realism (in all its variants), liberalism and neo-liberalism that need to be absorbed in academia. This has led to the emergence of newer IR currents having a strong research bent towards post-Western theorizing and whose spreading acceptance it is believed can create a more humane world because of a more culturally diverse understanding of the global order. But a serious lacuna in Indian IR is the relative absence of a strong current seeking to come to proper grips with the political economy of globalizing capitalism and how this must shape the IR agenda everywhere so as to address better today's unique dangers to the human species itself. Whether the community of IR scholars, well aware that India is an "emerging power" which will play an increasingly significant role in shaping the world order, will take up this responsibility remains an open question.

The dominant approach

So much of IR research has been little more than rationalization and legitimization from afar of that Indian foreign policy. From afar because the political leadership and policy bureaucracy, i.e., the decision makers/shapers, insulated themselves from the IR academy whose public role in serving as apologists or mild critics was less than that of a free, but politically speaking, largely supine mass media. This is now changing, but slowly. Up to the 1990s two government-funded think tanks – the

Indian Centre for World Affairs and the Institute of Defence Studies and Analysis (and their house journals) – provided minor recommendations within the existing framework of official thinking. With the accelerated insertion of the country into the global capitalist economy, some big Indian corporate houses have begun to exercise a degree of influence on foreign policy while a new levy of privately funded think tanks (including those being indirectly controlled by political parties) have emerged that make "policy-relevant" advocacy – not disinterested or critical academic study – their main concern when researching international matters. The Rajiv Gandhi Foundation, headed by Sonia Gandhi of the Congress Party, was established in New Delhi in 1991. The Vivekananda International Foundation and the India Foundation, both in New Delhi, were established after the new millennium and are headed by figures chosen by the leaders of the RSS/BJP. The RSS, or Rashtriya Swayamsevak Sangh (National Volunteer Corps), is the parent body of the ensemble of Hindu nationalist organizations, and the Bharatiya Janata Party (BJP) is its political-electoral wing currently in power at the center.

Even the one major study of current foreign policy by a group of independent analysts, which produced a report titled *Nonalignment 2.0*, broadly endorsed government policies, namely the shift economically to neoliberal capitalism, the Indo–US nuclear deal and nuclear weapons acquisition, and welcomed the fact that a stronger India could now play a more "responsible" and positive regional role. The report in contradictory fashion endorsed the closer tie-up with the United States even while warning against efforts to contain China, as if the second was not implicit in the first. All in all, it sought to portray an India operating in basic continuity with its past in supposedly pursuing strategic autonomy, hence the gloss contained in its title. This report, administratively supported by the government's National Defence College and by an autonomous think tank – the Centre for Policy Research, was presented in 2012. It has not proven noteworthy in the public domain where the dominant view is that past "nonalignment" (emphasizing economic self-reliance along with moral posturing) has deservedly died now that bloc politics has ended, a more self-assertive India is awakening and a globalizing capitalism is the main game in town.

These developments reflect a growing nexus between government personnel (active and retired) and some civil society organizations. Attempts to regularize connections between the government, the media and some university departments regarding discourses on IR, as in the United States, is still in the infant stage. The post of National Security Advisor was established only in 1998 as was a National Security Advisory Board that could bring in – among other civilian appointees – select academics. Insofar as Indian academics want to be policy influential, they can hardly be severe critics of either the neoliberal global economic order (let alone of capitalism) or dare to characterize Indian geopolitical behavior as expressing the ambitions of what I would call a regional imperialism in the making, while others would situate the Indian case in the wider category of emerging or emergent sub-imperial powers (Bond and Garcia 2016). Indeed, the bulk of work produced by Indian IR scholars that is policy orientated is realist in nature, reinforcing the current trajectory of promoting an "Asian NATO"; namely an alliance in all but name between the United States (as the lead power) in concert with Japan, Australia, India and South Korea, with supplementary help sought from other Southeast Asian countries for the purposes of "balancing" China (MacDonald 2002).

This is a perspective that appeals to Asian elites, since even more than Africa the Asian continent is replete with various nationalist tensions, making the pursuit of even milder forms of continental unity beyond the economic much more difficult. The United States sees China as the main challenger to its primacy in Asia and the world. Few voices in India – journalistic, political or academic – propose the development of an alternative "Asian Security system" that excludes the United States in the way, for example, that it would never tolerate an outside power involving itself in any "security framework" for the Americas. Such a framework carefully thought out and planned can greatly diminish intra-Asian rivalries by, for example, making disputed island territories in Eastern waters "regional entities" to be jointly administered for the mutual benefit of all the disputing parties.

One way of moving in this direction is the idea of building an Asian Collective Energy Security Grid with oil and gas pipelines running horizontally across the Asian landmass from Iran and beyond through Central Asia all the way to East Asia and vertically down to the countries of South and Southeast Asia. This would be highly beneficial cost-wise to both energy-producing and energy-consuming countries and was recognized as such by both. This would also deprive the United States of the leverage it has over Europe, China, India and Japan by virtue of its control of sea-lanes for tanker transportation from West Asia. In fact, former Indian Petroleum Minister Mani Shankar Aiyar in November 2005 actually set up a ministerial round table conference where representatives of key Asian producing and consuming countries came together to approve such a proposal. Aiyar, a maverick within the Congress Party, has always been its most critical voice on the neoliberal economic turn and on the strategic shift towards the United States. Aiyar's subsequent transfer from this post to a more junior cabinet position, to the obvious delight of the US administration, put paid to any further exploration of the idea (Vanaik 2014, 30).

Critical and non-realist IR currents: the specter of Eurocentrism

There are Indian scholars who would consciously buck realism's theoretical grip and comprehensively reject the idea that IR must serve Indian national interests. But from their ranks very few are attracted to constructivist and feminist approaches, and even fewer would see themselves as adherents of critical international theory, let alone operate within a broad neo-Marxist framework. Regarding this non-realist current, one scholar has suggested three "likely trajectories in Indian IR in the foreseeable future" (Behera 2013, 41): (i) local theorizing using Western derived concepts/frameworks to creatively understand India and South Asia; (ii) creating a niche approach drawing on India's intellectual resources dating to even the ancient past that Western practitioners are unfamiliar with and uninterested in to, for example, elucidate a distinctive Indian understanding of diplomacy; and (iii) using Indian intellectual resources to help fashion a post-Western IR by creating a space for equality of dialogue between plural views of IR that is devoid of assumptions of hierarchy and superiority, i.e., in opposition to a Eurocentric "imperialism of categories."

This last is a trope common to defenders of indigenism/nativism and to post-colonial theory (even if each takes different directions) and is by far the most innovative and influential trend among critical approaches. This post-Western IR positions itself as strongly critical of conventional IR theories and seeks to contribute to the making of a more humane global order precisely through an epistemic revolution that would reject Eurocentrism as well as recognize that there are "multiple modernities" (MM) that must now interface in ways that can promote greater collective understanding and respect. This group of Indian IR scholars can look forward to becoming stronger and more influential since it is part of a much wider intellectual stream in the social sciences generally that has moved toward accepting the paradigm of MM. The critique, methodology and substance of MM and post-Western IR go together. Whatever their virtues, they also constitute a diversion of sorts – intellectually and politically-practically – from what I believe *should* be the relationship of IR (in India and elsewhere) to policy, practice and activism today.

MM and the Indian search for a post-Western IR

The claim that modernity originates in Europe and then spreads outwards is rejected by scholars working in the MM tradition. Insofar as there has been a multiple reality of different cultures with different institutions, practices and mentalities shaping their respective political and civilizational histories, there is no place for a misleading master narrative about modernity that marginalizes non-Western voices and experiences by presenting European values and thought as universal and showing the way to others. What exist instead are multiple modernities. This discourse was effectively initiated at the turn of the new millennium by a Western revisionist scholar, S. N. Eisenstadt (Eisenstadt 2000). Many Indian origin contributors have since implicitly or explicitly endorsed this paradigm shift (Kaviraj 2005). Yet another IR school where Indian origin scholars have made seminal contributions is that of connected histories that indict MM for being insufficiently post-Western in the task of developing a truly global historical sociology that recognizes the global as the condition and not the consequence of modernity (Bhambra 2011c).

MM implies that alongside multiple diversities there is a common core across differences relating to institutions (mainly economic and political) created by the history and legacies of European colonial expansionism across the world. But even these function in ways different from their operation in the West. Yes, there is a special kind of newness about modernity as compared to passages of change in the past that justifies it being seen as a distinctive kind of change, hence that it is "modern." This does not mean MM advocates would accept that there is anything like a *profound* rupture between modernity and pre-modernity in that the rate, depth and scope of change in modernity is of an incomparably greater order. To accept this would then focus attention on the strongest explanatory candidate by far: capitalism. Rather, some would insist that acceleration is historically cumulative, average growth rates more in the nineteenth century than in the eighteenth, more in the twentieth than in the nineteenth, and which will be more in the twenty-first than in the twentieth (Mukhia 2013, 15). What would not be conceded here is that the very *regularity* of such accelerations (beyond economic ups and downs) is a function of the internal dynamics of capitalist competition and not of an "antecedent accelerating pace" (Mukhia 2013, 15).

There is, of course, a range of disagreements about how accelerated or changed today's modernity(ies) is/are from the past. The temporal differentiation from the pre-modern past is taken as necessarily less than the spatial differentiation between cultural-civilizational clusters, i.e., the cultural-civilizational continuity *within* each cluster is *the* key to explaining the very fact of MM. Logically enough this leads to a search for those long-standing essences or characteristics that are indigenous to that culture/civilization/society/nation or however else one may wish to describe it. This is where post-Western IR and the Indian contribution can come in. Insofar as IR has a philosophical grounding which is said to be Western, there is a need to broaden this philosophical base by, for example, learning from the history of Indian political thought and practice and also from other non-Western intellectual traditions. After all, even those scholars who believe that there is a somewhat obsessive and unbalanced critique of conceptual Eurocentrism would postulate a broader Eurasian modernity, pointing out the intellectual debt of ancient Greece to Egyptian, Persian and even the Indus Valley civilizations (Dirlik 1994).

An alternative universalism could then emerge that is more solidaristic because, unlike in the West, it is not based on fundamental binaries of thought and self. IR need not aim to be scientific-universal since to explain better much of human behavior, we need to grasp these spiritualized and non-scientific worldviews (Acharya 2011, 633–636). This Indian IR perspective is a reminder that the principles of Kautilyan statecraft as laid out in the *Arthashastra* is the real forerunner to realism as a theorization of realpolitik and therefore very much worth incorporating in the study of IR everywhere. More importantly, India's truly unique scale and longevity of "unity in diversity," its lived tolerances, its understandings of how to live with and accept inescapable differences, can offer lessons of global scope and application. Since social reality is decisively shaped by how we perceive it, IR is especially well placed to be an agent of transformation if it pluralizes itself to be genuinely dialogical and therefore better able to deal with local, regional and global problems through the promotion of a more peaceful and harmonious coexistence and cooperation.

The Indian contribution to this reshaping of the discipline will require mining the religiously inspired thought of figures like Gandhi and Tagore who believed in the reconciliation of opposites and unity through the recognition of differences. Most helpful perhaps would be the Vedic concept of Advaita or non-dualist monism rejecting binaries of the self and other, subject and object, creator and creation, and conducive therefore to the development of a fluid more harmonious, non-hierarchical self less imposing on others, wherein the sense of power is more inward-directed seeking self-mastery rather than, as in the West, other-directed.

This then is the direction being taken by the minority Indian IR current that wishes to contribute to the fashioning of a post-Western IR. This effort is not meant to install an Indian ethnocentrism, but to help develop a more refined and deeper understanding of IR as discipline and reality. As of now the analytical fruits are still very much in the early stages and are better understood as tentative propositions than detailed and systematized arguments.

A critique

To claim that the political philosophy and thought in the texts of ancient India and in the writings of modern Indian thinkers that are based on that intellectual heritage remain highly relevant is to claim a trans-historical autonomy of the political and ideological which is not shaped by the historically constituted and changing conditions of existence or by the interplay of the social forces related to those conditions that sought to reproduce and strengthen themselves at the expense of others. The fact that there are historically constituted forms of the state greatly limit the applicability of the political and ideological wisdoms of the past to grasping and improving the present, where the very notion of what constitutes desirable change and human empowerment will be so different. Put simply, the geopolitics of previous religiously legitimated territorialized empires or of self-perceived civilization-states is very different from the geopolitics of capitalist nation-states. IR need not shun those undeniably original intellectual endeavors to uncover the thought frames of that past but instead ask how practically purposeful those insights are for dealing with critical contemporary dilemmas.

This general line of thinking – searching in the Indian past from ancient to medieval to more recent pre-colonial times – for developing a distinctive understanding of IR today, though small compared to the dominant forms of (realist) discourse, is certainly larger than the miniscule few who would uphold the claim of those like Fredric Jameson that "the only satisfactory semantic meaning of modernity lies in its association with capitalism" (Jameson 2002, 12–13) and, therefore, that this capitalist modernity with its universalizing compulsions and processes of uneven and combined development is the real subject matter of IR. But for both MM and post-Western IR, it is Difference with a capital D that is paramount, and acknowledging and appreciating this epistemic and lived reality is all-important. Therefore, there are multiple forms of the emancipatory society, and each society will find its own (but not separate) way to greater emancipation since world emancipation must be a collective project the precondition of which for achieving success must be a recognition of these alternative paths.

Relegated, then, as an important concern is whether all differences are desirable. To escape moral relativism we must ask: "Who or what decides desirability?" It is not enough to glorify value pluralism because values clash and therefore rights clash, and there will have to be some adjudication over different claimants as to what constitutes a righteous social order. But there is moral learning and even moral progress over time and across societies through shared agreement. This means there is a weak foundationalism for a universal human condition because of a minimal commonality of instincts, needs, capacities, rationality and emotions. Also downgraded in importance are the undeniably common capitalist characteristics cutting across these societal differences. Indeed, capitalist modernity creates *common processes* that both unify *and* differentiate as never before. There are modern phenomena, the very variability of which is also testimony to their universality. There is the nation-state system no matter the social diversities within individual units. It makes more sense to talk of varieties of democracy, not of multiple democracies. In such democracies amid overall variability of legal structures each will have a core set of secular jurisprudences which will be fundamentally different from its past where customary laws, religion-based laws, kinship norms, and rules held sway. Is modern science and technology not cross-cultural in its making and adoption, though not in its uses and effects?

MM and post-Western IR enthusiasts in their culturally biased analytical frameworks give pride of place to the notion of "social hybridities" as the defining characteristic of the modern world order. However, the most important source for these multiple hybridities is, in fact, the capitalist development process that creates a dynamic of change in all human relations, practices and beliefs – whether economic, political, social, legal, cultural or ideational – whose inventive, destructive and combinatory powers are historically unprecedented. This is what is meant when one says that capitalism eliminates/preserves/distorts/limits/combines/originates, and in doing so necessarily makes all modernity hybrid! If this is the view of Perry Anderson, for Bruno Latour, hybridity means we have never been modern (Dirlik 2013, 8). The approaches that make hybridity the signature claim for an anti-universalism of sorts or the justification for decrying a false universalism because it is not a sufficiently cosmopolitan universalism do not adequately come to terms with the power or reality of capitalism. Does not capitalism carry with it features and values that intrude into *all* cultures/societies/civilizations such as commodity fetishism, forms of mass culture attendant upon the emergence of the hardware of mass communications, consumerism, money/wealth as the measure of social status? Is it not better (given the nation-state system) and capitalism's uneven and combined development to talk of varieties of capitalism than of multiple capitalisms, let alone of the more implausible notion of "alternative capitalisms"?

Indeed, insofar as it is the expansionist power of capitalist imperialism that has enabled Eurocentrism to masquerade as a universalism, it is deeply ironic, as well as debilitating, that there are postcolonial currents that while attacking the latter would deny the universalizing dynamic of the former that made this cultural-ideological ascension possible. Instead, this intellectual trend "throws the cover of culture over material relationships, as if one had little to do with the other . . . and diverts attention from the criticism of capitalism to the criticism of Eurocentric ideology"

(Dirlik 1994, 346–347). What gets lost here is the urgency with which we must now focus on the common universal dangers imposed by this globalizing capitalism.

What to address, what to suggest?

For the first time in history, the species itself is threatened by mass devastation through dangers humanly created. More than ever there is a need for a response that subordinates our differences to what we collectively share as global dilemmas. First, even as there are the most obscene and historically unmatched levels of wealth concentration and inequality, basic needs (which now go well beyond the eradication of malnutrition to include health, education, leisure, respect and personal dignity and freedom from fear) for so much of the world's population are and will remain unmet. This is not because of scarcity of resources but in spite of the fact that for some time now the age of such scarcity globally is finally over. Second, ecological limits of various kinds are in the process intersecting with profound negative consequences for the delicate metabolism that connects humans with nature. Third, the cloud of a nuclear conflagration and nuclear winter looms constantly over us even as it shifts its geographical positioning.

For all the disagreements about the purposes of IR or of the values that should shape its trajectory, in the face of these three global horrors, let the discipline stake out at least one non-controversial and yes, universal, value as its principal lodestar – a *secularly* grounded notion of human flourishing whose precondition of course must be the survivability of humans everywhere. The international today is largely constituted by a political economy of capitalist globalization mediated via a system of multiple nation-states. For the foreseeable future this will remain the terrain on which IR scholars/practitioners must operate, first to analyze, then to propose, to as many possible audiences (including governments) at the levels of the national, the international and the transnational.

To take the first two dilemmas: even as it can hardly be denied that actually existing capitalism has caused deprivation and despoliation on a grand scale, there is also a dividing line in the social sciences (including IR) and among the general public on how these two problems are to be resolved. Does this require management and reform, or must capitalism itself be transcended because its inner dynamics are incompatible with the achievement of equitable and ecologically sustainable development? The historical name given to the pursuit of this earthly transcendence has been socialism. Which side one takes on this divide will shape the public stands IR practitioners must take at home and abroad (this is no time, if there ever was, for retreat into an academic ivory tower when universities themselves are being corporatized); the specific policy proposals made or endorsed to governments both one's own and others; and the practical-political allegiances one should search to make with social forces, groups and movements that share one's programmatic vision and goals.

One cannot escape starting from where one is. A new internationalism cannot ignore national structures of power or the importance of respective citizen solidarities. Pursuing the common and universal goal of equitable and ecologically sustainable development will also require nationally differentiated policy advocacy, specific themes and demand slogans for mobilization. On the deprivation front, the call in an advanced industrialized country might be for a basic income grant sufficient for a decent existence. In India, soon to become the most populous country as well as the single largest home to the world's poorest and most destitute, it might, for example, be a demand for effective land rights to women (Agarwal 1994).

On the ecological front, India has witnessed massive deforestation and coastline and land degradation through ruthless exploitation of forest, marine and mineral wealth. Already the fourth biggest emitter of carbon gases and rising higher in global rankings, India hides behind its poor by pointing to its comparatively much lower per-capita rates of emissions when its huge "middle class" (this is not a median category as in the West but is constituted by the top 15 percent to 20 percent of the Indian population), which will soon enough exceed the US population, has a per-capita ecological footprint not much different from its advanced country counterparts. Yet taking together the media and academia, one can count on the fingers of two hands those who are strongly opposed to the ecological-cum-economic direction being taken by successive governments (Shrivastava and Kothari 2012). The Indian involvement at Conference of Parties 21 (COP21) reinforces this negative evaluation (Adve and Kothari 2015). The cultural turn by some of the more creative minds in Indian IR toward religious metaphysics (mainly Hindu Brahminical) and to the wisdoms of Gandhi, who lauded the comparative virtues of pre-industrial agrarian society, does emphasize the importance of the human–nature relationship; but like deep ecology, it does not distinguish between a dangerous anthropocentrism and a necessary philosophical anthropology.

Finally, what of the nuclear question? The research and teaching agenda of IR within academia is unavoidably influenced by struggles outside. The independent anti-nuclear movements of Western Europe, North America and Japan were among the largest in human history, mobilizing tens of millions. This stimulated a discourse – academic and public – that was wide and deep, creating counter-arguments to deterrence advocates, policy prescriptions of restraint and step-wise disarmament for governments and demand slogans for national and extra-national mass movements. Indeed, the UK was the only de jure nuclear weapons state where a major party of governance had twice when in opposition (but not in government) promised unilateral disarmament.

All this certainly played some part (how much is debatable) in promoting management of the nuclear arms race, regional and global restraint measures, geographical restrictions on deployment, even elimination of a whole class of nuclear-armed delivery vehicles. Yet, the most important impact of these movements was in the establishment and consolidation of a taboo on nuclear use even when nuclear weapons states were losing wars to non-nuclear opponents (Tannenwald 2007). This taboo has held up so far. However, even the strongest, most universal taboos are sometime, somewhere broken. Fear of a global holocaust was the crucial spur to the great mass movements of the Cold War era. When that era ended the fears and the movements subsided. Nonetheless, the danger of such a war erupting has not disappeared but has instead been regionalized.

Nevertheless, a deeply destabilizing global nuclear arms race between the United States on one hand and Russia and China on the other (with knock-on effects for India and Pakistan) has re-emerged because of the US decision to go in for Ballistic Missile and Theatre Missile Defense systems as part of its "full-spectrum dominance" strategy to militarize/nuclearize outer space. This is reason enough why nuclear restraint and disarmament should remain on the global agenda and a field of intervention for IR practitioners everywhere.

Of the three regions where nuclear tensions are of real concern – Northeast Asia, Middle East and South Asia – the last is easily the most serious since it is only here that a continuous Hot-Cold War for over six decades exists and shows no sign of ending between two now nuclear-equipped rivals. The bitter, long-standing conflict over Kashmir is being exacerbated by the growth of Muslim and Hindu communal forces, respectively, and religious polarization in Jammu and Kashmir province itself. The problem is not that India or Pakistan would assault the other out of the blue, but that once a conventional conflict breaks out an escalation dynamic sets in to reach a point where neither side would ever want to arrive – that is, considering pre-emptive use for fear of the other doing so first. India has declared a "no first use" doctrine but its practical preparations betray this pledge. Pakistan has declared willingness to use smaller-yield tactical or "battlefield" nuclear weapons should India's conventional forces intrude beyond a point into Pakistani territory. In the 1999 Kargil war, both sides readied their arsenal for possible use. Indian IR does try and address the India–Pakistan face-off, suggesting confidence building and other measures, but there is near unanimity inside and outside academia that India must retain nuclear weapons and only disarm as part of a multilateral process of total disarmament, all the while endorsing the government claim to being a "responsible" nuclear power (Vanaik 2015, 165–189). Since for most Indians making basic ends meet is a full-time preoccupation, the opposition to nuclearism in India and South Asia should be part of a wider opposition to an excessive militarism that has dangerous security implications as well as wasting resources that could otherwise be used for development. This stance should not be separated from opposing the Indian state's ambition to become a regional hegemon through partnership with the United States.

Conclusion

What effects will current trends in Indian IR have for IR elsewhere? Highlighted earlier are the three great global evils I believe must be given high priority on teaching, research, policy and activist agendas everywhere. Since India – perhaps more than any other country – best exemplifies the problems posed by this trident of issues, the task of Indian IR should be to unflinchingly and ruthlessly critique the policies and perspectives, nationally and internationally, that promote these dangers. It should seek links to progressive movements at home. It should aim to help institutionalize a wider South Asian solidarity and a much higher level of trans-Asian cooperation to address common problems. This would be one way of influencing positively IR practitioners elsewhere. Given the character of both the dominant realist and post-Western IR trends as laid out here, this is not going to happen soon.

India is a key node in a de facto Asian NATO headed by the United States, so for the realist community on both sides, deeper collaboration, academic and political and justified in the name of sensible IR thinking, is inevitable. India has also joined the BRICS grouping (Brazil, Russia, India, China and South Africa). This grouping hopes to have enough collective leverage to rearrange global economic and political institutions and structures of power, thereby enhancing the influence and authority of the respective member states. How effective it will be, given that there are serious contradictions related to unevenness within and differing alliance networks without, remains to be seen. In all likelihood, interchange among IR scholars belonging to these and other emerging powers is likely to grow and take broadly two directions. The major stream will be constituted by those who see their role as providing wise counsel and analysis about the pursuit of the national interest and how this can be best aligned with the collective endeavors and institutions of the BRICS and other bodies representing the interests of major aspirants to greater global and regional authority. Here, a more collective sharing of academic understandings of IR and more interaction between academia and policy makers can have practical policy payoffs for the states concerned – payoffs concerning the sustenance of a global capitalist order and also the rearrangement of nation-state power relations within.

The post-Western IR stream in India, no handmaiden of the state, will seek and find its counterparts in other BRICS countries and in other emerging powers to better institutionalize a collective process of discussion, research and interrogation to carry out the epistemic revolution that can create a stronger, more detailed vision of a genuinely more egalitarian universalism. This can more persuasively appeal to and shape the outreach to students and teachers and to the wider public in the civil societies of the countries concerned. Policy and practice could then, it might be argued, take a more radical and transformative turn.

If the first stream colludes with those upholding the capitalist order, the second would significantly diminish the relevance of political economy in favor of an unbalanced culturalism. Neither would accept that the principal subject matter of contemporary IR is capitalism itself. Therein lies the problem.

Bibliography

Acharya, Amitav. 2011. "Dialogue and Discovery: In Search of International Relations Theories." *Millennium*, 39 (3): 619–637.

Adve, Nagraj and Ashish Kothari. 2015. "A Flawed Climate Road Map." *Economic and Political Weekly*, 50 (42): 14–17.

Agarwal, Bina. 1994. *A Field of One's Own: Gender and Land Rights in South Asia.* Cambridge, UK: Cambridge University Press.

Behera, Navnita C., ed. 2013. *Political Science, Vol. 4: India Engages the World.* New Delhi: Oxford University Press.

Bhambra, Gurminder K. 2011a. "Historical Sociology, Modernity and Postcolonial Critique." *The American Historical Review*, 16 (3): 653–662.

Bhambra, Gurminder K. 2011b. "The Possibilities of, and for, Global Sociology: A Postcolonial Perspective." *Postcolonial Sociology, Political Power and Social Theory*, 24: 295–314.

Bhambra, Gurminder K. 2011c. "Talking among Themselves? Weberians and Marxist Historical Sociologies as Dialogue without 'Others'." *Millennium*, 39 (3): 667–681.

Bond, Patrick and Ana Garcia. eds. 2016. *BRICS: An Anti-Capitalist Critique*. New Delhi: Aakar Books.

Dirlik, Arif. 2013. "Thinking Modernity Historically: Is 'Alternative Modernity' the Answer?" *Asian Review of World Histories*, 1 (1): 5–44.

Dirlik, Arif. 1994. "The Postcolonial Aura: Third World Criticism in the Age of Global Capitalism." *Critical Inquiry*, 20 (2): 328–356.

Eisenstadt, S. N. 2000. "Multiple Modernities." *Daedalus*, 129: 1–29.

Jameson, Fredric. 2002. *A Singular Modernity: Essay on the Ontology of the Present*. London: Verso.

Kaviraj, Sudipta. 2005. "An Outline of a Revisionist Theory of Modernity." *European Journal of Sociology*, 46 (3): 497–526.

MacDonald, Juli A. 2002. *The Indo-US Military Relationship: Expectations and Perceptions*. US Dept. of Defense Report. Washington, DC: Allen Hamilton.

Mukhia, Harbans. 2013. *Subjective Modernities*. Occasional Papers in *History and Society* (new series) 1–20. New Delhi: Nehru Memorial Museum and Library.

Seth, Sanjay. 2011. "Postcolonial Theory and the Critique of International Relations." *Millennium*, 40 (1): 167–183.

Shrivastava, Aseem and Ashish Kothari. 2012. *Churning the Earth: The Making of Global India*. New Delhi: Penguin Books.

Tannenwald, Nina. 2007. *The Nuclear Taboo: The United States and the Non-Use of Nuclear Weapons Since 1945*. Cambridge, UK: Cambridge University Press.

Vanaik, Achin. 2015. *After the Bomb: Reflections on India's Nuclear Journey*. New Delhi: Orient Blackswan.

Vanaik, Achin. 2014. "Asian Studies beyond Borders: Where Do We Come from? Where Are We Going?" *Asian Studies*, 59 (3&4): 18–32.

12

UNDISCIPLINED IR

Thinking without a net

Laura Sjoberg

My education prior to graduate school consisted of a fairly traditional (American) breakdown of Political Science into American Politics, Comparative Politics, International Relations, and Political Theory. I walked into the introductory lecture in my PhD program with a fairly clear understanding of what IR was: I saw it as a subfield of Political Science with a focus on the international.

Perhaps unwittingly I had enrolled in a PhD program in International Relations, not in Political Science. I chose my graduate school based on my advisor – I wanted to learn from and, in the sort of arrogance you can only have when you are 20, teach policy relevance to J. Ann Tickner. So I had applied to the graduate program in which she taught. Ann was in IR, and it never occurred to me that IR was outside of Political Science, so I thought I knew what to expect. I was going to a PhD program that would let me focus on the part of Political Science that was IR, and within that feminist IR. Since most of my undergraduate coursework was either outside of the field completely or in comparative politics and political theory, I thought this would be great.

So then I walked into that introductory lecture in my PhD program. The lecture was given by Hayward Alker. I do not remember all of the content of it, but I remember some things that stood out. First, he told us how difficult it was to get a PhD, which I took as a challenge. But then came talk that I was less familiar with. Hayward characterized IR as an interdiscipline. He spoke with subtle but palatable disdain for the Political Science department that was right down the hall, and made it clear that what we would be doing in graduate school was what people did in Political Science graduate school. He then suggested that thinking about IR as a part of Political Science handicapped the potential of IR. The IR that he envisioned was one without limits, one where any intellectual tools that one could find might be applied to thinking about global politics usefully. What was exciting about IR to Hayward was its expanded "sandbox." Everything could be in IR, so IR had better tools – more tools, fewer disciplinary constraints – than other disciplines, especially, but not limited to, Political Science. It was not a discipline. It was an interdiscipline. It therefore transcended disciplinarity.

While I never really came to share Hayward's optimism and enthusiasm about the possibilities of IR, I did quickly become a student of his interest in thinking across disciplines and in picking up different tools to address different questions. My research has been as much in disciplinary geography, sociology, gender studies, and law as in "IR proper" (whatever that is), if not more so, and my recent dalliances have brought me into mathematics. This positions me somewhat awkwardly to assertions that IR is a coherent discipline for which a point can be determined. While seeing IR as a discipline is more comfortable to me than placing IR *within* Political Science, I do not think that the description that there is *an* IR – a discipline – is either accurate or normatively useful. Instead (along with Hayward), I think that if there is anything that makes IR unique, it is its interdisciplinary or undisciplined nature. I do not think IR is a discipline, and I think that is a good thing.

This chapter explores the virtues of IR as an undiscipline – suggesting that the comparative advantage of IR, or the potential comparative advantage of IR – is its lack of disciplinarity and the accompanying lack of foundation, which brings about a lack of clear rules for thought, knowledge production, and research. The disciplinary borrowing, or tool shopping, that has become characteristic of IR would be impossible were IR a proper "discipline" – and, with Hayward, I find that to be one of IR's greatest strengths.

The remainder of this chapter explores that attraction – the draw of undisciplined IR – and discusses some of the potential advantages of IR-as-undiscipline for the (loose) intellectual community of IR scholars and their corresponding body of scholarship. After a brief engagement of what undisciplined scholarship is/could be, the chapter explores two potential draws of such work: (i) putting exploration before coherence; and (ii) sampling diverse paths claiming contribution to IR.

The draw of the undiscipline/d

What was appealing to me about Hayward's characterization of IR as an interdiscipline was the virtually unbounded field of intellectual tools that interdisciplinarity made possible. Hayward, however, found IR's interdisciplinarity – the availability of multiple tools – useful precisely because it had the potential to make knowledge about global politics *better.* While he was neither a positivist (Robert Keohane's [1988] use of the term *reflectivist* as opposed to *rationalist* was in no small measure aimed at Hayward) or a dualist (in Patrick Thaddeus Jackson's [2010] terms), Hayward believed firmly that you could know the world *better* – more complexly, more deeply, in more ways – and that such *better* knowledge is not only possible, but the major payoff of the interdiscipline and ray of hope it generates also makes the world a better place along the way.

When I say that I came to share Hayward's view of IR as an interdiscipline, or even an undiscipline but not his optimism, I mean that I have never been sure of the potential for, or even desirability of, *better* knowledge about how the world works – causes, constitution, or signification in global politics. I worry that claims to progress, like claims to certainty, can be backwards and incorrect, and often have the violent effect of silencing their constitutive others. Claims to knowledge cumulation, which I recently argued (Sjoberg 2016) are fantasies, have the effect of creating a class division between knowledge that does contribute to cumulation and knowledge that does not achieve, or even reach for, those ends.

I share with Hayward some disdain for the Political Science department that was down the hall then and the one that now employs me. Unlike Hayward my career has depended on the ability to meet the disciplinary standards of those disdained Political Science departments with at least part of my research work. At least in my professional experience being in the United States, and having thus far chosen Political Science over gender studies or law, there is some of *my* IR and *my* research that is stuck in disciplinary Political Science as well. Disciplinary Political Science has rules – some written, many not – about what counts as research, which publication outlets count, and how knowledge is legitimated. Those rules are more rigid, and more unified, than any corresponding rules or norms in the interdiscipline of IR. The IR that is a part of Political Science is as a result narrower than the IR that is an interdiscipline or an undiscipline. As I live in both worlds simultaneously, I prefer the world of IR as an interdiscipline or an undiscipline. My preference is an attraction, a romanticization, and an engagement. That attraction helps me imagine what undisciplined IR, or IR as an undiscipline, might be.

Seeing undisciplined IR

As I alluded to earlier, my suggestion that IR be undisciplined is partly a suggestion that it free itself from any disciplines of which it might be considered a part and from the label of being a discipline itself. With the *inclusion* in disciplines comes *inclusion* in disciplinary rules, norms, and significations. With *identification* as a discipline comes a tacit requirement of establishing IR's own disciplinary rules, norms, and signification. Being an interdiscipline implies the ability to borrow from, traverse across, and journey through other disciplines, with a sort of imagined lack of tether to any particular foundation. While that lack of tether is often imaginary or illusory given the economic and political realities of doing this work *as a profession*, it is, nonetheless, an important image – one that allows borrowing, transversal, and journeying, even if it is within limits.

By replacing the term "interdiscipline" with "undiscipline/d," I am interested in moving even further away from disciplinarity. I think of an undiscipline as having four important features. First, an undiscipline is the constitutive opposite of a discipline. If a discipline is structured by coherence of inquiry, commonality of method, and intellectual polish, an undiscipline is unstructured by incoherence, methodological experimentation, and rogue inquiry. It is closer to anti-epistemological than epistemologically orthodox, "to break down the legitimacy of the distinction between 'contexts of discovery and justification,' and to develop an anti-individualist *and* anti-empiricist framework for the sociology of knowledge" (Shapin 1995, 297, emphasis mine). If, anti-epistemologically, knowledge (cumulation) is impossible, an undiscipline defiantly charges on producing, mirroring, and playing with it anyway, *knowing its own impossibility* and simultaneously engaging and rejecting it. Second, it follows that an undiscipline is *undisciplined*. Googling the word "undisciplined" finds these synonyms: *unruly, disorderly, disobedient, ill-behaved, recalcitrant, restive, wayward, delinquent, rebellious, refractory, insubordinate, disruptive, errant, out of control, wild, naughty.* While the undiscipline I envision is those things for a reason – that is, a rebel without a cause – it is those things *with purpose*. IR the undiscipline cannot be controlled by demands for methodological compliance; it cannot be brought to order by demands for political correctness; it cannot be contained by university or government rules about what is okay and what is not. Third, undisciplined IR goes in multiple directions – the search for coherence is replaced by scholars' searches for approximation of knowledge, for gratification, for justice, for rebellion. Undisciplined IR is neither coherent nor pluralist – it is not a lake or many tributaries flowing into one river. It is instead multidimensional and multidirectional – quantum, if you will (with credit to Wendt 2015). Fourth, underlying IR as an undiscipline is the claim/understanding/supposition that the traditionally understood goal/norm of disciplines – knowledge cumulation – is illusory and fantastical.

The argument that knowledge production/cumulation is illusory is based on a sense that disciplinary/disciplined standards for knowledge production are political and performative rather than given, objective, useful, or founded. I mean performativity where "performativity cannot be understood outside of a process of interability – a regularized and constrained repetition of norms" which resonate as "ritualized production" (Butler 1993, 60).

The iterative performance of standards of the measurement of knowledge has the impact of rendering uninhabitable the methodological, epistemological, and political space that falls outside of those performed standards, quelling dissent. Butler explains this process. She argues that "dissent is quelled . . . through threatening the speaking subject with uninhabitable identification" (Butler 2006, xix), since a dissenter has the choice between silence and being labeled a traitor, criminal, or otherwise evil. This trap between two bad options for dissenters limits dissent, which in turn limits what is heard, seen, and mourned, as well as choices of how life is lived, which Butler frames (in Levinas' [2005] terms) as "the surplus of every sociality over every solitude" (Levinas cited in Butler 2006, 128). Butler characterizes this as a policing of meaning, which is constitutive of human experience, both generally and specifically, in terms of serving a regulatory function in which political space deemed unacceptable is made uninhabitable conceptually. This makes statements like "the tests are robust" and "this article is good science" into disciplining signs without referents (Baudrillard 1993). The undisciplined and their undiscipline can form a resistance to these progressivist narratives.

This is not to advocate being "bad" for the sake of mischief (though I do not mean to exclude the possibility that such mischief could be, in some way, productive). Instead, it is to suggest that contrarian resistance to supposedly well-established disciplinary norms (e.g., Cynthia Weber's [1994] critique of the treatment of women and femininity in the discipline, or Robert Vitalis' [2015] history of the racism of the discipline), and the discomfort that those interventions produce, fly in the face of progressivist narratives about what makes knowledge in the Political Science while at the same time playing important normative and empirical roles. Undiscipline stands out in its importance and in its gravitas compared to ritually produced knowledge, which follows the implicit and explicit rules of disciplinary inquiry, whether in Political Science or in IR.

Exploration before coherence

One of the violent side effects of progressivist, disciplining projects is the price of admission, or violence of inclusion. As I mentioned earlier, disciplinarity has a narrowing effect. An uncritical look might suggest that the narrowing takes place mainly or exclusively by *exclusion* – who is left out of the disciplining flood and what work they do that is excluded. Some accounts of exclusion are people whom IR does not study or perspectives that it does not consider. For example, early feminist work in IR asked a fairly simple question – "where are the women?" – in response to women's absence on the pages of books and articles about global politics (Enloe 1989; Pettman 1996). Others have asked why American voices have often dominated IR, given how small a part of the global population Americans comprise (Hoffman 1977; Paolini 1999), or even critiqued the ways that the American academy is unrepresentative of the diversity of Americans (e.g., Turner, Gonzalez, and Wood 2008). Still others have written about the intersectionality of disciplinary silences on the basis of race, class, and sex (Chowdhry and Nair 2002; Mohanty 2003; Agathangelou and Ling 2004). The "bias" of IR inquiry towards a narrow segment of the population of the world and away from women, minorities, poor people, and residents of small states is related to, but does not fully reflect, disciplinary power politics along the positivist/post-positivist and qualitative/quantitative divides. In Agathangelou and Ling's (2004, 2) account, the "neoliberal imperium" of IR academia and the world that academia resides in "draws on and legitimizes neocolonial strategies of power based on race, gender, sexuality, and class to privilege the few at the expense of the many."

This is useful and important. The search for coherence and the force of disciplining exclude pioneers and explorers; this does not happen randomly but on axes of well-established disadvantage. Still, less attention is paid to the violence of *inclusion* (Haritaworn, Kuntsman, and Posocco 2013). While some who would change the undiscipline are left out of it, others are coopted by it, either by professional incentive or by the seductive feeling of compliance and belonging. A discipline is a hegemonic project that looks to order those within. As Agathangelou and Ling describe (2009, 2): "An overarching hegemonic project . . . encompasses states, governments, classes, and sets of ideologies that work in tandem to validate each other . . . a set of *social relations of power* expressed through daily interactions and the institutions that support them."

Along these lines, it is important to see how "the inclusive expansion of the neoliberal imperium to involve the queer other-within remains exclusive and violent towards its constitutive other(s) even as it appears gentler" (Sjoberg 2016; citing Puar 2006). The violence of inclusion is a vehement enforcement, replication, and naturalization of neat, clean, and bounded (faux) identities to replace the liminal and messy identities that would exist absent the cleanliness of liberal inclusion (Agathangelou 2013; Haritaworn, Kuntsman, and Posocco 2013; Scott 2013). IR's representation of bounded identities in both global politics and disciplinary inquiry serves to erase both intellectual and political messiness, alienation, and liminality. The violent reproduction of bounded identities shows stability, hiding liminality; shows certainty, hiding doubt; and shows stickiness, hiding mobility (Sjoberg 2012, 2016). Liminality is everywhere but almost nowhere visible. For example, queer theorizing shows the instability of sex/gender identities, showing that even those properties of people which we presume to be primordial are really liminal underneath systems that people build to make them appear otherwise (Sjoberg and Weber 2014). Translated to thinking about the availability of political space, this theorizing shows that the illusion of the safety of science and knowledge cumulation hides uncertainty and liminality under its claims to objectivity (empirical and normative) and clarity (Haritaworn, Kuntsman, and Posocco 2014). As such, "all the repressive and reductive strategies of power systems are already present in the internal logic of the sign," such that "that violence is an inevitable byproduct of signification" (Baudrillard 1981).

Following this argument, traditional standards of knowledge cumulation cover up both their own impossibility and their own violence. "The raced, sexed, and classed impacts of that masking and the recursive enactment of the standards despite (and at the expense of the visibility) of those impacts continue" (Sjoberg 2016). Baudrillard characterizes this as a break between signs (standards) and referents (the fantasy of the externally valid existence of standards of scholarship) which needs to be corrected (Baudrillard 1973). The corrective can be found in ambivalence, where

> only ambivalence, as a *rupture* of value . . . sustains a challenge to the legibility, the false transparency of the sign . . . questions the evidence of the use value of the sign (rational decoding) and of its exchange value (the discourse of communication),
>
> (Baudrillard 1981)

The intellectual work of ambivalence "*brings the political economy of the sign to a standstill;* it dissolves the respective definitions of symbol and referent" (Baudrillard 1981).

We have been taught concerning this standstill, though, that there is a possibility that things have to have meaning and progress has to be possible, lest we fail, and IR fails with us. Rethinking failure, though, provides another path – one that does not need to be forward or go forward. Failure is not "a stopping point on the way to success" but "a category levied by the winners against the losers" and "a set of standards that ensure all future radical ventures will be measured as cost-ineffective"

(Halberstam 2011, 184). "Research failure" (the opposite of "research success") "is not a weakness to be overcome, but a category constituted by the 'winners' as a demonstration of the 'losers' being inferior" (Sjoberg 2016). Within IR scholarship, the availability of the idea of failure and the stigma that it is paired with serve to reinforce as unquestionable regressive, violent, and unchanged standards of research success. After all, who would want to change the way that research is done if those changes create failure when there is a formulaic way to approach having success? Who would prefer to fail than succeed? Scholarship that challenges how knowledge is produced (or even if it is produced) is not only characterized as failed or bad scholarship, but, by extension, constitutes its researchers as failures as scholars. This cycle repeats when "we tend to blame each other or ourselves for the failures of the social structure we inhabit, rather than critiquing the structures . . . themselves" (Halberstam 2011, 35; citing Kipnes 2004). In this understanding, it is the privileged position which success holds that reinforces violent structures of power. Un-privileging success, and embracing failure, could serve a liberating function wherein such a move "dismantles the logics of success and failure with which we currently live" (Halberstam 2011, 2).

In this world, "under certain circumstances, failing, losing, forgetting, unmaking, undoing, unbecoming, not knowing may in fact offer more creative, more cooperative, more surprising ways of being in the world" (Halberstam 2011, 2–3). This is because:

> To live is to fail, to bungle, to disappoint, and ultimately to die; rather than searching for ways around death and disappointment, the queer art of failure involves acceptance of the finite, the embrace of the absurd, the silly, and the hopelessly goofy.
>
> (186–187)

Embracing *failure* to discipline, failure to produce scientific knowledge, and failure to live up to the constraining expectations of the rules of inquiry "allows us to escape the punishing norms that discipline behavior and manage human development" (Halberstam 2011, 3). Undisciplined IR, the failure of disciplined IR and its follower-after-death, then, provides a way to reject *both* traditional disciplinary narratives *and* the temptation to recast IR as a different discipline. In recognizing its own failure, IR can become undisciplined, and in that undiscipline there is space for exploration and difference.

The pressures for coherence and contribution cause distortion, singularity, and boredom. When I argue that the pressures for coherence cause distortion, I am thinking of the many cases where quantitative specialists have told me that they have finessed or manipulated data to get a clear result, or equally the many cases where qualitative specialists have told a small part of the whole story that "fits together." Rarely is the mess of real life – whether it is missing or messy data or lived internal contradiction – foregrounded in IR analyses. When I suggest that the pressures for contribution cause singularity, I am thinking of all of the times that IR scholars have held up Kuhnian or Lakatosian standards for knowledge contribution, both of which judge by how one's research is similar to, and serves as a friendly corrective of, other research in the field. When I suggest that pressures for coherence and contribution cause boredom, I am thinking of the many books and articles in the field that follow a formulaic approach to presenting argumentation and data and the many creative presentations that get less attention.

Diverse sampling of claims to contribution

A cure for this distortion, singularity, and boredom is to think of IR as a fantasy. Transitioning from thinking about IR as a discipline or interdiscipline to an undisciplined fantasy produces possibilities of exploring both unruliness and unrealities. Seeing IR as fantasy "displaces not only the centrality of order and meaning, but also challenges the stability of the traditional form and the primacy of the dominant narrative" (Casey 2012, 117), enabling a move from "problems of knowing to problems of modes of being" (Casey 2012; citing McHale 1987, 10). The purpose of this move is to unbound the narrative boundaries of the discipline to *acknowledge* their fantastical construction and the fantastical construction of all claims to research acumen.

Some readers may suggest that I have just turned this chapter into a pointless exercise of identifying IR as pointless – if IR is a fantasy, those readers might say, it is unreal and churlish. I would argue that those readers are being too quick to judge fantasy as insidious. It is our inherited understandings of science-as-research-success that is linked to a tendency to immediately reject the value of fantasy as scholarship. Instead, as I have argued before, the normative value of fantasy "is related to the normative value of the fantasy experienced or performed, and to the acknowledgment of a particular behavior or set of behaviors as fantastic" (Sjoberg 2016, building on Berlant 2000). One of the key identifiers of fantasy as a genre is the divorce of the sign and the referent – something IR has always and already been. Instead, fantasy is fully context dependent, where it is "a literature of desire" compensating for lack and loss (Scott 2011, 3, 5). As such, fantasy (including IR as fantasy) is a "literature of unreality" of stories where one object does not signify (Scott 2011, 10, 42). Right now, IR is a literature of unreality governed by rules of artificial pretense to reality. An undisciplined IR would be an IR that broke the boundaries of artificial pretense with imagination – imagined possibilities, imagined worlds, imagined knowledges. Dispensing with the pretense to disciplined/disciplinary inquiry would also create space to dispense with disciplinary standards, disciplining exclusions, and power structures that dominate both IR and the global political world it studies.

One could read this position as nihilist, but that would, in my view, be a misreading. My view is that "the fantasy of knowledge cumulation *itself* can be productive, *so long as it is recognized as a fantasy*" (Sjoberg 2016, emphasis in the original). The location of the value just changes. In this understanding, there is value in the process, in the exploration, in the risk, and in the bravery of *thinking without a net* rather than in the finished "scientific" product/project. There is value in the social relationships of scholarly communication rather than in the publication and citation of credited and credible science. There is value in teaching students to question teaching, rather than in teaching students. There is value in the enjoyment of the process of inquiry rather than in alignment with discipline/d expectations. Fantasies are fun, imaginative, and exploratory; the fantasy of knowledge cumulation *acknowledged as such* could be that.

Refusing to see that knowledge cumulation *is* a fantasy destroys almost all of these productive potentials. If IR research looks to produce finished scientific products, depth and breadth are often sacrificed for coherence, and creativity is often sacrificed for contribution to existing literatures. If scholars believe we are imparting knowledge to our students, we contribute less to their ability to question the world around them. If researchers hold a wounded attachment to meeting purportedly objective understandings of knowledge production, then competition, pride, and desperation can inhibit intellectual exchanges in scholarly communication. If scholars were to humbly walk away from the crutches of standards of success, the enterprise of IR could shift from the violent, liberal "helping everyone know" to an undisciplined space for diverse, fantastic intellectual work

While "helping everyone know" can be a well-intended goal, it often has the unintended effect of putting ways of knowing down to the inherited wisdom of how knowledge is properly produced. That can foreclose different ways of knowing, stifling creativity, diverse self-identification, and the utilization of the full toolbox of possible IR knowledges. That toolbox not only includes recently used tools of autobiography (Inayatullah 2010) and fiction (Jackson 2014) but also a wide variety of literary, visual, and advocacy tools that IR scholars rarely, if ever, find the freedom to use while they remain tied to disciplinary or interdisciplinary IR. An undisciplined IR would free space for more radical critique and more radical experimentation.

Conclusion

I have previously endorsed keeping IR up despite its necessary and overdetermined failure as a knowledge production enterprise (Sjoberg 2016). That endorsement is explicitly political – a political embrace of failure and liminality; it is also explicitly *affective* – a desire for failure and liminality, intellectually and personally. I write an advocacy for IR as a non-cumulative undiscipline, both because I think that it is an important intellectual/political critique and because I *want* it.

I have become uninterested in the ever-present questions about what IR scholarship adds. What is its contribution? How is the contribution identified? Were good methods used? Was the evidence high quality? How closely must you approximate science for your inquiry to count? If it approximates science, is it knowledge? If it is knowledge, is it progress? I have become uninterested intellectually because I think those questions are the wrong questions and in part because I have a negative emotional reaction to forcing my thoughts into those boxes. Those traditional questions seek discipline, and I look to undiscipline.

I argue that IR should give up pretense to foundation, substance, disciplinarity, and justifications for those things. But by giving up those things – and with them, a wounded attachment to knowledge cumulation, success, and coherence – it might be possible to find the *undiscipline* in IR – the out-of-control, disruptive space where innovation is not constrained by the will to knowledge, the will to success, or punitive rules of disciplinary membership. An IR that thinks without a net – that is not only undisciplined, but unhinged – looks more appealing to me than IR as a subdiscipline, a discipline, or an interdiscipline.

Undisciplined IR carries itself with the boldness of the rebel, the naughtiness of the delinquent, the exploratory drive of the unruly, and the stubbornness of the recalcitrant. In its last 50 years, IR has had some moments of undiscipline, with some impressive payoffs. But, more often, IR is a world of the disciplinary boundaries of politics/Political Science, the rules of inquiry of science, the ritualized production of a certain sort of knowledge in a certain sort of way. To the extent that a ritualized science has become the point of IR, I find IR to be pointless, meaningless, and uninspiring. My vision of IR as an undiscipline comes with a vision of the point of IR that is very different. For an undiscipline/d IR, the point of IR is in its very pointlessness. The conduct of inquiry in undisciplined IR is without rules, without requirements, without a net. The point of IR when IR is thinking without a net is the same as the point of circus performances without a net – they are more captivating, more daring, more brave, more committed, and more true to self for their lack of net, their lack of safety, and their independence. Undiscipline/d IR, thinking without a net, finds its point in its very unhinged nature. My IR, my undisciplined IR, is naughty, unruly, and rebellious – *with a cause* – of undoing the violence of politeness, rule following, and formula.

Bibliography

Agathangelou, Anna. 2013. "Queerness as Speculative Economy and Anti-Blackness as Terror," *International Feminist Journal of Politics* 15(4): 453–476.

Agathangelou, Anna and L. H. M. Ling. 2009. *Transforming World Politics: From Empire to Multiple Worlds.* New York: Routledge.

Agathangelou, Anna and L. H. M. Ling. 2004. "The House of IR: From Family Power Politics to the Poesies of Worldism," *International Studies Review* 6(4): 21–50.

Baudrillard, Jean. 1991 [1979]. *Seduction.* London: Palgrave Macmillan.

Baudrillard, Jean. 1981. *For a Critique of the Political Economy of the Sign.* St. Louis, MO: Telos Press.

Baudrillard, Jean. 1973. *The Mirror of Production.* St. Louis, MO: Telos Press.

Baudrillard, Jean. 1993. *Symbolic Exchange and Death.* London: Sage.

Berlant, Lauren. 2000. "The Subject of True Feeling: Pain, Privacy and Politics". In *Transformations: Thinking Through Feminism.* Edited by Sara Ahmed, Jane Kilby, Celia Lury, Maureen McNiel and Beverly Skeggs. 33–48. New York: Routledge.

Butler, Judith. 2006. *Precarious Life: The Powers of Mourning and Violence.* London: Verso.

Butler, Judith. 1993. *Bodies That Matter.* New York: Routledge.

Casey, Jim. 2012. "Modernism and Postmodernism". In *The Cambridge Companion to Fantasy Literature.* Edited by Edward James and Farah Mendlesohn. 113–125. Cambridge: Cambridge University Press.

Chowdhry, Geeta and Sheila Nair. 2002. *Power, Postcolonialism, and International Relations: Reading Race, Gender, and Class.* New York: Routledge.

Enloe, Cynthia. 1989. *Bananas, Beaches, and Bases: Making Feminist Sense of International Politics*. Berkeley: University of California Press.

Halberstam, Judith. 2011. *The Queer Art of Failure*. Durham, NC: Duke University Press.

Haritaworn, Jin, Adi Kuntsman, and Silvia Posocco, eds. 2014. *Queer Necropolitics*. New York: Routledge.

Haritaworn, Jin, Adi Kuntsman, and Silvia Posocco, eds. 2013. "Murderous Inclusions," *International Feminist Journal of Politics* 15(4): 445–578.

Hoffman, Stanley. 1977. "An American Social Science: International Relations," *Daedalus* 106(3): 41–60.

Jackson, Patrick Thaddeus. 2010. *The Conduct of Inquiry in International Relations*. New York: Routledge.

Jackson, Richard. 2014. *Confessions of a Terrorist: A Novel*. London: Zed Books.

Keohane, Robert O. 1988. "International Institutions: Two Approaches," *International Studies Quarterly* 32(4): 379–396.

Kipnes, Laura. 2004. *Against Love: A Polemic*. New York: Vintage.

Levinas, Emmanuel. 2005 [1972]. *Humanism of the Other*. Trans. Nidra Poller. Urbana-Champaign: University of Illinois Press.

McHale, Brian. 1987. *Postmodernist Fiction*. New York: Methuen.

Mohanty, Chandra Talpede. 2003. *Feminism without Borders: Decolonizing Theory, Practicing Solidarity*. Durham, NC: Duke University Press.

Paolini, Albert J. 1999. *Navigating Modernity: Postcolonialism, Identity, and International Relations*. Boulder, CO: Lynne Rienner Publishers.

Pettman, Jan Jindy. 1996. *Worlding Women*. Sydney: Routledge.

Puar, J. 2006. *Terrorist Assemblages: Homonationalism in Queer Times*. Durham, NC: Duke University Press.

Scott, Jessica. 2013. "The Distance between Death and Marriage," *International Feminist Journal of Politics* 15(4): 534–551.

Scott, Joan W. 2011. *The Fantasy of Feminist History*. Durham, NC: Duke University Press.

Shapin, S. 1995. "Here and Everywhere: Sociology of Scientific Knowledge," *Annual Review of Sociology* 21: 289–321.

Sjoberg, Laura. 2016. "The Closer You Look, the Less You See: Knowledge Cumulation in IR". In *Evaluating Progress in International Relations: How Do You Know?* Edited by Patrick James, Annette Freyberg-Inan and Ewan Harrison, pp. 156–72. New York: Routledge.

Sjoberg, Laura. 2012. "Toward Trans-Gendering International Relations?" *International Political Sociology* 6(4): 337–354.

Sjoberg, Laura and Cynthia Weber, eds. 2014. "The Forum: Queer International Relations," *International Studies Review* 16(4): 596–622.

Turner, Caroline Sotello Viernes, Juan Carlos Gonzalez, and J. Luke Wood. 2008. "Faculty of Color in Academe: What 20 Years of Literature Tells Us," *Journal of Diversity in Higher Education* 1(3): 139–168.

Wendt, Alexander. 2015. *Quantum Mind and Social Science*. Cambridge: Cambridge University Press.

PART FOUR
Engaging the world

13

MIND THE GAP

Defining and measuring policy engagement in IR

Catherine Weaver

There is much ado about the engagement between the academic study and practice of international relations today. Many in and outside of the discipline lament IR's peculiar myopia, commenting on the perceived lack of IR scholarship's policy orientation, relevance, and ultimately impact (A. Stein 2000; Lepgold and Nincic 2001; Nye 2008; Walt 2009; Mahnken 2010; Jentleson and Ratner 2011; Goldgeier 2014; Parks and Stern 2014). Some have even gone as far as to try to measure the gap through exhaustive surveys and content analysis of IR's top journals and books (Maliniak et al. 2012, 2015; Sharman and Weaver 2013a and b). Others have turned the question on its head, asking where policy makers themselves find IR scholarship meaningful to their work in the "real world" (Desch 2009; Avey and Desch 2014). Why does such a gap purportedly exist, and how can we address it? And if this gap continues to grow, what does this forebode for the very point of IR and its role in the world? In an era of increasing skepticism about the relevance of higher education and pressures to demonstrate impact through national performance assessments, such as the UK's Research Excellence Framework (REF) and Australia's Excellence in Research (ERA), this is not merely a question for pedantic debate. It is central to the question of how our discipline may survive.

To be sure, the extent and nature to which IR *should* be engaged with the policy world (in US terms) or "praxis" (in more British terms) is certainly a matter of legitimate debate on which there is no clear emerging consensus (Calhoun 2009; Jones 2009; J. Stein 2009). At the same time, there is increasing evidence that – normative questions aside – IR is, in fact, increasingly disconnected from the real world in terms of direct engagement with policy and activism.

For example, in a 2011 survey of 3,464 IR scholars in 20 countries carried out by the College of William and Mary's Teaching, Research, and International Politics (TRIP) program, only 11 percent of respondents reported that their research was primarily "applied" with direct policy applications in mind (versus basic research, or scholarship purely for the sake of knowledge). Only 15 percent reported their research was both, but leaning toward applied (Maliniak et al. 2012). When asked about the academic–policy divide, 37 percent reported that they thought the gap between was growing, and 39 percent reported it was the same as 20 to 30 years ago. Only 23 percent thought the gap was shrinking. In the updated 2015 TRIP survey, nearly 44 percent of IR scholars reported that they never engaged in issue advocacy, with only 11.65 percent reporting that they did so four or more times each year. TRIP's analysis of journal and book publications reveals an even starker divide. In a study of publications in the top 12 journals and top five book presses in IR, Sharman and Weaver (2013a) found that, on average, only 2.9 percent of journal articles use policy analysis and 12 percent contained policy recommendations. Books were slightly more likely to have some policy engagement: on average, 10 percent of books engage in policy analysis, and 19.6 percent offered policy recommendations.

In sum, in both the 2011 and 2015 TRIP surveys, over 90 percent of IR scholars said they think there should be a larger number of links between the academic and policy community. Yet this is not what we see when we make direct observations of what IR scholars are actually doing. So why is there such a disconnect between what we say we want and what we do?

Why the gap? A US perspective on incentives and socialization in IR

Why are we, as scholars intrinsically interested in engaging policy, so reluctant to do so? I offer some observations from the US system, in full recognition that national differences exist and merit further investigation. Ultimately, in the United States, I believe this all boils down to an obvious, but untested, claim: IR scholars may be intrigued by policy engagement, but they are poorly incentivized to devote scarce time and resources to endeavors that do not mesh with our profession's expectations and norms for hiring, tenure, and promotion. We do not engage in policy-relevant work because the risks are high, the payoffs are uncertain, and demonstrating our "impact" in the policy world is inherently difficult.

This academic–policy divide exists, and in fact may be growing, because of how we currently train and socialize our graduate students in doctoral programs in the United States. Simply put, our students are not well versed in how to speak to policy makers, and they are not encouraged to pursue research and publication paths that would invite those conversations. Area studies and careful case study work, so prized by policy makers, is increasingly eschewed by IR scholars. PhD students face inordinate pressures to "tech-up" in the fanciest methods *du jour*, publish in top academic journals, and get out of grad school as fast as possible. This certainly precludes time for learning additional languages critical to area studies, extensive fieldwork, or engaging in interdisciplinary coursework. More critically, pursuing a publication in *Foreign Policy*, writing op-eds, or spending time maintaining a serious policy analysis blog represents a tremendous opportunity cost for a young scholar hoping to land in the pages of *International Organization* or a top university book press before entering the tight academic job market.

Then, of course, come the tenure, promotion, and merit review processes. How many political science or IR departments in the United States (or elsewhere) – and their higher administrations – formally give credit for non–peer-reviewed work, even if it lands in the hallowed pages of *Foreign Affairs* or the *New York Times*? How many external reviewers are prompted to discuss (in positive terms) the policy relevance of a young scholar's work? Tenure and promotion processes, particularly at top-tier research institutions, arguably discourage such scholarship. Ironically, this seems to hold even for US policy schools, where op-eds and policy reports are often seen as the profligate icing on the cake of *real* research.

Moreover, in a discipline so obsessed with the mantra that "only things that can be counted count," some departments have reverted to practices of ranking publication outlets according to their perceived status or influence in the discipline, relying on "objective" indicators such as journal impact factor scores. As the top IR journals (defined as those with the highest impact factor scores and – critically – *peer reviewed*) show increasing signs of quantitative bias in what they choose to publish, this reifies incentives to select research questions based on the method that will get an author into a top journal rather than choosing a method and outlet best suited to answering an important research question that might peak the interests of policy makers. The result is an increasingly inward-looking discipline that values influence within its inner circles more than its sway with external audiences. The divide widens.

How, then, in the face of such strong professional norms and incentives, do we encourage the kind of scholarship that appeals to policy makers, practitioners, and activists? Merely talking about the academic–policy divide will not resolve it. We cannot rely solely on efforts to expose the academic–policy divide in hopes of shaming IR scholars into reorienting their research and publication strategies or rely on efforts to entice them into the policy fold through lucrative funding opportunities. More proximate logics of consequences and appropriateness will inevitably prevail.

Bridging the gap, part I: defining and measuring relevance and impact

With some trepidation, I argue that instilling value (and thus incentivizing) policy engagement in IR may require constructing the means to measure policy influence in a manner commensurate with how we measure scholarly influence. That, of course, begs the obvious question: How do we begin to empirically observe and measure policy influence and impact?

One relatively easy way – through various easy-to-quantify metrics such as Twitter followers and "retweeting" volume, blog activity, and media citations – may be less indicative of influence than self-promotion, with no guarantee that policy makers are actually listening or acting upon scholars' insights pushed through those channels. Grant activity may be another imperfect, but measurable, signal. Are scholars not only winning grants, but also being actively solicited, by public-sector agencies or think tanks for contracted work and future grant submissions? Can scholars in turn trace the impact of that work into the policies and practices of their "clients"? Is their work not only known in the policy circles (which may be a residual of many things), but discernibly "in demand"? And, if so, how do you measure that demand in a market of ideas?

Finally, the most direct measure of a scholar's impact or influence on policy might be the testimony of policy makers and practitioners themselves, elicited directly through polls or review letters, or indirectly assessed through serious mention of scholars and their work in policy speeches, testimonies, and legislation. Gathering such data would be onerous and subject to a host of arguments on sampling and measurement criteria. Moreover, which policy makers have sufficient status and credibility to evaluate scholars' work (especially since policy practitioners are arguably even more siloed in their areas of work than academics are)? How should they evaluate academic scholarship for policy relevance and impact? How many citations or mentions does it take to add up to some benchmark of policy impact or influence, and in what venues?

More questions than answers abound here, but I think breaking down the gaps between academia and the policy world requires serious dialogue on how we might observe and measure policy influence or impact (both of which should be distinguished from mere "presence," which can all too easily conflate aggressive networking with actual effects on policy). This goal of measurement ironically entails much more *qualitative* attention to the processes through which scholarly ideas attract attention, gain traction, and shape policy making at all levels. It also requires much more attention to the *sociology* of our own discipline and an open and honest discussion of the professional norms and incentives that deter transgressions outside our IR's ivory tower walls.

Bridging the gap, part II: a call for pragmatism

Ultimately, policy relevance/engagement/impact entail an approach to the study of international relations that embraces *pragmatism*, or more simply, "being useful." Like policy relevance or impact, pragmatism is better defined not by what it is, but what it is not. Friedrichs and Kratochwil (2009) argue that pragmatism is the corrective to a slew of pathologies in our discipline: an increasingly tendency toward reductionist thinking and manic deductive hypothesis testing, the obsession with Popperian-style positivism and the production of law-like statements, and a preoccupation with paradigm maintenance and theorizing. At the same time, the proffered alternative of pragmatism lacks clarity and punch. It is, in my best guess, a variation on Sil and Katzenstein's (2008) analytical eclecticism, an approach that adopts an abductive and reflexive epistemology and explicitly accepts the inter-subjective quality of social reality. Most promising, pragmatism is oriented toward useful knowledge. Ultimately, Friedrichs and Kratochwil provide us with a better explanation of how pragmatism serves as a strategy for knowledge generation than as a strategy for making that knowledge appealing, useful to, and impactful on a broader audience outside of academia. So how do we articulate a pragmatist approach that is clear in how it can help us generate knowledge useful to praxis? Next I offer more questions to guide this discussion than answers in hopes that this chapter can help fill in the blanks.

First, how do we *define* "useful knowledge"? Likewise, *to whom* is the knowledge we generate useful (*cui bono*?) and *how* is it useful (to what end?)? The answers to these questions also require us to be crystal clear on *why* it is important to orient research around the production of "useful" knowledge. Craig Calhoun, president of the Social Science Research Council, made a persuasive public speech in October 2009 to this effect, calling for social scientists to speak directly to public issues (Calhoun 2009). Yet the idea that our role as IR scholars should be to produce socially useful knowledge is not universally embraced in the profession. In my own experience, my suggestion that the field of IPE reorient itself toward more policy-relevant puzzles once provoked a vicious response from a senior scholar who insisted that "it is not our job to be public intellectuals or to engage in policy debates."[1] To give this scholar the benefit of the doubt, I presume this statement was made from the perspective that the value of social science is, in fact, its distance from the policy world, which presumably enhances the rigor of our knowledge production by granting us independence, objectivity, and patience.

The danger in this view lies not so much in the (mis)perceived objectivity of our disciplinary endeavors and misguided pursuit of "pure" knowledge. What is worrying here is that we believe that the knowledge we produce in the academic sphere will in fact remain intact in that realm, insulated from use and abuse by those in the public sphere. Thus, as the logic goes, self-selecting out of policy engagement in fact keeps us from having any negative impact on policy and practice. This line of argument is not only misguided, but it raises a series of questions for discussion in the pragmatist agenda: What is the appropriate relationship between academia and the policy community that defines the goals and parameters of engagement? How do we define our role as IR scholars producing socially useful knowledge vis-à-vis journalists or policy "experts" in think tanks (how are we different)? How do we ensure that the knowledge we produce reaches our intended audience without being adopted or coopted into policy debates in oversimplified or uncritical ways?

Moreover, *when* should the knowledge we produce be useful? Craig Calhoun (2009) laments in his speech that

> it is . . . true that many academic projects are driven by neither deep intellectual curiosity nor pressing public agendas, but simply by the internal arguments of academic subfields or theoretically aimless attempts at cumulative knowledge that mostly accumulate lines on CVs.

Being useful, for Craig Calhoun, means making social science directly responsive to public issues in "real time," "gathering new information and developing new knowledge in the context of rapidly changing social circumstances." This is easier said than done. In a profession that values probabilities and proof, working on emerging problems in real time means coping – quickly and flexibly – with environments where data are messy, ever changing, or just outright missing. It also means disseminating our research in a timely manner, which goes against the grain of publishing routines. If we are to be serious about a pragmatist approach that values being "useful," we have to think about the implications this would have on how we disseminate research and how the incentives, structures, and culture of our profession could be realigned to reinforce this goal. We do not, in the end, want the pragmatist approach to be the sole luxury of tenured full professors who no longer need fear the specter of publish or perish. Recent moves by our top journals in IR (such as *International Studies Quarterly*) to establish online forums and symposiums are productive steps toward this end.

Finally, what would make IR scholarship, approached from a pragmatist philosophy, really useful to a policy audience? For instance, how might a more pragmatic orientation in our scholarship empower IR to see and cope with Black Swans – those rare and unpredictable events that always seem to take policy makers (and academics!) by surprise? In Nassim Taleb's mind, Black Swans represent the unobserved risks that occupy and threaten the stability of social systems, and yet are consistently unobserved because they occupy "the statistical tails of the probability distributions of outcomes." As such, Black Swans – such as the 2008 financial crisis or the recent uprising in the Middle East and North Africa – "disappear from policymakers' fields of observation" (Taleb and Blyth 2011, 33).

Arguably, one distinctive aspect of pragmatism is its unwillingness to confine IR scholarship to linear, causal analysis obsessed with using theoretical abstractions to construct and then deductively test law-like generalizations about the social world. Instead, a pragmatist approach – more driven by policy puzzles and the end of being useful – pursues the study of complex systems, spurred by empirical observations that fall in or outside the 95 percent confidence interval. It investigates what may be in the "fat tail" and what to do about it.

So in the end, what does it means to be engaged with or relevant to policy? It means holding ideals and chasing puzzles (rather than "tests"). We must not only seek to generate knowledge, we must seek to be useful to the world beyond our university walls to those who hold power and – perhaps more importantly – those who do not. And yet, unfortunately, so many incentives and norms of the IR discipline today work against such priorities, subjugating us to the prerogatives of publish or perish and perpetuating the myopia and navel gazing that inhibit our willingness to bridge academic–policy divides where they continue to exist.

Conclusion: making IR matter in the world

Let us again consider for a moment the counterargument to all that I have written earlier. There is in fact good reason to argue that academia should maintain some gap or distance from the world of praxis, eschewing pragmatic approaches for a more rigid adherence to pure science. On the one hand, these arguments rest primarily on the notion that academic scholarship preserves room for objectivity in the face of political or organizational pressures to derive arguments and results that support selected policies and practices. Such arguments are firmly behind the backlash in the past 10 years against the revival of US Department of Defense funding for the social sciences through the Minerva Initiative. On the other hand, preserving such gaps also carves out space for academics to pursue more critical and normative arguments, protected by tenure and other job securities afforded by our discipline that would otherwise not exist in other sectors.

That said, the opportunity costs of ignoring the gap loom large. The neglect of more applied research that sincerely addresses and informs policy and praxis, as addressed in this chapter, restricts the tremendous luxury of learning (if not uncritically) from those who occupy the space we are studying. To that end, IR is making some modest progress with initiatives such as the Bridging the Gap program and the academic-run Monkey Cage series in the *Washington Post*. The Monkey Cage, in particular, is a forum in which serious IR scholarship is translated into clear language, reaching a much wider audience in a timely manner that empowers IR scholars to react publicly to issues of the day with serious analysis and prescriptions. It also allows those in the world of policy and practice to react to these ideas (as evident in the lively comments section that follows key posts). This is in fact a form of peer review that happens in the matter of hours, not months or years.

So what more can we do to adopt a more pragmatic approach to IR that empowers scholars to more effectively engage and have an impact on praxis? Here I offer a few preliminary recommendations to re-establish IR's relevance for the real world.

First, we need to think about how to boil down complex intellectual arguments and conclusions not just into "lessons" but into clear policy prescriptions that are feasible and desirable (Krasner 2008). More critically, the prescriptions need to be actionable: we must remain cognizant of the real-world political, economic, social, and cultural constraints that impede policy makers, practitioners, and activists from pursuing optimal courses of action. We must also be critically reflective of the way we articulate our conclusions and imply prescriptions. Policies are often very blunt instruments. Caveats and nuances, so prevalent in academic arguments, have little traction in the policy or activist world. Complex ideas must be delivered concisely and clearly, lest they be misinterpreted or co-opted toward other ends. Let us be true to our ideals, but let us also be empathetic to those who do not have the luxury of time or the capacity to slog through our dense analysis and disciplinary jargon to find *the point*.

Second, the direct and immediate impact of pragmatic engagement may not be obvious, and thus frustrating for those eager to reap the rewards of their work, so often conflated with "it was published in X journal and cited Y many times." Be patient. Recognize that most change in the world is not revolutionary, but incremental and not always distinguishable in causal terms. Be satisfied with participating and shaping debates and practice over time. For those of us on the other side of tenure, it is incumbent on us to remember these points when hiring or evaluating newer faculty.

Third, we should also duly recognize that our impact may be less on the level of strategic, high politics than less visible technical, operational, and discursive levels. We must also be cognizant of the elite-centrism that seems to permeate discussions of bridging the gap. This requires engendering an inclusive definition of practitioners and policy makers that includes activists and actors in the private sector, at all levels of policy decision-making and practice. Moreover, we need to be more reflective of our own inherent elitism and acknowledge how policy makers can teach us. Genuine praxis is a two-way street and must be based upon norms of intellectual exchange where we, as scholars, are willing to question and change our preconceptions and beliefs as the result of an exchange of ideas, as much, if not more than, we expect those in the world of policy and practice to do the same.

Fourth, let us not forget that one way of having genuine impact is through teaching. We hold enviable positions with respect to shaping the minds and actions of younger generations (and the occasionally older ones). Many of our students may decide to pursue careers in policy or activism because of ideas and values we have been able to cultivate in the classroom. Even if one never steps foot outside the Ivory Tower, it is possible to see and value the influence of our pedagogy.

Finally, consistent with the argument detailed throughout this chapter, I believe we need to think deeply and openly about the training, socialization, and incentives in our field that deter policy engagement. What structural constraints and norms exist that currently shape scholars' propensity to engage in policy-relevant scholarship and policy engagement? Which elements of these structures and norms need to be maintained to sustain the independence and objectivity of academic scholars, and which need to be broken down to encourage constructive engagement? These are the conversations that need to be broached, in departments, universities, editorial boards, professional associations, and even national assessment processes.

Ultimately, an IR scholar's decision to "bridge the gap" should be governed by the norms and rules of intellectual freedoms. As long as a scholar pursues a path of inquiry leading to the accumulation of knowledge and ideas in our field, the incentives and socialization structures that shape our profession should recognize and reward such work. The end goal here should be a more intellectually diverse and rich field that empowers us, as IR scholars, to not only critically reflect upon the politics of our time, but to attempt to change the world in which we live for the better.

Note

1 This was a statement offered by a prominent US IPE scholar during a roundtable discussion on "The Future of IPE," International Political Economy Society Annual Conference, November 18–19, 2008, University of Pennsylvania.

Bibliography

Avey, P. and M. Desch. 2014. "What Do Policymakers Want from Us? Results of a Survey of Current and Former Senior National Security Decision-Makers," *International Studies Quarterly*, 58(2): 227–246.

Calhoun, Craig. 2009. "Social Science for Public Knowledge." Speech delivered on October 10, 2009. Accessed July 7, 2016. http://publicsphere.ssrc.org/calhoun-social-science-for-public-knowledge/

Desch, Michael. 2009. "Professor Smith Goes to Washington," *Notre Dame Magazine*, Spring 2009.

Friedrichs, Jorg and Friedrich Kratochwil. 2009. "On Acting and Knowing: How Pragmatism Can Advance International Relations Research and Methodology," *International Organization*, 63: 701–731.

Goldgeier, James. 2014. "Addressing the Challenge – From above and below," *International Studies Quarterly*, online symposium on The Academic and Policy Worlds: Reflections on a Divide, September 2, 2014.

Jentleson, Bruce W. 2002. "The Need for Praxis: Bringing Policy Relevance Back In," *International Security*, 26(4): 169–183.

Jones, Lee. 2009. "International Relations Scholarship and the Tyranny of Policy Relevance," *Journal of Critical Globalisation Studies*, 1: 125–131.

Krasner, Stephen D. 2008. "Policy-Making and Academic Research: Why Wisdom May Not Result in Action." Bridging the Gap Working Paper #1, Robert S. Strauss Center for International Security & Law, University of Texas at Austin.

Lepgold, Joseph and Miroslav Nincic. 2001. *Beyond the Ivory Tower: International Relations Theory and the Issue of Policy Relevance.* New York: Columbia University Press.

Mahnken, Thomas G. 2010. "Bridging the Gap between the Worlds of Ideas and Action," *Orbis*, 54(1): 4–13.

Maliniak, D., S. Peterson and M.J. Tierney. 2012. "TRIP around the World: Teaching, Research and Policy Views of International Relations Faculty in 20 Countries." Published by the Teaching, Research, and International Policy (TRIP) Project, The Institute for the Theory and Practice of International Relations at the College of William & Mary, Williamsburg, VA.

Maliniak, D., S. Peterson and M.J. Tierney. 2015. "TRIP around the World: Teaching, Research and Policy Views of International Relations Faculty in 28 Countries." Published by the Teaching, Research, and International Policy (TRIP) Project, The Institute for the Theory and Practice of International Relations at the College of William & Mary, Williamsburg, VA.

Nye, Joseph N., Jr. 2008. "Bridging the Gap between Theory and Practice," *Political Psychology*, 29(4): 593–603.

Parks, Bradley C. and Alena Stern. 2014. "In-and-Outers and Moonlighters: An Evaluation of the Impact of Policy-Making Exposure on IR Scholarship," *International Studies Perspective*, 15(1): 73–93.

Sharman, J.C. and Catherine Weaver. 2013a. "Between the Covers: International Relations in Books," *PS: Political Science and Politics*, 46(1): 124–128.

Sharman, J.C. and Catherine Weaver. 2013b. "RIPE, the American School and Diversity in Global IPE," *Review of International Political Economy*, 20(5): 1082–1100.

Sil, Rudra and Peter J. Katzenstein. 2008. *Beyond Paradigms: Analytical Eclecticism in the Study of World Politics*. Basingstoke: Palgrave Macmillan.

Stein, Arthur. 2000. "Counselors, Kings, and International Relations: From Relevance to Reasons and Still No Policy Relevant Theory". In *Being Useful: Policy Relevance and International Relations Theory.* Edited by J. Lepgold and M. Nincic. 50–75. Ann Arbor: University of Michigan Press.

Stein, Janice. 2009. "Evolutionary Hubris, False Certainty, and Structural Skepticism: The Academic-Policy Divide," *Cambridge Review of International Affairs*, 22(1): 120–124.

Taleb, Nassim Nicholas and Mark Blyth. 2011. "The Black Swan of Cairo: How Suppressing Volatility Makes the World Less Predictable and More Dangerous," *Foreign Affairs*, May/June 2011: 33.

14

IR THEORY IN THE ANTHROPOCENE

Time for a reality check?

Stephanie Lawson

The disciplinary field of International Relations (IR) was formally founded in the immediate aftermath of World War One (WWI) with the express intention of contributing, at both an intellectual and practical level, to making the world a better place. Thus if IR has a point, it is to be located in this profoundly normative purpose. The early focus of the field was, understandably, on the causes of war and the conditions for peaceful interactions between states in the international sphere. These remain of central concern to the field, although the agenda has expanded considerably with attention now also directed at a range of other concerns from the global distribution of wealth and poverty to gender issues and the environment. Theoretical development has followed accordingly, and there are now a variety of contending approaches to how the field of international politics should be conceptualized and interpreted.

From an early stage, there has been considerable contestation over just what constitutes the basic "realities" of the field. One particularly influential approach that has long claimed superior insights into the nature of reality is, of course, realism. Its exponents take the view that to truly understand politics, international or otherwise, one must grasp certain harsh truths about the dynamics of power and the fact that it will invariably be used to the advantage of those who hold it, often ruthlessly. Realists have typically contrasted their position with those of a more liberal persuasion who envisage a world in which power may be controlled, mainly through institutions, and the potential for violent conflict minimized.

More recent theorizing has been critical of the almost exclusive focus on material power (that is, economic and military power), especially by realists, while much greater emphasis has been placed on the social construction of power relations. Thus attention has been drawn to the fact that many of the so-called realities of the political world, which have so often been presented as given by nature and therefore virtually unchangeable, are actually highly malleable. This approach has been evident in much post-Marxist critical theory, as well as in gender theory, both of which have sought to shed light on alternative realities.

More radical approaches incorporating postmodern or poststructuralist perspectives flatly reject the very idea of objective realities, truths, and positive knowledge, not just in the social and political world, but in a material or empirical sense as well. "Truth" is simply the product of an act of interpretation with no independent standpoint available from which to judge competing claims. Those who succeed in imposing truths generally do so through an act of power, thus creating a power/knowledge nexus (Lawson 2015, 159–169). This extends from moral or ethical claims through to those of the natural or physical sciences. Indeed, the status of modern science as a source of reliable knowledge, or even as a guide to probabilities, has been subject to some quite vitriolic attacks from this perspective. This constitutes a form of anti-science.

Other forms of anti-science have emerged in the world of practical politics over the last few decades, and nowhere has this been more evident than in relation to the impact of human activity on the natural environment. So profound has this impact become that the current epoch is increasingly referred to as the Anthropocene – a term that places humans front and center of the changing dynamics of the earth's physical system, with climate change now the most significant issue. The dangers posed by anthropogenic climate change to human survival, at least for a very significant proportion of the earth's population, appear set to rival those generated by other forms of human folly, including large-scale warfare. Indeed, climate change seems likely to become a source of increasing conflict around the globe as its impact on food production, the availability of water, the inundation of coastal areas, and a range of other developments that affect human security gather pace. The Anthropocene therefore brings into focus the very issues which were foremost at the time of the formal founding of IR and which provided it with its most basic point of departure – the causes of war and the conditions for peace.

Against this broad understanding of IR's purpose, and in light of the dangers posed by the Anthropocene, this chapter addresses some issues concerning the status of science, the phenomenon of anti-science (which sometimes presents in the form of pseudoscience), and the implications of theories of knowledge. The latter have been incorporated in certain approaches to the theorization of IR that reject outright the notion of "objective realities." With the notable exception of climate change, not all of the examples given in this chapter are associated directly with anthropogenic change, but are rather illustrative of the problem of anti-science in particular and, more generally, the relationship between politics and science in both a practical and intellectual sense.

The Anthropocene

There has been a growing conviction in recent years that the cumulative effects of large-scale industrial activity on the planet require a reconceptualization of the present geological era as the Anthropocene. This term was popularized by Paul

J. Crutzen, who shared the Nobel Prize in Chemistry for his work on the formation and composition of ozone (Crutzen 2010) and who proposed that data retrieved from ice cores from the late eighteenth century, around the same time that James Watt invented the steam engine, shows discernable changes in atmospheric concentrations of what we now call greenhouse gases (Crutzen and Stoermer 2000). The increasing currency of the Anthropocene in scientific literature could soon see the displacement of the Holocene – the term used to define the period dating from approximately 11,000 years ago when the last ice age ended, ushering in a period of congenial climatic conditions under which a whole variety of human civilizations have flourished, including modern industrial civilization.

No one has described more clearly than Marx and Engels the development of industrial society in the century preceding their own time, a period during which

> more massive and more colossal productive forces than have all preceding generations together were brought into being, along with the 'Subjection of Nature's forces to man, machinery, application of chemistry to industry and agriculture, steam-navigation, railways, electric telegraphs, clearing of whole continents for cultivation, canalisation of rivers, [and] whole populations conjured out of the ground . . .' and all leading to an absurd 'epidemic of over-production'.
>
> (Marx and Engels [1848] 2009, 47)

The issue of population growth mentioned here is also a key factor in the emergence of the Anthropocene. At the beginning of the Holocene, the total world population is estimated to have stood at around 5 million. It took until the late eighteenth century to reach 1 billion. As of January 2016 it stood at nearly 7.4 million (Geohive 2016) and is predicted to rise to over 9 billion by the middle of this century and exceed 11 billion by 2100 (UN News Centre 2015). Virtually all of this very rapid increase over the last two centuries is also due to advances in various areas of science and technology, from the development of vaccines against deadly diseases to the transformation of agricultural practices which now produce food on an industrial scale and which has itself had a massive impact on the earth's systems.

The idea of the Anthropocene obviously places humans front and center in the changing dynamics of the entire planetary ecosystem. Taken together, these changes are now said to be driving the sixth major extinction event in the earth's history. It is therefore scarcely an exaggeration to claim that humankind now "rivals some of the great forces of Nature in its impact on the functioning of the Earth system" (Steffen et al. 2011, 843). On climate change in particular, and the risks it poses to human security, this is not a minority view, but the consensus view of the vast majority of expert climate scientists (Nurse 2012, 4; see also IPCC 2014).

"Climate change denialism" is the phenomenon that directly challenges the reality of anthropogenic climate change, as identified by numerous scientific studies. It is therefore unsurprising that although it claims scientific credentials, climate change denialism is frequently branded as "anti-science." And because it is usually associated with the political right, it may be placed under the rubric of "conservative anti-science," as we see next.

Conservative anti-science

Critical studies in the United States have identified a range of anti-science and/or pseudoscientific views over a variety of issues from climate change denialism to "intelligent design" and which have typically been endorsed by leading figures on the Republican right (see Mooney 2005). Other examples from the recent past include the debate over the harmful effect of tobacco products, which saw vested interests in the tobacco industry attempting to discredit the findings of mainstream research in medical science in order to protect vested commercial interests (Oreskes and Conway 2010, 13). Industries producing asbestos, dichlorodiphenyltrichloroethane (DDT), and other highly dangerous materials adopted similar tactics. Much of the pseudoscience sponsored by such industries has been exposed as just that. Interestingly, some of the most prominent scientists supporting the tobacco lobby were to become leading figures in attempts to discredit the findings of the UN's Intergovernmental Panel on Climate Change (IPCC). One of these figures, US-based Fred Singer, has most recently attracted headlines for his denunciation of the 2015 UN Climate Change Conference in Paris, otherwise known as COP21, as "a radical, economy-wrecking and sovereignty-destroying UN climate pact" (quoted in Goldenberg 2015).

Industries associated with various forms of environmental degradation or with threats to human health have been supported by a range of conservative think tanks. Many of these are located in the United States and are funded in large part by those industries. They include the Alexis De Tocqueville Institution, the Cato Institute, the Enterprise Institute, the Heritage Foundation, and the Marshall Institute, among others (Oreskes and Conway 2010, 125). A recent study found that attacks on science had been increasing in later years while the "think tank" organizations promoting these were focusing less on policy issues (Readfern 2016). Although the phenomenon these organizations represent is not confined to the United States, the intellectual climate there has been particularly receptive to their views, which have been consistently pro-business and pro-industry.

The conservative anti-science camp also includes the conservative media. One of the United States' most popular radio broadcasters, Rush Limbaugh, once claimed that "science has become a home for displaced socialists and communists" while calling climate change science "the biggest scam in the history of the world" (quoted in *Nature* 2010). Fox News, with its genuinely ironic banner of "fair and balanced" reporting, is also well known for deliberately propagating doubt about climate change. It was an enthusiastic purveyor of the so-called "climategate" scandal which emerged after a sophisticated hacking operation into the emails of climate scientists at the University of East Anglia in the UK. This exercise attempted to portray these scientists as part of a global conspiracy promoting a myth of climate change for their own nefarious purposes. The release of emails purporting to expose this conspiracy was timed just ahead of the Copenhagen Summit on Climate Change in December 2009. A second release of emails occurred just before a further UN conference in Durban in 2011. Both incidents were found to be an attempt to discredit the science, and the scientists, involved in climate research and to therefore cast doubt on the veracity of findings concerning anthropogenic global warming (see Parliament, UK 2011).

On the religious right, creationists have put the most extraordinary spin on scientific findings in such fields as carbon dating, geological time scales, fossil studies, DNA research, and evolutionary biology more generally (see Institute for Creation Research 2016). More recently, one organization of evangelical Christians in the United States, The Cornwall Alliance for the Stewardship of Creation, has joined in the global warming debate on the denialist side, publishing "An Evangelical Declaration on Global Warming":

> We believe Earth and its ecosystems – created by God's intelligent design and infinite power and sustained by His faithful providence – are robust, resilient, self-regulating, and self-correcting, admirably suited for human flourishing, and displaying His glory. Earth's climate system is no exception. Recent global warming is one of many natural cycles of warming and cooling in geologic history. . . . There is no convincing scientific evidence that human contributions to greenhouse gases is causing dangerous global warming.
>
> (quoted in Stenger 2013)

One point emerging from all this is that much conservative anti-science actually attempts to present itself as scientific in order to gain respectability. The religious right promotes "creation science" and argues that the concept of "intelligent design" deserves a place in school science curriculums. "Science" is, after all, a word that usually carries authority, weight, and prestige and therefore provides a mantle of legitimacy for claims made in its name.

The focus shifts next from the political right to the political left, or more especially the green/left, which is scarcely immune to anti-science or pseudoscientific claims. As we shall see, one particular movement associated with ecologism endorses the authoritative scientific consensus with respect to anthropogenic climate change while rejecting a significant scientific consensus in another area. I place this under the rubric of radical anti-science as it appears in many respects to be diametrically opposed to the kind of conservative anti-science described earlier.

Radical anti-science and ecologism

Environmental thought and the variety of "green theories" generated over the last few decades have spawned a bewildering variety of approaches to the issue of the anthropogenic impact on the earth's systems. It is possible nonetheless to identify two distinctive strands of green thought which have been conceptualized under the respective rubrics of "environmentalism" and "ecologism," with the latter denoting a more radical approach to both the interpretation of environmental problems and their solutions. Ecologism regards mere environmentalism as tantamount to a managerial reformism that will not bring about the thoroughgoing changes to patterns of production and consumption or the relationship between the human and non-human worlds, which they believe are essential if an environmental catastrophe is to be avoided and which also require a conceptual shift from anthropocentrism to ecocentrism. This was set out in one of the earliest and best-known forms of ecologism – "deep ecology" – a term coined in the early 1970s by Norwegian philosopher, Arne Næss, who sought to distinguish his more radical approach from the "human-first" (anthropocentric) value system of "shallow" environmentalism.

Here we must note that deep ecology and kindred approaches are distinct from the regular scientific study of ecosystems known as ecology. Ecolog*ism* is an ideological approach based in turn on an explicit normative value system – hence the "ism." So influential has it become that it has succeeded in changing the general public understanding of what ecology is, as reflected in expectations among some students enrolling in introductory ecology courses to gain not just factual scientific knowledge but spiritual and moral enlightenment as well (Westoby 1997, 166). Deep ecology is just one form of ecologism, but for present purposes I use the term more generally to denote ideological ecologism as distinct from the regular scientific study of ecosystems, and the ecologists – that is, the scientists – who study them.

Like creation science, deep ecology has a spiritual dimension, although it is very different from the anti-science of the creationists and is certainly diametrically opposed to the anti-science of climate change deniers, industrial lobbies, and the like. Indeed, the deep ecology view of nature is said to derive from "a scientific insight into the interrelatedness of all systems of life on Earth" combined with the idea that anthropocentrism needs to be replaced with ecocentrism (Context Institute 1997). But the endorsement of science by deep ecologists and green parties turns out to be highly selective when it comes to certain areas where it conflicts with their ideology.

One area in which those subscribing to ecologism have clashed head on with a strong scientific consensus concerns transgenic engineering, more commonly known as genetic modification (GM). The technology has a range of applications, including in medical science where, for example, genetically modified bacteria are used to produce insulin for treating diabetes. But the focus has been mainly on food and agriculture. The scientific consensus at present is that GM crops do not pose a significant environmental threat and the food they produce is safe to eat (Nurse 2012; Council for Science and Technology 2014). This is supported by a European Union study which analyzed a decade of research on the effects of GM crops on both the environment and human health and which concluded that the risks were no higher with GM plants than with conventional plants and organisms. The study noted that an estimated 2 trillion-plus meals had been consumed without a single health effect being observed (EU 2010; EuropaBio 2014).

Resistance to GM technology is also motivated by its association with profit-driven industries. The question of vested interests is, of course, an important one, as emphasized earlier. But the organic food industry also has vested interests, which include propagating a certain level of fear about GM food products. The more persuasive their own narratives, the greater the profits for the organic food industry. Much the same, incidentally, can be said of the complementary and alternative medicine (CAM) industry, with its implicit claim to being more "natural" and therefore healthier than regular (scientifically tested) pharmaceutical products, which are portrayed as guilty by association with "Big Pharma." Both the organic foods and CAM industries, however, are themselves multi-billion-dollar enterprises.

In summary, the position taken on either climate science or GM food, as well as a range of other issues, appears to depend more on one's ideological beliefs than it does on the scientific consensus on these issues. And even when people do have some relevant scientific knowledge, an ideological commitment often means cherry-picking of evidence to match that commitment, or sometimes the deliberate distortion of evidence. This applies as much to the opponents of GM agricultural science, who generally regard themselves as politically progressive, as it does to the politically conservative opponents of climate science. Of course, a scientific consensus does not represent an unassailable truth about any given matter, nor is it immune from challenge on any particular matter on the basis of new evidence. But it remains the most reliable guide for non-scientists – that is, for the great majority of the public at large – on such important matters as the safety of products such as vaccines and insulin, which have saved millions of lives, as well as the likely impact of uncontrolled climate change.

Anti-science in social and political theory

The third group discussed here brings us back to our point of departure. It consists of those whose epistemological position amounts to another kind of denialism – namely, that there is a real world "out there" that exists independently of subjective beliefs. It stands in contrast with a belief that Einstein observed as lying at the basis of all natural science, and that is "in an external world, independent of the existing subject . . . even if it can only be conceived by way of speculation" (quoted in Newton 1997, 160; see also Devitt and Sterelny 1999, 12). Rather, the reality of the material world itself is mediated and indeed 'constructed' through social processes and all the subjectivities that these entail.

Moderate forms of social constructivism accept material realities while emphasizing the importance of the ideational processes of interpretation, which can give rise to different meanings and constructions. Such moderate forms are not "anti-science" but rather maintain a critical perspective on the way in which power may be exercised in any context, including that of science studies and science policy. More radical approaches, however, claim that language does not merely represent, but actually constitutes, reality, which can therefore only ever be relative (see Bertens 1995, 9; Blackburn 2005, 69). Within this latter camp much effort has been expended in debunking objective realities and the epistemic authority of any science that purports to have discovered such realities.

Debates around these issues have given rise to the so-called "science wars," a phenomenon which is rather simplistically, although not altogether inaccurately, depicted as being waged between "scientific realists," which includes most scientists, on the one hand, and relativists on the other, mainly from among the ranks of postmodernists/poststructuralists within the humanities and social sciences. The most notorious manifestation of this "war" was the hoax perpetrated by physicist Alan Sokal (1996) who submitted an article to the journal, *Social Text*. Entitled "Transgressing the Boundaries: Towards a Transformative Hermeneutics of Quantum Gravity," the article was complete nonsense from a scientific point of view but deployed the distinctive language and style of a postmodern critique of science:

The article was reviewed, accepted and published. One point to emerge was that not only did the editors (and probably the readers) of Social Text know nothing about science, but that the dangers in "the systematic disparagement of modern science: emerging from this particular quarter were little different from, and indeed in some cases supported, equally disparaging views coming from the conservative right" (Gross and Levitt, 1998, iv–v). This view has something in common with Jürgen Habermas's depiction of the postmodern/poststructuralist camp, as occupied by "young conservatives" for their perceived anti-modernism (Habermas 1981).

My intellectual sympathies are with Gross, Levitt, and Sokal, not because I subscribe to the absolute authority of science by any means, let alone to the alleged superiority of positivism in social science over alternative methodologies, often described by its critics as "scientism" (see Puchala 2013, 15). I have spent most of my academic life deploying historical/interpretive methods to critique discourses of power and the strategies used by elites to legitimate their own positions at the top of socio-political hierarchies, while making them appear natural to subordinate elements. I am therefore only too aware of how the power/knowledge nexus works in social and political contexts – science studies and science policy among them. But exposure of the machinations of power in such contexts is one thing. The denial of any objective realities in the material world is another. Indeed, a dogmatic relativism is just as absolutist as a dogmatic universalism, and both entail a certain closure of discourse (see Lawson 2006, 161).

It is very much to be doubted that what scientists are actually studying when they engage with the natural or physical world, or the particular parts of it in which they specialize, is an intersubjective mental construct. The behavior of electromagnetic fields, the properties and interactions of elements, the activity of tectonic plates, the processes of cell division – all go on independently of any human perception of them, let alone of our naming them in language and analyzing them in discourse. They were certainly going on well before modern humans with their over-sized brains even existed. We are a product of these processes, not them of us.

Acceptance of the general idea of the social construction of reality, and of all its political implications when it comes to the exercise of power, should not entail rejection or dismissal of the way in which the natural or physical sciences pursue knowledge of the material world of nature from the smallest of individual entities to the largest possible agglomeration of particles and forces which we call the universe, and all things in between, including the human brain itself. Furthermore, humans obviously have a very significant impact on the material world of nature through various forms of intervention. And we can read this impact in the material evidence for an Anthropocene – a term which logically assumes the objective reality of a world affected very deeply by human activity.

None of the critiques of anti-science touched on here mean that we cannot also recognize science as a human enterprise with deeply subjective and normative elements which even the strictest of methodological protocols cannot eliminate, especially given all the political, commercial, moral, and other pressures placed on its practice. Furthermore, the norm of objectivity in science is exactly that, a norm. However, we may well say that it is a good one to observe as far as it is (humanly) possible. And there are many other norms in the practice of science, and in the study of social science for that matter, that we widely regard as good, and a considerable body of ethics that distinguishes good practice from bad practice from both a procedural and normative point of view.

Most scientists would be the first to acknowledge the difficulties of producing an unassailable truth about some aspect of the material world. Certainly, climate scientists are at the forefront of acknowledging the problems involved in making accurate predictions about what the immediate, let alone the long-term future, of climate change will actually produce. At the same time, we would be hard put to find anyone in the radical anti-science camp with so little trust in the laws of physics and the technologies of aeronautical engineering that it would prevent him or her from stepping on a plane to attend an academic conference, the occasional failure of the technology (or its human operators) notwithstanding.

Conclusion

Those who accept that material realities exist and that the arrival of the Anthropocene is a "known known" generally treat it as more than just an objective fact to be viewed dispassionately, for it has deeply subjective dimensions and is loaded with moral significance. Unlike the Holocene, the Anthropocene is, almost by definition, a *problem*, and not just a scientific or environmental one. It is deeply political and economic, requiring a sea change in dominant models that rely on endless, unsustainable, economic growth (see Gillings and Hagan-Lawson 2014, 8). The Paris Agreement, reached in December 2015 when 195 countries adopted the first universal climate agreement, signaled at least a move in the right direction in committing to a significant reduction of greenhouse gas emissions, although this addresses only part of the problem. The future of human security will require much more.

We have formal political recognition of the dangers of anthropogenic change at a global political level and, through the UN and its agencies, we have some key institutions of world politics that are essential to the task of addressing the problems it generates and in which scientists are also engaged. What has been lacking, of course, is that form of energized, proactive consciousness known as "political will." But this has been lacking not just among many political leaders but among ordinary people on the ground. Among those of us in the academic study of politics who teach it to the next generation and who may wield some degree of influence in the wider public and political sphere lies some of the responsibility for educating both public opinion as well as policy makers.

The degree to which we can do anything effective, however, also rests to some extent on the relationship between our discipline and the humanities and social sciences more generally and the cluster of disciplines in the natural or physical sciences. There is certainly still some sense in which the two distinctive "cultures," as described by C. P. Snow in his famous Rede Lecture of 1959 (Snow 2012), exist between these clusters – and with all the prejudices that attend them. For our own part, prejudice against science as such does not serve us well, and what the Sokal hoax exposed is that critiques of science emanating from some quarters of the humanities and social sciences have simply gone too far. Certainly they had gone far beyond the kind of healthy critical stance characteristic of good social science practice, which also requires high standards of evidence and argument, as well as serious peer review of research prior to dissemination of results.

This by no means necessitates mimicking the natural sciences as some forms of positivism have attempted and which has actually generated some of the hostility toward science evident in much post-positivist work in the social sciences. Neither does it mean devaluing empirical and quantitative studies. Methodological pluralism is a strength rather than a weakness of any discipline. What is required, in addition, is respect for the integrity of other disciplines at a time when the relationship between both the practical and the academic study of politics on the one hand, and science on the other, has never been so important. If IR – and its theorization – in the contemporary world is to contribute to making it a better place, then it is indeed time for a reality check.

Bibliography

Bertens, H. 1995. *The Idea of the Postmodern: A History*. London: Routledge.

Blackburn, S. 2005. *Truth: A Guide*. Oxford: Oxford University Press.

Context Institute. 1997. "Introduction to Deep Ecology." http://www.context.org/iclib/ic22/zimmrman/

Council for Science and Technology (UK). 2014. "GM Science Update." http://www.gov.uk/government/uploads/system/uploads/attachment_data/file/292174/cst-14–634a-gm-science-update.pdf

Crutzen, P. 2010. "Anthropocene Man." *Nature*, 467. 14 October. S10, http://www.nature.com/nature/journal/v467/n7317_supp/full/467S10a.html

Crutzen, P. and Stoermer, E. 2000. "The Anthropocene." *Max Planck Institute for Chemistry IGBP Newsletter* 41. May, http://www.mpic.de/en/honors-and-awards/the-anthropocene.html

Devitt, M. and Sterelny, K. 1999. *Language and Reality: An Introduction to the Philosophy of Language*. 2nd edition. Cambridge, MA: MIT Press.

EU (European Union). 2010. "A Decade of EU-Funded GMO Research (2001–2010)." Directorate-General for Research and Innovation Biotechnologies, Agriculture, Food. EUR 24473 EN. 17 June, ftp://ftp.cordis.europa.eu/pub/fp7/kbbe/docs/a-decade-of-eu-funded-gmo-research_en.pdf

EuropaBio. 2014. "Are GM Crops Safe for Human and Animal Health and the Environment?" http://www.europabio.org/are-gm-crops-safe-human-and-animal-health-and-environment

Geohive. 2016. "Current World Population (Ranked)." http://www.geohive.com/earth/population_now.aspx

Gillings, M. and Hagan-Lawson, E. 2014. "The Cost of Living in the Anthropocene." *Earth Perspectives*, 1(2): 1–11.

Goldenberg, S. 2015. "US Climate Deniers Call Paris Summit 'A Threat to the World'." *Guardian*, 27 June 2015, http://www.theguardian.com/environment/2015/jun/26/us-climate-deniers-call-paris-summit-a-threat-to-the-world

Gross, P. and Levitt, N. 1998. *Higher Superstition: The Academic Left and Its Quarrels with Science*. Baltimore: Johns Hopkins University Press.

Habermas, J. 1981. "Modernity versus Postmodernity." *New German Critique*, 22: 3–14.

Institute for Creation Research. 2016. "ICR's Approach to Scientific Investigation." http://www.icr.org/how-we-do-research/

Lawson, S. 2006. *Culture and Context in World Politics*. Basingstoke: Palgrave Macmillan.

Lawson, S. 2015. *Theories of International Relations: Contending Approaches to World Politics*. Cambridge: Polity Press.

Mooney, C. 2005. *The Republican War on Science*. New York: Basic Books.

Nature. 2010. "Editorial, Science Scorned." 467(133), 8 September, http://www.nature.com/nature/journal/v467/n7312/full/467133a.html

Newton, R. 1997. *The Truth of Science: Physical Theories and Realities*. Cambridge, MA: Harvard University Press.

Nurse, P. 2012. "Advising Society on Science." Anniversary Address, Royal Society, 30 November, https://royalsociety.org/people/paul-nurse/

Oreskes, N. and Conway, E. M. 2010. *Merchants of Doubt: How a Handful of Scientists Obscured the Truth on Issues from Tobacco Smoke to Global Warming*. New York: Bloomsbury Press.

Parliament, UK. 2011. "The Reviews into the University of East Anglia's Climatic Research Unit's emails." http://www.parliament.uk/business/committees/committees-a-z/commons-select/science-and-technology-committee/inquiries/100831-new-inquiry–reviews-into-crus-e-mails/

Puchala, D. 2013. *Theory and History in International Relations*. New York: Routledge.

Readfern, G. 2016. "Era of Climate Science Denial is Not Over, Study Finds." *Guardian*, 7 January, http://www.theguardian.com/environment/planet-oz/2016/jan/07/era-of-climate-science-denial-is-not-over-study-finds

Snow, C. P. 2012. *The Two Cultures*. Cambridge: Cambridge University Press.

Sokal, A. D. 1996. "Transgressing the Boundaries: Towards a Transformative Hermeneutics of Quantum Gravity." *Social Text*, 46/47: 217–252.

UN News Centre. 2015. "UN Projects World Population to Reach 8.5 Billion by 2030, Driven by Growth in Developing Countries." http://www.un.org/apps/news/story.asp?NewsID=51526#.VqPatUugGlc

Westoby, M. 1997. "What Does 'Ecology' Mean?" *TREE* 12(4): 166.

15

UN STUDIES AND IR

History, ideas, and problem-solving

Thomas G. Weiss

The analysis of international organization (IO), and especially the United Nations (UN), is integral to the field of international relations (IR), although far too many colleagues view it as an after-thought, if a thought at all. The point of departure for my and many others' interest in the field has been to understand better world politics in order to address more effectively concrete trans-boundary problems, particularly those that threaten human survival with dignity (Weiss 2009, 2014). Because global problems – which are rising not diminishing in number – require global solutions, the study of the successes and failures of the system of universal membership in intergovernmental organizations has increasing, not decreasing, salience.

Long before the Conference of the Parties deliberations in Paris in December 2015 (COP21), it should have been obvious that many of the most intractable contemporary problems are transnational, ranging from climate change, migration, and pandemics to terrorism, financial instability, and proliferation of weapons of mass destruction and that addressing them successfully requires actions that are not unilateral, bilateral, or even multilateral but rather global. Everything is globalized – that is, everything except politics. The policy authority and resources necessary for tackling such problems remain vested in individual states rather than collectively in universal-membership institutions. The classic collective action problem is how to organize common solutions to common problems and spread costs fairly. The fundamental disconnect between the nature of a growing number of global problems and the current inadequate structures for international problem-solving and decision-making goes a long way toward explaining the fitful, tactical, and short-term local responses to challenges that require sustained, strategic, and longer-run global perspectives and action.

If the field of IR, and IO within it, is to inform better policy choices – a central if not the only purpose of international relations – it should be more historically informed, reflect more accurately the contribution of big ideas, and help solve real-world problems. As a community of scholars and students, we customarily fall short on all three tasks, and it is worth asking "so what?" and "why?" My practical experience in, as well as research and teaching about the UN, inform the answers.

History remains a tough sell

The United Nations Organization resulted from the gathering in San Francisco from April to June 1945, but planning had begun long before the end of the second worldwide war within a generation that was "to end all wars." Seventy years later, it is essential to recall that the UN Conference on International Organization was not a stand-alone event. The successful cooperative ventures during WWII had strengthened the political will of populations and reinforced the diplomatic bonds among their leaders. The United Nations was in evidence not only in the trenches and in the air but also in a commitment to collaboration and multilateralism and robust intergovernmental organizations, which were viewed as realist necessities, not as liberal playthings.

As a lifelong student of the world organization, I was largely unaware of the history from 1 January 1942 – when 26 Allies signed the Declaration by United Nations – until the actual founding of the world organization, by my ignorance was altered by recent work (Plesch 2011; Plesch and Weiss 2015). Drilling deeper into this history complicates conventional wisdom, and it gets in the way of the parsimony of which IR specialists are so fond. The elegance and simplicity of such theorizing are in fact ill-suited to capturing the multiplicity of interests and interpretations, of cultures and countries that shaped responses to that armed conflict, let alone today's world order.

In interpreting events, historians tend to emphasize continuity, whereas political scientists emphasize change (Weiss and Wilkinson 2015). The plea by the former to learn lessons from the past to address today's and tomorrow's problems has too little resonance for social scientists (Carr 1961; Macmillan 2009). Despite exceptions (Buzan and Lawson 2013), for those and especially Marxists who have long emphasized the march of history, the ahistorical quality of much contemporary social science and international relations is undoubtedly striking and perplexing. The professional premium for formulating the simplest theoretical depiction of causal mechanisms confronts an enemy in history, which definitely complicates matters but also can shed light and make fundamentals clearer (Williams, Hadfield, and Rofe 2012). Self-doubt, puzzlement, and reflection flow naturally from historical analyses in a way that they do not from the abstract theorizing, which is the common bill of fare that typically makes or breaks the careers of IR scholars. The lack of appreciation for what drives change and continuity in the way that our world is organized over very long periods of time typically renders international relations as a broad intellectual undertaking ahistorical.

Oxford University's Andrew Hurrell (2002, xiii), for one, chides those in the IR field for the affection for and affliction of "relentless presentism." That any computer's spell-check does not like the noun in that expression suggests something more sinister in our classrooms and research. "History" might be something that we introduce to students in the opening lectures of an introductory international relations class, but we tend to cite carefully or circumscribe it. We either cherry-pick illustrations to treat history as an empirical treasure trove wherein we can find examples that fit – or can be made to fit – the way that we choose to explain the world, or we concentrate so narrowly on concepts or particular issues that the lessons from studying broader historical phenomena are obscured.

My "discovery" of the wartime history of the United Nations points the way toward essential insights for today's study of international relations. The rediscovery of the lost or the suppressed is a recurring theme in literature, mythology, and history from the Renaissance to Western popular fiction since WWII – for example, *Lord of the Rings* and *The Chronicles of Narnia* and *Star Wars*. The UN at war provides a startling illustration. The wartime alliance of United Nations was formed in January 1942, some three and a half years before the 26 June 1945 signing of the UN Charter in San Francisco and its entry into force on the following 24 October. The wartime UN reflects both idealism and vision that the actual post-war institution does not and that contemporary analyses also do not.

That practical idealism of the 1940s should shock us from the twin complacencies that we are doing the best that we can and that our best today is better than yesterday. The ancient Greeks would appreciate the tragedy if we allow ourselves to drift into catastrophe in the twenty-first century, having discarded or forgotten lessons learned at such cost in the twentieth century's international relations.

Reference is often made to the collapse of the temporary, fuzzy-headed idealism at the end of the war with the double shock of Hiroshima and the acute tensions between the West and the Soviet Union. Little, if any, attention, however, is paid to the earlier and potent mix of realism and idealism that was relevant for Lend-Lease but apparently is irrelevant today in Washington, where "we don't do social work." However, the essentially free food, oil, and arms for all Allies between 1941 and 1945 was in fact an essential US contribution in WWII, alongside, of course, its industrial and military muscle. "It is not impossible that post-war organization will be the product not of one embracing covenant or constitution," one commentator wrote already in July 1942, but "learning to work together on everything from ships and tanks to tea and quinine" (Wild 1942, 94).

Indeed, a host of Allied efforts – including international criminal justice, post-war reconstruction, decolonization, international development, regulated world economic activity, public diplomacy, and forward-looking agricultural and educational policies – provided the foundations for post-war stability in addition to sustaining the wartime military enterprise. The proverbial bottom line was evident: no one sought a return to the chaotic pre-1914 world despite the abject failure of the League of Nations. Unilateral military might was not viewed as a viable future policy option.

The establishment of the UN system was absolutely central to policy making and decision-making about the postwar era – not least as a means to reduce Washington's direct financial requirements. At a moment when one might have expected the disaster of the failed Kantian experiment of the League of Nations to have produced Hobbesianism on steroids, those at the helm were resolute that multilateralism and the rule of law, not going it alone and the law of the jungle, were the best foundations for the postwar order. In fact, the bleak contrast was with the Third Reich and Imperial Japan, the epitomes of the right of might and lawlessness.

The combined national decisions to work together and to construct the subsequent organizations for peace and prosperity central to the original mobilization against fascism reflect an enlightened Realism about the merits of multilateralism and international cooperation in a variety of economic and social spheres. It was not John Mearsheimer's (1994/95) famous "false promise of international institutions" but rather a genuine cooperative strategy that motivated peoples and kept states allied. Multilateralism was a tangible tactic and strategy. The postwar vision was more than mere propaganda, although "business as usual" quickly returned as the default option with the Cold War's onset (Cull 1995; Brewer 2009).

As a lifelong student of the behavior and misbehavior of the world organization, it is embarrassing to admit my ignorance about the UN's wartime origins. My own "value," such as it was – both as an international civil servant from the mid-1970s to mid-1980s and subsequently as a consultant and advisor – was an ability to extrapolate from recent experience. IR specialists, like commissioners of blue-ribbon panels or professional pundits, are paid for insights about today. We are compensated to extrapolate from yesterday's headlines. A long-term perspective stretches back to the latest public opinion poll and forward planning to the next one. As an illustration of the limits of such customary approaches for understanding IR, others joined me as members of the IO choir singing about the UN's renaissance in 1991 when nothing was impossible after the Persian Gulf War. And then a few years later in 1994, nothing was possible in the face of mass murder in Rwanda, and 1999 was the *annus mirabilis* or *horribilis*, depending on one's view, with bullish efforts and both Kosovo and East Timor.

So, my first proposition that would help IR contribute to helping address global problems is the following: all social scientists should become back-of-the-envelope historians. Remembering Martin Luther King's admonition to keep in mind the "long arc of history," we should take a deep breath. More in-depth history would slow us down and help us move away from the "gee-whiz" character of too many analyses that also weakens the value of policy ruminations and recommendations that find their way into the hands of governmental, inter-governmental, and non-governmental actors.

Ideas remain peripheral

While constructivists have emerged as a visible intellectual factor in studying the shape and outcomes of international relations, they remain more marginal than either of the two dominant IR theories, realism and liberal institutionalism, and more peripheral still to IO analyses (Walt 1998; Snyder 2004). My experience with the United Nations Intellectual History Project (UNIHP) illustrates the largely under-explored role of international organizations in the generation of ideas, norms, standards, and principles, which are concrete reflections of essential contributions to global problem-solving that should be more integral to analyses in international relations.

One of the UN's most distinctive legacies resides in its character as a purveyor of ideas and as a norm and standard setter, which draw in particular on the strength of its universal membership (Jolly, Emmerij, and Weiss 2009). If such problems as terrorism and climate change require participation by major and minor powers, the UN's role would appear beyond question. Quite surprising for the appreciation and evaluation of the contribution of international organizations in the twentieth century, there had been no intellectual history of the United Nations and its efforts to establish global norms. The value of institutional memory was appreciated better by both the World Bank and the International Monetary Fund, which have invested substantially in documenting their institutional histories, including their contributions to policy ideas (de Vries 1969, 1976, 1985; Mason and Asher 1973; Kapur, Lewis, and Webb 1997; Humphreys 2000; Boughton 2001). Once again, why IO analysts had overlooked this dynamic is a puzzle because international organizations live or die not as a result of another training program or irrigation project, but rather of the quality and relevance of the policy ideas that they put forward and advocate and that member states adopt or reject.

Although much has been written in general about the world organization and a few specialized agencies have undertaken official histories, no systematic intellectual history had been made of the UN's essential normative products (Shaw 2001; Murphy 2006). This absence was especially puzzling because ideas and the formulation of norms and standards are one of the main ways by which the United Nations can fulfill its Charter-based purposes. This omission was remarkable for an organization that routinely gives policy advice on economic and social development issues, humanitarian aid, human rights, and human security. Nor, for that matter, have other organizations of the UN system taken on the task.

An intellectual history should do at least four things. First, it should attempt to trace the ideas that an organization has identified, albeit recognizing that most ideas have many and distant origins. Second, it should examine the quality, validity, and timing of these ideas. Third, it should identify missing ideas and why they are absent. Fourth, it should specify which areas in the future require improved ideas and how the organization should change in order to give the emergence of relevant ideas in good time a better chance of coming to fruition.

It is important not to over- or under-state the UN's contributions in this or any arena; but it also is essential to understand them better if the current generation of intergovernmental organizations are to help address global problems. The UN's contributions take the form of adding value at one of eight distinct steps: providing a forum for debate; generating ideas and policies; giving them international legitimacy; promoting and advocating their adoption for policy; implementing or testing them at the country level; generating resources to pursue them; monitoring progress; and, admittedly too infrequently, acting to bury ideas that seem inconvenient or excessively controversial. For readers who like alliteration, Margaret Joan Anstee described these eight roles as forum, fount, font, fanfare, framing, funding, following – and funeral. The UN achieves influence in many ideational ways through efforts in headquarters and at the country level. And that makes a difference.

UNIHP's 16 books and 80 oral histories represent a start on tracing and documenting the itinerary of an enormous set of contributions (Weiss et al. 2005). This particular output was largely unanticipated in 1945 and remains peripheral today for too much thinking about the world organization's pluses and minuses and about the implications for the analysis of IO and IR. Nonetheless, the following list helps to capture the impact and potential of many UN ideas that should be part of any history of the role of international organizations in the twentieth century: promoting human rights for all (Jain 2005; Normand and Zaidi 2007); providing an international economic framework for national development policies (Jolly et al. 2004); quantifying the world by providing a statistical framework to measure and to compare progress in many economic and social areas (Ward 2004); changing the debate about trade and development (Toye and Toye 2004); setting global goals; proposing development policies that combine economic growth with poverty reduction, productive employment creation, and better income distribution (or human development and human security (MacFarlane and Foong-Khong 2006; Stokke 2009); and bringing issues of environment and development to global attention, most recently the threat of global warming, along with gender and population issues (Schrijver 2010). There were debits as well – including a late reaction to the Washington Consensus, weak responses to the problems of the poorest countries and to HIV/AIDS, too little attention to culture, and inadequate consideration of inequality. However, the balance sheet shows a solid surplus.

This cursory summary fails to do justice to the details of this history, and other observers could formulate and calculate a different ledger and balance sheet. However, the point is that the United Nations has added value to the world of policy ideas, normative priorities, and standard setting – all of which are essential elements of an IR field that could and should fill knowledge gaps and thereby provide guidance toward better global governance (Weiss and Thakur 2010). If IR is to understand better, interpret, and act upon the threats to human survival with dignity – the point of departure for this chapter – this arena is *the* comparative advantage of the universal United Nations, and it may be its greatest legacy. It may also be the main leverage for addressing the planet's ills, ranging from terrorism to pandemics, from mass atrocities to proliferation of weapons of mass destruction.

In order to gain a better perspective on how this particular angle of IO analysis would improve the contribution of IR to solving global problems, it is worth pondering what the world would have been like without the UN. One undoubtedly can imagine a world without many of the concerns elaborated earlier or with such concerns having come on stream later than they did – human rights in 1948, women's rights in 1975, and the human environment in 1972. It would have been a much poorer world and, at its core, much less humane than the one to which the present world organization aspires and, at its best, contributes and helps achieve. Other ideas were ignored or could have been pursued more vigorously or with less political correctness. At the same time, the UN's intellectual work could have been much worse. It could have been smothered by caution, controlled by secretaries-general and other senior officials who allowed too little scope for creativity within international secretariats, who lacked any vision, and who were dominated by dogma.

Instead, and from the very outset, the UN has managed to attract many individuals with outstanding intellectual and leadership capabilities. The Charter, the Universal Declaration of Human Rights, and the continuing attractiveness of the humanitarian values and peace missions in many parts of the UN system remain central to the world body's work. At each stage of its life, individuals and some governments have argued passionately for maintaining this vision and for applying its values to the contemporary international system. This is not an inconsiderable achievement.

So my second proposition is the following: IR and IO within it would benefit if more scholarly work would probe when, where, and why ideas matter within specific country, intergovernmental, and civil society contexts. In terms of future research, the international norm diffusion literature needs to move to where the rubber really hits the road in national contexts and more systematically document impact in the way that Beth Simmons (2009) has for human rights. And international secretariats should not shy away from recruiting the best and the brightest of intellects at all levels like the 10 persons with substantial experience within the United Nations and its policy processes who won the Nobel Prize in Economics: Jan Tinbergen, Wassily Leontief, Gunnar Myrdal, James Meade, W. Arthur Lewis, Theodore W. Schultz, Lawrence R. Klein, Richard Stone, Amartya Sen, and Joseph Stiglitz (a former World Bank chief economist now closely associated with the UN). The bottom line for solving global problems is this: "People matter. Ideas matter" (Emmerij, Jolly, and Weiss 2001, 214).

Practice and theory remain in silos

The chasm is well known between those who observe and theorize, on the one hand, and those who act, on the other hand. And this generalization certainly applies to IR and IO. Yet, if scholarship is to help inform global problem-solving, the distance between theory and practice must diminish. Moreover, the generalization is not invariably true, and there are well-known exceptions, which is one reason why as president (2009–2010) of the International Studies Association, I chose "Theory versus Practice" as the theme for the annual meeting (Weiss and Kittikhoun 2011). In the preceding 48 years of annual meetings by the largest professional association of IR specialists, this topic had never provided a thematic focus.

The reasons for the gap and the ways to bridge it are not unknown, including pertinent analyses from over two decades ago by Alexander George (George 1994; Girard, Eberwein, and Webb 1994; Hill and Beshoff 1994; Nincic and Lepgold 2000; Jentleson 2002; Anderson 2003; Nye 2008, 2009b). Stereotypes – not all of which are untrue – about the two belligerent camps and their clashing cultures remain a dominant perspective in department corridors and academic promotion panels. To most scholars, the development of theory is highly valued, regardless of practical applications. Simplification and generalization are of the essence. Social scientists may ask "so what?" but do so usually in the context of theory building and not because a specific answer is actually necessary to advance a research profile or career. Some scholars might even go so far as to deny any requirement for theories and methodologies to be applied outside the academy. While that view can be tolerated and even respected, there definitely should also be room in the academy for those who apply themselves to problem-solving.

The misuse of scientific knowledge for the pursuit of political agendas is cited as one reason to assume the role of detached critic who remains above the policy fray. At the same time, many practitioners and activists associate academic "theory" not only with abstraction *but also* irrelevance because *sui generis* conditions make generalizations implausible. Theories too rarely offer good guidance for practitioners because "unreal" assumptions and – to repeat that awful term – "parsimony" are not useful when events are unpredictable and do not follow the neat patterns used in simplifications to construct theories and models. In an IR field with multiple contending perspectives – representing the have nots, gender, race, and the list goes on – the simplest of explanations hardly seems relevant to capture the variety of views surrounding contested topics. Seemingly permanent academic debates make theoretical propositions appear of doubtful utility in comparison with personal interpretations, selective historical memory, or even intuition and anecdotes. As one senior UN official once snapped at me, "My 30 years of experience in multilateral diplomacy exceeds some professor's 30 years of reading about it."

Given the paucity of resources and the excess of demand for international help and succor, the success and survival of various types of international cooperation require moving beyond a divide that presents practitioners as privileged guardians of insights about the real world and scholars as gadflies. Is the gap between the two worlds actually growing? Are "Scholars on the Sidelines" as Joseph Nye (2009a) argued in an op-ed in *The Washington Post* in April 2009? Which of these stereotypes are more myths than truths? What is the influence of scholars (or persons with advanced degrees) on policy formulation and execution? What accounts for influence or the lack thereof? What type of future engagement should be possible for scholars within specific institutions?

The gap may not be as deep or mysterious as often imagined, but it is still more prevalent than absent, more hurtful than helpful. For instance, in the case of the US foreign policy establishment, despite some high-profile academics with IR credentials serving in senior government positions (e.g., Henry Kissinger, Zbigniew Brzezinski, Condoleezza Rice, Stephen Krasner, and Ann-Marie Slaughter), the devaluation of policy-relevant scholarship in the academy (e.g., in courses, journals, job markets, and tenure decisions), along with the increased role and visibility of think tanks and the limited interest of foreign-policy makers in theory per se, provides explanations for why scholars and their work seemingly have little traction.

Nonetheless, some academics, especially those with access to "track two" – that is, informal but semi-official dialogue – have offered consequential inputs at early stages of negotiations and in institution building for the design of, for example, regional organizations and banks or trade regimes. A crucial factor is the capacity of academics that successfully penetrate the world of policy to determine how to address the specific knowledge needs of practitioners through the generation of new policy ideas, constitutive localization, validation and legitimization of government ideas and policies, and occasional dissent.

In the case of the UN system, as suggested earlier, prominent scholars have had an impact in fostering ideas and policies, including human development, climate change, the global compact, sovereignty as responsibility, and human security. Of the three-headed UN monster – the first UN of member states, the second UN of staff members, and the third UN of those closely associated with the world body but independent from it – scholars and activists constitute a key part of the "third UN" whose contributions have included research, policy analysis, and idea mongering (Weiss, Carayannis, and Jolly 2009). They have been able to exert influence as consultants, commissioners, and temporary staff members. The phenomenon of institutional cross-dressing – or the movement among posts in government, the international civil service, and civil society (including universities) instead of spending a career in one type of organization – is a reality. This pattern also means that more and more former officials may be attached for a portion of their careers to the academy or think tanks.

There is no excuse for the chasm between theory and practice in the making of foreign policy or intergovernmental organizational policy to be as wide as it appears because there are a surprisingly large number of serious scholars and graduate students who are interested in policy work, and of practitioners who respect social science tenets and themselves have advanced training and appreciate the power of ideas and analysis. If learning rather than spurning lessons is a prerequisite for addressing menacing trans-boundary problems, there should be not only more tolerance within the academy for policy-relevant scholarship, but also more room and more rewards in regular IR departments rather than only in schools of public policy for those whose research and teaching endeavor to understand and formulate recommendations about how to address global challenges. Moving in this direction should not be bad news for theorists, as many key debates in foreign policy overlap with academic causal arguments. Moreover, such a focus should broaden the career prospects of PhDs who face stiff competition and diminishing demand in the current academic job market. More research and project–based connectivity to the policy world and crossover from both sides would be beneficial to bridging the gap.

My third proposition thus is: there should be more rewards in IR for research and generation of knowledge that can have an influence in the real world in real time – on governments, international organizations, the media, nongovernmental organizations, and the for-profit sector. It should be possible to alter the training, socialization, and incentives within the IR field to reward those who attempt to identify ways to improve the human condition.

Conclusion

How full or empty is the international relations glass in the second half of the second decade of the twenty-first century? As a concentration for students, it remains popular and growing so that those whose livelihoods depend on enrollment may heave a partial sigh of relief. At the same time, as an academic pursuit, Rorden Wilkinson and I have argued that IR is fragmented and atomized, and we have gone so far as to indicate that it is teetering on the abyss of irrelevance (Weiss and Wilkinson 2014). One way to back away from the brink is to return to debating the grand questions that used to sustain international relations. I have suggested that those of us who analyze international organizations could help move in that direction and – to return to the metaphor – put more liquid in the IR glass by being more historically informed, analyzing more thoroughly the contribution of big ideas, and helping specifically to address concrete problems. If the IR field, and IO within it, is to better inform policy choices, decision-making, and ultimately action – as indicated, a crucial if not the only reasons to be in the field – the community of scholars and students should do better than in the past in accomplishing these three tasks.

Bibliography

Anderson, Lisa A. 2003. *Pursuing Truth, Exercising Power: Social Science and Public Policy in the Twenty-First Century*. New York: Columbia University Press.

Boughton, James M. 2001. *Silent Revolution: The International Monetary Fund, 1979–1989*. Washington, DC: IMF.

Brewer, Susan A. 2009. *Why America Fights: Patriotism and War Propaganda from the Philippines to Iraq*. New York: Oxford University Press.

Buzan, Barry, and George Lawson. 2013. "The Global Transformation: The Nineteenth Century and the Making of Modern International Relations." *International Studies Quarterly* 57(3): 620–634.

Carr, Edward Hallett. 1961. *What Is History?* London: Pelican.

Cull, Nicholas John. 1995. *Selling War: The British Propaganda Campaign against American 'Neutrality' in World War II*. New York: Oxford University Press.

de Vries, Margaret G. 1969. *The International Monetary Fund, 1945–1965: The Twenty Years of International Monetary Cooperation*. Washington, DC: IMF.

de Vries, Margaret G. 1976. *The International Monetary Fund, 1966–1971: The System under Stress*. Washington, DC: IMF.

de Vries, Margaret G. 1985. *The International Monetary Fund, 1972–1978: Cooperation on Trial*. Washington, DC: IMF.

Emmerij, Louis, Richard Jolly, and Thomas G. Weiss. 2001. *Ahead of the Curve? UN Ideas and Global Challenges*. Bloomington: Indiana University Press.

George, Alexander L. 1994. "The Two Cultures of Academia and Policy-Making: Bridging the Gap." *Political Psychology* 15(1): 143–172.

Girard, Michel, Wolf-Dieter Eberwein, and Keith Webb. eds. 1994. *Theory and Practice in Foreign Policy Making: National Perspectives on Academics and Professionals in International Relations*. London: Pinter.

Hill, Christopher, and Pamala Beshoff. eds. 1994. *Two Worlds of International Relations: Academics, Practitioners and the Trade in Ideas*. London: Routledge.

Humphreys, Norman K. ed. 2000. *Historical Dictionary of the IMF*. Washington, DC: IMF.

Hurrell, Andrew. 2002. "Foreword to the Third Edition." In Hedley Bull, *The Anarchical Society*, vii–xiii. New York: Columbia University Press.

Jain, Devaki. 2005. *Women, Development, and the UN: A Sixty-Year Quest for Equality and Justice.* Bloomington: Indiana University Press.

Jentleson, Bruce W. 2002. "The Need for Praxis: Bringing Policy Relevance Back In." *International Security* 26(4): 169–183.

Jolly, Richard, Louis Emmerij, Dharam Ghai, and Frédéric Lapeyre. 2004. *UN Contributions to Development Thinking and Practice.* Bloomington: Indiana University Press.

Jolly, Richard, Louis Emmerij, and Thomas G. Weiss. 2009. *UN Ideas That Changed the World.* Bloomington: Indiana University Press.

Kapur, Devesh, John P. Lewis, and Richard Webb. 1997. *The World Bank: Its First Half Century.* 2 vols. Washington, DC: Brookings Institution.

MacFarlane, S. Neil, and Yuen Foong-Khong. 2006. *Human Security and the UN: A Critical History.* Bloomington: Indiana University Press.

Macmillan, Margaret. 2009. *The Uses and Abuses of History.* New York: Random House.

Mason, Edward, and Robert Asher. 1973. *The World Bank since Bretton Woods.* Washington, DC: Brookings Institution.

Mearsheimer, John. 1994/95. "The False Promise of International Institutions." *International Security* 19(3): 5–49.

Murphy, Craig N. 2006. *The United Nations Development Programme: A Better Way?* Cambridge: Cambridge University Press.

Nincic, Miroslav, and Joseph Lepgold. eds. 2000. *Being Useful: Policy Relevance and International Relations Theory.* Ann Arbor: University of Michigan Press.

Normand, Roger, and Sarah Zaidi. 2007. *Human Rights at the UN: The Political History of Universal Justice.* Bloomington: Indiana University Press.

Nye, Jr., Joseph S. 2008. "International Relations: The Relevance of Theory to Practice." In *Oxford Handbook of International Relations.* Edited by Christian Reus-Smit and Duncan Snidal. 648–660. Oxford: Oxford University Press.

Nye, Jr., Joseph S. 2009a. "Scholars on the Sidelines." *The Washington Post*, 9 April.

Nye, Jr., Joseph S. 2009b. "The Question of Relevance." In *The Future of Political Science.* Edited by Gary King, Kay Lehman Schlozman, and Norman H. Nie. 252–255. New York: Routledge.

Plesch, Dan. 2011. *America, Hitler and the UN.* London: Tauris.

Plesch, Dan, and Thomas G. Weiss. eds. 2015. *Wartime Origins and the Future United Nations.* London: Routledge.

Schrijver, Nico. 2010. *Development without Destruction: The UN and Global Resource Management.* Bloomington: Indiana University Press.

Shaw, D. John. 2001. *The UN World Food Programme and the Development of Food Aid.* Basingstoke, UK: Palgrave Macmillan.

Simmons, Beth A. 2009. *Mobilizing for Human Rights: International Law in Domestic Politics.* Cambridge: Cambridge University Press.

Snyder, Jack. 2004. "One World, Rival Theories." *Foreign Policy* 145: 53–62.

Stokke, Olav. 2009. *The UN and Development: From Aid to Cooperation.* Bloomington: Indiana University Press.

Toye, John, and Richard Toye. 2004. *The UN and Global Political Economy: Trade, Finance, and Development.* Bloomington: Indiana University Press.

United Nations Intellectual History Project (UNIHP). Accessed 1 December, 2016. http://www.unhistory.org

Walt, Stephen M. 1998. "International Relations: One World, Many Theories." *Foreign Policy* 110: 29–46.

Ward, Michael. 2004. *Quantifying the World: UN Ideas and Statistics.* Bloomington: Indiana University Press.

Weiss, Thomas G. 2009. "What Happened to the Idea of World Government?" *International Studies Quarterly* 53(2): 253–271.

Weiss, Thomas G. 2014. *Governing the World? Addressing 'Problems without Passports'.* Boulder, CO: Paradigm.

Weiss, Thomas G., and Anoulak Kittikhoun. guest eds. 2011. "Theory vs. Practice: A Symposium." *International Studies Review* 13(1): 1–154.

Weiss, Thomas G., and Ramesh Thakur. 2010. *Global Governance and the UN: An Unfinished Journey.* Bloomington: Indiana University Press.

Weiss, Thomas G., and Rorden Wilkinson. 2014. "Global Governance to the Rescue: Saving International Relations?" *Global Governance* 20(1): 19–36.

Weiss, Thomas G., and Rorden Wilkinson. 2015. "Continuity and Change in Global Governance." *Ethics & International Affairs* 29(4): 397–406.

Weiss, Thomas G., Tatiana Carayannis, Louis Emmerij, and Richard Jolly. 2005. *UN Voices: The Struggle for Development and Social Justice.* Bloomington: Indiana University Press.

Weiss, Thomas G., Tatiana Carayannis, and Richard Jolly. 2009. "The 'Third' United Nations." *Global Governance* 15(1): 123–142.

Wild, Jr., Payson S. 1942. "Machinery of Collaboration between the United Nations." *Foreign Policy Reports* 18(8): 94–106.

Williams, Andrew J., Amelia Hadfield, and Simon J. Rofe. 2012. *International History and International Relations.* London: Routledge.

16

BEYOND THE "IVORY TOWER"?

IR in the world

Peter Newell and Anna Stavrianakis

What is the point of IR in relation to today's world beyond the university? Should individual academics and the discipline of which we are a part engage with the array of state, corporate, civil society actors, and global governance institutions that govern the world in different ways? If so, on what issues, and how? How might we think about the relationship between our research and teaching and the world of policy, politics, and practice broadly understood?

These are old questions for IR, yet ones that have become increasingly prominent in recent years given the changes in the political economy of higher education and the erosion of public funding for academic research in the context of neoliberal austerity and state rollback in many parts of the world. Academia is being increasingly asked to demonstrate its relevance, its impact, and its value for (public) money. At the same time the focus of the discipline of IR has changed over time. Compared with the early predominance of preoccupations with questions of the "high" politics of war, security, and to a lesser extent economy, there is now a broader range of issues dealt with in IR such that there is more scope for critical and activist engagements with a wider range of actors than state-based military and foreign policy actors. Work on peace studies, feminism, post-colonialism, development, and the environment has broadened and enriched the discipline. This brings into focus a wider range of potential targets of impact and influence-oriented work with different parts of the state and international organizations, as well as relevant actors among civil society and the private sector.

The range of potential engagements and avenues for pursuing them is, of course, vast. This immediately opens up questions about the contested understanding of what counts as "engagement" and "policy," what forms they take, and what we mean by "research," especially given IR's traditional tendency to be very theoretically driven. The assumption, often misplaced, is that only more empirically grounded areas of IR gain any traction with policy audiences, despite the historical role of major theoreticians in advising governments about their foreign policy and the contemporary demand for academic input on policy committees dealing with issues of justice and ethics in international relations, for example. Conversely, many NGOs and think tanks also produce research and undertake fieldwork, often working with academics. So the co-production of academic work with and for others muddies the supposed divides between research and policy and between theory and practice. Likewise, the overlap between state, market, and civil society actors observed in the growing popularity of public–private partnerships, the delegation and sharing of authority with non-state and private actors, and privileged roles afforded to business actors within the state, seconded as advisors, experts, and policy "users," means it is not always obvious where policy is made and who the appropriate target for influence is. Identities of "researcher," "activist," "policy maker," and "citizen" are also often looser, more fluid, and context specific than many accounts allow. Many of us engage in some combination of roles as citizen, activist, and academic depending on the issue and the spaces available or closed to us.

In this chapter we take up these issues as follows. First we outline the historical and contemporary context of policy relevance in IR. Then we outline three types of interaction: engagement, activism, and scholarship as practice. Then we show how these types play out in our own work on climate change (Newell) and the arms trade (Stavrianakis). We conclude with some reflections on the implications for how we think about and practice policy engagement.

Engagement, activism, and scholarship as practice

The concern with policy relevance is hardly a new one, even if the terminology around it changes with the times. The social sciences have long had an intimate relationship with state power. Geography, anthropology, political science, economics, and sociology, as well as IR, all grew up as modern academic disciplines in tandem with western state interests. Currently, a variety of terms are used to refer to scholarly interaction with those beyond the confines of the university. We group these into three types: policy engagement, activism, and scholarship as practice.

Policy engagement involves technical, problem-solving approaches that seek to integrate scholarly research into policy making, taking up invited spaces without troubling the parameters of policy per se (e.g., Armijo and Rhodes 2015; Bertucci et al. 2014; Cox 1981). In this vein, the issue is one of relevance *for* policy and sharing of "best" practice. The central element of "paradigm compatibility" (Eriksson and Norman 2011) in which researchers seek to speak the same language as those they are engaging with, is usually implicit rather than explicit. *Activism*, meanwhile, accepts the premise of engagement and impact, but in an oppositional manner, be it Marxist, Feminist, or Post-Structuralist (e.g., Edkins 2005; Eschle and Maiguaschca 2007; Herring 2006). One useful way of thinking about the differences within this approach is the distinction between activism that takes "anti" forms and that which takes "counter" forms, in which the former opposes dominant power and the latter attempts to diffuse power (Stavrianakis and Selby 2012). It is often assumed that the policy engagement model speaks to the needs of state power, whereas the activist model engages with critical civil society. But this assumes a problematic "state power bad/ NGOs good" dichotomy. IR has come in for criticism for its long-standing role as handmaiden of the western world in extending and legitimating its dominance in global affairs (e.g., van der Pijl 2014), even if this position is contested within the discipline from critical sub-currents such as Critical Terrorism Studies or Critical Security Studies (Booth 1995). Beyond this, scholars may choose to engage with policy for the purposes of critical research. There are difficult political choices to be made around participation and engagement in public debates and policy controversies in terms of reputational and other immediate risks, as well as being forced to declare "which side you are on." While any engagement is shot through with power, engagement with powerful actors requires particularly complex navigations and accommodation on all sides. The historical imbrication of intellectual curiosity with state power means, simultaneously, that scholarship is always already in a relationship with powerful social forces, but not necessarily beholden or subservient to them. Meanwhile, NGOs and campaign groups may themselves either unwittingly buttress state or corporate power by forming alliances and partnerships, what is often dismissively labeled "cooption," or have positions that are otherwise open for critical scrutiny. Challenges to the status quo are not necessarily progressive, and the status quo is not always regressive.

A third strand insists on *scholarship as a practice* in its own right: this questions the binary between "theory" and "activism," "relevance" and "engagement" (e.g., Eriksson 2014; Reus-Smit 2012; Zambernardi 2016). Rather than taking a position "for" or "against" activism, this approach opens up a discussion of how we have come to see theory and activism as distinct and the ramifications of this. In this view, scholarship and teaching are practices to be valued in their own right, engaged with the world, even if not instrumentally oriented toward practical change. This disavows the distinction commonly drawn between academia and the "real world:" scholarship and teaching are already in and of the world and valuable as practices in and of themselves. Teaching, in particular, is probably the most important form of engagement, activism, or practice most scholars will engage in during their careers.

This tripartite set of positions still does not leave us with nuanced, disaggregated accounts of how practical change happens or of the role of scholarship in this. Engaged research is often keen to move beyond the actually existing world while recognizing the need to solve immediate and short-term real-world problems along the way. Scholars and students all operate according to different theories of change guided and informed either by our worldview or theoretical understanding of how the world works and for whom. A more practice-based account of negotiating change would draw attention to some of the following explanations of the relationship between research, activism, and policy in IR.

First, *different political contexts* shape how much scope there is for policy influence or to be openly critical of state or corporate policy. IR is strongest in the United States and Western Europe where, in theory at least, channels are available to debate policy, articulate critiques, and engage in direct mobilization without fearing for your life. This is clearly not the case in large parts of the "majority world." Without dismissing the very real existence of threats to researchers in the richer part of the global system, there are clearly additional and distinct challenges associated with contesting elite policy in conflict-torn or authoritarian settings. What it is safe to say, when, and to whom are functions of the character of different political systems. This is not to idealize liberal democratic systems or richer states and the space they ostensibly give to engaging researchers. Many such political systems, as well as "open" multilateral UN policy processes, are very adept at engaging in elaborate rituals of participation while protecting powerful actors from policy shifts threatening to their interests (Newell 2010). It nonetheless remains the case that there is an understandable tendency on the part of IR scholars to target "safe" spaces of policy and politics for intervention and those states and governments which, ostensibly at least, are willing to engage in some degree of dialogue, which are generally located in the heartlands of the discipline in the UK and North America where, conveniently, global political power is also heavily concentrated.

Second and relatedly, there is *uneven capacity and resources among states and institutions* in terms of their willingness or openness to engage with academics. States in the global South are potentially more dependent on external input from experts, whether it is scientific, technical, or legal advice, or research of various kinds where there is limited in-house capacity. Leading IPE scholars at Argentina's FLACSO research institute regularly sit on the Argentine delegation at trade negotiations, given their knowledge of trade policy. Experts in international law also often have a key and privileged role. To take one example, small island states in the UN climate-change negotiations are some of the most vulnerable countries in the world to the effects of climate change, yet have limited capacity and power to shape outcomes at the international level. The demands of tracking and intervening effectively in climate policy debates place an onus on high levels of legal and scientific expertise, which mean governments from the islands often invite NGOs such as the London-based international legal NGO FIELD (Foundation for International Environmental Law and Development) on to their delegations to benefit from their legal advice and understanding of how the process works (Newell 2000). In this sense researchers and activists play on, and have to navigate, structural inequalities between states to make their voices heard.

Third, the *targets of policy influence* are not static or fixed. Many academics target their "home" state and feel they have a legitimate call on their representatives. Citizenship entitlements encourage us to look to "our" nation-state even in the knowledge that its willingness or ability to regulate or constrain key economic actors is often compromised. This is the case, for example, with those trying to hold transnational corporations to account: to challenge their ability to forum-shop between different institutions in multiple spaces to get the outcome they want, by calling on individual governments to set common rules to regulate their conduct. NGOs, movements, and unions try to mobilize globally to match the power of capital to do the same. For IR academics, the political and theoretical overlap here. As citizens we are often pushed to engage nationally, yet as scholars we have a duty to think about the international and about the political and geographical sources of power to be investigated, challenged, or supported.

Fourth, there is a *political economy of funding* that shapes IR's relationship to activism and policy. In contexts of low or tied state funding and a strong overlap between IR researchers and the policy communities they study, there are both enhanced chances of impact and fewer spaces for more critical or activist interventions which might jeopardize the access and flow of financial support from the state to research institutes. Many leading IR research institutions also clearly play on and benefit from their convening power, which make them a safe space for free and frank (but unattributed) dialogue captured in the notion of "Chatham House Rule" named after the location of the Royal Institute for International Affairs in London. For those largely dependent on one donor the stakes are even higher with regard to not causing offense to principal sponsors. The disciplining and censoring effects are rarely explicitly enforced, though sometimes this is also the case. Yet it is clear that to be overtly critical and public in condemnation of government policy is to risk internal censure and reduced financial support. A generic and pernicious fear of "biting the hand that feeds" has the potential to screen in and out of debate convenient and inconvenient truths. Funding for activist research in IR also faces a precarious funding environment with cuts in the budgets of foundations (such as Ford and Rockefeller) for work with and for civil society in the wake of the financial crisis.

Fifth, the nature and degree of access and the scope for influence is also a product of the nature of the *issue area* that IR academics work in. It is clearly harder to shape ministries and parts of the state dealing with "high" politics of core state strategy around security and economy where secrecy and confidentiality are at a premium. This poses a key challenge for the discipline of IR given the weight afforded to those areas of study in the discipline and somewhat easier for other issue areas such as health, environment, and development where weak bureaucracies sometimes seek allies among academia and NGOs to reinforce their position in internal battles over resources, power, and influence. The same is to some extent true of corporations where those parts of the company most open to engagement are often the least powerful internally.

It also needs to be recognized that any attempt by IR researchers to generate change or impact through their work has different starting points for entering the conversation, not only in terms of individuals' access and networks, but also in terms of how much meaningful scope there is to *shift the terms of debate.* Often in practice this means engaging on others' terms in order to be heard. Examples might include those we illustrate later around the arms trade and the lack of space to seriously debate the merits of the UK's Trident nuclear program given the open hostility and mockery by military leaders of the UK Labour Party leader Jeremy Corbyn's position that he would not be willing to use nuclear weapons. In relation to environmental issues the relevant parallel might be the difficulty of questioning the use and effectiveness of payments for ecosystem services in the face of such widespread policy support for market mechanisms. Certain framings are seemingly non-negotiable for researchers and activists.

Sixth, there is the question of the *positionality of academics* when it comes to the types of engagement academics are willing and able to contemplate. There are issues of seniority and age, security of contract, and gender. In terms of stage of career, how much safety academics have in their job to speak out and potentially antagonize employers and funders has a key bearing on who is able to speak out on what issues. At our own university controversies over the offering of an associate position to NATO official Jamie Shea, around the privatization of some university services (the 235 campaign), or around fossil fuel divestment ("fossilfree Sussex") have involved many IR academics in ways which have led to difficult negotiations about when to speak out and to whom and in what capacity. In the more conservative context of the US system, in terms of both the tenure system and the political culture which inhibits junior scholars from stepping out of line or upsetting managers who have the power to withhold tenured employment from them, research aimed at policy elites and incremental change appears to be a far safer bet. In the UK, the Research Excellence Framework, which places increasing emphasis on demonstrating non-academic impact culture, has similar effects by rewarding more senior figures with ample access to policy elites to generate impact.

Engaging on climate change and the arms trade

How do these factors that constrain, enable, and shape the role of IR scholarship play out in practice? In what follows, we offer two sets of brief personal reflections on engaged scholarship around climate change (Newell) and the arms trade (Stavrianakis). Newell has engaged with these dilemmas and pressures through working closely with a range of campaigning organizations from the earliest days of his research career. During his PhD he worked at Friends of the Earth UK and Climate Network Europe in Brussels. More recently he has been working with Carbon Market Watch, based in Brussels, on exposing flaws in global carbon market mechanisms and their impact on more marginalized groups in particular. Central among these has been the Clean Development Mechanism (CDM), a UN market-based offset mechanism created under the 1997 Kyoto Protocol that allows richer countries, with legal obligations to reduce their greenhouse gas emissions, to pay poorer ones for projects that reduce these emissions more cheaply. In return, developing countries are meant to receive local sustainable development benefits, such as jobs, technology, and improved health and environmental outcomes.

His research highlighted a number of key governance deficits in relation to participation, accountability, coordination, and capacity, which are inhibiting the ability of governments to realize sustainable developmental benefits from CDM projects. It examined these governance issues at a range of levels, from the UN's CDM Executive Board, to national governments that have responsibility for approving and screening projects, down to local bodies that oversee consultations and participation with local communities about the risks and benefits of projects they are asked to host. Controversially, it found widespread evidence of collusion, corruption, and exclusion in decision-making and project approval processes. It found that decision-making tends to revolve around tightly knit networks of project developers, financiers, regulators, and auditors, while many key stakeholders are not adequately consulted. The research also found many examples of a "revolving door" between national officials, project developers, and verification agencies, often even occupying more than one role at the same time. The research highlighted the need for redress mechanisms and efforts to monitor and evaluate whether or not sustainable development benefits are being delivered by projects, as well as to ensure that adequate opportunities are provided for participation in and consultation over the projects. The findings were supportive, therefore, of a wave of NGO concern about the effectiveness and beneficiaries of carbon markets.

Timing – doing research that was useful and relevant to the debate at an opportune moment – was crucial to the relationships Newell was able to form. A sense of a legitimacy crisis among key UN bodies and corporate carbon traders seeking to defend themselves from criticism increased governments' and NGO actors' receptivity to what he was saying, in seeking to reform carbon markets in the case of the UK government, for example, and to reduce their use in the case of several NGOs (Newell 2014). Such was the sensitivity of the issue in late 2011, amid growing scandals around the social and human rights impacts of CDM projects and questions around gaming and fraud in the buying and selling of permits, that the Chair of the UN's CDM Executive Board attended Newell's final project workshop to debate the issues.

Recognition of expertise was another key factor. An Economic and Social Research Council (ESRC – one of the main academic funding bodies in the UK) "leadership fellowship" generated resources to facilitate the research having an impact on policy and helped Newell to secure access to key players through meetings hosted by the ESRC with government officials and others. A self-reinforcing circle was generated between research and recognition whereby opportunities for "invited engagement" increased. For example, the UN CDM Executive Board – the highest governmental decision-making body on carbon markets – held a closed retreat in September 2011 to discuss challenges facing the CDM in the wake of the crises engulfing global carbon markets noted earlier. Newell was included among the "well-known leaders and thinkers in this area" and produced a briefing note for the participants based on his research.

This episode also points to the uneven openness and receptivity of different parts of the state to research critical of international governance actors. His research was used by the UK government's Department for International Development (DfID) in its submission to the UN regarding the reform of carbon markets. This department has a somewhat more skeptical position toward the role of carbon markets in combatting climate change than other parts of the UK government, and hence was more disposed to draw on research that was critical of the way carbon markets function. This is a good example of how actors can use research and the support of expert networks to bolster their own positions in policy battles with more powerful actors.

Finally, Newell's experience illustrates the challenges and dilemmas of proximity to activists. His relationship with Carbon Market Watch has helped to promote his research among activists, and it has also provided an important vehicle for getting access to key UN bodies. Yet proximity to activists has also brought challenges and dilemmas. Being considered too close to a group like Carbon Market Watch has led to criticism from government and carbon traders, who claim the closeness discredits the neutrality of the findings of his work: a convenient way of delegitimizing research that questions policy orthodoxies. Criticism also comes from more radical movements with whom leading scholars are aligned, who view any such engagement as misplaced and lending legitimacy to a problematic solution to climate change (Lohmann 2012). On other occasions, however, he has played precisely on the fiction of scholarly objectivity and neutrality accorded to academic research when presenting findings to UK parliamentary select committees and parliamentary groups. Arguments are heard differently depending on who is making them, and academics can often say things that their more politically situated allies cannot. Overall, his experience has been that the boundaries between research, activism, and policy are blurred and problematic given the frequent interchange between different roles and the fact that academics occupy many of these roles simultaneously.

Several of the same themes emerge in Stavrianakis' work on arms transfer control. She, too, has worked with NGOs and campaign organizations and faced some of the same dilemmas and tensions. In her case, it was the process of doing PhD research on NGO strategies in relation to the arms trade that pushed her politically more toward the critical, "outsider" end of the activist spectrum. The more she learnt about the arms trade, the more oriented toward activism she became. Yet her experience has been that academia provides the freedom and autonomous space to say things that cannot be said in an NGO or campaigner capacity. In this sense, her research is not directly *for* NGOs or campaigners. During interview work for her research, for example, she was repeatedly struck by not only the variety of opinions among NGO staffers, but how radical and critical the views often were of those who worked within "insider" organizations. Yet those "personal" views could not be translated into their organizations' policy and strategy. This led her to think increasingly about the structural disciplining of NGOs and about the ways that academic and NGO/campaign research can be made to complement each other.

Over the past decade or so, she has moved between oppositional activism and questioning the binary between theory and activism. She has experienced this as a recursive move in and out of engagement and in and out of theory, in which activism and scholarship inform each other, but remain distinct as social activities. This highlights the importance of translation (Stavrianakis 2006) but also is suggestive of how varied the political space is. Some arguments can be heard politically and are thus ripe for direct policy activism, whereas others are beyond the pale. For example, a term's sabbatical spent in Saferworld's China team led directly to policy-relevant briefing papers – welcomed, in part, because of the way the UK government's Foreign and Commonwealth Office has effectively outsourced its research capacity to insider NGOs, given funding cuts and changes to the character of the civil service. Meanwhile, academic articles that explore the ramifications of the Arms

Trade Treaty for liberal states' arms transfer practice (e.g., Stavrianakis 2006, 2010, 2016) grew out of, and also shaped, engagement with practitioners (diplomats, NGO staffers, experts) through participant observation at NGO and diplomatic meetings. This sort of work has policy ramifications, but does not readily lead to policy-relevant recommendations. This is in contrast to her research on the imperial relations of racialized gun control and the problem of methodological nationalism. This sort of research is too far removed from where the policy debate is to have any practical application: the battle is so politicized that there is very little space for engagement that broadens the boundaries. Hence, it is harder to trace the impact of the latter on policy (whether of the state, corporations, or NGOs): it is not obvious who the target audience is or what immediate change might be possible.

There are several key practice-based issues that Stavrianakis has found repeated over the years. These include the importance of paradigm compatibility, or speaking the same language as those with whom scholars are engaging. Given her research trajectory and political orientation, this has been easier with NGOs than with government departments, and within government, easier with elements of the Foreign and Commonwealth Office (FCO) and DfID than the Ministry of Defence (MoD) or Department for Business, Innovation and Skills (BIS), now split into International Trade, and Business, Energy and Industrial Strategy. Relatedly, she has been faced with the question of whether she is engaging with practitioners (whether NGO or government) to influence them, to share knowledge with them, or to conduct research on them. With some NGOs it has ended up being the former two elements; with the MoD it has ended up being the latter. Even with NGOs and campaign groups there are lines of argument beyond the political pale or strategically beyond the bounds of what can usefully be said. NGOs are often seen as the "good guys" against governments, but their positions are also circumscribed by politics. This puts academics in a difficult position when they are seen to criticize or not be on board with more progressive actors. This often results in an "ivory tower" criticism. But to return to the model of scholarship as practice outlined earlier, there remains a value in academics' autonomous positioning to articulate uncomfortable positions based on their research.

On the other hand, it is important to reflect on the ways academics are disciplined in a variety of ways. For Stavrianakis, her experience has been one of wanting to be seen as reliable, respectable, or reasonable: not only to get access to the MoD, FCO, and other "hard" elements of the state, but also to be able to talk to them, for us to hear each other. Yet any listening or hearing is always on their terms. Here the fiction of objectivity is useful but troublesome and limited – it is shot through with power relations. Attempting to use her position as an academic by acting as an expert witness in an Information Tribunal case brought by an anti–arms trade activist, she was repeatedly accused by government barristers of being a mouthpiece for Campaign Against Arms Trade – an anti-arms group with whom she has developed a relationship over the years. Her expert knowledge has been generated in part through involvement with activists; but when she used that knowledge as an ostensibly disinterested expert (the precondition for being called as an expert), there was an attempt to discredit her by more powerful actors. This illustrates the challenges of engagement: as academics we are autonomous but not disconnected and have to negotiate the political terrain at each turn.

Conclusion

Reflecting on similarities and differences across these two case studies and how they relate to the three types of interaction outlined, it is evident that there are practical issues that resonate with the policy engagement model. Timing, windows of opportunity, serendipity, speaking in the same terms as interlocutors, and so on are all significant practical challenges. There are also larger political issues at stake that speak to the second and third models of activism and scholarship as practice. These include the useful but troublesome fiction of disinterested scholarly neutrality, the role of research in generating a sense of crisis, the potential to bolster the position of weaker actors that require support, and the difficulties of creating openings for articulating different views in policy debate. These challenges give a different slant to the way we evaluate the impact of research beyond the university. Rather than valorizing research that is useful to state policy or enhances competitiveness (the explicit aim of the ESRC, for example), the key criterion could be whether research holds power (be it states or capital or civil society) to account. As UK citizens and UK-based academics, the key question is how to hold state power in the core of the international system to account. In both cases, that state power is allied to the power of capital – and at times to the power of NGOs. For example, in the case of the arms trade, while the MoD and BIS operate in tandem with military capital, DfID and parts of the FCO have (weaker) alliances with NGOs, so NGOs are integrated into the operation of state power (Stavrianakis 2010). So the question of whom to hold to account, and for what, is more complicated than we might initially think.

These issues mean we require a more nuanced view of where and how impact happens and with or to whom, taking into account all of the contingencies earlier about available spaces, risks involved, and the nature of the issue. Understanding the nature of the relationship between academia and the world beyond the university is inherently political. Failure to address the politics of engagement means we run the risk of powerful academics having powerful voices with powerful people, creating a self-reproducing dynamic and diminishing the prospects of progressive change. Thinking about where power is located and how it operates requires us to go beyond homogenizing accounts of key actors (be they states, corporations, international organizations, or NGOs) without being naive about the scope for autonomy and the willingness of powerful actors to engage with researchers and act on their findings.

Bibliography

Armijo, L. E. and S. Rhodes. 2015. "Can International Relations and Comparative Politics be Policy Relevant? Theory and Methods for Incorporating Political Context." *Politics & Policy*, 43 (5): 611–646.

Bertucci, M. E., F. Borges-Herrero and C. Fuentes-Julio. 2014. "Toward 'Best Practices' in Scholar – Practitioner Relations: Insights from the Field of Inter-American Affairs." *International Studies Perspectives*, 15 (1): 54–72.

Booth, K. 1995. "Human Wrongs and International Relations." *International Affairs*, 71 (1): 103–126.

Cox, R. 1981. "Social Forces, States and World Orders: Beyond International Relations Theory." *Millennium* 10 (2): 126–155.

Edkins, J. 2005. "Forum: Ethics and Practices of Engagement: Intellectuals in World Politics." *International Relations*, 19 (1): 63.

Eriksson, J. 2014. "On the Policy Relevance of Grand Theory." *International Studies Perspectives*, 15 (1): 94–108.

Eriksson, J. and L. Norman. 2011. "Political Utilisation of Scholarly Ideas: The 'Clash of Civilisations' vs. 'Soft Power' in US Foreign Policy." *Review of International Studies*, 37 (1): 417–436.

Eschle, C. and Maiguashca, B. 2007. "Rethinking Globalised Resistance: Feminist Activism and Critical Theorising in International Relations." *The British Journal of Politics and International Relations*, 9 (2): 284–301.

Herring, E. 2006. "Remaking the Mainstream: The Case for Activist IR Scholarship." *Millennium*, 35 (1): 105–118.

Lohmann, L. 2012. *Beyond Patzers and Clients: Strategic Reflections on Climate Change and the 'Green Economy'*. Dorset: The Corner House.

Newell, P. 2000. *Climate for Change: Non-State Actors and the Global Politics of the Greenhouse*. Cambridge: Cambridge University Press.

Newell, P. 2010. "Democratising Biotechnology? Deliberation, Participation and Social Regulation in a Neo-Liberal World." *Review of International Studies*, 36 (2): 471–491.

Newell, P. 2014. "Dialogue of the Deaf? The CDM's Legitimation Crisis." In *The Politics of Carbon Markets*. Edited by Stephan, B. and R. Lane. 212–236. London: Routledge.

Reus-Smit, C. 2012. "International Relations, Irrelevant? Don't Blame Theory." *Millennium: Journal of International Studies*, 40 (3): 525–540.

Stavrianakis, A. 2006. "Call to Arms: The University as a Site of Militarised Capitalism and a Site of Struggle." *Millennium*, 35 (1): 139–154.

Stavrianakis, A. 2010. *Taking Aim at the Arms Trade: NGOs, Global Civil Society and the World Military Order*. London: Zed Books.

Stavrianakis, A. 2016. "Legitimizing Liberal Militarism: Politics, Law and War in the Arms Trade Treaty." *Third World Quarterly*, 37 (5): 840–865.

Stavrianakis, A. and J. Selby. 2012. "War Becomes Academic: Human Terrain, Virtuous War and Contemporary Militarism: An Interview with James Der Derian." In *Militarism and International Relations: Political Economy, Security, Theory*. Edited by Stavrianakis, A. and J. Selby. 59–73. Routledge: London.

Van der Pijl, K. 2014. *The Discipline of Western Supremacy: Modes of Foreign Relations and Political Economy, Volume III*. London: Pluto.

Zambernardi, L. 2016. "Politics Is Too Important to Be Left to Political Scientists: A Critique of the Theory – Policy Nexus in International Relations," *European Journal of International Relations*, 22 (1): 3–23.

PART FIVE

Imagining the future

17

ESCAPING FROM THE PRISON OF POLITICAL SCIENCE

What IR offers that other disciplines do not

Justin Rosenberg

For many writers, the question of "what has been the unique contribution of IR to the social sciences and humanities?" has a simple and depressing answer: not very much.[1] Ever since IR was founded, the intellectual traffic has been almost entirely in the opposite direction: we import concepts and methods from other disciplines, but we have not produced any big ideas that are taken up elsewhere (Brown 2013, 485; Buzan and Little 2001, 19–21; Halliday 1994, 7). What should we make of this peculiar situation? And what can we do about it?

This chapter addresses these questions in three steps. First, it argues that IR has never quite been established as a field *in its own right*. It emerged as an extension of Political Science and has remained trapped within a borrowed definition of its subject matter. This "prison of Political Science" explains our failure to produce ideas that can travel to other disciplines. Second, however, this was not a necessary outcome. On the contrary, IR rests upon a fundamental fact that is full of implications for the social sciences. This is the fact that the human world comprises a *multiplicity* of co-existing societies. Knowing how to take intellectual possession of this fact and how to draw out its implications for other fields – these are the key to reversing our intellectual trade deficit and developing ideas that can travel creatively. Finally, the chapter considers one such idea – that of "uneven and combined development" – which could become a successful export from IR because it carries the importance of the international directly into the subject matter of other disciplines.

The prison of Political Science

What is the prison of Political Science? A powerful illustration can be seen in one of IR's founding texts: E. H. Carr's *The Twenty Years' Crisis* (1981). It lies about a third of the way through the book, at the start of Chapter 7. This is where Carr switches from criticizing his opponents and starts to lay his own foundations for the new discipline – and it looks at first as if he gets off to a flying start.

"Man," he tells us in the opening sentence, "has always lived in groups" (Carr 1981, 95). This is indeed the universal fact about the human world that must be the starting point for our discipline: the co-existence of multiple social entities. Surely, if he now reflects on this, he will uncover both the distinctiveness of this object of study and its implications for social existence in general. And the discipline of IR will be firmly established.

Alas, this is not what happens. When Carr talked about humans living in groups, his use of the plural word – "groups" – was almost incidental. He was not referring to the *co-existence* of multiple societies. What he actually meant was that humans always live in a group of some kind – they are social animals. And even this was just a means of getting to the foundational statement he *really* wants to make, which is a statement about *politics*: *because* individual humans always exist in a group, he says, "one of the functions of such a group has been to regulate relations between its members." He immediately adds: "Politics deals with the behavior of men in[side] . . . organized . . . groups" (Carr 1981, 95).

From here, Carr goes on to add three further points. First, in groups, people behave in both egoistic and cooperative ways. Second, although the *political* group, the state, is unique in being a compulsory association, it too exhibits this duality because it rests on both coercion and legitimacy. And finally, all this is no less true of *international* politics than of *domestic* politics. The "infancy" of "the science of international politics" (Carr 1981, 1) lies in the fact that it has not yet come to terms with this twofold character of its subject matter. Only when its initial utopian hopes have been balanced by realist analysis will this new field pass out of its infancy and become a social *science*.

In one sense it is hard to object to this reasoning. After all, Carr calls his chapter "The Nature of *Politics*" (Carr 1981, 95, emphasis added). And his basic point is Aristotle's undeniable claim that because humans live in groups, there is an irreducibly political dimension to their existence. Nonetheless, there is a real problem here. Carr is supposedly laying the foundations for a discipline of IR. However, the way he does this is not to identify what features of its own the international might uniquely contain. It is rather to extend the premises of Politics into the international. IR becomes an extension of the study of Politics or Political Science. And to see *why* this is a problem, we need to think for a moment about the nature of academic disciplines.

The study of the human world is distributed across a range of social sciences and humanities. People often lament this fragmentation, yet the division of labor does bring benefits too. Each discipline foregrounds a particular dimension of social reality and makes it the object of an organized enquiry. It analyzes both this dimension in itself and its wider significance for human affairs. As a result, the analysis surely goes much deeper than it would otherwise have done.

Geography, for example, specializes in the spatial dimension of human and natural existence – both what space means for society and how space is itself socially constructed in different ways in different places. It is thus about spatiality. Similarly, History ultimately subtends on our existence in time – which explains its preoccupations with historical specificity, causal sequencing, and narrative forms of explanatory method. Temporality is to History what spatiality is to Geography. Sociology is grounded in the fact that individual human lives are always carried on within wider structures of social relations. "Society" is its special object. It is no wonder that the "agent-structure debate" is perennial to this discipline. Sociology is, after all, the original home of the very idea of social *structure*. One last example: Comparative Literature is not just the study of the different national traditions of creative writing. At a deeper level, it is also about the properties of language itself – and how by extension the social world at large, which is also linguistically mediated and produced, exhibits properties of textuality that invite hermeneutic deconstruction and analysis.

In each of these four cases an academic discipline rests upon a specific feature of social reality – spatiality, temporality, social structure, and textuality. Yet this specialization is also the secret of their *trans*-disciplinary potential. Precisely *because* each has taken possession of something that is in fact *general* to the social world, their local investigations produce concepts that can suddenly travel and be applied right across the human sciences. We see this happening again and again – whether it is the "spatial turn" coming out of Geography; the Braudelian idea of temporal "conjuncture" from History; Wallerstein's World-Systems Theory which originates in Sociology; or poststructuralist and postcolonial theories today in which literary scholars like Edward Said, Homi Bhabha, and Gayatri Spivak have played such a prominent role.

In all these cases, the reason that a given discipline can speak to other disciplines (and has something to say to them) is precisely because it has specialized in a particular feature of social reality that is nonetheless general to the social world. So the question arises: What general feature is the special preserve of IR enabling *us* to speak to other disciplines in our *own* language about *their* particular subject matter?

If we ask this question of *The Twenty Years' Crisis*, the answer actually is "nothing." IR emerges from its infancy not by finding its own voice and object but by accepting that it is simply an extension of another discipline, the "science of politics." Only when the same assumptions are accepted for *international* politics as have been since Aristotle recognized for politics – only then will the *science* of IR exist.

Here we can see the foundations of the prison being laid. If IR is just a subfield of Political Science, then the only identity available for it becomes a negative one: it studies politics but in the absence of central authority. Thus the international itself becomes associated with the narrow version of it provided by political realism. And once that has happened, the possibility of IR producing ideas that can travel to other disciplines evaporates.

Even the work of Kenneth Waltz, who certainly did assert the distinctiveness of the international, has two characteristics that *prevent* it from having trans-disciplinary significance. First, he defined international theory as international *political* theory: it emphatically did *not* embrace a wider condition of internationality with implications beyond Political Science. Second, Waltz conceptualized the international as separate from, and counter-posed to, the domestic realm. About that domestic social world, neorealism – quite literally – had nothing to say, except to note how different it was from the world of international politics that existed alongside it.

Of course, realism has not had the field to itself in IR. Numerous other approaches have rejected both the narrow statist definition of the international and the idea of an autonomy of geopolitics. The sheer range of these alternatives – from liberalism, Marxism, and feminism through to constructivism, post-colonialism, queer theory, and so on – accounts for much of the vibrancy of IR today. Yet how many of these challenges have replaced realism with theories of their own that are based on the unique properties of the international? The answer, it seems, is none. Perhaps this is because they regard the idea of the international as part of the toxic legacy of realism (with its insistence on the "anarchical" inevitability of power politics and war). This is understandable, but it carries a high price. It leads them to conclude that international affairs must be shaped by other aspects of the social world, and they are best interpreted by ideas imported from the disciplines that study those aspects. Alas, this merely replaces one problem with another: if you declare that Sociology, or History, or Anthropology holds the key to understanding IR's subject matter, then IR is effectively turned into a subfield of Sociology, History, or Anthropology. The downside to IR's wonderful openness to the other disciplines is that if we have no deep ontology of our own, we become in effect *everybody's* subfield.

So we should hardly be surprised that no big ideas have traveled outwards from IR. Any such ideas would have to be about the unique importance of the international for the human world. However, the realists have defined it too narrowly for this role. And the anti-realists have steered clear of the uniqueness of the international because they associate it with realist claims about anarchy and power politics that they are determined to refute.

I call this situation "the prison of Political Science" for three main reasons. First, its ultimate source lies in the continuing failure of IR to emancipate itself from Political Science. Second, this situation confines IR within the premises of an alien discipline, preventing it from developing freely and realizing its own potential as a viewpoint on the world. And finally, just like in a real prison, IR can *receive* visits but it cannot repay them. It can import ideas from outside, but it cannot send anything back in return. Whatever significance the international holds for the wider social sciences, it never becomes visible. It remains locked inside the prison.

Yet it need not be so. Just like other disciplines, IR has an ontology of its own, one with enormous significance for all the human sciences. This ontology is not the property of any one particular approach. It is our shared inheritance as a discipline. And it is our way out of the prison of Political Science. To find out what it is, we need only return to the big question: If Geography subtends on our existence in space, and if Sociology analyzes the relational quality of human life, what general feature of the social world provides IR with its deepest ontological premise?

The consequences of multiplicity

No matter how much we twist and turn it in our hands, the word "international" always ends up presupposing the same basic thing: namely that human existence is not unitary but multiple. It is distributed across numerous interacting societies. This multiplicity is the basic fact about the human world that justifies the existence of IR as an academic discipline. No other discipline – not even Political Science – subtends fundamentally on this fact. It is uniquely our ontological premise.

This has remarkable consequences for all the social sciences. Some of these consequences are half-known to us already; but we half-know them under the negative sign bequeathed to us by Political Science – the sign of the *absence* of overarching government. We do not yet know them under the positive sign of the international – the co-*presence* of multiple interacting societies. And when it comes to IR finding its own voice among the disciplines, switching signs makes all the difference in the world. So what are these consequences?

Co-existence

The first and most profound one is this: at its highest level, the human world does not culminate in a single authority, nor does it just tail off into empty space; instead, it opens out into a lateral field of co-existing societies. This field of co-existence adds a whole new layer of social reality beyond the internal structures of any individual society. The result is not simply that the human world is bigger. It also contains a whole extra *kind* of social phenomena: inter-societal relations, inter-societal behavior, inter-societal ethical norms, and inter-societal causality. In other words, multiplicity generates the international itself as a dimension of the social world. It is the special remit of IR to bring this dimension into focus and construct it as an object of study. Will doing so just lead us back to realism? To find out, we must unpack the other consequences of multiplicity.

Difference

The second consequence is *difference*: for the *quantitative* multiplicity of societies is also a *qualitative* one. We know this empirically: societies differ from each other in all kinds of ways – size, power, culture, history, and so on. However, difference is also a *necessary* consequence of multiplicity itself. Why?

The reason is partly that multiple societies must vary in their geographical location. They are therefore differently influenced by the physical variety of the earth itself. Yet difference also obtains because the distribution of social development across more than one society *allows* it to take different forms in different places at the same time. One of the most distinctive attributes of humans as a species is our ability to construct our social existence in radically different ways, and for those ways themselves to undergo historical development and change. Multiplicity converts this attribute into a concrete variety of societies that actually coexist in space and time. Thus the international inscribes difference and multi-linearity into the nature of social development itself.

Interaction

Yet multiplicity is not just about co-existence and difference. It also compels societies into *interaction*. This is because it imposes a common condition on all societies: all confront the fact that the human world extends beyond themselves. And that is a source both of dangers and of opportunities. It is a danger because processes occurring outside can become threats to a society's interests or even survival. During the nineteenth century, dozens of Asian and African societies were overwhelmed because the industrial revolution elsewhere had increased the power of European states whose very existence had barely been known to them before. It is also an opportunity because differences between societies can be the basis for trade and for importing knowledge and resources produced by differential development elsewhere.

So multiplicity leads to interaction because societies *have* to manage their external environment through diplomatic and military means in order to survive; and if they want to benefit from the opportunities of difference, they must also develop structures of interdependence. All modern societies do both of these all the time. This is international relations as mainstream IR theory knows it – geopolitics and interdependence. However, the implications of multiplicity do not stop there.

Combination

Interaction brings with it a fourth consequence: no society undergoes a history that is truly uni-linear and self-enclosed. All societies are ongoing combinations of local patterns of development with external influences and pressures of all kinds. This can apply even to their most apparently indigenous elements. What could seem more English than the English language? Yet we know that it is actually a mixture of the Latin, Saxon, Norse, and French languages, among others. And those different ingredients are not just linguistic influences: they are the sedimentation in language of the influence of the Romans, Saxons, Vikings, and Normans on Britain's social and political history too. This has a dramatic implication both for IR and for all the other social sciences. It shows that the international dimension is not simply a matter of external relations: through interaction, multiplicity reaches into the inner constitution of societies themselves.

Dialectical change

Finally, if human societies are multiple, varied, and interactive, then it also follows that the process of *world* development cannot be uni-linear or even just multi-linear. It must be a fully dialectical process – shaped, that is, by interactions among different societies, and not just by the logic (or logics) of development internal to them as individual social formations.

Consider this example. In 1620, Francis Bacon wrote that the modern world was marked off from the past by the impact of three main inventions: gunpowder, the printing press, and the magnetic compass (Bacon 1960, 118). Between them, he wrote, these inventions had done more than any empire or religion to lift Europe out of the darkness of the Middle Ages. Unknown to Bacon, all three of these had originated in China and had been transferred to Europe through processes of indirect trade and communication.

This is not, however, simply a general point about interconnection: when they arrived in Europe, these Chinese inventions were inserted into a different social setting and they therefore developed in new directions and with results that they never had in China. The same can be said of the transfer of classical Greek learning from the Arab world to Europe at the start of the Renaissance – or indeed of the original translation of Greek philosophy into Arabic 300 years before. In all these cases, the dialogical transfer of something out of one society into another sets in train a new and different process of development that inflects the wider course of world development itself. And conversely, viewed in that wider frame, even the rise of the West turns out to have been rooted in a dialectical causality generated by the interactions of multiple societies.

Co-existence, difference, interaction, combination, dialectics: What do these five points tell us about the subject matter of IR? They tell us that the international is even more significant than we normally think. It certainly *is* the field of geopolitics and interdependence that realist and liberal theories say it is; but it is also the implications of societal multiplicity for all the so-called "domestic" aspects of social life too – for social structures, economic systems, intellectual production, cultural phenomena, and so on. To put it another way: a discipline of IR should certainly try to understand what happens in international politics, but it should also elaborate the significance of societal multiplicity for the social world as a whole.

This is our passport out of the prison of Political Science. It means that we finally have something to say to other disciplines about *their* subject matter. Instead of talking only about the significance of class, gender, language, and so on for IR, we can also explore the significance *of the international* for class, gender, and language too. This may even be something these other disciplines need and want to hear. One of the knottiest problems in the social sciences is the problem of "methodological nationalism" – unwittingly thinking of social change as entirely internal to individual societies. It is a problem that goes all the way back to the classical social theorists themselves, including Marx, Weber, and Durkheim. At a deep theoretical level, they conceptualized society in the singular and therefore failed to theorize the consequences of multiplicity for social reality. From this intellectual source the problem is carried into contemporary theory where, as many writers – from Theda Skocpol (1973) to Zygmunt Bauman (1992) to Ulrich Beck (2007) – have observed, it continues to hamper social analysis.

In his book, *Intimations of Postmodernity*, Zygmunt Bauman quails at the thought of what it would take to overcome this problem. Modeling the inter-societal space, he says, is a harder challenge "than anything the sociologists tried to grasp intellectually in the past" (1992, 65). Surely IR ought to have the solution? Societal multiplicity is, after all, the general feature of reality that is specific to us as a discipline. Alas, locked inside Political Science, it has not been available to other disciplines in a form they could use. Indeed, as the problem of methodological nationalism attests, the international has been the missing piece of the jigsaw of the social sciences. Yet if we reground IR in its own ontology of multiplicity, that piece can finally be put into place.

Of course, for that to happen, we now need ideas that operationalize all this – ideas that make the international exportable to other disciplines by showing its importance for their subject matter. Fortunately, we already have at least one such idea: the theory of uneven and combined development.

Uneven and combined development

This theory was originally formulated outside IR by Leon Trotsky at the start of the twentieth century. Yet it works precisely by operationalizing the five consequences of multiplicity outlined earlier. This enabled Trotsky to overcome a major instance of methodological nationalism at the time. Let us first recall what this instance was and then examine how Trotsky's theory re-imagines the international in a way that carries its significance beyond the discipline of IR.

At the start of the twentieth century, Czarist Russia was undergoing rapid capitalist development, but it was not retracing the experience of the Western countries as the *Communist Manifesto* implied it should. Marx and Engels had expected capitalism to create "a world in its own image" wherever it spread (Marx 1973, 71). State-led industrialization in Russia, however, was producing quite different social structures from those of Western Europe. And since the Russian Marxists drew their worldview from the *Manifesto*, they were increasingly left without a coherent political analysis and strategy. The root of their problem lay in their assumption that all societies had to pass through the same stages in order to develop – a belief that ignored the impact of international relations on social change. It was this problem that Trotsky solved by arguing that modern world development was not unilinear but was rather uneven and combined.

He began by invoking the first two consequences of multiplicity: for 'unevenness' meant that capitalism had emerged into a world of *co-existing* societies of *different* kinds and levels of development. Next, he argued that this unevenness produced a mixture of dangers and opportunities that intensified international interactions. On the one hand, the growing power of capitalist states imposed a geopolitical "whip of external necessity" (Trotsky 1932, 5) onto all other societies: if they could not reproduce this power inside themselves, they would be consumed by the European empires – as indeed most of them were. On the other hand, this same historical unevenness gave them a paradoxical opportunity too which Trotsky called the "privilege of historic backwardness": they did not *have* to retrace the slow, haphazard development of the pioneers; they could import the latest technological and financial results from outside. In this way, co-existence and difference among societies created the possibility of *accelerated* development among late-comers such as Russia.

Yet it also meant that late-comers would not become copies of the pioneer societies. Russian Czarism had no intention of transforming itself into a British-style constitutional monarchy. On the contrary, Czarism was importing foreign inventions and resources in order to shore up its own survival. The result, therefore, was not repetition, but *combination* – or, as Trotsky called it, "combined development." Elements of modern capitalist society were being grafted on to a semi-feudal social structure to produce a unique hybrid of the old and the new, in which the original sequence of developmental stages was being compressed and even re-ordered. What Trotsky was discovering here was the difference that societal multiplicity was making to the history of capitalist world development. And he realized that as a result of this difference, the overall shape of that process was dialectically altering too.

Trotsky referred to this big picture as the "social structure of humanity" (1962, 9). He argued that it did not comprise a homogeneous world of capitalist states that were just at different stages of a uniform development. Instead, East–West interactions had produced peculiar social structures in the catch-up societies, making them paradoxically *closer* to anti-capitalist revolution than were the advanced Western societies where Marx had expected the first revolutions to occur. In this way, the international – conceived as uneven and combined development – had dialectically transferred the trigger of world revolution away from the Western countries. This was an outcome that Marx's largely unilinear theory could not have foreseen. Trotsky's analysis now transformed it from a baffling contradiction into an enabling condition of political action.

One need not share Trotsky's Marxism to see the significance of this move. The inner logic of his idea is the exact inverse of E. H. Carr's in *The Twenty Years' Crisis*. Carr argued from the nature of politics to the nature of the international. Trotsky's idea, by contrast, is all about how deeply the *international* can reshape the dynamics of *political* development and change. And by inverting the direction of the analysis in this way, it looks like the kind of big idea that could be exported from IR into the other social sciences.

After all, the world today is full of striking instances of combined development. The largest, in every sense, is surely China, a country that endured a whip of external necessity so intense and prolonged they call it "the century of humiliations." Using the privilege of historic backwardness, Chinese industrialization is now occurring on an even more accelerated, compressed scale than the other late developers before it. And like others before it, Chinese combined development is also producing a peculiar hybrid social formation. Capitalist industrialization organized by a semi-feudal Czarist monarchy was weird enough; capitalism presided over by a communist state is surely the weirdest, most paradoxical combination so far.

Yet it is far from being the only one. In Saudi Arabia, a tribal system of politics has been grafted onto an industrializing society, so that the state – which owns the wealth of society – is itself the property of a 7,000-strong extended family of princes. The forcing together of the old and the new does not come more extreme than that. Yet a significant chunk of the world's energy supply rests on this peculiar political hybrid (and the events of 9/11 showed how just how unstable this hybrid could be). Meanwhile in Iran, a theocratic revolution that has no precedent in *Shia Islam*, let alone the textbooks of Western social theory, has been locked in a confrontation with the great powers over its use of advanced nuclear technology. "Islamic Republic" – the very name announces the fusion of traditional and modern elements. Because we live with these examples every day, we forget how truly peculiar they are. Their existence could never be explained by internal development alone – international pressures and opportunities have created these hybrids and woven them into the social structure of humanity. They demonstrate the relevance of Trotsky's idea in contemporary social analysis.

Yet, they also do something else. They help us finally correct the balance between IR and Political Science. For nearly a century now, political realists have defined IR as a subfield of Political Science. *We* – that is, those of us working in IR – already know that it is much more than that. The consequences of societal multiplicity extend across all the different fields of human action and thought. Yet among these different fields is, of course, Political Science itself. If it now turns out that the real-world political systems studied by Political Science have themselves been interactively produced, and this is what explains their individual peculiarities, then it must follow that in this respect Political Science is a subfield of IR.

The point is worth savoring, though we should not press it in an imperialistic way. The logic of our argument about academic disciplines is that *all* are subfields of all the others with regard to the particular aspects of social reality those others have made their own. All should be importers *and* exporters of ideas. The anomaly of IR is that it has so far been only an importer; and this is because it had not found an independent foundation of its own, but instead has been locked inside Political Science.

Conclusion

We can press this argument one step further using an example from comparative literature. Trotsky notes at one point that "Russian thought, like the Russian economy, developed under the direct pressure of the higher thought and more developed economies of the West" (1962, 173–74). That sounds like a mechanical formula. Yet it need not be. It could be the first step in an extension of "uneven and combined development" from the social sciences to the humanities. There it could provide a framework for uncovering the international history of ideas and of cultural production in particular. And a brilliant example of what that might mean has been provided by the Brazilian writer Roberto Schwarz (1992).

Schwarz analyses the rise of the Brazilian novel after national independence in 1822. He argues that this literary trajectory was part of a wider cultural process in which a new Brazilian intelligentsia was scrambling to assemble what were then seen as the accouterments of a modern civilized society. The European novel, a literary form that gave expression to the new kinds of private and public identity associated with bourgeois society, was among the most prominent of these accouterments. Brazil must therefore produce novels of its own.

There was a problem, however. Unlike England and France, nineteenth-century Brazil was not a bourgeois society. On the contrary, it was based on aristocracy, clientilism, and slavery. This did not provide the basis for the plot form of the European novel, which explored the fate of socially constructed individuals adrift in a depersonalized world of commercial relations. The result of this mismatch was a first generation of Brazilian novels that were necessarily superficial and inauthentic – not engaging with the reality of Brazilian society at all. The real history of the Brazilian novel began only later, when both the plot form and the narrative voice of the novel were redesigned by the next generation. Only then could they express both the different production of individuals in Brazil and the different inner meaning of European ideals when they were transplanted into Brazilian society. The result was not just the creation of an authentic Brazilian literature; it was also a further development of the literary form of the novel itself, which expanded its possibilities beyond the European originals that had been so slavishly copied at the start of the process.

This example rediscovers in the sphere of cultural production exactly those consequences of multiplicity that lie at the heart of IR's social ontology: the coexistence and variation of multiple societies, the pressures and opportunities this creates that lead to interaction, the innovation of new forms which emerge from the process of hybridization, and finally the dialectical structure of the overall process itself. What Schwarz has reconstructed here is an episode in the uneven and combined development of the novel as a modern literary form.

And what goes for the novel also goes for music, film, architecture – even clothing fashions and cookery. In fact, there is an international relations of just about everything, just like there is a spatiality and a sociology and a politics of everything. And that is because societal multiplicity, like spatiality, social structure, and politics, is a *general* feature of the human world.

Applying uneven and combined development in these other fields will enable them to incorporate the international, but it will also enrich *our* conception of the international itself as we follow its causality into one area of life after another. Schwarz's analysis of the nineteenth-century Brazilian novel is as much a case study in international relations as is Mearsheimer's (2014) critique of Western policy in Ukraine. Both explore the consequences of societal multiplicity for a particular aspect of the human world.

As the centenary of IR approaches, then, it is time to leave behind the prison of Political Science. When we reflect on the consequences of multiplicity, we find that the foundations for an independent discipline already exist. If we look outwards, we start to discover the enormous constitutive significance of the international for the social world in all its dimensions. As we piece together the different elements of this, IR surely *can* become a producer of big ideas for the social sciences and humanities. And if that is the case, then when the centenary of IR arrives, we will indeed have every reason to celebrate.

Note

1 This chapter is an edited version of the 2015 EH Carr Memorial Lecture, delivered at the University of Aberystwyth in October 2015. An expanded version of the lecture has been published as Rosenberg (2016). I am grateful to Sage for permission to reproduce material from the original lecture here.

Bibliography

Bacon, Francis. 1960. *The New Organon and Related Writings*. Edited by Fulton H. Anderson. New York: Bobbs-Merrill.

Bauman, Zygmunt. 1992. *Intimations of Postmodernity*. London: Routledge.

Beck, Ulrich. 2007. "The Cosmopolitan Condition: Why Methodological Nationalism Fails." *Theory, Culture and Society*, 24 (7–8): 286–290.

Brown, Chris. 2013. "The Poverty of Grand Theory." *European Journal of International Relations*, 19 (3): 483–497.

Buzan, Barry and Little, Richard. 2001. "Why International Relations Has Failed as an Intellectual Project and What to Do about It." *Millennium: Journal of International Studies*, 30 (1): 19–39.

Carr, E. H. 1981. *The Twenty Years' Crisis 1919–1939, an Introduction to the Study of International Relations*, 2nd Edition. Basingstoke: Macmillan.

Halliday, Fred. 1994. *Rethinking International Relations*. Basingstoke: Macmillan.

Marx, Karl and Engels, Friedrich. 1973. "Manifesto of the Communist Party." In *The Revolutions of 1848: Political Writings, Volume I*. Edited and Introduction by David Fernbach. 62–98. Harmondsworth: Penguin.

Mearsheimer, John. 2014. "Why the Ukraine Crisis Is the West's Fault." *Foreign Affairs*, September–October 2014, 1–12.

Rosenberg, Justin. 2016. "IR in the Prison of Political Science." *International Relations*, 30 (2): 127–153.

Schwarz, Roberto. 1992. *Misplaced Ideas: Essays on Brazilian Culture*. London: Verso.

Skocpol, Theda. 1973. "A Critical Review of Barrington Moore's *Social Origins of Dictatorship and Democracy*." *Politics and Society*, 4 (1): 1–34.

Trotsky, Leon. 1932. *The History of the Russian Revolution*. New York: Pathfinder.

Trotsky, Leon. 1962. *The Permanent Revolution/Results and Prospects*. London: New Park Publications.

18

THE FUTURE OF FEMINIST INTERNATIONAL RELATIONS

Adrienne Roberts

This chapter seeks to draw attention to current discussions taking place over the past, present, and future of feminist International Relations (IR). These discussions, which have occurred in a number of different forums over the past several years, center on a shift that has taken place in feminist IR scholarship over time. Whereas much of the early feminist IR scholarship that emerged in the late 1980s and 1990s sought to apply a gender lens to issues traditionally associated with war, peace, and security *as well as* issues related to the global political economy, by the early 2000s, it is argued, these two areas of research were increasingly de-linked and separated into distinct feminist security studies (FSS) and feminist international political economy (FIPE) literatures. For those engaged in this discussion, this de-linking is generally posited as an unfortunate development, which has had the effect of analytically separating questions about war/peace, in/security, and borders from questions about the global economy and the production–reproduction nexus. The result, it has been argued, has limited the ability of either body of work to adequately account for the intersections between these social processes and therefore to offer a sufficiently holistic account of global politics.

Part of the concern, expressed by people like Lisa Prügl, is that FSS has overshadowed FIPE to become the "most visible research field in feminist IR during the past decade" (Prügl 2011, 112). That is, while the FSS work focused on questions and theories of war, militarism, peace, and security is readily identified with the label of feminist IR, other areas of feminist research (which includes research into the international political economy as well as issues of global governance) are much less so. As someone who works in the area of FIPE, I am interested in asking the following: What is to be gained by returning to a more integrated feminist IR? What, if anything, might be lost in the process?

In order to answer these questions, this chapter begins, first, by offering an overview of feminist IR and the debate about the need to address cleavages within this scholarship. While I am broadly sympathetic to much of what is being suggested, I argue that there is actually very little by way of critical interrogation of the similarities and/or differences between SS and IPE in either its feminist or non-feminist forms. Second, drawing on the broader resistance of many IPE scholars to being subsumed under the banner of IR, I suggest that there may actually be very little to gain from "re-subsuming" FIPE under the banner of feminist IR. This is not least because several decades after the first feminist interventions in the discipline, IR remains a rather inhospitable place to do feminist research. Third, while I am not advocating a move back toward an integrated feminist IR per se, I nonetheless agree that there are important insights provided by FSS scholarship, as well as critical (but not explicitly feminist) IR scholarship that can usefully be taken forward within feminist scholarship *outside* of IR. While this chapter mainly focuses on feminist research, it has implications for IR more broadly as it raises questions about "the point of IR" for scholarship that identifies itself with IPE and/or other areas of the social sciences. Contrary to what many of those working within the field of IR suggest, it is not at all clear that this is the only, or the best, place from where to engage in critical research, writing, and teaching about global politics.

To feminist IR and back again

Feminist thought began to be applied to IR relatively later than it did to other areas of the social sciences. Nonetheless, when it did emerge in the 1980s and 1990s, it offered a forceful critique of the gender-blindness of both positivist and post-positivist approaches. Without offering a detailed overview of feminist IR scholarship, which has been done in a number of excellent recent collections (Tickner and Sjoberg 2013; Tickner 2014; Shepherd 2015; Steans and Tepe-Belfrage 2016), ultimately, this work has exposed the ways gendered meaning systems inform how we produce knowledge about the world. Whereas mainstream IR scholarship has tended to focus on the so-called "high" politics of war and interactions between state actors, feminists have suggested that this is a "masculinist knowledge enterprise" (Prügl 2011, 112) that marginalizes women's experiences, their voices, and their contributions to constituting the "international." It also creates dichotomies and hierarchies between the masculine and the feminine, which are not about men and women per se, but rather about the privileging of a host of behaviors that are considered to be masculine, up to and including the supposedly objective search for "truth" that underpins the dominant positivist approaches to the study of IR (Peterson 2005).

Feminist scholarship challenges the conventional understanding of IR as a discipline concerned with power struggles between sovereign states operating under conditions of anarchy. Rather, feminists understand IR to involve "the identification and explanation of social stratifications and of inequality as structured at the level of global relations" (S. Brown quoted in Runyan and Peterson 2014, 18). Here, power is viewed in much broader and more complex ways, and it operates at a range of levels, from the household to the global, and through a range of social structures, including the structures of sexism, racism, classism, and heterosexism (2014, 34).

Given these challenges to the way that the IR discipline has been framed, it is unsurprising that feminist IR has drawn heavily from feminist (and other critical) work done within other disciplines, including sociology, anthropology, development studies, legal studies, gender studies, and more. It is perhaps also unsurprising that many of the early feminist IR scholars came from outside of the discipline. For instance, Cynthia Enloe's immensely influential *Bananas, Beaches and Bases: Making Feminist Sense of International Politics*, first published in 1989, was not originally written for an IR audience. As she explains:

> What happened is that the women inside of the IR camp, picked it up and they did the hard work of using it to break open some discussions. Spike Peterson and Ann Tickner, people who were already 'inside of' IR, said 'We will take this and use it.' Then, they kind of adopted me and brought me into IR.
>
> (Schouten and Dunman 2012)

For Enloe, along with a number of other pioneering feminist scholars, the emphasis put on the "personal" and the household as levels of analysis, the attention given to a multiplicity of power relations, and the focus on overlapping structures of inequality led to analyses of international politics that linked questions about war, militarism, peace, and security to those about the global economy, the division of labor, and unpaid work. Along with Enloe, Ann Tickner has tended to employ a view of feminist IR as being concerned with questions of war and militarism alongside questions of political economy. One of her key contributions to feminist IR is rooted in her framing of security as involving national security, along with ecological and economic security. This is not merely the case with work published in the 1980s and 1990s, as people like Ann Sisson Runyan and Spike Peterson (2014), for instance, have continued to emphasize the co-constitutive nature of changes in global security, global political economy, and global governance (see also Peterson 2003).

Nonetheless, it has been observed that whereas much of the early work in feminist IR had a broad conception of global politics, since the turn of the millennium there has been a growing divergence within feminist IR scholarship, particularly between feminist work in security studies and feminist work in international political economy, with the former being more readily identified with IR than the latter. In 2011, Lisa Prügl suggested that a quick survey of the program of the International Studies Association (ISA) conference pointed to the visibility of FSS within the field, as almost half of the panels sponsored by the Feminist Theory and Gender Studies Section focused on security – a dramatic increase from a mere 3 out of 24 panels in 2001 (2011, 112). A similarly quick survey of the ISA 2015 program shows an impressive 28 FTGS-sponsored panels on security, war, and/or militarization. In contrast, there were only 5 panels that could be clearly identified as IPE, while another 28 were on topics that do not easily fall into either camp, covering a wide range of things such as diplomacy and peace processes, international organizations, global health, sexism in the academy, and queering global politics.

While this anecdotal evidence about the ISA suggests an exciting array of feminist IR scholarship, it also seems to confirm the cleavage between FSS and FIPE, which has been explicitly discussed at these conferences. At the ISA in 2012, for instance, this theme was visited in a panel entitled "Feminist International Relations: Towards an Integrated Analysis," while in 2014, it was the topic of a roundtable entitled "Feminist Security Studies and Feminist Global Political Economy: Crossing Divides and Rebuilding Bridges." The contributions to the latter roundtable were subsequently published in a special section of *Politics & Gender* in 2015 (volume 11, issue 2) edited by Juanita Elias. While the contributors to the special section differ on a number of counts, the general tone of these discussions suggests that there is a need to move toward re-integrating FSS and FIPE perspectives in a way that more closely resembles the work of early feminist IR scholars.

While I am generally sympathetic to much of what is being suggested in the debates, I would also argue that much more needs to be done to critically interrogate the ontological, epistemological, and methodological similarities and/or divisions between SS and IPE in both its feminist and non-feminist forms. Instead, in these discussions, IPE ends up being, to use the terminology of Laura Sjoberg (2015), a *lens* that, when used in conjunction with an SS *lens*, can help to make sense of the lived experiences of conflict and violence. Yet, this notion of being used in conjunction with SS – or with IR more broadly – stands somewhat in tension with the claims of IPE scholars that their framing offers a more holistic (or "totalizing") analysis of global politics that accounts for the mutually constitutive nature of politics and economics (Steans and Tepe 2010). That is, given that the "economic" is not separated from politics (including the politics of militarization and war), it is unclear how this could operate as a separate lens from that used to understand these processes.

Far from simply focusing on "economic" processes, much FIPE begins from the ontological starting point that the ways human beings organize to meet their productive and reproductive needs forms the basis of a particular society (Bakker and Gill 2003; LeBaron 2010). Here, the point is that productive and reproductive social relations are the foundations upon which other politico-economic processes are built, even though it is in the interest of some to project "the economic" as a separate (and apolitical) sphere (Roberts 2016). Thus, even Tickner's multifaceted definition of security fails to capture the essence of much FIPE, which is more concerned with problematizing the gendered category of "the economic" (Benería 2003) than it is with interrogating the conditions under which "economic security" can be achieved.

For their part, within these debates, many of the FIPE scholars have suggested that they have already integrated "security" questions into their work by developing broader political economy analyses of violence, particularly "everyday" forms of violence experienced by women in the home, in the workplace, in travel, or in public spaces (Elias and Rai 2015; True 2012; 2015). This is an important point (and one to which I return later in the chapter), as it emphasizes one of the key areas of overlap between FIPE and FSS scholarship: the need to focus on "everyday life," up to and including the supposedly personal experiences of non-elite women and men (see also Allison 2015). However, the focus on everyday violence is only one part of what FSS aims to do. It seeks to reformulate mainstream approaches to traditional security issues, foreground the roles that women and gender play in conflict and conflict resolution, and complicate what it means to achieve "international security" (Sjoberg 2009: 184). In other words, much (but by no means all) FSS engages with mainstream SS and IR scholarship in a way that FIPE does not (for critical reflections on this engagement, see Lobasz and Sjoberg 2011).

As various contributors to this debate have suggested, part of the division between these two areas of research is linked to their different theoretical and methodological orientations, with much FSS being influenced by post-structuralism and its related methods (particularly discourse analysis) and FIPE being more closely linked to Marxism and/or institutionalism and a methodological preference for interrogating "material" relations. While some are optimistic about the ability to bring these theoretical traditions together (Hudson 2015), it is not immediately clear how this will be done given long-standing debates between these theoretical traditions (see, for instance, Bieler and Morton 2008). While debates between post-structuralist and Marxist traditions are perennial, there are also a number of feminist scholars who work comfortably at their intersections, with Spike Peterson (2003) standing out as a particularly notable example of someone working across the material-discursive divide (see also Marchand and Runyan 2000; Griffin 2011). In other words, it is not clear that a theoretical reconciliation is needed to bring these approaches into greater conversation.

In raising these issues, my aim is not to suggest that there is nothing to gain from promoting more interaction between FSS and FIPE scholarship, as this is surely a worthwhile endeavor. What is less obvious, however, is that this discussion should occur under the banner of a broadened IR. It is to this point that I now turn.

What's the point of IR for feminism?

The relationship between IR and IPE is contested. For many, IPE is believed to have originated in 1971, when Susan Strange founded the International Political Economy Group (IPEG), which later became a research group within the British International Studies Association (BISA). While the group was originally focused on a narrow range of issues, including how to resuscitate the fixed exchange-rate system, it is argued that developments in the 1970s (including wars in the Middle East that affected oil prices) led to a widening of the scope of IPE and to the diffusion of this field of inquiry (Murphy and Nelson 2001). There is also a debate within the field of IPE about its own internal coherence, with Benjamin Cohen (controversially) arguing that there are two distinct schools of IPE: an American School characterized by the "twin principles of positivism and empiricism" and a British School driven by a more normative, interpretive, and ultimately "critical" agenda. In both instances, he argued, the aim is to study "the complex linkages between economic and political activity at the level of international affairs" (Cohen 2007,

197). Taken together, these approaches position IPE as a relatively new area of study that is derived from political science, to which it brings insights from the discipline of economics.

Others, however, would disagree with these origin stories of IPE, arguing that it is problematic to view IPE simply as a merging of politics and economics. Luke Ashworth, for instance, offers a different history of IPE, arguing that it has important links with the tradition of political economy, which is distinct from "economics" and goes back much further to the eighteenth century. Focusing on Britain in the 1950s, Ashworth points out "that the study of international affairs *was* IPE," and many of the early IR scholars associated with this period "took a political economy approach to international problems" (Ashworth 2011, 11). In contrast to the characterization earlier, there is a large amount of critical IPE scholarship that begins from the starting point that the dichotomy between states and markets is a false one (Higgott and Watson 2008), and the task of IPE is not to bring an "economic" perspective to bear on political science – or, for that matter, IR – but rather to develop its own holistic approach to world order (Cox 1981; Cox 1987).

While some would certainly argue that IPE falls under the broader umbrella of the discipline of IR, the purpose of raising these debates is to show that this is contested. At a number of universities (including my own place of work, the University of Manchester), undergraduate and/or post-graduate programs in IPE are separate from those in IR. Research groups often fall into these different categories, as do job appointments. There is also a tendency for IPE scholars to publish in and read different journals than IR scholars and to seek out different academic presses (Malinlak and Tierney 2009, 9–10).

Part of the IPE critique of IR focuses on its preoccupation with questions of "high politics," its failure to understand the interplay between the "international" and the domestic, its inability to adequately account for cooperation and interdependence, and its problematic tendency to see "politics" and "economics" as separate. As Sandra Whitworth observes, these are also feminist critiques of IR more broadly (Whitworth 2006; see also Marchand and Runyan 2000). While IPE has not necessarily done a better job of incorporating feminist frameworks into its core – though there is some research to suggest that IPE scholars value women's contributions to the field more than other IR scholars do (Malinlak and Tierney 2009, 13) – it may nonetheless be better suited to the type of interdisciplinary inquiry that informs feminists research than IR. Given this broader context, what is the point of IR for feminists and for feminist international political economists in particular?

Decades after its initial interventions, feminism remains in an uncomfortable position within IR. This has never been far from the minds of feminist IR scholars, who have continually reflected on this troubled relationship. This is partly because feminism is an explicitly self-reflective endeavor (Ackerly and True 2010). It is also because of a deep-seated frustration among feminists whose attempts at widening (and internationalizing) the field of IR have been ignored by mainstream scholars who do not consider them to be doing IR at all. In a famous article entitled "You Just Don't Understand," Ann Tickner (1997) explained that a key misunderstanding between feminists and IR theorists relates to the question of epistemology. In an interview 15 years later, Tickner reiterated this argument, noting that while there has "been some acceptance of the subject matter with which feminists are concerned, it is a more fundamental and contentious question as to whether feminists are recognized as 'doing IR' in the methodological sense" (Riffkin-Ronnigan 2013).

Thus, there is both an epistemological and a methodological misunderstanding. Tickner notes:

> [a]s the field broadens its concerns, IR may see issues that feminists raise as legitimate, but how we study them still evokes the same responses that I brought up fifteen years ago. Many of the questions that feminists ask are not amenable to being answered using the social scientific methodologies popular in the field, particularly in the US.
>
> (Riffkin-Ronnigan 2013)

Marysia Zalewski also makes this point, noting that "there is a great deal of feminist work being done on international politics, although you might not find most of this work in IR." She went on to note that "feminist scholars have made massive inroads in constituting international politics in theory/practice – though not (always) as a 'contribution' to IR" (Schouten 2009).

The continued invisibility of feminist contributions to IR came to light at the 9th Pan-European Conference on International Relations in 2015 when the conference organizers decided to name the conference rooms after eminent IR theorists. All 18 of the IR theorists who gave their names to the conference rooms were men of European origin. The invisibility of my own research area within IR was made evident when, at the "What's the point of IR?" conference (upon which this volume is based), a senior scholar in the field asked me about my research. After explaining that I was researching corporate-driven gender equality agendas, which include campaigns such as Nike's "Girl Effect" and Coca-Cola's 5x20 initiative, she asked, "And does anyone take that work seriously?"

Feminist global politics outside of IR

According to Judith Squires and Jutta Weldes, "[w]hile most feminist scholars see feminist research as having the potential to transform IR, many now wonder if IR is the right place for 'a more radical rethinking of what properly constitutes I/international R/relations' to begin with'" (quoted in Tickner and Sjoberg 2013, 224). In line with this latter group of critical scholars, I would suggest that there is no need to return to a more "integrated" feminist IR scholarship. Rather, I would argue that a more fruitful way forward would involve strengthening interdisciplinary discussions about the gendered nature of global politics more broadly.

This could take place as part of a broadened feminist IPE (in the critical "British" tradition), for instance, which could include many of the insights of feminist scholars in IR along with feminist scholars in other disciplines. The potential for

FIPE to be a truly interdisciplinary endeavor is demonstrated in the wide range of scholarship brought together in the *Handbook of the International Political Economy of Gender*, which I co-edited with Juanita Elias (2017). This collection includes chapters written by people who identify themselves as IPE, along with those working in the areas of SS, IR, political economy, political theory, comparative politics, geography, development studies, migration studies, queer studies, and gender studies.

However, I am less concerned with advocating a broadened FIPE agenda than I am in suggesting that IR is not the *only* place where sustained conversation between feminists interested in global politics can take place. As Georgina Wayeln (2006) has pointed out in her rejoinder to Tickner's (1997) article, despite the many potential points of contact between IPE and feminist critiques of IR, IPE "still does not understand" the importance of gender as a constitutive force in global politics or the effects of global processes on gender relations. Nonetheless, critical IPE shares much in the way of common ontological and epistemological ground with feminist approaches (Wayeln 2006, 164) and may be a more hospitable home from which to continue to debate the intersections of security and political economy. Jacqui True's (2012) work on the political economy of violence against women is an excellent example of such engagement occurring within an IPE framework.

While I believe that these conversations need not wed themselves to the field of IR, there are important moves taking place within IR that can and should be taken forward. While feminists instigated some of these moves, some have also been instigated by critical IR scholars who do not associated themselves with gender scholarship; and some advances have been promoted by feminist and non-feminist scholars alike, sometimes without acknowledging each other's contributions.

One important turn in IR scholarship is the focus on how "everyday" social relations both affect and are affected by global politics (Elias and Rethel 2016; Elias and Roberts 2016). As Cynthia Enloe (2013) has suggested, the "mundane" matters when we conceptualize broader processes of global change. This is because, on the one hand, global processes are predicated on a host of daily activities that allow these processes to take place. We cannot have global trade or national armies without workers and soldiers who need to be birthed, fed, clothed, and cared for. On the other hand, global processes affect people "on the ground" in myriad ways as the international is *always* personal. Outside of feminist perspectives as well, the "everyday" has become an increasingly popular framework in SS (Jarvis and Lister 2013; Vaughan-Williams and Stevens 2016) and IPE (Hobson and Seabrooke 2007; Davies 2016). The everyday turn thus provides important openings for future engagement between feminist and other critical scholarship and will be central to future feminist work on global politics (be that work inside or outside of IR).

IR has also made some important inroads into identifying its own colonial origins and in offering alternative histories that have the potential to greatly expand how the cannon is viewed within the discipline (Hobson 2012; Blaney and Tickner 2013; Shilliam 2010; 2015). Of course, this is not a task that is particularly new, as it has a long history in post-colonial and feminist IR. In 1996, Jindy Pettman (1996) asked how the discipline of IR could be "worlded," which entailed, in part, the inclusion of the different worlds of those outside of the power centers (and not from dominant classes) into understandings of global politics. Others have continued to develop this notion of "worldism" (Agathangelou and Ling 2009) and to otherwise challenge the Western- and male-centric history of IR scholarship and propose alternative futures. IPE has much to learn from this reframing of the past and present of the discipline, and this must be a central part of feminist and critical scholarship looking forward.

Conclusion

Reflecting on the concluding session of a conference on feminist IR (the proceedings of which were later published in an edited volume), Ann Tickner and Laura Sjoberg argue that feminist scholars have the tools to embark on the mission of "rewriting IR," as well as offering advice and guidance in the policy arena (2013, 232). I am less certain that this is the case and more skeptical about the claims emerging for the need to bring FIPE "back into" IR. However, I am also aware of the need to avoid "[b]uilding, brick by metaphorical brick, new intellectual barriers [that] would deprive all of us, trying to make sense of politics in all its myriad guises, of crucial feminist insights" (Enloe 2015, 436). Thus, while this chapter is intended to be provocative and to challenge a number of assumptions about IR, it should be understood as a productive engagement about the future of feminist thought inside and outside of IR. It should be understood as seeking to build bridges rather than walls, even if those bridges take us outside the field of IR.

Bibliography

Ackerly, Brooke A., and Jacqui True. 2010. *Doing Feminist Research in Political & Social Science.* Basingstoke: Palgrave Macmillan.

Agathangelou, Anna M., and L.H.M. Ling. 2009. *Transforming World Politics: From Empire to Multiple Worlds.* London: Routledge.

Allison, Katherine. 2015. "Feminist Security Studies and Feminist International Political Economy: Considering Feminist Stories." *Politics & Gender* 11 (2): 430–34.

Ashworth, Lucian M. 2011. "Missing Voices: Critical Ipe, Disciplinary History and H.N. Brailsford's Analysis of the Capitalist International Anarchy." In *Critical International Political Economy: Dialogue, Debate and Dissensus.* Edited by Stuart Shields, Ian Bruff, and Huw Macartney, 9–26. Basingstoke: Palgrave Macmillan.

Bakker, Isabella, and Stephen Gill. 2003. "Ontology, Method, and Hypotheses." In *Power, Production and Social Reproduction.* Edited by Isabella Bakker and Stephen Gill. 17–41. New York: Palgrave Macmillan.

Benería, Lourdes. 2003. "Economic Rationality and Globalization: A Feminist Perspective." In *Feminist Economics Today: Beyond Economic Man.* Edited by Marianne A. Ferber and Julie A. Nelson. 115–33. London: University of Chicago Press.

Bieler, Andreas, and Adam David Morton. 2008. "The Deficits of Discourse in IPE: Turning Base Metal into Gold?" *International Studies Quarterly* 52 (2): 103–28.

Blaney, David L., and Arlene B. Tickner. Eds. 2013. *Claiming the International: Worlding Beyond the West.* London: Routledge.

Cohen, Benjamin. 2007. "The Transatlantic Divide: Why Are American and British IPE So Different?" *Review of International Political Economy* 14 (2): 197–219.

Cox, Robert. 1981. "Social Forces, States and World Orders: Beyond International Relations Theory." *Millennium: Journal of International Studies* 10 (2): 126–51.

———. 1987. *Production, Power, and World Order: Social Forces in the Making of History*. New York: Columbia University Press.

Davies, Marr. 2016. "Everyday Life as Critique: Revisiting the Everyday in IPE with Henri Lefebvre and Postcolonialism." *International Political Sociology* 10 (1): 22–38.

Elias, Juanita, and Shirin M. Rai. 2015. "The Everyday Gendered Political Economy of Violence." *Politics & Gender* 11 (2): 424–29.

Elias, Juanita, and Lena Rethel. Eds. 2016. *The Everyday Political Economy of Southeast Asia*. Cambridge: Cambridge University Press.

Elias, Juanita, and Adrienne Roberts. 2016. "Feminist Global Political Economies of the Everyday: From Bananas to Bingo." *Globalizations* 13 (5): 1–14.

Enloe, Cynthia. 2013. *Seriously! Investigating Crashes and Crises as If Women Mattered*. Berkeley: University of California Press.

———. 2015. "Closing Reflection: Militiamen Get Paid; Women Borrowers Get Beaten." *Politics & Gender* 11 (2): 435–38.

Griffin, Penny. 2011. "Poststructuralism in/and IPE." In *Critical International Political Economy: Dialogue, Debate and Dissensus*. Edited by Stuart Shields, Ian Bruff, and Huw Macartney, 43–60. Basingstoke & New York: Palgrave Macmillan.

Higgott, Richard, and Matthew Watson. 2008. "All at Sea in a Barbed Wire Canoe: Professor Cohen's Transatlantic Voyage in IPE." *Review of International Political Economy* 15 (1): 1–17.

Hobson, John. 2012. *The Eurocentric Conception of World Politics: Western International Theory, 1760–2010*. Cambridge: Cambridge University Press.

Hobson, John, and Leonard Seabrooke. 2007. *Everyday Politics of the World Economy*. Cambridge: Cambridge University Press.

Hudson, Heidi. 2015. "(Re)Framing the Relationship between Discourse and Materiality in Feminist Security Studies and Feminist IPE." *Politics & Gender* 11 (2): 413–19.

Jarvis, Lee, and Michael Lister. 2013. "Vernacular Securities and Their Study: A Qualitative Analysis and Research Agenda." *International Relations* 27 (2): 158–79.

LeBaron, Genevieve. 2010. "The Political Economy of the Household: Neoliberal Restructuring, Enclosures, and Daily Life." *Review of International Political Economy* 17 (5): 889–912.

Lobasz, Jennifer, and Laura Sjoberg. Eds. 2011. "The State of Feminist Security Studies: A Conversation." *Politics & Gender* 7 (4).

Malinlak, Daniel, and Michael J. Tierney. 2009. "The American School of IPE." *Review of International Political Economy* 16 (1): 6–33.

Marchand, Marianne, and Anne Sisson Runyan. 2000. "Introduction: Feminist Sightings of Global Restructuring." In *Gender and Global Restructuring: Sightings, Sites and Resistances*. Edited by Marianne Marchant and Anne Sisson Runyan. 1–22. London: Routledge.

Murphy, Craig, and Douglas Nelson. 2001. "International Political Economy: A Tale of Two Heterodoxies." *British Journal of Politics and International Relations* 3 (3): 393–412.

Peterson, V. Spike. 2003. *A Critical Rewriting of Global Political Economy: Integrating Reproductive, Productive, and Virtual Economies*. London: Routledge.

———. 2005. "How (the Meaning of) Gender Matters in Political Economy." *New Political Economy* 10 (4): 499–521.

Pettman, Jan Jindy. 1996. *Worlding Women: A Feminist International Politics*. London: Routledge.

Prügl, Elisabeth. 2011. "Feminist International Relations." *Politics & Gender* 7 (1): 111–17.

Riffkin-Ronnigan, C. 2013. "Theory Talk #54: Ann Tickner on Feminist Philosophy of Science, Engaging the Mainstream, and (Still) Remaining Critical in/of Ir." *Theory Talks* http://www.theory-talks.org/2013/04/theory-talk-54.html

Roberts, Adrienne. 2016. *Gendered States of Punishment and Welfare*. London: Routledge.

Runyan, Anne Sisson, and V. Spike Peterson. 2014. *Global Gender Issues in the New Millennium*. 4th ed. Boulder: Westview Press.

Schouten, P. 2009. "Theory Talk #28: Marysia Zalewski on Unsettling Ir, Masculinity and Making IR Theory Interesting (Again)." *Theory Talks* http://www.theory-talks.org/2009/04/theory-talk-28.html

Schouten, P., and H. Dunman. 2012. "Theory Talk #48: Cynthia Enloe on Militarization, Feminism, and the International Politics of Banana Boats." *Theory Talks* http://www.theory-talks.org/2012/05/theory-talk-48.html

Shepherd, Laura J. Ed. 2015. *Gender Matters in Global Politics: A Feminist Introduction to International Relations*. 2nd ed. Abindgon: Routledge.

Shilliam, Robbie. Ed. 2010. *International Relations and Non-Western Thought: Imperialism, Colonialism and Investigations of Global Modernity*. London: Routledge.

———. 2015. *The Black Pacific: Anticolonial Struggles and Oceanic Connections*. London: Bloomsbury Academic Press.

Sjoberg, Laura. 2009. "Introduction to Security Studies: Feminist Contributions." *Security Studies* 18 (2): 183–213.

———. 2015. "From Unity to Divergence and Back Again: Security and Economy in Feminist International Relations." *Politics & Gender* 11 (2): 408–13.

Steans, Jill, and Daniela Tepe-Belfrage. 2010. "Introduction – Social Reproduction in International Political Economy: Theoretical Insights and International, Transnational and Local Sitings." *Review of International Political Economy* 15 (5): 807–15.

Steans, Jill, and Daniela Tepe-Belfrage. Eds. 2016. *Handbook of Gender in World Politics*. Oxford: Edward Elgar.

Tickner, J. Ann. 1997. "You Just Don't Understand: Troubled Engagements between Feminists and IR Theorists." *International Studies Quarterly* 41: 611–32.

———. 2014. *A Feminist Voyage through International Relations*. Oxford: Oxford University Press.

Tickner, J. Ann, and Laura Sjoberg. 2013. *Feminism and International Relations: Conversations About the Past, Present and Future*. Abingdon: Routledge.

True, Jacqui. 2012. *The Political Economy ofViolence against Women*. Oxford: Oxford University Press.

———. 2015. "A Tale of Two Feminisms in International Relations? Feminist Political Economy and the Women, Peace and Security Agenda." *Politics & Gender* 11 (2): 419–24.

Vaughan-Williams, Nick, and Daniel Stevens. 2016. "Vernacular Theories of Everyday (in) Security: The Disruptive Potential of Non-Elite Knowledge." *Security Dialogue* 47 (1): 40–58.

Wayeln, Georgina. 2006. "You Still Don't Understand: Why Troubled Engagements Continue between Feminists and (Critical) IPE." *Review of International Studies* 32 (1): 145–64.

Whitworth, Sandra. 2006. "Theory and Exclusion: Gender, Masculinity and International Political Economy." In *Political Economy and the Changing Global Order*. Edited by Richard Stubbs and Geoffrey Underhill. Oxford: Oxford University Press.

19

A METHODOLOGICAL TURN LONG OVERDUE

Or, why it is time for critical scholars to cut their losses

Samuel Knafo

Perspectivism, the idea that knowledge is always only a perspective on world politics, never a fully objective account of it, is perhaps the main foundation behind the emergence of critical approaches in the 1980s and 1990s. In Robert Cox's famous words, "[T]heory is always for someone and for some purpose" (Cox 1981: 128). As a first step, this idea became a tool to highlight how mainstream approaches concealed class, patriarchal, or colonial interests, and more generally worldviews under the pretense of universal claims. Emphasizing the need for other perspectives was also a means to break the walls erected by the mainstream to cast out of the discipline a series of social concerns that critical scholars wanted to tackle. Yet critical scholars rarely took the second step of working out the reflexive implications of perspectivism for the way they carry out their own work. Usually employed as a relativizing device, a means to celebrate diversity (Weldon 2006; Levine 2012), the perspectival nature of knowledge was never taken to place its own methodological demands on critical scholars. And yet, the very fact that we know that we always have to settle for a perspective, rather than an objective view on the world, implies that difficult decisions will have to be made which cannot be based on the evidence or simply justified in the name of normative commitments.

This chapter argues that the future of the discipline, or at least of its critical approaches, should be cast in the font of a methodological turn. Building on recent literature, which seeks to highlight the importance of methodology (Ackerly, Stein, and True 2006: Salter and Mutlu 2012; Hamati-Ataya 2013), I contend that it is time for critical scholars to move beyond their long infatuation with ontology in order to reflect concretely on the demands that perspectivism places on critical scholarship. For the challenge of critique does not consist in open promises to recognize complexity, but in the sober recognition that doing so forces us to make more difficult decisions as to what should be left out. In that respect, I will argue that the difficult part is not to open up doors, but rather to decide on which door to close.

To make this point, I proceed in two steps. First, I reflect on the resistance of critical approaches toward methodology and why they often see it as standing in the way of critique. As I will show through various examples, this problem can be observed in a variety of approaches such as radical constructivism, neo-Gramscianism, feminism, or poststructuralism, which all reject positivism by invoking some form of perspectivism but without drawing out the methodological implications of this recognition. The second section of the chapter takes a step in this direction. It argues that the epistemological critique directed at mainstream approaches should be turned back onto critical approaches and used as a building block for an alternative methodology. For many of the problems attributed to the mainstream also represent, I argue, key stumbling blocks for critical scholars.

Critique and the resistance to methodology

What is the point of methodology? The issue is central to what we take to be the purpose of IR. For positivism, methodology is the defining feature of scientific knowledge claims and what marks out the knowledge about world politics that this discipline generates. In that respect, the purpose of methodology is to test claims and validate them as legitimate and objective through the rigorous collection, organization, and manipulation of facts about world politics. This ambition, however, was challenged by non-positivist scholars who progressively demoted the place given to methodology in the practice of knowledge production. Generally, non-positivists criticized the emphasis given to methodology as smacking of academicism, as if the goal was simply to produce knowledge of a certain quality, rather than knowledge which could make a difference. Perspectivism was central to this concern with the transformative effects of knowledge because making a difference often came to be seen as developing a different perspective on world politics which could inform a new practice. In the process, non-positivists thus turned away from the idea that methodology defines what is at stake in IR (i.e., the production of scientific claims as defined by methodology). This critique of methodology involved three arguments:

A tool to silence dissent?

The first reason is that methodology came to be seen as a disciplinary device used by mainstream scholars to silence more critical scholarship. This stems partly from the history of IR as a field of study which saw numerous attempts to discipline dissent on methodological grounds. In particular, the emergence of critical approaches in the 1980s and 1990s took place in the face of various attempts to dismiss them for their inability to live up to so-called scientific standards (Keohane 1988). Critical scholars were repeatedly asked to translate their work in positivist terms, with methodology being offered as a scientific common ground that could be used to test different theories. In response, neo-Gramscians, feminists, and poststructuralists all took aim at positivism (Lapid 1989: Harding 1992), criticizing how it introduces highly conservative biases by seeking to make world politics quantifiable and amenable to empiricist enquiries.

Although the critique of positivism raised a lot of important points, one of the unfortunate outcomes of this debate was that critical approaches often came to conflate methodology with positivism (Jackson 2011: 186). The result was a powerful stigma attached to methodology. It is striking that critical scholars now often depoliticize this aspect of their own work precisely to steer clear of any suggestion that they may themselves use methodology as a disciplinary device. Avoiding methodological debate has thus meant that IR discussions continue to be concerned mostly with theoretical programs defined by ontology – that is, what we deem to be the main structures, actors, and processes which shape world politics, rather than modes of enquiry. In other words, we are usually more concerned with debating about how to conceive of world politics, rather than with the concrete ways we actually produce knowledge, as if ontology is a more legitimate terrain for disagreement than methodology. Ironically, critical scholars thus often seem to internalize the positivist assumption that engaging issues of methodology meant defining what counts as a scientific procedure and thus who is considered to be a legitimate or scientific interlocutor. This was a task they rightly refused to consider. But, in sacrificing methodology in the process, they lost sight of their epistemological concerns.

A constraint on critical thinking?

Second, the reluctance of critical scholars to engage with methodology goes beyond a concern with those seeking to impose a standard of proper scientific conduct upon others. There is also a resistance on the part of critical scholars to the idea of methodological commitments because they are seen to constitute constraints on critical thinking (Wendt 1992: 393). It is not uncommon to see critical scholars oppose strict formalizations of their mode of inquiry on the basis that this would deter innovation and critical thinking, an idea which draws support from the philosophy of science, in particular the work of Paul Feyerabend (see Wight 2006: 240).

This is largely the legacy, once more, of the post-positivist debate when it became fashionable to claim that critical thinking requires flexibility and imagination too often hemmed in by the tight parameters of mainstream science. Robert Cox put forward a famous articulation of this problem with his characterization of the field of IR as divided between "problem solving theory and "critical theory." According to Cox, trying to define tightly the methodological parameters of our studies traps our thinking within rigid frames that are not conducive to the goal of challenging our own assumptions. Methodological rigor, Cox argued, has forced positivists to adopt ahistorical perspectives that take for granted the premises upon which the social order is established (Cox 1981: 129). By contrast, critical work, more interpretative in nature, is bound to appear less rigorous even if it is more promising for generating rich critical insights. This is precisely because remaining open to unexpected findings about history requires flexibility.

This settlement has meant that there is an asymmetry at the heart of the critical project. Critical scholars are often keen to challenge the objectivity and scientific nature of mainstream approaches, presenting them for "what they are": specific perspectives parading as universal accounts. Yet critical scholars mostly avoid subjecting themselves to the same standards. They rarely develop a reflexive strategy to deal with their own biases and often claim instead the privilege of awareness. From this perspective, knowing that knowledge is only a perspective can help critical scholars avoid reifying world politics by being more careful and open to other viewpoints (Levine 2012). In other words, realizing that claims only represent a perspective should encourage us to be self-critical, more aware of our normative biases, and open to challenging what is "simply a heuristic" (Gill 1993). But such a strategy built on good intentions only betrays an inordinate belief on the part of critical scholars in their ability to perceive their own social conditioning; as if reflexivity, or the ability to challenge what we take for granted, is a matter of awareness rather than technique (or methodology). *Knowing that our viewpoint is only a perspective does not mean that we understand what is specific about it.* The result is that too often critical scholars conclude that the epistemological problems they are pointing to apply only to specific perspectives unaware of the real nature of knowledge, when in reality it concerns the very fact that we all work on the basis of a perspective. Coming to grips with our own perspective is a fundamental challenge for all approaches. It applies as much to critical scholars as it does to the mainstream they criticize.

Committing critique to ontology?

A third reason for why methodology continues to be neglected is that, having rejected the idea that critique should subject itself to an ideal of science, or knowledge production, most critical scholars privilege ontology as a lens to direct their enquiries. Believing there is no point in worrying about a scientific method because methodology cannot live up to the ambition of producing objective knowledge, they confined methodology to more applied tasks for scholars doing fieldwork or relying on data manipulations. In this new role, methodology was mostly a matter to be dealt with on a case-by-case basis rather than framed as an integral part of a broader critical strategy of enquiry that could be defined *a priori*. Patrick Thaddeus Jackson thus observes that IR scholars came to focus mostly on what he calls methods – that is, the concrete "techniques for gathering and analysing bits of data" – which were expected to be relevant to a specific research project rather than with methodology per se, understood here as a broader concerns "with the logical structure and procedure of scientific enquiry" (2008: 131). For broader strategic decisions about how to structure their studies, they relied mostly on ontology and theories about the nature of world politics, rather than on epistemology, or more generally considerations about the nature of knowledge. Epistemology was used mostly as a tool of critique to show the limits of positivism, not as a starting point for thinking about how to produce knowledge claims.

That ontology came to be seen as a substitute for methodology was a direct product of perspectivism. For the shift to ontology was only possible because perspectivism blurs the lines between ontology and methodology. It suggests that our choice of ontology (i.e., our template for understanding the nature of world politics) is itself a normative and political commitment. It is not based on truth or absolute necessity and is never a simple recognition of "what is." Ontology can then be conceived *as a commitment* to a worldview that sets its own priorities (e.g., determining what are the main dynamics, actors, institutions, and discourses that shape world politics). From there, it can be easily interpreted as a methodology in its own right in that it sets out a program and tells us what to focus on. But this meant a shift in what was considered important when framing our studies, with scholars usually focusing on setting out their priorities (the aspect of world politics they wish to emphasize), rather than being explicit about how they deal with facts or treat the evidence, which had been the traditional concern of methodology.

Closing the door on common sense

What is the point of IR if we have only a perspective? It cannot simply be to affirm our right to produce knowledge claims without having to worry about whether it is objective or not. As I argued, the point for critical scholars was to authorize the production of a different type of knowledge. This often meant highlighting how world politics was socially constructed and thus amenable to be transformed and re-constructed. However, in seeking to make space for new priorities, concerns with methodology too often receded to the background. Perspectivism was thus often treated as a mere ethical injunction to act responsibly with knowledge and to recognize its temporary, partial, and fluid nature.

In this last section, I want to argue that there is more to perspectivism. The fact that knowledge always comes in the form of a perspective has too often been treated as a justification for abdicating any pretense to science, when in fact it should have increased the stakes of methodology. For the recognition of the open relationship of knowledge to world politics implies that more choices about framing have to be made. These are not simply a matter of setting our priorities. They involve epistemological concerns which stem from the very process of producing knowledge and which are somewhat independent of our object of research. This is why methodology should be a much more integral part of critique because what is at stake is the development of new capacities to engage with world politics.

I make three points for why a methodological turn is now a necessary step for critical scholarship to build the capacities to come to terms with the challenges of perspectivism. These all point to the fact that the difficult problems that perspective poses for critique do not come from the fact that we interpret from somewhere (i.e., from our specific biases about world politics). *They stem from the work that needs to be done to establish a relationship to an object* (Knafo 2016). As I argue later, when we seek to carve a perspective on world politics, we often have to make compromises that sometimes undermine key aspects of the critical project. For example, we abstract from social complexity in order to gain some distance, thus reifying the very world we are keen to problematize. This is precisely what methodology is meant to address. It should represent a set of counters to navigate the pitfalls associated with the development of a perspective. It should not be reduced simply to an ethical call about how to deal with perspectives once we already have them.

Capitalizing on the epistemological resources of critique

The first reason why we need this methodological turn is that critical scholars have missed an opportunity to capitalize on many of their epistemological insights about the nature of knowledge. Epistemological contributions have usually been geared toward criticizing other positions rather than developing strategies of critical enquiry (Jackson 2011: 186). Yet there is a trove of valuable ideas here to be mined. A central, yet simple, idea behind this text is the Nietzschean notion that a perspective can be established only if we take a lot out of the frame. In other words, if we took everything into consideration, there would be no perspective, nothing that would stand out. This is an easy critique that has been articulated against naïve versions of objectivity. However, few use this as a framing device despite the fact that there is much to gain to reflect on this question, as I will argue later.

A similar insight is the observation that meaning crystallizes through contrasts and differentiation, as pointed out in numerous discussions of identity formation. And yet there are few systematic comparative approaches in IR that exploit differentiation as a strategy of analysis. In fact, poststructuralists have usually taken the opposite road of deconstructing difference, making it more and more difficult to settle the terms of their own perspective (i.e., on what basis are they to establish differentiation to locate their interventions).[1] While scholars do compare along historical lines, very little spatial comparisons are made. It is my contention that there are many ideas like these that are begging to be developed more fully from a methodological standpoint.

Making good on our claims to reflexivity

The second reason for turning to methodology is that it is the only platform we have to make good on our claims to reflexivity. As often pointed out, perspectivism puts a great onus on reflexivity because of the specific nature of our knowledge (Bourdieu and Wacquant 1992). Yet there are few reflexive hooks embedded in the very structure of critical enquiries.[2] We may be aware that we need to be reflexive, but good intentions are not enough. The challenge is to develop techniques to actively question our own assumptions. This is a task which ontology cannot fulfill since it grounds the very perspective we are seeking to problematize. We need something else to provide us with an angle and give us a perspective on our own perspective: a means to gain some distance. This is why reflexivity requires a framing device which is different from our ontology, a commitment distinct from the priorities we set at the ontological level and which can "work against the grain."

This intuition is brilliantly captured by non-IR scholars such as Quentin Skinner and Bruno Latour (Skinner 1978; Latour 2005) who turn, each in their own way, methodological framing into a lens to destabilize our understanding of social reality.[3] When social reality seems too seamless or transparent, this is usually because we take too much for granted. As a result, methodology must provide an anchor to work against the thrust of our ontologies.

To give a concrete example, one can refer to the work of Skinner who speaks of the importance of destabilizing how we interpret political theory. When looking at an author writing in a different age, he argues, we are often struck by what are general conventions of the time. Take the example of Karl Marx. It is common for scholars reading him to place the emphasis on the labor theory of value. Yet this theory was a widely held convention at the time and associated in fact with liberalism and particularly the influential work of David Ricardo. It would thus be wrong to single out this theory as the defining contribution of Marx. This type of problem led Skinner to emphasize the need to rely on comparisons with other authors such as Ricardo, in order to grasp how Marx mobilizes the conventions of his age, such as the labor theory of value, for a specific purpose. In this respect, Skinner's great insight is to turn contextualization into a reflexive tool meant to challenge what we take to be an author's contribution, rather than a means to explain why an author is doing what she is doing. It is an effective framing device that has little to do with how Skinner thinks of politics but which can help, for this very reason, to destabilize our assumptions.

In this respect, methodology is a key register to frame our analysis because it provides space to gain distance from our assumptions. This can be possible only if we are clear about the distinction between methodology and ontology and if we can establish our methodological strategies on the basis of principles that have more to do with our understanding of how knowledge works (i.e., epistemology) rather than ontology, precisely so that they do not map onto one another. For the goal is to entertain a productive tension between two forms of commitments (ontological and methodological) and the space this tension creates to challenge our own assumptions.

Ultimately, ontology seeks to capture what is most important about the world and thus it is always liable to be conflated with reality as if it was justified by the fact that this is how the world is. When we keep the lines blurred, we are giving ourselves what is often an irresistible invitation to fall back on such justifications. In that respect, drawing a clear distinction between ontology and methodology represents the quintessential reflexive move, a form of ethical rigor that stops us from falling back on the easy but unfounded claim that our enquiries are based essentially on "reality."

Making complexity count

The third reason is that methodology is a vital tool to create accountability. This was, of course, key to the methodology of positivism. For the point was not simply to define what constitutes scientific knowledge but also to determine what needs to be established so that others can understand how conclusions are reached. In that respect, objectivity was something that needed to be demonstrated or established. Yet, in dismissing the positivist concern with objectivity, critiques of positivism mostly lost sight of this issue of accountability. Limited accountability about the process of knowledge production meant that critical scholars often multiplied the promises as to what they wished to look for, leading to vast expansive agendas which could never materialize. Calls were made on a regular basis to remediate reification, reductionism, or determinism by bringing back social complexity in the form of history, agency, social relations, difference, and intersectionality. Yet, critical scholars often failed to live up to their ambitions. Constructivists who insisted on the importance of agency rarely succeeded in making space for it in their studies (Checkel 1998). Historical Materialists who emphasized history so often reduced it to a set of examples to draw upon in order to illustrate dynamics established at more deductive and theoretical level (Knafo 2010). Poststructuralists who sought to do away with grand narrative often ended up grounding their analysis in broad sweeping claims about modernity, governmentality, or western civilization.

Such examples highlight once more that the main challenge is not to recognize social complexity, but to make it count. It is easy for Foucauldians to insist on the need to account for the micro-configurations of power, but it makes little difference if most studies continue to rely on overly general ideas about governmentality. Setting standards for accountability in knowledge production thus constitutes a recognition that what matters is not our intentions, but what we actually do. This is why we need to be much more concrete and precise about how we wish to track the work of history, agency, and difference in our accounts so as to enable others to assess how well we live up to our promises.

That this represents a real issue is best reflected in the fact that many of these vectors of complexity have led to the formation of intractable dualisms that have now become central preoccupations for the whole IR discipline. Dualisms such as the opposition between theory (general) and history (specificity), between structures and agency, the global and the local, the national and the international, the state and the market, or more recently the human and nonhumans all attest to recurrent difficulties we confront in coming to terms with world politics when seeking to factor in complexity.

As I mentioned initially, the real difficulty lies in the challenges involved in the very process of crafting a perspective on world politics. We may wish to capture the complexity of history, to register the agency of people, or the specificity of social relations, but we also look for powerful claims about world politics that often depend precisely on taking this complexity out of the equation. Simply describing a wide set of facts is of little use. They need to be streamlined in order to establish a compelling perspective, and this creates difficult trade-offs we need to acknowledge. Indeed, it is easier to speak of power by looking at structural features or to explain broad regimes such as neoliberalism by abstracting from historical specificities. But this is also why reification is such a difficult problem to deal with. Developing a perspective on world politics usually pushes us to drop complexity out of the equation because it is convenient to do so.

This is why I argue that coming to terms with perspectivism is to recognize finally that critical scholars need to cut their losses and accept that they cannot have it all. Making space for complexity is only possible if we accept that the general terms in such binaries must be cast out so that we are forced to develop alternative strategies for gaining perspective on world politics. In that respect, methodology must serve as a corrective lens to make history, agency, specificity, and more generally difference count as more than simple variations on a common theme. This will happen only if we relinquish the misguided hope that these binaries can be overcome through some form of dialectical model that takes both sides into account, or is simply transcended by dismissing the very existence of the problem in the first place. Instead, we need a methodological rigor to force us on a new terrain. We need to learn to speak about power and inequality without relying on the idea of structural power (Knafo 2010), to analyze liberal governance without relying on the overly general concept of the market (Knafo 2013). For this, one cannot rely on thinking about how power or world politics works and fall back on ontology. We need to be strategic about how we can make this social complexity stand out through various framing devices such as the one proposed by Skinner to think of political theory. It is only then that we can finally make good on the promises of critique.

Conclusion

Any discussion about the future of a discipline is usually bound to have advocates for bringing "back in" new things that need to be taken into consideration. This, of course, helps enrich our discussions. Too often, however, it ends up adding to the ever-growing wish list of critical approaches. Rapidly, we get overwhelmed by new agendas that propose to take an increasing number of things into account, making it harder to make decisions. As the calls multiply, we risk becoming paralyzed by complexity and lose our critical edge. It is precisely because this trade-off is a difficult one that we need a strategy, one that does not rest on how we see world politics but on what type of knowledge we wish to produce.

Critical scholars may be tempted to brush off such concerns as a conservative ploy to kick away the ladder, but in fact this may be said to apply first and foremost to the more established critical approaches which never took this step and only added to the layers of what they consider important to take into account. There is a genuine trade-off which must be taken seriously. What is at stake is not setting in stone all of the issues that should be of concern to the field of IR, but rather to recognize that the laudable critical goal of expanding what we take into account also comes with its own set of pitfalls. Bringing more layers requires a more robust methodological framing to make complexity count, one that can enable us to avoid overloading our concerns by strategically narrowing the lens.

In making this argument, I have emphasized that many academic debates should be resolved on methodological grounds rather than ontological ones. For critical scholars have too often exaggerated the naivety of others, as if the mainstream is not reflexive, and overestimated their own abilities to come to terms with social conditioning. The turn to methodology is a necessary move mandated by the ethic of accountability. Perspectivism has too often been used to make the mainstream accountable while lowering the demands placed upon critique. In that respect, there is great promise in coming to terms with perspectivism because the limitations attributed to the mainstream are often stumbling blocks for critical approaches themselves. These problems are not issues that can be avoided. We have to learn to work with them. While methodological commitments can often be constraining, the point is precisely that they should force us to go in places where we would not otherwise venture. As a means to challenge our assumptions, they are crucial in stopping us from settling back on our common sense and overly relying on our own judgment.

Notes

1 One may argue that deconstruction represents the culmination of the poststructuralist ethos of destabilizing perspective, an attempt to solve the inherent contradiction between recognizing the necessity of perspective while seeking to avoid biases.
2 Too often critical scholars insist on the need to bend over backwards in order to grasp from where their perspective comes, but this has often turned reflexivity into a peripheral affair, one focused on the self and mostly separated from the actual analysis of world politics (see Knafo 2016).
3 Actor Network Theory has had a profound impact in thinking about methodology, but too often scholars unfortunately dropped the methodological framing and read the approach in ontological terms.

Bibliography

Ackerly, B., M. Stein and J. True. 2006. "Feminist Methodologies for International Relations." In *Feminist Methodologies for International Relations*. Edited by B. Ackerly, M. Stein and J. True. 1–16. Cambridge: Cambridge University Press.

Bourdieu, P. and L. Wacquant. 1992. *An Invitation to Reflexive Sociology*. London: University of Chicago Press.

Checkel, J. T. 1998. "The Constructivist Turn in International Relations Theory." *World Politics* 50 (1): 324–348.

Cox, R. W. 1981. "Social Forces, States and World Orders: Beyond International Relations Theory." *Millennium: Journal of International Studies* 10 (2): 126–155.

Gill, S. 1993. "Epistemology, Ontology and the 'Italian School'." In *Gramsci, Historical Materialism and International Relations*. Edited by S. Gill. 21–48. Cambridge: Cambridge University Press.

Hamati-Ataya, I. 2013. "Reflectivity, Reflexivity, Reflexivism – IR's Reflexive Turn – and beyond." *European Journal of International Relations* 19 (4): 669–694.

Harding, S. 1992. "After the Neutrality Ideal: Science, Politics, and Strong Objectivity." *Social Research* 59 (3): 567–587.

Jackson, P. T. 2011. *The Conduct of Inquiry in International Relations*. London: Routledge.

Keohane, R. 1988. "International Institutions: Two Approaches." *International Studies Quarterly* 32 (4): 379–396.

Knafo, S. 2002. "The Fetishizing Subject of Marx's Capital." *Capital and Class* 76: 183–213.

Knafo, S. 2010. "Critical Approaches and the Legacy of the Agent/Structure Debate in International Relations." *Cambridge Review of International Affairs* 23 (3): 493–516.

Knafo, S. 2013. *The Making of Modern Finance: Liberal Governance and the Gold Standard*. London: Routledge.

Knafo, S. 2016. "Bourdieu and the Dead end of Reflexivity: On the Impossible Task of Locating the Subject." *Review of International Studies* 42 (1): 25–47.

Lapid, Y. 1989. "The Third Debate: On the Prospects of International Theory in a Post-Positivist Era." *International Studies Quarterly* 33 (3): 235–254.

Levine, D. J. 2012. *Recovering International Relations: The Promise of Sustainable Critique*. Oxford: Oxford University Press.

Salter, M. and C. Mutlu. Eds. 2012. *Research Methods in Critical Security Studies: An Introduction*. London: Routledge.

Weldon, S. L. 2006. "Inclusion and Understanding: A Collective Methodology for Feminist International Relations." In *Feminist Methodologies for International Relations*. Edited by Ackerly B. Brooke, M. Stern and J. True. 62–88. Cambridge: Cambridge University Press.

Wendt, A. 1992. "Anarchy Is What States Make of It: The Social Construction of Power Politics." *International Organization* 46 (2): 391–425.

Wight, C. 2006. *Agents, Structures and International Relations: Politics as Ontology*. Cambridge: Cambridge University Press.

20

SUBVERTING THE "INTERNATIONAL"

Imagining future as past

Yongjin Zhang

Anniversary is always an occasion for celebration, reflection, and contemplation. The fiftieth anniversary of IR at Sussex is no doubt a distinctive landmark for disciplinary development at Sussex, past and future. However, unlike the 50-year-old versed in the Confucian learning who would like to claim, as the Sage did, that "At fifty, I know the decrees of Heaven," disciplinary IR at 50 at Sussex, like anywhere else, cannot claim to know any of Heaven's decrees for its future. Rather, it seems steeped in anxieties not just about striking changes of IR as a discipline in the last 50 years, but equally about what the future may hold for the discipline we have been collectively constructing and reinventing. In what follows, I offer four brief exercises of thought and imagination, reflecting first, from the vantage point of 2015, upon the dynamic evolution of the discipline in the past 50 years, as the material world of international relations underwent profound, and sometimes unforeseen, transformations. Yet, instead of gazing into a possible future of the discipline, I propose a modest intellectual project – a global history of international thought – that builds on the legacies of Martin Wight and Sussex IR as an ongoing endeavor to subvert the still paradigmatic, but parochial, understanding of the "international" that continues to hinder the healthy development of the discipline. In so doing, my intervention also pays tribute to IR at Sussex.

1965 and after: IR and/at Sussex

Imagine you were in Sussex in 1965 as a student of IR. You would have been taught by Martin Wight, among others. There would have been no escape from such Wight (1966) questions as "Why is there no international theory?" The history of European political thought would have been central to your learning of IR theory (Kavan 2015). If you have stayed on as an academic, whether at Sussex or anywhere else, you would have grown up – intellectually if not otherwise – with the legendary "great debates" of this contentious discipline. You would have witnessed personally and may even have contributed to the inter-paradigm debates and to battles lost and won by what David Lake (2011) called "evil isms" – realists, neo-liberal institutionalists, Marxists, constructivists, and a host of critical, post-positivist, and reflectivist theoretical approaches. You would have had a personal story to tell, reminiscent of an intellectual journey you have embarked on in pursuit of knowledge. You would have probably taught your students – with all good intentions – a number of disciplinary "myths," among which is the proliferation of theories as the putative progress of an academic discipline. As a student at Sussex in 1965, you could never have imagined the disciplinary anxieties, false promises, and unanticipated twists and turns, and yes paranoia, too, through which that adolescent discipline called IR would have evolved and thrived in the way that it has. Nor could you have ever imagined that the "international" would have been so stretched and become so encompassing that it is now inclusive of almost all human activities with its complexity.

In 1965, students and scholars studying and residing at Sussex, and anywhere else, were living in a material world and international order appreciably different from that which we have come to inhabit today. The Cold War was raging, and the third generation of the Berlin Wall was just being put up to replace the old construction. The year 1965 was three years after the Cuban Missile Crisis, but three years before Apollo 8, the first manned flight to the moon, the Paris Uprising, and the Prague Spring, all in 1968. It was a time when MAD (Mutually Assured Destruction) was regarded as the most rational and effective way to maintain international security in the nuclear age and when the bipolarity underscored by the superpower rivalry and the nuclear confrontation was thought to be perpetual. It was 26 years before the end of the Cold War and the collapse of the Soviet Union in 1991, which would shock the discipline out of its malignant complacency.

In 1965, translational relations and complex interdependence were only just knocking at the door of the discipline. If multinational companies had begun to make their impact felt in world economy, the entry of "globalization" into the lexicon of the discipline was still decades away. The "international" was otherwise relentlessly subverted daily by rising social movements from below such as anti–Vietnam War protests, the Civil Rights movements, second-wave and third wave feminism, and Greenpeace (1969–1971), although the discipline at the time was oblivious of them. The world was definitely not flat, even in the 1980s. The information revolution was at best on the distant horizon. Google, YouTube, Facebook, Twitter, WeChat – and the virtual world they have created for us today – were simply and plainly beyond popular imagination, not to speak of gene editing, which would potentially and profoundly change the meaning of being human.

No student or scholar of IR at Sussex in 1965 and after could ever have envisaged either the profound and sweeping political, economic, and scientific and technological transformations of their future material world or the rapidly changing intellectual universe of IR they have helped construct. How can we, then, be expected to peer into what the future holds for the material world of international relations and IR as a discipline in the next 50 years?

2015: Past and present of a still inchoate discipline

In 2015, what was envisaged in 1965 as the future of IR had fast receded into the past. *The Future of International Relations: Masters in the Making* published no earlier than in 1997 (Neumann and Waever 1997) – which purported to offer a glimpse of the future of the discipline – can probably now be better read as part of the disciplinary historiography. With hindsight, it is not difficult to see that the material world of international relations has unleashed relentlessly dramatic changes in the last 50 years, and is constituted of surprises ranging from the non-violent end of the Cold War, the collapse of the Soviet Union, and the terrorist attacks of 9/11, to global financial crises and the exigencies of climate change. Central concerns in the core conversations in IR have been accordingly expanded from questions concerning war and peace, order and justice, to those related to prosperity and growth, rights and freedoms, and most recently, to the survival of the biosphere and the planet, exploring how humanity can live an ethical life. Though the indictment of IR as a "failed discipline" in the wake of the end of the Cold War is sometimes contested, it is not uncommon to lament in the intellectual world of IR how insular and incomprehensibly narrow-minded the debates between neorealism and neoliberalism look in retrospect and what a blinkered tunnel vision of world politics they both offer. More often than not, arguments are made, undoubtedly contentious, as to why and how problem-solving theories, in particular neorealism, help perpetuate the hegemonic practice of Cold War politics and the way the Cold War as a distinctive historical era disciplined the discipline.

The divide between rationalism and reflectivism (call it positivism vis-à-vis post-positivism if you like) as a vanishing intellectual fashion perpetuates, perhaps unwittingly, the "paradigm wars" in disguise and is a signal example of how IR remains fundamentally riven by epistemological differences, i.e., differences over what constitutes true knowledge and by methodological disagreement as to how best to pursue that knowledge. The ontological, epistemological, and methodological debates in IR theorization – largely inspired by its closer and more recent engagement with the debates in the philosophy of social science – have, however, led to the proliferation, some would say an explosion, of IR theories. More profoundly, these meta-theoretical debates challenge what we think constitutes IR, and by the same token, what are theories of IR. In so doing, they expand the field of enquiry and lead to the legitimation of intellectual pluralism constitutive of a wide range of theoretical approaches and accounts that reveal different worlds of IR to explain and to understand.

Even with a cacophony of contending theoretical perspectives offering a multiplicity of understandings of global politics as never before, the discipline of IR today, while seemingly convinced of – no doubt inaptly – its own methodological and theoretical breakthroughs, is paradoxically uncertain about its legitimation as science. While it shows unconvincing confidence and emotions about its past and present, it remains at best ambivalent and at worst confused about its future. If the disciplinary future of IR cannot be foretold, however, few would dispute that the discipline of IR has been invented and reinvented in a century of wars and revolutions and that the disciplinary IR as a world made of knowledge is a social world constructed through human reflections and scholarly efforts. Changing worldviews, abandoned theoretical paradigms, fresh points of contestation, exposed intellectual traps, and inspiring critical insights all reveal the nature of the constructed knowledge of IR.

Today, the contentious question of progress in the studies of international relations, in terms of knowledge gains and improved understanding of global politics, continue to haunt this arguably healthier discipline, even when "increased sophistication in theory and method, greater communication and learning across theoretical boundaries, and more artful borrowing from other fields" seem to have been clearly registered in evaluating the current state of the discipline (Reus-Smit and Snidal 2008, 5). As much as in 1965, the American academy of IR – the largest and best funded – continues to serve "both as power house and as control tower" to use E.H. Carr's (1961, 147) metaphors for the studies of IR. Stanley Hoffmann's characterization of IR as an American social science in 1977 remains largely intact, even when flourishing diversity in the discipline "as having many mansions, and many different views of the world, each coherent, plausible and intellectually defensible" (Richardson 1990, 141) has been accepted more than ever before, and is sometimes celebrated. Not surprisingly, perhaps, the discipline continues to be obsessed with power and the powerful and "does not reflect the voices, experiences, knowledge claims, and contributions of the vast majority of the societies and states in the world" (Acharya 2014, 467).

Symptomatic of the inchoate nature of the discipline, IR as a discipline continues to wrestle with and agonize over – now as in 1965 – two basic yet fundamental questions to the legitimacy and vitality of the discipline. The first is the question of relevance and sense of purpose. *What's the point of IR?* is a poignant question informed manifestly by the disciplinary anxieties. It is telling that in celebrating 50 years of IR at Sussex, the conference organizers asked "Where does IR's practical importance and value lie?," What should IR's practical functions and purposes be?," Who and what is IR for?," and "Whose interests should IR serve?," among the key questions that are identified for reflection and debate.

At one level, this is related to the ever-increasing demand that IR scholarship speaks to the most pressing social, political, economic, and ecological problems and dilemmas of the contemporary world. This demand for IR scholarship to address real-world problems is more than the classical contention about academic IR resisting the siren song of policy relevance, though it does hark back to a classical debate on the relations between theory and practice (Wallace 1996, Booth 1997, Smith 1997). Neither is it simply a matter of favoring or opposing "advisers who whisper in the prince's ears principles that justify the prince's acts" (Hoffmann 1981, 28). It goes beyond the role of the intellectual to say truth to power (Said 1996, 184–185). If it is accepted that IR consists of practical discourses as a distinctive political practice, promoting its policy relevance is no more (or less) legitimate than advocating political resistance, emancipation, and purposive change of the chaotic world. However, to the extent that social sciences "were born in the services of the modern state and whose goal was producing research that could be of use to policy makers" (Tickner 2006, 386), it poses an acute dilemma for IR scholars and scholarship. On the one hand, there is always a danger of knowledge being coopted by power, hence the nagging anxiety about the appropriate relationship between IR scholars and policy makers. Even if it is accepted that the academy can never be neutral to power as an integral part of the social and political fabric that criticizes and justifies power, policy advocacy and public engagement that are seen as purposively engineered political projects are likely to endanger the discipline's legitimacy. On the other hand, there is a deep concern that "the divorce between scholarship and policy-making has gone too far" in the pursuit of different types of social knowledge of IR. As Henry Nau (2008, 635–637) puts it,

> Scholarship and statesmanship, theory and practice, the academy and policy worlds, while they are different, are nevertheless joined at the hip, and neither can succeed, even within its own realm, without the other. . . . Social knowledge, which is evolutionary, is the product of an inevitable partnership between scholarship and policy-making.

At a more general level, this concerns how to make social science matter, and more specifically, how "we may successfully transform social scientific research into an activity performed in public for publics" (Flyvbjerg 2011, 25). This raises a number of searching questions about knowledge production and formation in IR. Outstanding among them are knowledge-for-what and knowledge-for-whom questions. If, following Michael Burawoy (2009, 200), we recognize the distinction between instrumental and reflexive knowledge and accept that "each knowledge has its own distinctive character – its notion of truth, power, legitimacy, and accountability" how can we strike a balance between instrumental knowledge and reflexive knowledge production in IR that is complementary? What danger is likely to be posed by the domination of instrumental over reflexive knowledge, or vice versa, in our production of IR scholarship?

The other basic yet fundamental question that has caused and continues to provoke deep and chronic anxieties is the question of disciplinary status and science. One recent account of the disciplinary history based on the philosophy of social science has constructed its narrative about all four great debates in terms of IR's unrelenting but less-than-successful quest for its scientific status, which continues to be as contentious as ever (Kurki and Wight 2008). To be sure, no one would argue today – and least of all accept – that IR as a discipline is still in a pre-paradigmatic state. The onward march of scientism in social science, in particular the belief that the science of nature could be extended to a science of humanity, has certainly left indelible marks on the quest for IR to be a science. Positivism – as a prevailing account of what science means and is – has made irresistible inroads into and is deeply entrenched in the efforts to create a "science" of IR that is ostensibly value free in the production of knowledge. Nowhere is this more conclusively demonstrated than in the core theoretical conversations in the heartland of the discipline, the United States, where the dominance of positivism as a philosophy of science in the disciplinary imagination is overwhelming, so much so that many may feel that the garden of natural science is no longer "an intellectual paradise from which he [or she] has lamentably been excluded" (Ayer 1967, 7).

It is the advance and dominance of positivism in the disciplinary IR that has triggered meta-theoretical debates surrounding the philosophy of social science in IR. These debates concerning ontological, epistemological, and methodological assumptions take the consideration of whether IR can be a science right back to a prior question of what science is and to a battle on the terrain of the philosophy of science. Can IR as a social science model the natural sciences in its disciplinary pursuit? This is among a number of contentious questions raised at the heart of this consideration. Scientific realism may have mounted a credible challenge to positivism. It may have provided a meaningful alternative account of what science is and means for social science. It may have advanced a set of persuasive arguments that social science should not attempt to copy the natural sciences and should abandon its pretense to emulate the natural sciences in producing cumulative and predictive theory. However, the validity of scientific realism's account of science continues to be hotly contested. It is far from clear whether scientific realism as a new philosophy of social science has provided, and indeed can provide, a secure philosophical foundation upon which IR as a discipline can claim its legitimation as science. Is IR a science or an art? What does the "scientific" study of world politics entail? Now as then, these questions remain unanswered and may prove unanswerable in any conclusive manner.

As the discipline of IR races toward the centenary of its fabled birth in the ashes of World War I, the dynamic character of IR is perhaps best illustrated by our changing understanding of the "international." In the rear-mirror view of the disciplinary growth, it is clear that the "international" in both our material world and intellectual understanding has been constantly and unforgivingly subverted from all directions in the last 50 years. The iconic feminist claims that "the personal is international" and "the international is personal" are good examples (Enloe 1990, 196–201). Indeed, where the "international" begins or ends – if it has indeed a beginning and an ending – remains a central question much debated yet unresolved in the discipline among contending paradigms (Dunne, Hansen, and Wight 2013, 420). To the extent that both the material world of international relations and the intellectual impulses of IR have changed dramatically between 1965 and 2015, however, these changes present us with an apparent and curious paradox today. While the material world of international relations has become irreversibly personal, local, transnational, global, virtual, and even extraterrestrial, the discipline of IR that we have constructed continues to slide, seemingly irremediably, into a Eurocentric cul-de-sac wedded to a colonial view of the world, unable to break free even from its Westphalian straitjacket and its obsession with anarchy. The dominant paradigmatic understanding of the "international," in other words, is parochial and mired in modern European history.

Between 1965 and 2015: Martin Wight, David Armitage, and beyond

Imagine that Martin Wight were a panelist at the celebration of 50 years of IR at Sussex. What would have been his reflections on the discipline today? He may feel relieved that "why is there no international theory?" has become more or less a moot question. He would be deeply dismayed at the inexplicably parochial nature of disciplinary enquiries 50 years on. He would be scathingly skeptical of any self-assured celebration of theoretical proliferation and progress. He would be bewildered at the invention of the "English School," of which he is said to be one of the founding figures. If he were pushed to speculate on the future of the disciplinary IR, he would probably ask rhetorically: "How could a discipline that is so scandalously negligent of its own past know what its future holds?"

In his search for intellectual foundations for international theory more than 50 years ago, Martin Wight engaged in a series of enterprising and pioneering efforts to construct what emerged as the three traditions of international thought by joining in the conversation with classical political philosophy. In one of his teaching notes in the 1950s, Wight pushed for efforts to ruminate among classical political theory for relevant ideas, citing the following from Alexis de Tocqueville in his presidential address to the Académie des Sciences Morales et Politiques in Paris in April 1852:

> It is unbelievable how many systems of morals and politics have been successively found, forgotten, rediscovered, forgotten again, to reappear a little later, always charming and surprising the world as if they were new, and bearing witness, not to the fecundity of the human spirit, but to the ignorance of men.
> (Wight 1991, 5)

For Wight, drawing inspiration from T. S. Eliot, "[t]here is only the fight to recover what has been lost and found and lost again and again" (1991, 5), i.e., what has been neglected, forgotten, and even repressed in the history of international thought.

As a tribute to Martin Wight and to IR at Sussex, let me make a humble and modest submission, not about any speculations of the future of IR, but concerning what we could and should do to ensure a healthy future development of IR. If it is generally accepted that the future of disciplinary IR lies, at least in part, in subverting the present paradigmatic, yet parochial, understanding of the "international," then one viable intellectual project is to seek a *global* renaissance in the history of international thought. This project can build upon, but critically must go beyond, the project tentatively envisaged by Martin Wight in the 1950s and the 1960s at the London School of Economics as well as at Sussex. Such a renaissance has to be truly global, inclusive of international thought of different civilizations; and the *longue dureé* intellectual history of the international should go into deep world history beyond the Enlightenment and the Renaissance. The purpose of this project is not, however, to search for any foundations – ancient, pre-modern, modern, or post-modern – of international thought but to understand the contested nature of the "international" and its implications for the "dare-not-to-know" future of the disciplinary IR.

Three fortuitous disciplinary developments in recent decades, among others, have made this project both imperative and possible. The first of these developments is a diverse range of collective and concerted efforts to overcome the "great divide" between comparative politics and IR in general, and to bridge the theoretical and institutional gap between political theory and international relations theory in particular in the trans-Atlantic political science community. These two sub-fields, in Brian Schmidt's (2002) assessment, have come together again after a rift between the two developed in the 1950s that came to define them respectively.

The second development, and certainly of more importance to the proposed project, is the acclaimed "international turn in intellectual history" in trans-Atlantic IR substantively pursued in the last decade by David Armitage and Duncan Bell, among others. This has led to "a renaissance in the history of international thought" in trans-Atlantic IR, as the 50-year rift between intellectual history and IR came to an end as the "dawn of a historiographical turn" as studies of international relations began to explore how those neglected, forgotten, and repressed historical ideas play constitutive roles in shaping our understanding of the present (Bell 2001, Armitage 2004). In David Armitage's (2013, 1) rather upbeat assessment, international intellectual history – i.e., intellectual history of the international – has developed within just over a decade between 2000 and 2013 from a field that "had neither a local habitation nor a name," "had no common agenda, no coherent body of scholarship and no self-identifying practitioners," and "occupied no territory on the broader map of contemporary historiography" to "an identifiable field, with an expanding cannon of works, a burgeoning set of questions and a fertile agenda of research." This signals a return to a tradition in social science research, which sees that history and theory as "inextricably linked," and "not only are they both inseparable; they are also in a specific sense interminable" (Runciman 1969, 174).

Beyond the trans-Atlantic IR, there is a third fortuitous disciplinary development, which I would refer to as an "international turn" in the studies of ancient Chinese political thought, where ancient Chinese history and philosophy have been rediscovered, excavated, explored, and interrogated in search of international thought in China's deep history and classical Chinese philosophical works. This happens most notably, though not exclusively, in recent Chinese studies of IR. Three projects are worth mentioning as significant indicators of this notable "international turn," namely, the so-called Tsinghua Approach led by Yan Xuetong (2011) to rediscover international thought in ancient China, Qin Yaqing's (2012) efforts to reinvent Confucian relationalism in IR, and Zhao Tingyang's (2009) attempt to reinterpret the classical concept of *Tianxia* (all under heaven) to foster an all-inclusive worldview and imagine a world that is of all and for all.

In claiming an "international turn" in the studies of ancient Chinese political thought, I take "international thought" to mean, following Robert Jackson, principally three inquiries, namely, "an inquiry into the fundamental ideas and beliefs involved in the arrangement and conduct of world affairs over time"; "an inquiry into the values at stake" such as peace, security, independence, order, and justice, among others; and an inquiry "into the language and discourse of world affairs" (Jackson 2005, 1). Such an understanding of international thought is trans-temporal as well as trans-historical. It does not necessarily share the assumptions taken to be fundamental and foundational for modern international thought, as Armitage (2015, 117) has stipulated, namely,

> the separation of the domestic and the foreign; the primacy of states over all other actors in the external realm . . .; international law as the positive law of a system of states under conditions of international anarchy; and the states-system as a self-policing club with its own hierarchical standards of admission and exclusion.

This claim of an international turn also assumes that international thought as a body of knowledge as understood earlier can be (re)discovered and (re)constructed through close and contextual readings of classical canons of ancient Chinese history and philosophy and by creative interpretations of ideas and concepts articulated by key classical thinkers in ancient China. This is no doubt a contestable assumption, though.

There is no evidence to suggest that these two seemingly unconnected yet parallel "international turns" as distinctive intellectual development in the trans-Atlantic and the Chinese IR scholarly communities are remotely aware of each other. Chinese scholars pioneering the international turn mentioned earlier are blissfully unaware of the renaissance in the history of international thought in the trans-Atlantic IR. Intellectual historians in the trans-Atlantic IR have not taken any notice of the international turn in Chinese exploration of ancient history and philosophy. Both have, however, brought back the humanist tradition in political thought in exploring the international in the *longue dureé* as a critique of and a correction to increasingly posivitistic IR theorization, which posits a separation between the subject as observer and the object as observed, as "the ancient perspective sees both observer and observed as reciprocally interacting in an unpredictable process of change" (Cox 2008, 86). Their respective attempts at (re)discovering and resurrecting the forgotten system of morals and politics in historical Europe and ancient China show shared intellectual commitment to historicizing ideas and concepts fundamental to IR theory construction, and indeed to what is counted as our knowledge of IR in general.

A more important point I wish to make is that to the extent that this international turn in the exploration of ancient Chinese political thought adds a global dimension to and complements the renaissance of the history of international thought, it also helps highlight the limits and problems of the international turn in intellectual history in the trans-Atlantic IR evaluated by David Armitage and exemplified by his own works. Three questions can be raised in this regard.

First, what is "international thought"? David Armitage (2013, 7) defines international thought as "theoretical reflection on that peculiar political arena populated variously by individuals, peoples, nations and states and, in the early modern period, by other corporate bodies such as churches and trading companies." Is this definition too limiting and too bound up with the European historical experience? Is such understanding of international thought parochially embedded in culturally specific and historically situated experience and philosophical edifice? What has been excluded from such a definition? If historical writings on war and peace, diplomacy and law, sovereignty and the state are indeed what come to define the study of IR since Thucydides (Armitage 2004, 99), what about those historical writings before the early modern period and beyond Europe? Putting it differently, is there international thought before early modernity in Europe? Can international thought as "an historical corpus of reflection on the international" (Armitage 2015, 129) be found in the non-European world?

This leads to the second question, the question of *longue dureé* in the historiography of the international. Armitage (2012) argues strongly for the importance of *longue dureé* intellectual history, exemplified by his personal endeavor to explore the intellectual history of civil war as a "big idea" from ancient Rome to the present. Yet, he is convinced that it is correct "to see the full emergence of the international as post-dating the Renaissance, not least when historiographical analysis converged with natural jurisprudence in the works of Pufendorf and Vattel" (Armitage 2015, 125). He anchors foundations, if not the origins, of modern international thought firmly in the age of European empires and states and traces them back genealogically to the Enlightenment thinkers in the long eighteenth century. The deep historical linkage between the imperial and the international in its modern incarnation is well acknowledged and affirmed but not problematized (Armitage 2013). This view of *longue dureé* intellectual history of the international has serious historiographical implications, not in the least because it may lead to the production of what one critic of Armitage calls "a new master narrative in which the revolution of 1776 comes to occupy a similar status to the 1648 Peace of Westphalia in the historiography of International Relations" (Hutchings 2014, 492). It may also come to legitimate the exclusion of *longue dureé* intellectual histories – European as well as non-European – that have enabled as well as conditioned the full emergence of the international in its modern manifestations in the long eighteenth century.

The final question is where to look for international thought? Armitage's own exploration of the intellectual history of the international has relied heavily on British historiographical sources. His excavation of international thought has been mostly performed by looking into the canonical works of principally British political thinkers from Hobbs to Locke. In responding to his critics, Armitage acknowledges that international thought in its various manifestations needs to be reconstructed "high, middle and low" in such resources as "manuals for diplomats; collections of treaties (and the texts of the treaties themselves); the works of journalists and publicists," among others (Armitage 2015, 125). Although he has warned against the "dangers in relying on predominantly Western historiography for conceptions of the international" (Armitage 2015, 126), his own works have rarely moved beyond

Western historiography. The pivotal historical moments when ideas concerning the when and where the international changed are all found in European history.

This is where and how the international turn in the exploration of ancient Chinese political thought complements the renaissance in the history of international thought in the trans-Atlantic IR. In the words of Terry Nardin (2014, 101), "[T]he enterprise of international intellectual history is likely to become more inclusive as the study of ideas, thinkers, and texts in languages other than European ones, and by scholars in other parts of the world, increases." This suggests that a lot beyond the European historiography needs to be interrogated and scrutinized for international thought. If Armitage (2015, 120) is right in claiming that theology remains "one of international thought's foundations that is yet to be fully excavated," one could legitimately ask, in the true Wightian spirit, what non-Western historiography, for example, that of the Axial Age (Bellah and Joas 2012), remains to be fully excavated in constructing a truly global intellectual history of the international in the *longue dureé*? Can a Confucian tradition of international thought be meaningfully constructed not necessarily as a coherent intellectual edifice but as the grinding of the intellectual optics through which the world is seen and understood in the past and at present, perilous as such an enterprise may be? How can the excavation of the international in ancient Chinese political thought contribute to a comparative historical research project considering the international turn in intellectual history in the trans-Atlantic IR? And indeed, how is the putatively universal as we understand it today constituted by the historical particularities we study and scrutinize?

2065: imaging future as past

Imagine then 50 years from now, in 2065, when another conference is held here to celebrate 100 years of IR at Sussex attended by scholars and students of the twenty-first-century generations. How different would the material world of international relations and the intellectual terrain of IR be in 2065 from what we know today? Dare we imagine the "internationals" in 2065? Would the School of Global Studies in Sussex be called by another name, say, the School of Planetary and Virtual Sphere Studies? "What the future will bring us, we do not know," as Karl Popper (1972, 376) cautioned us 60 years ago. What we do know is that IR is an extraordinarily resilient discipline and that what we envisage today as the future of IR will be invariably looked upon as part of disciplinary historiography and intellectual history. The question is: What would that conference say about the future that we imagine today of the discipline as the past?

Bibliography

Acharya, Amitav. 2014. "Global International Relations and Regional Worlds: A New Agenda for International Studies." *International Studies Quarterly* (58): 647.

Armitage, David. 2004. "The Fifty Years' Rift: Intellectual History and International Relations." *Modern Intellectual History*, 1 (1): 97–109.

Armitage, David. 2012. "What's the Big Idea? Intellectual History and the Longue Dureé." *History of European Ideas*, 38 (4): 493–507.

Armitage, David. 2013. *Foundations of Modern International Thought.* Cambridge: Cambridge University Press.

Armitage, David. 2015. "Modern International Thought: Problems and Prospects." *History of European Ideas*, 41 (1): 116–130.

Ayer, A. J. 1967. "Man as a Subject of Science." In *Philosophy, Politics and Society* (Third Series). Edited by Peter Laslett and W. G. Runciman. 6–24. Cambridge: Cambridge University Press.

Bell, Duncan. 2001. "International Relations: The Dawn of a Historiographical Turn?" *British Journal of Politics and International Relations*, 3 (1): 115–126.

Bellah, Robert N. and Hans Joas. Eds. 2012. *The Axial Age and Its Consequences.* Cambridge, MA: Harvard University Press.

Booth, Ken. 1997. "A Discussion: A Reply to Wallace." *Review of International Studies*, 23 (2): 371–377.

Burawoy, Michael. 2009. "Can Public Sociology Travel as Far as Russia?" *Laboratorium*, 1 (1): 197–204.

Carr, E. H. 1961. *What Is History?*, 2nd edition. London: Penguin.

Cox, Robert. 2008. "The Point Is Not Just to Explain the World but to Change It." In *The Oxford Handbook of International Relations.* Edited by Christian Reus-Smit and Duncan Snidal. 84–93. Oxford: Oxford University Press.

Dunne, Tim, Lene Hansen and Colin Wight. 2013. "The End of International Relations Theory?" *European Journal of International Relations*, 19 (3): 405–425.

Enloe, Cynthia. 1990. *Bananas, Beaches, and Bases: Making Feminist Sense of International Relations.* Berkeley: University of California Press.

Flyvbjerg, Bent. 2011. "Making Social Science Matter." In *Social Science and Policy Challenges: Democracy, Values and Capacities.* Edited by Georgios Papanagnou. 25–56. Paris: UNESCO Publishing.

Hoffmann, Stanley. 1981. *Duties beyond the Borders: On the Limits and Possibilities of Ethical International Relations.* New York: Syracuse University Press.

Jackson, Robert. 2005. *Classical and Modern Thought on International Relations: From Anarchy to Cosmopolis.* Basingstoke: Palgrave.

Kavan, Zdenek. 2015. "Memories of IR at Sussex," in What's the Point of IR Conference Pack. 25–33. Accessed December 10, 2015. http://whatsthepointofir.com/conference-pack/

Kurki, Milja and Colin Wight. 2008. "International Relations and Social Science." In *International Relations Theories: Discipline and Diversity*, 3rd edition. Edited by Tim Dunne, Milja Kurki and Steve Smith. 14–35. Oxford: Oxford University Press.

Lake, David. 2011. "Why 'Isms' Are Evil: Theory, Epistemology, and Academic Sects as Impediments to Understanding and Progress." *International Studies Quarterly*, 55: 465–480.

Nau, Henry. 2008. "Scholarship and Policy-Making: Who Speaks Truth to Whom?" In *The Oxford Handbook of International Relations.* Edited by Christian Reus-Smit and Duncab Snidal. 635–647. Oxford: Oxford University Press.

Neumann, Iver B. and Ole Waever. Eds. 1997. *The Future of International Relations: Masters in the Making.* London: Routledge.

Popper, Karl R. 1972. *Conjecture and Refutations: The Growth of Scientific Knowledge*, 4th edition. London: Routledge and Kegan Paul.

Qin, Yaqing. 2012. "Culture and Global Thought: Chinese International Theory in the Making." *Rivista DIDOB d'Afers Internacionals* 100: 67–89.

Reus-Smit, Christian and Duncan Snidal. 2008. "Between Utopia and Reality: The Practical Discourses of International Relations." In *The Oxford Handbook of International*

Relations. Edited by Christian Reus-Smit and Duncan Snidal. 3–37. Oxford: Oxford University Press.

Richardson, James L. 1990. "The Academic Study of International Relations." In *Order and Violence – Hedley Bull and International Relations*. Edited by J.D.B. Miller and R. J. Vincent. 140–185. Oxford: Clarendon Press.

Runciman, W. G. 1969. *Social Science and Political Theory*. Cambridge: Cambridge University Press.

Said, Edward. 1996. *Representations of the Intellectual: The 1993 Reith Lectures*. London: Vintage Books.

Schmidt, Brian. 2002. "Together again: Reuniting Political Theory and International Relations Theory." *British Journal of Politics and International Relations*, 4 (1): 115–140.

Smith, Steve. 1997. "Truth and Power: A Reply to William Wallace." *Review of International Studies*, 23 (4): 507–516.

Tickner, Anne. 2006. "On the Frontline or Sideline of Knowledge and Power?" *International Studies Review*, 8 (3): 383–395.

Wallace, William. 1996. "Truth and Power, Monks and Technocrats: Theory and Practice in International Relations." *Review of International Studies*, 22 (3): 301–321.

Wight, Martin. 1966. "Why Is There No International Theory?" In *Diplomatic Investigations: Essays in the Theory of International Politics*. Edited by Herbert Butterfield and Martin Wight. 17–34. Cambridge, MA: Harvard University Press.

Wight, Martin. 1991. *International Theory: The Three Traditions*, edited by Gabriel Wight and Brian Porter. London: Leicester University Press and Royal Institute of International Affairs.

Yan, Xuetong. 2011. (translated by Edmund Ryden) *Ancient Chinese Thought, Modern Chinese Power*, edited by Daniel Bell and Sun Zhe. Princeton: Princeton University Press.

Zhao, Tingyang. 2009. "A Political World Philosophy in Terms of All-under-Heaven (Tian-xia)." *Diogenes*, 56 (5): 5–18.

INDEX